RED, WHITE, AND BLUE
LETTER DAYS

Red, White, and Blue Letter Days

An American Calendar

Matthew Dennis

★ ★ ★ ★ ★

Cornell University Press

Ithaca & London

First published 2002 by Cornell University Press

Printed in the United States of America

Library of Congress Cataloging-in-Publication Data
Dennis, Matthew, 1955–
   Red, white, and blue letter days : an American calendar / Matthew
Dennis.
      p. cm.
   Includes bibliographical references and index.
   ISBN 0-8014-3647-8 (cloth : alk. paper)
   1. Holidays—United States—History. 2. United
States—Historiography. 3. Memory—Social aspects—United States. 4.
National characteristics, American. I. Title.
   GT4803.A2 D46 2002
   394.26973—dc21

                          2001006501

Cloth printing   10 9 8 7 6 5 4 3 2 1

For my parents
Jeanne and Irving Dennis and
Pamela and Ronald Reis

CONTENTS

ILLUSTRATIONS

ACKNOWLEDGMENTS

*I*N WRITING a book as wide ranging as this one, I've found it difficult to decide what to leave out. But here, where I cannot forget anyone, I fear—ironically in a book about memory, history, and identity—the consequences of an imperfect memory and my failure to identify all those who have helped me. But let me try.

I thank various institutions and the people behind them: the National Endowment for the Humanities for a summer fellowship, the Beinecke Rare Book and Manuscript Library (especially the generosity of Ralph Franklin and George Miles), and the University of Oregon for fellowship support that aided my research. The American Antiquarian Society offered the help of its wonderful staff and the opportunity to examine its incredible collections.

Thanks to the Supreme Council, Knights of Columbus, for access to their archives and library, and to the archivist Susan Brosnan for her help. And I thank Chad Wall, Nebraska State Historical Society, for his assistance.

Various people have heard or read portions of the book, as lectures, talks, and draft chapters. I thank them for their attention, references, and suggestions: Peter Agree, Jack and Shirley Barton, Raymond Birn, Richard Maxwell Brown, Andrew Burstein, Joanne Chaison, Shaul Cohen, Philip Deloria, Jeanne and Irving Dennis, Ralph Franklin, David Glassberg, Emily Greenwald, John Hench, Derek Hoff, Graham Hodges, Peter Hoffenberg, Frederick Hoxie, Nancy Isenberg, Paul Johnson, Jane Kamensky, Jack Maddex, George Miles, Patrick Miller, John Murrin, Simon Newman, Peggy Pascoe, William Pencak, Susan Pezzino, Niko Pfund, Earl Pomeroy, Daniel Pope, Yuri Rasovsky, David Reis, Ronald Reis, Jonathan Sassi, Douglas Seefeldt, Nina Silber, Lyn Spillman, Quintard Taylor, Len Travers, Jeffrey Wasserstrom, Erik Weiselberg, and Richard White. And thanks to my editor at Cornell University Press, Sheri Englund, and to Karen Hwa and Kathryn Gohl.

The writing of this book has been informed in important ways by the fieldwork of everyday and holiday life—it has been, in a sense, celebrated into existence. I thank my fellow celebrants at numerous fetes: the Birn-Hatches, the Baxter-Cohens, the Kirtners and Kirtner-Goldenbergs, the Wood-Raiskins, the Morgen-Longs, Leo Altmann and family, the Dennis family, the Reis and Tamarkin families, and other mixed multitudes.

I extend special thanks to Pamela Reis, who read several chapters and offered incisive suggestions, to David Waldstreicher and Leigh Schmidt, who thoughtfully critiqued the entire manuscript and signaled numerous ways to improve it, and most of all to Elizabeth Reis, who read draft after draft and devoted herself to this project and to an even more important one—our family. Lizzie, along with our children, Sam and Leah Reis-Dennis, make every day a banner occasion.

RED, WHITE, AND BLUE
LETTER DAYS

Introduction

Identity, History, and the American Calendar

The kind of history that has the most influence upon the life of the community and the course of events is the history that common people carry around in their heads. . . . Whether the general run of people read history books or not, they inevitably picture the past in some fashion or other, and this picture, however little it corresponds to real past, helps to determine their ideas about politics and society.

Carl Becker, "What Are Historical Facts?"

---

*O*N JULY 4, 1986, I found myself swept up in the hoopla surrounding the centennial celebration of the Statue of Liberty. As New York's streets surged with millions of celebrants, as tall ships and pleasure crafts clogged the harbor, and as fireworks exploded overhead, amid the cacophony I heard a woman remark that she had come to see history in the making. How could this be? Nothing of great historical significance was actually occurring; no battle was being won or even fought, no piece of landmark legislation was being enacted, no disaster was being unleashed. In fact, these events simply celebrated and commemorated an earlier commemoration. Nonetheless, the woman-in-the-street was correct. She and the rest of us, as our collective weight tilted lower Manhattan into its bay, were indeed making history. History, after all, is not the past itself but, rather, our memory, interpretation, and representation of it. The past cannot be re-created, but history certainly can be, by professional historians or by anyone else who remembers or invokes the past and applies such invocations in the present. And we do it all the time. Such public commemorations are among the important moments when histories common and elite, popular and academic, commingle in public, sometimes volatile ways. At such moments, Americans do make history—that is, they define themselves and their place in a collective national past.

This book probes the malleable meanings of American history, changing notions of American national and local identities, and the shifting contents of public memory, through explorations of key annual public holiday celebra-

1

tions (and the less frequent anniversaries of significant events) that commemorate the American past, especially the foundation of the American nation and its principles. The creation of an American civic calendar during the early American period distinguished the new nation from Europe, promoted nationalism, and helped to define who and what was American. Yet as the United States was transformed in the nineteenth and twentieth centuries, negotiation of American identity—both national and particular—and reinterpretation of the nation's history continued. This study, then, examines the particular use of civic ritual, history, and myth that occurs periodically but purposefully throughout the year during public, political holidays—holidays that provide a fertile ground for working out the meaning of a diverse, even multicultural America.

From the perspective of the early twenty-first century in the United States, it is easy to dismiss the political importance of public holidays and their rites—parades, barbecues, shopping—despite the significant scholarly work on popular and festive culture of the last several decades.[1] Bread and circuses, meaningless spectacles and self-indulgent leisure, or windy orations and self-serving electioneering: such phenomena inhabit American political holidays and can inhibit us from taking them seriously. Yet such fetes deserve more careful scrutiny. Commemorative acts can be matters of consequence, even matters of life and death. Consider, for example, a recent Independence Day observance, halfway around the world, in northern India.

India marks its Independence Day on August 15. In Srinagar, in the Kashmir Valley, celebration was subdued on Independence Day 2000. People feared both the Indian security forces deployed in the Kashmiri summer capital and militant groups that might greet the occasion with deadly explosive devices. And most inhabitants rejected the notion that they were in fact part of the Indian nation. Ghulam Muhammad explained, typically, "I am a Kashmiri, not an Indian." Since 1989 in the State of Jammu and Kashmir, some twenty-five thousand people have died in conflicts between separatists, Islamic holy warriors, and Indian forces. On the August 12, instead of pledging allegiance to the nation, Kashmiris like Muhammad declared, "We want our freedom." The holiday's only official, public event occurred in the morning at Bakshi Stadium, which both militants and the military seemed to agree people should not attend. While militants called a strike, a state police spokesman on hand reasoned, "Who would want to attend anyway? . . . People are afraid to die." A rousing speech, a brass band, and army regiments all played to empty seats.[2] In the Kashmir Valley, Independence Day carried such intense meaning that no parade was possible.

Or consider another contested terrain where parades, despite their explosiveness, occur regularly and weightily. On each July 12 in Northern Ireland, the Orange Order—a traditional organization of militant Protestants—aggressively marches in their bowlers and orange sashes through the streets of Lurgan, Portadown, Lisburn, Belfast, and other disputed sites in the troubled province, to celebrate the victory of King William III, the Prince of Orange, over Jacobite foes at the Battle of the Boyne in 1690, a triumph that confirmed the Protestant ascendancy in Ireland. These marches, purposefully choreographed to proceed through Catholic neighborhoods, inevitably ignite violence. To avert bloodshed, authorities sometime ban the Orange Order processions along these routes, and such prohibitions typically produce new demonstrations, which themselves become marked by clashes with soldiers and police or among rival Protestants and Catholics. Much of the tension and frustration of thirty years of conflict in the most recent edition of the Troubles is expressed in these "loyalist" and other "nationalist" and civil rights parades, which—in the words of one student of the Irish parading tradition—have "long been a barometer of the political situation" in Northern Ireland.[3]

If "the past is a foreign country," the reverse may be true as well—that a foreign country can be our past, perhaps even our present. The exoticism of Northern Ireland and northern India festivity may be more apparent than real. In the United States too, parading as well as other holiday rites have functioned as barometers of the political situation. Sometimes commemorative events have produced violence and bloodshed, and sometimes authorities have cancelled observances to protect lives and property. In the late eighteenth century, Federalists squared off against Antifederalists as each sought to celebrate themselves into political preeminence, sometimes stooping to fisticuffs on the Fourth of July. In the nineteenth century, riots sometimes erupted during Independence Day as marginalized groups—such as African Americans in Philadelphia in the 1830s and 1840s or Irish Americans in New York in the 1850s—paraded in the streets and into the political arena, while other Americans sought to brutalize and exclude them. The potential for violence similarly hovered around Labor Day, which originated in the late nineteenth century essentially as a festive general strike, whereas Memorial Day signified an aversion to internecine violence, expressed the nation's sorrow over its losses in the Civil War, and signaled its commitment to reconciliation and reunion. Immediately following the First World War, Armistice Day (later Veterans Day) was the scene of a riot and lynching of a labor activist in Centralia, Washington. As recently as 1992, the prospects of mayhem persuaded Denver to cancel its traditional Columbus Day parade, targeted by the American Indian Movement for protest and disruption. About that time, the famous New York City St. Patrick's Day parade was the site of internal quarreling when organizers refused to allow the Irish Lesbian and Gay Organization to march under its own banner. Court fights and public disputes, on this and other issues, have kept the controversy alive and alienated some participants. Even Thanksgiving Day has seen its violent moments, not merely on the football field but in the streets of Plymouth, Massachusetts, in 1997, for example, where Native American activists and police tousled and mace was used not in mincemeat pies but to facilitate arrests.

In such instances—and in many others treated throughout these pages—commemorative activities mattered greatly to Americans and reflected the state of American politics, nationally and in various local contexts. Not only cataclysmic commemorative events, but light, apparently trivial observances of American public holidays—such as picnics, popular amusements, and bargain mongering—are mirrors of political and cultural life, revealing plenty about the material conditions of the United States and its citizens' identities, historical consciousness, and political attitudes. If American public holidays have often become moments of apparently apolitical fun and leisure, lying dormant within them nonetheless is the potential for political consequence, controversy, even transformation. Though traditional and sometimes trivial, American political fetes remain works in progress, as Americans continue to reinvent themselves and their nation through historical celebration, often with surprising results.

This book emerged originally from my interest as a historian of early America in discovering the actual origins of holidays that celebrated events from the colonial and revolutionary past—holidays such as Thanksgiving, the Fourth of July, and Columbus Day. Students asked me questions, like "What really happened at the First Thanksgiving?" Or, "If Columbus was such a villain, why do we celebrate Columbus Day?" I tried to provide historical answers, peeking especially into the earliest eras of American history. The more I looked—in the nineteenth and twentieth as well as the seventeenth and eighteenth centuries—the more I noticed Americans actively engaged in defining themselves and competing politically with each other through their commemorations of earlier landmark events and heroes, often rehearsing history in a fashion that could be remarkably at odds with modern historians' reconstructions of that same American past. From the privileged distance of our own present, it can be tempting to correct these "errors," and even to belittle those who made them (sometimes consciously and cynically, but often inadvertently and benignly). Similarly, merchants and advertisers have colonized the American calendar, moving in to sell their products by linking them, often tenuously, with the occasion or casting consumption as a patriotic act. In other instances, they have worked diligently to persuade consumers that proper observance of festive occasion demands the purchase of their products or services. Such merchandizing has trivialized American commemorations, added little to historical education in the United States, and at times become offensive. On the other hand, advertising executives and window dressers have often played a critical role in promoting and staging public holidays, and their work has met with as much popular appreciation as elite depreciation. It sells Americans short to depict them simply as mindless consumers, helplessly manipulated by admen, who foist upon them goods they cannot resist. If nineteenth- and twentieth-century Americans felt the constraints of industrial, mass culture, which commercialized—among other things—their public calendar, they acted (and continue to act) in ways that did not always conform to the plans and expectations of capitalist elites.

In the pages that follow I am less interested in passing judgment and condemning bowdlerization—declaring historical actors somehow inauthentic or inaccurate, insincere or insidious—and more committed to understanding how and why particular historical narratives, heroes, images, and celebratory rites emerged at certain times, in specific ways, and in particular settings in American history. My purpose is thus more descriptive and analytical than prescriptive and judgmental. Nonetheless, I have been struck, continually, by the creativity of commemorators and celebrants, the complexity of the public arenas they have constructed through festivity, and the varied politics they have practiced on such holiday occasions.

This book could not have been written without the pioneering work upon which it builds. Can we remember a time when scholars have produced so much about memory? Within the historical profession and the humanities in general, numerous scholars have sought with great energy and success to understand the nature of public memory, historical consciousness, and national identity.[4] This volume is not a work of historical theory, and it does not attempt to assay specifically the riches of this historiography, which is wide ranging and diverse. Nor is it a work of comparative history, despite the brief examples drawn from recent events in India and Ireland above. But as this volume focuses on the history of the United States and its colonial past, it draws on the historical, theoretical, and comparative insights of these writers, especially their emphasis on the constructed nature of historical consciousness; the impact of nationalism, region, class, religion, race, ethnicity, and gender in determining individual or group configurations of memory and history; and the way that presentation and interpretation of the past is not simply imposed from above but is, rather, pluralistic, contested, and negotiated.

The influential French social theorist Pierre Nora argues provocatively that "memory is constantly on our lips because it no longer exists." He laments the disappearance of *milieux de mémoire*—"settings in which memory is a real part of everyday existence"—and sees modern interest in historical sites (*lieux de mémoire*), "where a residual sense of continuity remains," as a poor substitute for what we have lost. Memory in the modern world, in his view, has evaporated—having been forgotten or never really absorbed by ordinary people; it has become merely residual (in public memory sites) or archival, with much stored but little remembered or understood. For Nora, a chasm exists between memory and history. "Memory is life, always embodied in living societies and as such in permanent evolution, subject to the dialectics of remembering and forgetting, unconscious of the distortions to which it is subject, vulnerable in various ways to appropriation and manipulation, and capable of lying dormant for long periods only to be suddenly reawakened." History, on the other hand, is reconstruction, "always problematic and incomplete," and operates through analysis and critical discourse; "history belongs to everyone and to no one and therefore has a universal vocation," whereas memory "wells up from groups that it welds together."[5]

Although such distinctions add complexity to our understanding of people's relationships to their pasts, memory and history—particularly popular historical consciousness—seem hopelessly entangled in the United States and, as in the English word "history" itself, used simultaneously to refer to the past and our representations of it. Few historians would argue that history, even as practiced by academic writers, is not in permanent evolution, affected by the changing life circumstances of individuals and societies, subject to swings of the pendulum of styles and fads, vulnerable to manipulation, appropriation, and distortion. Yet popular memory, particularly in the pluralistic United States, is constructed, incomplete, and itself at least partially dependent on formal history, which filters into popular consciousness. The world explored in this book is more amphibious than the one Nora has described; in this book, academic history, popular memory, mass culture, and commerce all commingle (often amid conflict), producing hybrid constructions of the American past and American identities.

Nora is right to suggest that modern nations "no longer speak of 'origins' but rather of 'inceptions,'" as they emphasize historical discontinuity, radically new beginnings. Yet the people of the United States, who lack the romantic past of a French medieval peasantry (whose members embody Nora's notion of "true" memory), and who emerged as a nation in the rupture of the American Revolution, nonetheless cultivate a sense of origins and continuity no less important because it is a mere two hundred, rather than two thousand, years old. Is it not the case, for example, that most Americans see "pioneers" as old and traditional, even if they appreciate them as path-breakers and innovators in a bygone time? I view the transformations of consciousness and historical representation with less nostalgia for the past or dread for the present and future than do scholars such as Nora, even while I appreciate the problems of our modern and postmodern condition.[6]

Students of commemoration and collective memory have effectively shown that modern peoples—social and political collectives since the eighteenth century—celebrate themselves into existence and nurture a common identity through public, festive rites. They emphasize birth or rebirth in these rites to distinguish themselves from others. They invent traditions and obscure the novelty of their creations to lend them the sanctity of antiquity, and they do so to construct and maintain group boundaries, whether national, ethnic, racial, religious, or social. Purposeful remembering requires purposeful forgetting, as collective pasts are assembled through an editing process that leaves much on the cutting-room floor. Commemorations are not merely the ephemera of national and particular identities but a significant means of constituting and expressing those definitions of the self, community, or nation that stem from people's historical and material circumstances. But who is the "they" here? Who are "the people," and what defines them collectively? Who works to make such identification plausible and necessary? Whose interests does such identification serve? And how strongly do various citizens feel such allegiance? Historians of American commemoration, popular history, and identity have been able to offer provocative but partial answers. My subject is the overwhelmingly complex array of people in the United States, with both common and distinctive identities, multiple and overlapping senses of themselves—as Americans, as hyphenated Americans, as denizens and sojourners, as others. More specifically, unlike most other studies, mine focuses on the performance of public holidays, on Americans' practicing their social, cultural, and political identities in the public sphere, and I do so over the several hundred years of the American past. Answering Hector St. John de Crévecoeur's impossible, old question—"What then is the American, this new man?"—is less important to me than gaining a sense of the arena and the ways in which Americans have argued about who they are and what their country means. And though I am sometimes surprised and troubled by their answers, my work does not join the discourse of declension that has become conventional, berating Americans for their lack of historical interest or knowledge, or for their abandonment to commercialized leisure or heritage. It might seem like an act of hubris to take on such a large, interdisciplinary subject, confronting the United States as a whole and spanning four centuries of history; it would have been less daunting and fraught with risk to have concentrated my analysis chronologically and focused more closely on a particular region or group. But it seemed important to seek broader historical answers to bigger questions about American culture and politics.

Red, White, and Blue Letter Days examines the cultural and political work that occurs on American public holidays, from the creation of the American ritual calendar in the colonial, early national, and antebellum periods—which laid the groundwork for the development of what Thomas Bender has called a "public culture" in the United States—through the reshaping of that calendar in the later nineteenth and twentieth centuries. My intention, however, is not primarily to delineate a historical chronology, which simply traces the accumulation of customs and traditions; instead, the narratives of each chapter and the book as a whole take readers backward and forward in time as they analyze the presentist approaches of commemorators and celebrants in various presents, from the colonial period to the year 2000. The chapters are ordered in a rough, chronological fashion, based more or less on when each commemoration emerged in the cultural and political life of the United States as a national fete. But American public holidays appeared simultaneously, waxed and waned in popularity, were transformed by other events and constituents, or even reborn as Americans played on the "mystic chords of memory," which sought to link their own times to ancient moments in the national history. Clearly, a simple, one-damn-thing-after-another approach to this history would not serve its complexity well. The book's six chapters together explore variations on a common set of themes, which will emerge more clearly and systematically by beginning with Independence Day and Thanksgiving, continuing with Columbus Day and Presidents' Day (originating in celebrations of George Washington's and then Abraham Lincoln's birthdays), and finishing with "St. Monday" (which treats Memorial Day and Labor Day) and the newest American political holiday, Martin Luther King Jr.'s Birthday.

Readers will find both more and less than the titles of these chapters advertise; none of the essays delivers an exhaustive documentary history of the holiday in question, but each ranges beyond its red-letter day to place the fete in a larger context and to consider related or contrasting celebrations. Thus in my essay on Independence Day I consider festivals of freedom among African Americans, such as Juneteenth; my chronicling of Thanksgiving relates it to another Pilgrim festival, Landing Day; the cultural and political significance of Columbus Day becomes clearer in light of a brief consideration of St. Patrick's Day; and I measure the St. Mondays of Memorial Day and Labor Day in relation to Armistice Day (and Veterans Day) and May Day.

What is the relationship between these public holidays and American history? Those who hear the philosopher George Santayana's adage about the consequences of failing to learn from history, it seems, are condemned to repeat it.[7] I will not. Certainly Americans have learned from their collective past, and they commemorate it through their national public holidays, but it is even more striking to observe citizens "remembering" that history on holidays, not to learn but to teach or preach, not to express gratitude or to promote historical knowledge in a neutral fashion but to promote their own agendas. Americans are able to display distinctively ahistorical inclinations even as they "make history," using the past to build, paradoxically, connections with distant and obscure eras while bypassing or avoiding more immediate or controversial historical events. Many seem to prefer public remembrances of a vague, more malleable past, better suited to use in their present. Contesting such history "making," Americans have also sought to unmake and remake the past, sometimes by finding alternative heroes and historic events to celebrate, sometimes by laying claim to conventional ones, and sometimes by disturbing the shallow graves of the more troubling historical problems (such as slavery and its legacy) that the powerful sought to bury. Finally, to further fracture Santayana's now clichéd words, some Americans have forgotten or simply abandoned the collective historical past, yet they have been condemned to repeat it blissfully through celebration. Avoiding politics—that is, stridently partisan politicking and its deployment of historical briefs—many have used their commemorative days as holidays, as occasions for noncontemplative leisure and amusement. As the chapters of this volume suggest, such modes of celebration, though not consciously political or historically minded, nonetheless embody American politics, define celebrants, and help shape their understanding of American history.

The United States' public calendar became thicker and more complicated as the country's history lengthened. And though all American political fetes, not just election day, could offer platforms for electioneering, they increasingly became moments for social and cultural politics, allowing Americans a voice beyond the voting booth. If, as they became routine and formulaic, they became politics as usual, they could nonetheless also serve the interests of those Americans pursuing a politics of the unusual. During the early American republic, only two political holidays were widely celebrated—Independence Day and George Washington's Birthday—symmetrically placed in the second and seven months amid other localized or religious feasts. Both nurtured union and nationalism among American celebrants and symbolized the birth of a new people and polity, and both offered a forum to contest the nature and achievement of national promise. As the Civil War approached, each continued to provide tools to mend the distended Union, and each could be claimed by North and South as an origin rite, even after the war came.

By the end of the Civil War, two additional holidays were incorporated into the national calendar—Thanksgiving and Memorial Day—and like the Fourth of July and February 22, they promoted union and reunion. These two fetes maintained the symmetry of America's yearly cycle, supplying autumn and spring holidays to balance the summer and winter celebrations of American nativity. Thanksgiving emphasized the inclusive memory of a more distant time of colonial origins, conceived in terms more social and domestic than political. Memorial Day observances focused on mourning, on the bravery and loss of both the blue and the gray, and ultimately sought reconciliation through an implicit agreement not to remember the issues that had produced the war—issues that lingered in postbellum America—slavery and racial discrimination.

In the latter half of the nineteenth century, however, as life became even more complex—with unprecedented industrial production, massive urban growth, new immigration, labor unrest, innovations in racial discrimination, and the rise of new forms of commercialized culture—the United States' public calendar became more crowded and conflicted and less symmetrical. Lincoln's Birthday, Labor Day, and Columbus Day found their places in the American festive, political cycle. The new hero Lincoln, paired with Washington, represented both liberation and rebirth and increased state power. Labor Day recognized the growing power of labor but sought to institutionalize a moderate working-class Americanism. (Subsequent attempts to create a Loyalty Day out of May Day in the 1930s represented a more aggressive effort to repress labor radicalism.) And Columbus Day became a venue to assert the legitimacy of ethnicity and, for the state and civic elites, to acknowledge American pluralism (even if some sought to Americanize and contain it). By the early twentieth century, then, the American calendar had become both denser and lighter: it contained more holidays, but not all were equally weighty or compelled wide participation. Americans increasingly picked their commemorative spots, and they honored them more and more—or seemed to neglect them—through private celebrations, or through indulgence in new forms of commercialized leisure. As public holidays commanded more attention from the state—with sponsored programs and parades—ironically they became vernacular in new ways, becoming more recreational, diverse in observance, and commercialized. Holidays could be simultaneously state-sponsored, store-bought, sincerely celebrated, and homemade. And like the newest public holiday in the United States calendar—Martin Luther King's Birthday—they remain public arenas in which American identity, principles, promise, policy, and history might be debated.

Red, White, and Blue Letter Days stresses the impact of pluralism in American life and on the nation's calendar, as various factions of hyphenated Americans (ethnic, racial, and religious) have systematically expanded the definition of citizenship through appropriation or invention of "traditional" American celebrations. This volume confronts the gendered nature of such festive occasions and the roles of women as well as men in their sometimes conflicted and changing expression. And it addresses regional and sectional fault lines that have opened and closed in American history, often conspicuously during public holidays. The history and history-making considered here had losers as well as winners, for Americans have not been equally enthusiastic about embracing received memories in holiday fetes, or equally empowered to reject or reshape mainstream notions of American history and identity. Indeed, the mainstream, to the extent that such a thing existed, was constituted in part through its opposition to marginal others. Less powerful or less privileged Americans have challenged dominant opinions and entrenched arrangements during potent holiday moments, while they have simultaneously sought to integrate themselves and claim the rights of first-class United States citizenship. Such participation in official commemorative events—and the affirmation of the state or authorities that taking part suggested—could enlist critics in their own marginalization. But the potential existed, and was sometimes realized, that this participation would become subversive and transformative as well.

Each chapter in this volume addresses such matters of inclusion and exclusion, and the identities—local and national, unified or conflicted—molded and expressed by celebrants during the festive events chronicled. Americans used these commemorations to practice nationalism (in various forms) as well as localized or particular affinities, often simultaneously and sometimes without contradiction. African Americans perhaps confronted the ambiguities of such identification most starkly, which the African American writer, publisher, and leader W. E. B. Du Bois articulated most clearly as "two-ness"—a "double-consciousness" that for American blacks represented "two souls, two thoughts, two unreconciled strivings; two warring ideals in one dark body."[8] Other Americans who benefited from the privileges of race, gender, or wealth could more easily conflate, or avoid confronting consciously, their divided strivings toward an American national identity, on the one hand, and identification with particular sections, classes, or partisan causes on the other. If, as the saying goes, all politics is local, many Americans found a way to construe their particular political practice—serving their race, ethnicity, religion, region, or class—as legitimately American, nationalistic, and even nonpartisan. And the public arena at commemorative moments offered a perfect venue for this political alchemy.

In an Independence Day 2000 editorial, the *New York Times* observed, "The unintended irony of American history is that every group that comes to the equality of collective freedom for the first time, whether emancipated slaves or enfranchised women or newly arrived immigrants, has reinstructed the rest of us in its value." It may well be that the historical trajectory of most American political fetes, like the fireworks on the Fourth of July, is one that flares initially with solemn and reverential commemoration and then descends toward the relatively mindless, forgetful, apolitical indulgence of leisure. Yet disaffected Americans—not only grateful newcomers—have been a critical force in keeping the meaning and import of American political holidays fresh and conspicuous through their dissent, challenges, and critiques, often boisterously expressed in the American public arena on these extraordinary occasions. More than pundits who bemoan the declension of American holiday observances, critics who commandeer our official fetes and condemn American failures to realize the principles or honor the legacies of celebrated events and heroes—or who question the very validity of those principles or nobility of those champions—garner public attention and prod Americans to reconsider who they are and what they stand for.

By focusing on the public arena at special annual or anniversary moments when participants implicitly define themselves and their country, assert their values, pursue their interests, and try to make money, this book attempts to examine American pluralism, democracy, and (in the twentieth century especially) corporate culture at work. This is a history of a place and process—the American public arena—a significant if unstable site where politics are practiced and history and meaning are produced. I hope that such a history can inform our understanding of Americans' changing relationships with each other, their nation, and their past and, more broadly, provide new, historical perspectives on the contours of American modernity and postmodernity.

Carl Becker's insight—that societies are most influenced by "the history that common people carry around in their heads" and less by the books of academic historians (however accomplished they are)—might challenge us to look carefully at those occasions and locations where popular history is produced, in streets and dining rooms, in newspapers and sheet music, in orations and jokes, in monuments and trinkets.

★ ★ ★ ★ ★ ★ ★ ★ ★ ★ ★ ★ ★ ★ ★ ★ ★ ★

CHAPTER 1

Political Fireworks

American Independence Day, 1776–2000

All politics is local.

    Thomas P. (Tip) O'Neill

HE FOURTH OF JULY—Independence Day—is the oldest, most public of American political holidays. And although it celebrates the birth of the United States as a nation in 1776, the festival is as essentially local as it is national. As with other national holidays—even those explicitly nationalistic in intent—the Fourth of July celebrates its celebrants as distinctly local exemplars of American-ness. Parades and picnics and fireworks displays are not federally sponsored events generally but rather emerge through the organizational work of local civic groups and individuals. Even as they nod toward events in the distant past and conceive of their actions as celebrations of the nation, revelers practice that nationalism locally. Americans think nationally and act locally; or rather, they think that they think nationally, while they express local or particular versions of American identity and history. Of course, Independence Day celebrations have their standard formulas, and communities imitate each other's versions of local Fourth of July festivals. Fireworks, parades, orations, and barbeques are accustomed fixtures. But Americans do not simply adhere to a nationally programmed festival and conform to prescribed images. Rather, they imagine themselves, however particular they might be, as essential, prototypical Americans and imaginatively assimilate (or exclude) others within the national boundaries, evaluating the others' claims to citizenship on the basis of the criteria established by their own ideal image.

Even in an age saturated with national commerce and communication, the meaning and practice of Independence Day remain beyond the easy control of national political or commercial brokers, ironically because of the traditional weakness of the American state in matters of culture as well as because of the undisciplined, even chaotic nature of the postmodern media. Paradoxically, both scenarios—limited and diffuse guidance, and informational overload—

create space for Americans to make of the holiday what they will, including even apparently mindless indulgence and diversion. Yet if Independence Day now strikes some of its celebrants as meaningless or devoid of politics, we cannot take their word for it but must probe more deeply. There are patterns to the complex and diverse ways that Americans have constructed or ignored the Fourth of July, and this chapter examines these patterns historically, from 1776 through the late twentieth century.

The collective memories of Revolution and national birth are a natural resource for Americans, a sort of cultural, social, and political capital. Like all resources, this one is better appreciated and more valuable to some than to others, and it is conserved or exploited differentially by various citizens. Abundance of privilege, safety, or prosperity may allow some citizens to neglect the sober rites of gratitude prescribed for them on Independence Day, enjoying instead a bacchanalian summer festival. Others (including inhabitants seeking citizenship or the full measure of rights associated with it), who are marginalized socially and politically, may indulge in similar escapist fetes. But often we see them instead employing the memory of 1776, and the radical implications of the Declaration of Independence in particular, to critique American society and polity and to promote reform, sometimes even revolution.

Identity and the boundaries of American citizenship and public life are fundamentally at stake during the Fourth of July. The Fourth presents an opportunity to define, delimit, or expand—while celebrating—the American nation. Orations and editorials, banquets and parades, have excluded as well as included, signaling who is and who is not (or is not legitimately) American. Historically Independence Day has marked a moment of possibility to contest or reshape such boundaries: territories displayed their patriotism and made their case for statehood; new citizens by the thousands have taken their oaths of allegiance to the United States; abolitionists have decried the hypocrisy of slavery in a land in which "all men are created equal"; African Americans have continued to seek true equality; women have declared and pushed for equal rights; unions have contended for greater economic democracy; American Indians have displayed their own patriotism, sometimes sincerely, sometimes ironically, and sometimes to cover traditional rites proscribed by their wardens.

Commercialization has only made such questions of political boundaries and national identity more complicated because Independence Day is also an economic resource. Since the early nineteenth century, merchants have hawked souvenirs and other wares appropriate to the day; it hardly seems possible today to celebrate the Fourth without a wide variety of products that advertisers tell us we need to do it up right. More deeply, identity itself—even political identity as an American citizen—is fundamentally shaped by advertising and consumption. Clothed in the flag—sometimes literally—manufacturers of consumer items creatively deploy the memory of American nativity, not to cultivate national feeling or historical insight but to sell products. Ironically, such apparent trivialization of the Fourth of July by American commerce seems to serve a nonmaterial need among American citizens: their preference to avoid, when possible, the sordid world of American popular politics. Since the beginnings of the republic, Americans have decried factionalism and sought to avoid the nasty give-and-take of conventional political conflict, preferring instead the tranquility of consensus. Needless to say, such political concord proved illusory, and Independence Day—so charged with political meaning and power—could not easily be insulated from partisan manipulation. Thus, while some continued to employ the Fourth of July to further political agendas or to promote reform, commercialization, even trivialization, of the holiday offered other Americans a pleasurable escape from the political contention they found discomforting. Nonetheless, although the economic and political forces of mass culture impinge on ordinary Americans, offering possibilities and limiting imagination, celebrations of the Fourth retain a protean quality: uniformly commemorating the birth of the American nation, they can vary according to historical times and particular circumstances.

Declaring Independence

When Americans declared their independence in 1776, they committed a revolutionary act, and throughout the War for Independence their commemoration of that event served the partisan goals of their revolutionary party. If today Americans continue to mistake commemorations for the unique referent events they celebrate, in the 1770s and early 1780s such ambiguity made sense. To establish American independence, revolutionaries needed to fight and to celebrate their new republic into existence. Nowhere was the mix of celebration and martial struggle, of commemorating an event and effecting it, clearer than in New York City in July 1776. There, on July 9, following a public reading of the Declaration of Independence, soldiers and new citizens toppled and destroyed the city's gilded-lead equestrian statue of King George III, which had stood on the Bowling Green only since 1770, when it had been erected by subjects grateful for the removal of the Townsend duties. Was this boisterous demonstration essentially a celebration of a document drafted elsewhere, in Philadelphia on July 4, or was this unceremonious funeral for a king its own event, festive but political and even military in nature? By necessity, of course, it was both. The nineteenth-century historian Mellen Chamberlain complained that Congress's declaration was eclipsed "by the glory of its annunciation."[1] How could it have been otherwise? The Continental Congress had adopted the Declaration on July 4 and ordered that it be printed and sent to "the several Assemblies, Conventions & Committees or Councils of Safety and to the several commanding officers of the Continental troops that it be proclaimed in each of the United States & and at the head of the army." As the scholar of early America Jay Fliegelman has shown, the Declaration of Independence was written to be read aloud. Indeed, it was "publication"—the act of making the Declaration public, through the performance of public readings—and popular acclamation through spontaneous celebrations that gave the Declaration its power, which made it less a document than an event. That event was national in scope, but it was realized locally, as in New York City, and in towns, villages, and encampments from Maine to Georgia.[2]

Contemplating the historical implications, John Adams wrote his now famous letter to his wife Abigail, declaring that "the second of July will be the most memorable epocha in the history of America. I am apt to believe it will be celebrated by succeeding generations as the great Anniversary Festival." In this instance, Adams's prophecy bore fruit. If his Independence Day anticipated the commonly recognized red-letter day by forty-eight hours, we might forgive him. July 2 was the day that Congress officially resolved to declare Independence. More significantly, Adams's call for a national festival suggests perhaps a multiday commemoration. The Medieval Latin *epocha*, or "epoch," connotes a period of time characterized by a distinctive development or memorable event (or series of events). Adams's word choice reflected his sense that the occasion being celebrated was a process—indeed, the beginnings of a process initiated well before July 2—not merely a discrete occurrence. Although Adams could "see the rays of ravishing light and glory," he nonetheless remained "aware of the toil and blood and treasure that it will cost us to maintain this Declaration and support and defend these States." Establishing Independence was not the work of a day; the revolution would be a protracted struggle and would require considerable popular support. Looking to the future, Adams offered his prescriptions: it should be commemorated, he wrote, "by solemn acts of devotion to God Almighty, solemnized with pomp and parade, shows, games, sports, guns, bells, bonfires, and illuminations, from one end of the continent to the other from this time forward, forever more." Adams's list mingled apparently frivolous diversions with sober, religious rites. Ironically, this compound of the sacred and profane recapitulated traditional celebrations of the king's birthday. As with the upending of George III's statue in New York, or the rush to remove the King's Arms from all public places, Americans popularly inverted this birthday rite in order to represent the death of the king and the birth of the republic.[3]

Partisans of the revolution thus staged impromptu, sometimes massive declarations of joy and republican assent. In Philadelphia on July 8, John Nixon of the Committee of Safety read the Declaration to a mass gathering from a balcony perched above the State House yard. According to Adams, "Three cheers rended the welkin [sky]," and battalions "paraded on the Common and gave us the feu de joie, notwithstanding the scarcity of powder. The bells rang all day and almost all night."[4] That night bonfires lit up the city, as did individual houses illumined with candles set in windows. Such actions were repeated elsewhere, in rural as well as urban areas, as the Declaration was read publicly and endorsed by the people at court houses, crossroads, public squares, and churches, with processions, musket salutes, "animated shouts," toasts, and even violence against royal or loyalist property. These were local celebrations of a continental event, an event

Fig. 1. The Declaration of Independence being "published"—that is, being publicized through public reading and "ratified" by popular acclamation. Engraving from Edward Barnard, *New, Comprehensive, and Complete History of England* (London, 1783). Courtesy of Knight Library, University of Oregon.

that was truly national only to the extent that the nation's far-flung constituents endorsed it through virtually simultaneous acts of affirmation.

By contemporary standards, news spread quickly along the eastern seaboard, although it was August before word of the Declaration reached the southernmost colony of Georgia. Committees of Safety sent express riders to distant counties; ministers were directed to read the Declaration to their congregations in Massachusetts; in New York, General George Washington issued his officers copies and ordered them read to assembled troops with a sober, "audible voice"; and no doubt the substance of the Declaration or quickly printed broadsides themselves found their way into private letters. Many would read the Declaration—or have it read to them—from printed copies, especially as they appeared in American newspapers. On July 6, the Declaration was printed in the *Pennsylvania Evening Post*, by July 9 it was printed in the

German-language *Pennsylvanischer Staatsbote*, by July 11 in the *Maryland Gazetteer*, and by July 20 in the *New Hampshire Gazette*. Before the month ended the Declaration had appeared in at least thirty American newspapers.[5]

As numerous contemporary scholars have stressed, the American Revolution developed in the context of an emerging public sphere, a public arena of communication and interaction that was self-created and autonomous relative to the state. Critical to this process was print, which enlarged the audience for news, information, and ideas; indeed, publication in print increasingly constituted that audience, making it "possible to imagine a people that could act as a people and in distinction from the state," argues literary scholar Michael Warner. Such a reading public could understand itself to be virtually limitless—unable ever to assemble or to encounter each other all at once—yet vitally connected through the common act of reading. Moreover, publication could reproduce, extend, even simulate the experience of some citizens for those distant from the site of events. Localized public activities—whether riots, battles, parades, orations, banquets, or toasts—reported in newspapers continentally, could be read by others without direct involvement and incorporated sympathetically as collective memories, or they could be imitated to produce new events. If, as the political scientist Benedict Anderson argues, modern nations are "imagined communities," then a new republican print culture, especially through the dissemination of politically charged festive experience, helped rebellious subjects imagine themselves as citizens of the United States.[6]

But not all Americans imagined themselves equally committed to the new rebel regime. Were all houses acceptably illuminated in Philadelphia on July 8, 1776, or did some windows remain dark, not because of Quaker aversion to such practices but because those with loyalist sentiments resided within? During the Fourth of July celebration of 1777 in that city, Connecticut representative William Williams reported great expenditures on liquor, powder, and candles and concluded on July 5 that "much Tory unilluminated glass will want replacing." A Continental officer in Philadelphia similarly noticed some Tory houses, which remained dark and "whose Windows Paid for their Obstinacy." Independence Day demonstrations of joy could thus also function as partisan expressions of intimidation and exclusion. In Huntington, Long Island, townspeople animated by news of the Declaration violently drew the boundaries between patriot and loyalist by tearing the name of George III from a local flag and by fashioning an effigy of the king suitable for execution. But this royal effigy was no ordinary ritual object; they made "its face black like Dunmore's Virginia regiment," and they "adorned" its head "with a wooden crown stuck full of feathers like . . . Savages." In their symbolic regicide and intimidation of lurking loyalists, Huntingtonians celebrated the Declaration and expressed solidarity with other revolutionaries by suggesting who had no legitimate claim to citizenship: African American slaves, specifically those who sought freedom in service with Virginia's royal governor, Lord Dunmore, and American Indians, who defined for white Americans the "savagery" that colonial civilization stood against.[7]

Independence Day remained a tool of these partisans, who ceremonially and wishfully declared as fact that which they hoped to accomplish through their war. The day continued to be celebrated as an anniversary during the military struggle, beginning in 1777, and with the successful completion of the war, marked by the Treaty of Paris in 1783, the United States continued to witness its celebration, with particularly exuberant eruptions of festive and political energy with the ratification of the Constitution in 1788.

Although elimination of the vanquished Tories seemed to transform the partisan holiday into a universally beloved national fete, the Fourth of July retained its tendency to inspire political contention, or its utility as a moment suitable for giving voice to party interests as well as nationalism. Given the sanctity of the Revolution and its place in the new myth of American nativity, such a development seems almost inevitable. Americans sought both to sanctify their own opinions and measures by constructing them as legitimate legacies of the Revolution and to claim rights promised in the Declaration but unfulfilled in their contemporary United States.[8]

The Independence Day festivals of 1788, for example, displayed both the spontaneous popular joy and the orchestrated political demonstrations that could commingle on or around July 4. In some cases, they expressed staunch political opposition through street theater and violence. On July 2, Congress announced officially that the Constitution, drafted in Philadelphia during the previous summer, had garnered the approval of the requisite nine states and was therefore enacted as the new frame of government for the United States. In the preceding months, towns and cities in ratifying states had staged processions locally to hail the unfolding national event, and in Carlisle, Pennsylvania, rioting and injury accompanied celebration of the state's ratification in December 1787.[9]

By July 4, 1788, with the necessary nine federal pillars erected (Virginia's ratification on June 25 made it ten), in Philadelphia a carefully planned Grand Federal Procession—the greatest spectacle in the city's history—marked the occasion with pageantry and pedagogy. Some five thousand marchers participated, forming a line that stretched a mile and a half and took three hours to pass spots on the three-mile parade route. Soldiers on foot and horse, dignitaries, bands, carriages, and great floats thrilled the multitudes. The procession was itself a carefully crafted play, beginning with a chronological pageant of American history from 1776 to the present, featuring local leaders and elites, and offering as its climax a Constitution float crowned with a thirteen-foot-high eagle, and the Carpenters' Company float, the Grand Federal Edifice, featuring a dome supported by thirteen Corinthian columns, "raised on pedestals proper to that order, . . . ten columns complete and three left unfinished." The procession continued with a marching exhibition of the city's crafts and trades. Squeezed onto large platforms atop carriages, craftsmen and mechanics plied their trades and displayed their machines and tools. Mariners escorted the thirty-three-foot-long "Federal Ship *Union*," which carried twenty mounted guns and an enthusiastic crew of twenty-five men and boys. At the procession's terminus, Union Green, some seventeen thousand people sat down to a banquet, arrayed in a circle of tables surrounding a space five hundred feet in diameter, where organizers placed the Grand Federal Edifice and the Federal Ship *Union*.[10]

As James Wilson observed in his oration marking the occasion, such public activities, like the present formal but festive procession, "may *instruct* and *improve*, while they *entertain* and *please*. . . . They may preserve the *memory*, and engrave the *importance* of great *political events*. They may *represent*, with particular felicity and force, the *operation* and *effects* of great *political truths*."[11] The Federalist organizer Francis Hopkinson designed the parade to construe as "truth" the idea that the new federal Constitution represented the legitimate culmination of the American Revolution. Participants—whether as marchers or spectators—were the objects as well as the embodiment of that Federalist lesson.

Federal processions elsewhere similarly seemed to display unity and nationalism through their festive recognition of the Constitution's ratification. In New Hampshire, the ninth state to ratify, one editor claimed that ratification produced a "hardly conceivable joy . . . diffused through all the ranks of citizens." But such an assertion likely misrepresented the feelings of New Hampshire's clearly divided populace. In states that had not yet given their assent to the new frame of government, claims that ratification processions and other popular political demonstrations in July 1788 were simply celebratory and expressed unanimity are more problematic. Although festive in their performance, they nonetheless functioned as an unsubtle means of persuasion, as Antifederalist critics of the Constitution could not help but notice. In Wilmington, North Carolina, "illuminations, bonfires, and other demonstrations of joy" heralded the news that Virginia had ratified. These celebratory acts would also have exerted pressure on state delegates, who were sixteen months away from ratification themselves. With ratification by ten states by late June,

New York became the chief battleground. In Albany on July 4, as historian David Waldstreicher writes, "plans for a joint [Federalist-Antifederalist] celebration in the morning gave way by midday to a full-scale street battle." While members of the militia marched about town firing their guns, Antifederalist opponents burned a copy of the Constitution. In the melee, one person died and several others were wounded. More violence might well have erupted in other towns had not some Federalists and Antifederalists opted to celebrate Independence Day separately.[12]

In New York City, the festive, political season continued beyond the Fourth of July with a grand procession on July 23, which displayed as much partisanism and exhortation as it did celebration. Heralding the new Constitution seemed less important perhaps than persuading state delegates upstate in Poughkeepsie to make New York the United States' eleventh pillar. Thirteen guns fired at ten o'clock began the proceedings, which continued with a march of twenty-six groups in ten divisions down Broadway to the Bowling Green, where George III's equestrian statue had stood. Soldiers, historical personages, tradesmen, scholars, and dignitaries, with banners, skits, music makers, and floats, including a fully manned twenty-seven-foot federal frigate, coursed through the streets. As in Philadelphia, the New York procession culminated in a banquet, this one feeding some six thousand people, seated symbolically at ten massive tables measuring 440 feet long, arranged like the spokes of a fan. Within three days after this spectacular political performance and act of persuasion, New York delegates voted to ratify the Constitution.[13]

If Federalists won the battle to appropriate the Fourth of July and have it serve their cause in the 1780s, by the 1790s and the early nineteenth century the tables had turned and Independence Day became a Democratic Republican festival. With the Declaration of Independence assuming its place in Fourth of July ceremonies as a sacred text, the political party of its acknowledged author, Thomas Jefferson, promoted its own partisan purposes. It is in this era that the day and the document assumed a new life, one that few of America's Founding Fathers could have anticipated. To paraphrase the Progressive era historian Carl Becker, the ongoing political struggle of Independence Day was not merely the celebration of home rule but of who should rule—and share the rights of citizenship—at home.

Claiming Independence

Thomas Jefferson's simple words, approved by the Second Continental Congress and ratified popularly by masses of Americans in 1776, turned out to be as much promise and provocation as declaration. "We hold these Truths to be self-evident, that all Men are created equal, that they are endowed by the Creator with certain unalienable Rights, that among these are Life, Liberty, and the Pursuit of Happiness." What did Jefferson and his colleagues mean? Did "men" mean mankind—men and women, whites and blacks, newcomers and natives—or did it mean white men? In a sense, this question was moot from the start. Less important than authorial intention was popular reception—the Declaration meant what the people took it to mean, as English radical John Wilkes recognized in a 1777 parliamentary speech. Although disparaging the Declaration's literary quality, Wilkes observed that it was "drawn up with a view to captivate the people"; for Wilkes this was "the very reason why I approve it most as a composition, as well as a wise political measure, for the people are to decide this great controversy. If they are captivated by it, the end is attained."[14] The meaning and power of the Declaration's words, in short, were political and thus unstable. After resting in relative obscurity for fifteen years, and after its deployment in partisan discourse in the 1790s, the Declaration achieved its present sacred status some thirty years later. By that time, its pronouncements about the legitimacy of separation from Great Britain were increasingly overshadowed by its apparent endorsement of "*the native equality of the human race,* as the true foundation of all political, of all human institutions," to quote Peleg Sprague's Hallowell, Maine, Fourth of July oration of 1826.[15]

Perhaps the Declaration of Independence was, as historian Pauline Maier writes, "a peculiar document to be cited by those who championed the cause of equality." Its claims about equality referred to persons in a state of nature, not those living under civil government; it was written by men, many of whom were lifelong slaveholders, who in 1776 trained their focus on severing ties with Britain, not on framing a new political system; and being neither a constitution nor a bill of rights, for any state or national government, it could claim no particular, ongoing legal authority. Nonetheless, from the start, the implications of the Declaration's language did not go unnoticed. Immediately in 1776, in an antislavery essay, Lemuel Haynes, the twenty-three-year-old black minuteman from western Massachusetts, used the Declaration's key lines on equality as an epigraph. "I think it not hyperbolical to affirm," Haynes concluded, "that Even an affrican, has Equally as good a right to his Liberty in common with Englishmen."[16] In the early 1780s in Massachusetts, where the language of equality was clearly inscribed in the state's bill of rights, such words allowed several slaves to win their freedom in arguments before the Supreme Judicial Court. Increasingly, the sacred status of the Declaration lent its text—or selections from that text—a unique moral authority that various groups sought to enlist in their efforts to claim rights or to reform the republic.[17]

The firm association of the Declaration of Independence with the Fourth of July, and the growing interpretation of the text as an instrument of equality and freedom, infused Independence Day with potential power and meaning as a festival of liberation and reform. In the 1790s, abolition societies in Pennsylvania and Maryland began to hold their annual meetings on the sacred day. In New York and New Jersey, gradual emancipation acts took effect on July 4 (in 1799 and 1804, respectively); by 1817, New York required that all slaves born before July 4 in that year be freed no later than Independence Day, 1827. Southern states were equally attuned to the symbolism of the Fourth of July, as Thomas Jefferson Randolph's 1831 emancipation proposal to the Virginia legislature suggests; the measure, if it had been successful, would have freed slaves born after July 4, 1840. Southerners similarly displayed their understanding of the power—or the danger—of Independence Day, which could nourish the contagions of liberty, by their efforts to prohibit blacks from attending white Fourth of July celebrations, and perhaps by sponsoring on many plantations purposefully nonpolitical midsummer holidays on July 4, featuring relaxation, recreation, and feasting for slaves.[18]

The American Colonization Society—founded in 1816 on the dubious proposition that the solution to America's slavery problem lay in the removal of slaves (and blacks generally) from the United States and their transportation to colonies in Africa—quickly laid claim to Independence Day as the occasion to promote its plans. Their campaigns to persuade ecclesiastical bodies and individual clergy to adopt "rites applauding the merits of colonization" during the 1820s helped transform the Fourth of July in some places into "a virtual colonization holiday," in the words of one historian. By the 1830s, however, with the emergence of radical abolitionism and the increasing rejection of colonization as a viable strategy to end slavery in America, new Independence Day exercises developed. Oberlin College students set July 4 aside as a day of devotion to abolitionist activities, for example, or for labor to raise funds to support their cause. William Lloyd Garrison, among the staunchest of white abolitionists and later publisher of the *Liberator*, commemorated the day by playing against tradition; in the mid-1830s he called it "the time-honored, wine-honored, toast-drinking, powder-wasting, tyrant-killing Fourth of July —consecrated, for the last sixty years to bombast, to falsehood, to impudence, to hypocrisy." An antislavery almanac for 1843 included the following verse, appropriate for July:

> Oh God! what mockery is this!
> Our land how lost to shame!
> Well may all Europe jeer and hiss,
> At mention of her name!
> For while she boasts of LIBERTY,

'Neath Slavery's iron sway
Three millions of her people lie,
On Independence day.

Writing in Horace Greeley's *New-York Daily Tribune* on July 4, 1845, the feminist and Transcendentalist Margaret Fuller remarked on the joylessness of Independence Day when America stood "soiled," its "great inheritance, risked, if not forfeited," as its citizens acquiesced to "extend Slavery as one of our 'domestic institutions.'" "For what is Independence," she asked, "if it does not lead to Freedom?" On July 4, 1854, passage of the Kansas-Nebraska Act drove Garrison to burn copies of the Fugitive Slave Act as well as the United States Constitution, which Garrison termed a "covenant with death" and a violation of the Declaration of Independence's sacred truths.[19]

Although some African Americans in the North similarly employed the Fourth of July as a day to reflect publicly on revolutionary principles and to condemn the United States' failure to achieve liberty and equality for millions of slaves, others chose to boycott Independence Day in favor of separate festivals of black freedom, or they stayed away as a matter of safety on a day known for its violence against blacks appearing in public streets and squares filled with giddy white celebrants.[20] The Fourth of July received its greatest boost as an African American holiday with the celebration of New York State Abolition Day in 1827, marking the culmination of the state's gradual emancipation process. The New York African American community held two celebrations. The first on emancipation day itself—the Fourth of July—was private and church-centered. From the pulpit of the African Zion Church in Manhattan, the Rev. William Hamilton hailed the regeneration of New York: "This day has She been cleansed of a most foul, poisonous and damnable stain." On July 5, some two thousand black New Yorkers marched in splendor with the accompaniment of music through the city's streets, to the delight of countless other African Americans. According to an eyewitness, "the sidewalks were crowded with the wives, daughters, sisters and mothers of the celebrants, representing every state in the Union." Although white coachmen and carters behaved insultingly to the processors, no violence marred the occasion, which culminated in an oration and banquet.[21]

For the next eight years, African Americans commemorated the occasion in some eighteen separate festivals in five states, often on July 5. Although celebrations typically pivoted around church activities—sermons, hymns, and prayers—they increasingly included activities, like those in New York City, staged out of doors—parades, gun salutes, banner displays, community banquets, and toasts. Such public exercises, as historian Shane White has shown,

Fig. 2. "Fourth of July Celebration, or, Southern ideas of Liberty—July 4, '40," by William Rhinehart. An abolitionist view of the Fourth of July under slavery. Courtesy of the American Antiquarian Society.

explicitly displayed free blacks as citizens, both to themselves and to whites, as they performed their identity as both African and American. The *Rochester Daily Advertiser*, chronicling the events of July 4, 1827, in its city, reported,

> The extinction of that curse by the laws of our State was marked by appropriate rejoicing on the part of the African race of the neighborhood. A procession of considerable length and respectable appearance, preceded by a band of music, moved . . . through the principal streets to the public square, yesterday forenoon, where a stage and seats were erected for the speakers and audience.

After an address by a black clergyman, officials read the relevant act and then the Declaration of Independence. Finally, the gathering heard an oration by Austin Steward, a local resident and former slave who had escaped bondage in Virginia in 1813. Steward's words mixed jubilation with sorrow: "we will rejoice though sobs interrupt the songs of our rejoicing, and tears mingle in the cup we pledge to Freedom."[22]

Twenty-five years later, the citizens of Rochester heard perhaps the most powerful challenge to thoughtless celebration of Independence Day ever voiced when the invited speaker, Frederick Douglass, asked, "What, to the Slave, is the Fourth of July?" Linking American revolutionaries with abolitionists, Douglass embraced the principles of Independence Day but rejected the festival's celebration of freedom as premature, hypocritical, even obscene. "Are the great principles of political freedom and of natural justice, embodied in the Declaration of Independence, extended to us?" he asked. "I am not included within the pale of this glorious anniversary! Your high independence only reveals the immeasurable distance between us," Douglass answered. "Fellow citizens, above your national, tumultuous joy I hear the mournful wail of a million! whose chains, heavy and grievous yesterday, are today rendered more intolerable by the jubilee shouts that reach them." For Douglass, "the character and conduct of this nation never looked blacker to me than on this Fourth of July."[23]

> What, to the American slave, is your Fourth of July? I answer: a day that reveals to him, more than all other days in the year, the gross injustice and cruelty to which he is the constant victim. To him, your celebration is a sham; your boasted liberty an unholy license; your national greatness swelling vanity; your sounds of rejoicing are empty and heartless; your denunciation of tyrants brass-fronted impudence; your shouts of liberty and equality hollow mockery; your prayers and hymns, your sermons and thanksgivings, with all your religious parade and solemnity, are to Him mere bombast, fraud, deception, impiety and hypocrisy—a thin veil to cover up crimes which would disgrace a nation of savages.[24]

Although the Fourth of July remained as indispensable for American radicals and reformers attempting to make political points as it was for mirthful celebrants attempting to avoid them, the bitter knowledge that slavery endured in the United States tempered African Americans' joy and inspired some to find a less ambiguous temporal site to celebrate freedom.

Some black leaders chose July 5—proximate enough to Independence Day to align it with the principles of the Declaration of Independence and to draw attention to their boycott of a day steeped in hypocrisy. And by observing July 5, black celebrants could avoid confrontation with the white revelers who monopolized public spaces on the Fourth.[25] As early as 1807, black Bostonians staged a parade on July 16 to mark the abolition of the foreign slave trade by Great Britain, Denmark, and the United States; a July 14 festival became an annual African American event there beginning the next year. Elsewhere, as in New York and Philadelphia, January 1—the day in 1808 when the ban took effect, and the date of Haitian Independence in 1804—commanded support among some African Americans as an appropriate holiday of freedom. But given persistent violations of the law and the continuation of an internal slave trade, not to mention slavery itself, and in some cases in the face of white opposition, even violence, the January 1 holiday declined, until it was reinvigorated in 1863, when President Abraham Lincoln's Emancipation Proclamation took effect.[26]

With the emancipation of some 670,000 slaves in the British West Indies in 1834, their day of liberation—August 1—assumed an important place in the African American calendar. The day became the most widely commemorated and most enduring of the antebellum freedom holidays in the United States, according to historian William B. Gravely, who has identified some 150 recorded black observances in fifty-seven different locations in thirteen separate states between 1834 and 1862. "Coming in the wake of the Fourth of July," the committee of the Banneker Institute in Philadelphia proclaimed in 1858, August 1 "gives abolitionists a fine opportunity to expose the hollow-heartedness of American liberty and Christianity, and to offset the buncombe speeches made upon our national anniversary."[27]

Although white commemorations also occurred, following the recommendation of the *Liberator* that all abolitionists celebrate the day, August 1 remained fundamentally a black festival, a proximate black alternative to the Fourth of July. Lacking true ownership of Independence Day, African Americans—at least northern free blacks—could "display banners, burn powder, ring bells, dance and drink whiskey" on August 1, according to Frederick Douglass. Indeed, Douglass noted, "a few . . . carried this 4th of Julyism a little too far." But if West Indian Emancipation Day could be a time of abandon, it nonetheless retained a seriousness of purpose, especially in its celebrants' efforts to develop black community, autonomy, and self-determination while working to abolish slavery. Douglass defended the commemoration of August 1 against criticisms from other black leaders that the holiday celebrated black passivity—liberation as a gift of the British government—and from white abolitionists who saw in it an inappropriate independence among African Americans. Addressing a West Indian Emancipation Day audience in Canandaigua, New York, in 1857, Douglass acknowledged that a certain "class of Abolitionists don't like colored celebrations, they don't like colored conventions, they don't like . . . any demonstrations whatever in which colored men take a leading part." He remained defiant: "I hold it to be no part of gratitude to allow our white friends to do all the work, while we merely hold their coats." Stressing black agency, in the West Indies and the United States, Douglass replied to black critics, "What [British abolitionist William] Wilberforce was endeavoring to win from the British senate by his magic eloquence, the slaves themselves were endeavoring to gain by outbreaks and violence."[28]

For northern African Americans, August 1 was unavoidably linked with the Fourth of July, as an alternative, relocated feast of African American freedom. It was a time, like the Fourth of July, "to preach the DECLARATION OF INDEPENDENCE, till it begins to be put in PRACTICE," according to one orator in 1834.[29] Whether on July 4 or 5, or August 1, such ceremonial moments provided opportunities for political persuasion and mobilization as well as for celebration. Even the conventional, self-satisfied white American Fourth of July proved crucial as a backdrop and platform for black critics such as Frederick Douglass, drawing attention to their message.

With the Union victory in the Civil War and black emancipation, West Indian Emancipation Day fell into irrelevance for most African Americans. A new sacred date, January 1, 1863—marked by Lincoln's Emancipation Proclamation—would be commemorated as an African American holiday, renewing the New Year's Day fete that had heralded the abolition of the slave trade in 1808. Yet this liberation, and the sense that blacks too would finally share the promise of the American Revolution, produced massive black celebrations of the Fourth of July in the wake of emancipation. Jacob E. Yoder, a teacher in a Freedmen's Bureau school in Lynchburg, Virginia, wrote in his diary on July 4, 1866, "A remarkable day in the history of this country. This is a day of rejoicing not only for the white people of this vast country but also for the late slaves of the Southern States. They seem to be generally inclined to select this day as an anniversary day to celebrate their emancipation." In Washington, D.C., on July 4, 1865, the first national celebration ever sponsored by African Americans took place under the sponsorship of the Colored People's Educational Monument Association. Elder D. W. Anderson's opening prayer declared to thousands present on the White House grounds that "the backbone of the slave-mongers' rebellion is broken, [and] we stand before Thee, O God, a nation redeemed by the commingled blood of the Anglo-Saxons and Anglo-African races." Officials read the Declaration of Independence and various letters dispatched to the committee, including one from Frederick Douglass. Douglass's letter and the orations that followed used the opportunity to celebrate "the Jubilee of Freedom," mourn Lincoln's death, demonstrate African American worth and respectability, and advocate black citizenship and suffrage. "The prophecy of 1776 will not be fulfilled," wrote Douglass, "till all men in American stand equal before the laws."[30]

Delayed word or implementation of emancipation postponed freedom celebrations in many places throughout the South; as a result, commemorations of freedom emerged in various communities at different times, often near July

4 on the calendar. Local traditions thus set aside different days for similar purposes; May 8 (Mississippi), May 22 (Florida), and May 28 (Alabama and Georgia), June 19 (Texas), August 4 (Missouri) and August 8 (Kentucky and Tennessee), and other days became occasions of localized African American jubilation. Juneteenth, for example, continues to commemorate Gen. Gordon Granger's landing at Galveston, Texas, on June 19, 1865, and his reading of General Order No. 3 proclaiming that "all slaves are free." Word quickly spread throughout east Texas, western Louisiana, southwestern Arkansas, and southern Oklahoma, setting off spontaneous celebrations. But the origins of many of these festivals are often obscure; celebrants themselves explain simply that on that day their ancestors learned they were free. Significantly, many festivals, like Juneteenth, proved to be as proximate to Independence Day, temporally and politically, as West Indian Emancipation Day had once been.[31]

The history of these Emancipation Days and their relationship with America's Independence Day are complex, as complicated as the history of African American struggles for equality and civil rights since the Civil War. Although some blacks ignored the Fourth of July—in the words of Mrs. Lula Bass, a Columbus, Georgia, schoolteacher, because "we didn't care nothing 'bout those white folks' day"—and favored their own separate celebrations, others embraced the Fourth of July and abandoned local Emancipation Days when racial integration seemed to hold real promise. As a Juneteenth celebrant told one scholar in the 1970s, "the younger generation of blacks have been taught that they're part of this country and that the Fourth of July is the day for them to celebrate." With integration, and with black migration to cities, "this type of celebration began to die down." As Mrs. Bass explained, "We have become culturized. . . . We've been picking up these other folks' culture. We had our own day [May 28], but now . . . everything is their day."[32]

Yet the shift toward a multicultural Independence Day, and the eclipsing of particular black celebrations of freedom, has not been steady or uniform; indeed, as progress toward racial justice stalled, or as African Americans sought to build community on the basis of a separate collective memory, black Emancipation Days have been cultivated or reborn. Locally, celebrations such as Juneteenth have not only been preserved, they have been spread beyond the region of their origin, as far afield as Milwaukee, Wisconsin, and Eugene, Oregon. And nationally, new holidays—Martin Luther King Jr.'s Birthday, for example—have been created that express African American history, pride, and community. Most likely, the Fourth of July will remain an ambiguous moment for African Americans, an experience that black columnist William Raspberry recently described as "feeling like a bastard at a family reunion": "We'd rather be here than not; where else, after all, would we be? And yet we're sure that many of our fellow celebrants see our presence at this American birthday party as faintly embarrassing—as not quite legitimate." In short, the rites of the national Independence Day do not resolve but, rather, express the characteristic "two-ness" of African Americans, in W. E. B. Du Bois's famous phrase, the double consciousness and conflict of being both black and American.[33]

National Rebirth: Re-Declarations of Independence

"I first took up my abode in the woods [at Walden Pond] . . . by accident . . . on Independence day, or the fourth of July, 1845," Henry David Thoreau wrote in *Walden*.[34] But the particular date for commencing this experiment in simple living was hardly an accident. Like other reformers, Thoreau understood the sacred quality of the Fourth of July, when Americans contemplated their national origins and judged the country's performance against its principles and ideals. Antebellum white reformers consistently found the nation wanting for its failure to fulfill the promises of liberty and equality inscribed in the Declaration of Independence. Indeed, Thoreau himself used the occasion of July 4, 1854, to address an audience at Framingham Grove, outside Boston, on the topic "Slavery in Massachusetts," condemning the state's complicity in enforcing the Fugitive Slave Act.[35] Before the same gathering, the abolitionist Wendell Phillips was forced to admit that "the Fourth of July never was a day of Liberty—never until the abolitionists used it." The Declaration merely "undertook to separate the connection betwixt the colonies and Great Britain." "It becomes us," Phillips argued, "to take one step further than they ["our fathers"] dared to take, and to add to Independence, *Liberty*—which they dared not add."[36] But if the slavery question preoccupied men like Phillips and Thoreau, it was not the only blight that reform-minded Americans considered on the Fourth of July. The national birthday proved an equally suitable time "to take one step further" to confront the evils of drink, irreligion, the plight of children, women's oppression, and worker exploitation.

Although Temperance—or the crusade against alcohol—had its roots in the late eighteenth and early nineteenth centuries, it began to achieve national prominence in 1825, following six stirring sermons delivered and subsequently published by the evangelical minister Lyman Beecher. The American Society for the Promotion of Temperance emerged as a national organization in 1826, advocating total abstinence from hard liquor. The movement grew in the 1830s, with the backing of a numerous newspapers, pamphlets, and enthusiastic supporters, and by 1836 the American Temperance Union had become the movement's national umbrella organization. The Fourth of July represented both a problem and an opportunity for Temperance advocates: traditionally celebrations were often intemperate, boozy fetes, yet the holiday recalled the birth of the American republic, dependent on the virtue of its citizens. Temperance societies therefore sponsored their own, liquor-free gatherings, at which their adherents and converts might celebrate the day respectably on Temperance principles. In New York City in 1844, for example, the American Temperance Union's almanac for 1845 reported, "the usual public nuisance of booths around the Park, for the sale of intoxicating liquors, was not allowed." Instead, the park fountain was cleaned, four tons of ice were added, and citizens were supplied with tin cups and "bountifully refreshed with pure ice-water." These and other such celebrations, the editors concluded, "must gladden the heart of every patriot, philanthropist, and Christian, as an assurance of the perpetuity of our free and noble institutions."[37]

Temperance enthusiasts on such occasions employed the language of the Revolution and sought to declare their independence from King Alcohol. The Fourth of July cold-water toasts of the Washington Temperance Society in 1844, for example, declared:

The day we celebrate—Our fathers rejoiced on the return of this anniversary, that they were freed from British allegiance—We, as Washingtonians, have greater reason to rejoice that we are freed from the shackles of King Alcohol, "clothed and in our right minds."

King George 3d and King Alcohol. The first had his armies destroyed by Washington; the latter by Washingtonians.

The day we celebrate—May it no longer be desecrated to the use of that which *blows* away the senses—knocks out the *understanding*—gives a sort of freedom for a while, and then liberty to lie in the gutter.

Our Nation—By the copious shedding of American blood, once redeemed and freed from the power of King George; may we, her faithful sons, true to our Tetotal pledge and Temperance principles, continue to labor untiringly and unwaveringly in our blessed cause, until all men are emancipated from the power and bondage of King Alcohol.[38]

The Sunday school movement similarly sought to subdue the evils of the traditional, bacchanalian Independence Day and to employ the Fourth of July in the interest of reform. Evangelical Protestants in the early nineteenth century saw Sunday schools as a means to educate working children on their days off. More broadly, Sunday schools represented a more aggressive attempt by evangelicals to challenge the infidelity they perceived around them and to transform the nation into a truly Christian commonwealth. By the 1830s, organizers sought to use the Independence Day holiday didactically as well as recreationally for their scholars, who should be shielded from the drinking and carousing of immoderate celebrations. The Sunday school children's Fourth of July fete thus became a religious and civic institution. In Rockdale, Pennsylvania, for example, the Calvary Sunday school managed to take control of the district's Independence Day event in 1837. At least six hundred young students and their teachers, and an equal number of spectators, convened to salute the nation's birthday with "a rational and proper celebration of the day." According to Clementina Smith, a teacher and administrator of the school, "It was the happiest day I ever passed."[39]

By 1860, Thomas Starr King's oration before the Episcopal Sunday School Mission Celebration in San Francisco seemed conventional. Welcoming the crowd "to a children's celebration of the Fourth of July," King congratulated the organizers for their inauguration here of "a new method of honoring and enjoying our National holiday." "Such methods of signalizing this day are not unknown in other portions of our Country," he continued, noting the growing cooperation of public authorities, especially in the East. "Let us hope," King declared, "that this is to be only the Commencement of a series of celebrations in which the children of the city, without distinction of sect and party, shall find provision made for their entertainment, and channels opened for their glee." Despite the venue, King's speech assumed a typical, if less bombastic form and made few adjustments for the youth of his audience. Near his closing, King spoke directly to the children, acknowledging, "You have not been interested much in what I have been saying. You have not understood much, if anything, of the vague speech I have used."[40] Nonetheless, even when orators fell short, Sunday school Fourth of July celebrations remained committed, as a patriotic duty, to moral reform and the inculcation of Christian beliefs and practices among America's children.

Sunday school advocates were less able than others to quote the language of the Declaration of Independence, although they tried to convince the public that America's founders envisioned a fully Christian republic.[41] Women's rights supporters faced a serious problem as well, stuck as they were with the words "all men are created equal." Claiming to embody the spirit of the Revolution, women could simply rewrite the letter of the Declaration and assert their "unalienable rights," as they did at Seneca Falls in July 1848. Elizabeth Cady Stanton's close revision declared, "We hold these truths to be self-evident: that all men and women are created equal." And it went on, like the Declaration of 1776, in a systematic indictment—of "man," not merely of George III—for the "repeated injuries and usurpations on the part of man toward woman, having in direct object the establishment of an absolute tyranny over her."[42]

Ironically, even this declaration emerged from the temporal margins of the conventional Independence Day fete, on July 19, 1848. Since 1776, women's participation in public celebrations of the Fourth of July had been marginalized. Respectable women were welcome spectators at parades and suitable guests at banquets and balls, but they seldom appeared as themselves—that is, as real women, not as allegorical figures—in public processions, as orators, or as toastmasters. Indeed, as politics broadened to include working-class white men, and as it focused more specifically on electioneering, women found themselves systematically excluded. Women represented national unity, nonpartisanism, and virtue. But their representation by proxy in the public sphere—by fathers and husbands—allowed little actual participation, beyond safe, symbolic demonstrations of assent to male rule, or efforts to inspire male duty and bravery in times of war.

Fig. 3. "The Fourth of July Orator," from *Every Saturday: An Illustrated Weekly Journal,* July 9, 1870. By the 1870s, this engraving provided a nostalgic view, invoking images of a classic, old-fashioned Fourth of July. Courtesy of Knight Library, University of Oregon.

Relegated to a domestic world, middle-class women, as republican mothers, were charged with the cultivation of morality among America's citizens. But as a generation of women's historians have shown, such a responsibility would draw women into public space in the interest of moral reform, as realms beyond individual homes were domesticated by the middle class in the nineteenth century. Moreover, as historian Nancy Isenberg demonstrates, women involved themselves more broadly in the ongoing debate over political rights in the antebellum period and challenged male rule as a tyranny of the majority. They became politically active through their devotion to antislavery, temperance, and other moral reform efforts, and they could demonstrate this activism at specialized Fourth of July festivals. But, even more significantly, women convened "spontaneous conventions"—unofficial bodies that existed outside of the state and the party system—to affect the revisions of state constitutions, which almost every state undertook between 1830 and 1860. Independence Day provided women private enjoyment and the occasion to become proper spectators, reinforcing their roles as listeners and granting approval to masculine displays. Less often did it serve women's aspirations to refashion themselves as political actors.[43]

Before the 1840s, we get only the barest hint of such a possibility. In early national America, both Federalist and Democratic Republican women could toast the rights of women at their teas, but they could not do so in a public forum—to act publicly as partisans would undermine their claims to virtuous womanhood, whereas to act as women rendered them politically mute. In a Fourth of July oration published anonymously in the Hartford, Connecticut, *American Mercury* in 1800, the Jeffersonian speaker extended his (or her?) indictment of inequality to the disabilities suffered by women:

> those principles of freedom, which embrace only half mankind, are only half systems. . . . Our daughters are the same relation to us as our sons; we owe them the same duties, they have the same science, and are equally competent to their attainments. The contrary idea originated in the same abuse of power, as monarchy and slavery.

But the public articulation of such ideas was rare and disembodied through the early nineteenth century, lacking the context that Elizabeth Cady Stanton, Lucretia Mott, and other women's rights advocates would work to build after 1830.[44]

In postbellum America, women reformers continued to maintain a diverse agenda, but they focused more closely on the cause of women's suffrage. On the occasion of the United States' centennial, the National Woman Suffrage Association used the Fourth of July to issue another Declaration of Rights for Women. At a meeting of the association in May, its president, Matilda Joslyn Gage, took seriously Abigail Adams's 1776 appeal to her husband to "remember the ladies": "We are determined to foment a rebellion, and will not hold ourselves bound by laws in which we have no voice or representation." Susan B. Anthony successfully urged that suffragists attend the Fourth of July festivities at the Centennial Exposition in Philadelphia and that women throughout the United States "meet in their respective towns and districts on the 4th of July 1876, and . . . declare themselves free and independent, no longer bound to obey laws in whose making they have had no voice, and in presence of the assembled nations of the world, gathered on this soil to celebrate our national Centennial, to demand justice for the women of this land."

Despite discouragement from Centennial organizers, Anthony presented a copy of the woman's declaration at the ceremony and read it aloud from a band platform in the shadow of Independence Hall.[45]

For Susan B. Anthony and other women's rights advocates, the principles of the Fourth of July were a resource and Independence Day itself an opportunity to promote their cause and reform the United States. Their efforts broadened the public sphere by forcing their way in, on the Fourth of July and other occasions, but they could also participate in the politics of exclusion to the extent that they failed on those occasions to represent (or even expressed hostility toward) the interests of citizens of different ethnicities, races, or classes. As these diverse interests increasingly represented themselves, the American public sphere became more fractious and cacophonous in the later nineteenth century. The Fourth of July remained a natural time for the festive detonation of social and political firecrackers.

For generations, beginning in the 1790s, the Fourth of July was celebrated as a sort of American Labor Day. In 1795 in New York, for example, the General Society of Mechanics and Tradesmen joined with the city's Democratic Republican societies, including the Tammany Society, and a trade union of barrel makers, the Cooper Society, in a joint Independence Day celebration. Indeed, if the Fourth of July was increasingly transformed into a Democratic Republican festival by the turn of the nineteenth century, in northern urban areas this occurred in large part through the local activities of white workingmen who supported and identified with the party of Jefferson. Independence Day parades consisted largely of marching mechanics and artisans who elaborately displayed themselves and honored their toil as they celebrated the United States' political birth.

In the early nineteenth century, especially after 1820, American cities expanded rapidly, and in the wake of a transportation revolution that linked cities, towns, and hinterlands into a new commercial network, cities like Philadelphia became centers of manufacturing. Although the shift toward mass production in large factories came gradually, urban workers—even those laboring in workshops and smaller manufactories—saw their lives transformed by the restructuring of work and the application of new values and expectations promoted by an emergent business class. The rapid growth of American industry increasingly eroded traditional crafts, encouraged a shift toward less skilled wage labor, and produced greater social and economic inequality. For many, these unsettling trends seemed to signal the decline not merely of prosperity or economic "competency" but of independence itself. Moreover, as businessmen developed a new ethos, drawing heavily from evangelical Protestantism, to promote discipline, self-control, and morality among their workers, they clashed with older, preindustrial patterns of male sociability that could be noisy, inexpedient, and drunken. For urban workingmen in the first half of the nineteenth century, then, the Fourth of July often assumed a new political meaning: from an uncomplicated, apparently consensual celebration of the new American republic, Independence Day became an occasion to preserve working-class independence or to signal and promote the unfinished business of the American Revolution.

In Philadelphia, for example, threats to the craft system, reductions in rates or wages, and increased expectations by employers regarding the quality or quantity of production prodded wage earners to form trade unions and, in the 1830s, to band together into the General Trades' Union of the City and County of Philadelphia. In 1835, a general strike—the first in American history— proved temporarily successful in achieving a ten-hour workday; more generally, it suggested that more rigid class divisions and a more adversarial relationship had developed, separating working people from those in the new middle class.

In large part, the new reform activity of the men and women of this class— temperance being one example—was directed at working people, particularly men, whose traditional revelry in the public streets and squares on the Fourth of July, Christmas and New Year's, or muster days was increasingly defined as uncouth and immoral. Public festive sites, like State House Square and Center Square in Philadelphia, where working people gathered on Independence Day to celebrate with great mirth and feats of drinking, were threatened by those who sought to tame such festivity and impose discipline and order on the metropolis. By 1823, booths dispensing alcohol were banned, and as we have seen, new, temperate fetes competed with traditional ones for public space. Over the course of the nineteenth century, middle-class Americans increasingly privatized their Independence Day celebrations, progressively withdrawing from public spaces to commune and celebrate in countryside retreats or private halls. Laboring people had fewer options for their festivity, and they continued to occupy public streets and squares, where their celebrations attracted greater attention and criticism. For working people beset with new rules of labor and social comportment, the Fourth of July could be a moment to express their independence simply by ignoring the gospel of employers and reformers and abandoning themselves in the frivolity and drunkenness of traditional celebration. Indeed, for some workers, like those at the small textile mills on Brandywine Creek, efforts to celebrate the day were rendered explicitly radical following employers' attempts to force them to work. For them, to mark Independence Day required a strike.[46]

By the 1830s, then, the Fourth of July had become a different sort of Independence Day for working people. Its parades, banquets, and festivals became an occasion not merely for merriment but for asserting rights, for making new demands on their own behalf, even for rewriting the Declaration of Independence. George Henry Evans, an English immigrant, editor, and founder of the New York Working Man's Party, wrote and published the Working Man's Declaration of Independence in December 1829. In 1834, a Declaration of Rights of the Trades' Union of Boston and Vicinity followed, a more liberal paraphrase of the 1776 Declaration that justified labor association and argued "that labor, being the legitimate and only real source of wealth, and the laboring classes the majority and real strength of every country, their interest and happiness ought to be the principal care of Government and any laws which oppose or neglect those interests, ought not to exist." An 1830 editorial, "The Fourth of July," in the *Mechanics' Free Press* of Philadelphia had urged "working brethren" not to fail to celebrate the day and compared contemporary conditions to the crisis of the Revolution; instead of foreign enemies, they faced a domestic one, the "nonproductive classes of society." Other workingmen likened their unions to "that *Holy Combination* of that immortal band of *Mechanics*" who dumped tea into Boston Harbor in December 1773.[47]

This resort to the principles and experiences of the Revolution, as interpreted by later generations, persisted. In 1844, New England shoemakers offered their own rewriting of the Declaration of Independence, charging that employers "have robbed us of certain rights," and New England textile workers planned unsuccessfully to stage a general strike for July 4, 1846, which they declared "a second Independence Day." The tradition continued among American laborers, beyond further re-declarations by George Henry Evans in the 1840s, to Ira Steward's Second Declaration of Independence to promote the eight-hour day in 1879, to the Socialist Labor Party's Declaration of Interdependence in 1895, to the Continental Congress of Workers and Farmers' New Declaration of Independence in 1933. Labor leaders found object lessons, precedents, and inspiration in the American Revolution, and the Fourth of July continued to serve working people as an occasion to build solidarity and celebrate themselves, while they protested injustice, claimed rights, and asserted their independence.[48]

Yet for others, the festivity and principles of Independence Day rang hollow, leading some labor activists in the 1880s to invent an alternate vehicle to express their hopes and flex their political muscle—Labor Day. In 1894, the San Francisco Labor Council, for example, refused to participate in the city's official Fourth of July celebration because the parade would include military units—federal troops had just been used to break the Pullman strike. In defiance, the *Coast Seamen's Journal* published on July 5 a bitter poem, "Fireworks," that pronounced "life, liberty, and the pursuit of happiness" to be "Life without the means of livelihood, / Liberty to starve, . . . / [and] Happiness, provided you're easily satisfied." It mocked Independence Day:

The Glorious Fourth! Hurrah!
Fire off your guns and crackers—
Chinese crackers at that—
Toot your horns, wave your flag, yell
And comport yourself generally like a dod-rotten lunatic.
Why?
Because this is the Glorious Fourth,
The day we struck for independence. . . .
Independence of what?
Taxation without representation.
What about the strike on the railroads?
Hush! That's anarchy.[49]

The sarcasm of these lines at least suggests the hope of protest and potential social and political change. Those of the "Song of an Italian Workman," from Rochester, New York, express only irony and the hopelessness of finding a good job in America, land of opportunity:

Nothing job, nothing job,
I return to Italy;
Comrades, laborers, good-bye;
Adieu, land of "Fourth of July."[50]

"Fireworks," the Fourth of July poem from the *Coast Seamen's Journal*, illustrates not only the radicalism of the late-nineteenth-century labor movement but some of its limitations as well, with its exclusionist, anti-Chinese language—"Chinese crackers"—reflecting the ethnic and racial tensions and divisions that undercut working-class organization. By the 1840s, anti-immigrant feeling had produced a nativist movement that sometimes laid claim to the Fourth of July. In Philadelphia in 1844, for example, the American Republican Party staged a Grand Native American Procession on July 4 to promote its proposal to limit citizenship rights to men of U.S. birth and to curtail Catholic (and Irish) civil rights. An aggressive, reactionary act, the procession nonetheless employed the standard symbols of America's founding moment and claimed a conservative purpose—to protect church and country. The nativists' political targets—Irish Catholic Philadelphians—failed to be provoked, but a riot erupted nevertheless the next day, as nativists attacked St. Philip Neri Catholic Church in the largely Protestant Southwark neighborhood, the rumored site of an arms cache. Irish and nativists clashed in New York as well, as on July 4, 1852, when the Ancient Order of Hibernians organized its own parade, which they hoped to join to the city's official one. Clad in green and arrayed with banners, the marchers ran into trouble when they reached Abingdon Square in Greenwich Village, first with an annoyed stagecoach driver who objected to having his way blocked, and then with the congealing mob of nativists, including the notorious nativist gang the Short Boys. The violence ended when the Ninth Ward police (with their own nativist sympathies) intervened, only to indict the bloodied Hibernians for rioting.[51]

If hostility and grim economic conditions generally impelled some immigrants to say "Adieu, land of 'Fourth of July,'" and to return to their motherlands, those who stayed found themselves divided into their own ethnic and racial enclaves. Ironically, not only did class solidarity and national feeling often fail to overcome such division, even on the Fourth of July, but by the late nineteenth century in industrial cities like Worcester, Massachusetts, as Roy Rosenzweig has shown, immigrants often chose to observe Independence Day collectively among their hyphenated countrymen and countrywomen. Indeed, in 1882, as the middle classes retreated into private celebrations, the only public Fourth of July demonstration in Worcester—bands and parading—was that organized by the Irish residents. Like the Irish, Worcester's Swedish and French Canadian communities celebrated separately, sometimes even in smaller religious and fraternal constituencies within their ethnic groups. And each group seemed to use the Fourth as much to demonstrate and cultivate its ethnic identity as to trumpet its American one. For these immigrants, the cultural politics of Independence Day, while vital, nonetheless left them divided against each other not only on the Fourth of July, but on election days, workdays, and picket lines.[52]

Declaring Interdependence: Region and Nation on the Fourth of July

In 1790 about two-thirds of the nearly four million white Americans lived within some fifty miles of the Atlantic Ocean; only about 100,000 whites had settled west of the Appalachian Mountains. By 1800, that number had increased to nearly 400,000, and within a decade more than a million white citizens of the republic resided in "the West," that is, principally in the Ohio Valley. From 1790 to 1820, the United States population had doubled, to nearly ten million, but now two million white Americans inhabited nine new states and several territories in lands that they had entered only within the previous fifty years. The story of this westward migration is well known and carries with it a sense of inevitability. Yet it was not certain during the early years of the republic that the United States would stretch from the Atlantic to the Pacific, or that westering settlers would cultivate or maintain their connections, as citizens, to the nation.

If the integration of the West into the United States now seems as if it was foreordained, the disintegration of the Union along a North-South fault line strikes us as equally inevitable, given the rupture of the Civil War. Yet, while particular identities and interests increasingly distinguished North (or East, that is, New England especially) from South and informed local and national politics, such regionalism—and its connection to nationalism—was often ambiguous, contingent, and complex. Our common notion is that essential differences divided northerners and southerners from the beginning, and that the federal government chartered in the Constitution, along with decades of compromise in Congress, delayed but could never disarm the explosion of North-South tensions. Some contemporary scholars, however, have argued convincingly that United States nationalism preceded regionalism, that American nationalism created the context for and enabled sectionalism.[53]

The United States after the Revolution was a "roof without walls," according to historian John M. Murrin. American nationalism was the product, not the cause, of the American Revolution. By declaring and effecting independence, colonists—now citizens—had severed the one tie they all shared, that which bound them to Great Britain. Their revolutionary settlement required that they follow this destructive act with a constructive one—that they erect a nation and forge a new, national identity. For much of the republic's early history, Murrin argues, the Constitution alone performed much of this nationalizing work. "In the architecture of nationhood, the United States had achieved something quite remarkable. . . . Americans had erected their constitutional roof before they put up the national walls."[54]

This feat was no less remarkable, perhaps, if we acknowledge that Americans' commitment to U.S. nationalism was hardly less solid or widespread than was their commitment to localism. Indeed the two were intertwined. As historians Edward L. Ayers and Peter S. Onuf have argued, "From the Revolutionaries' perspective, local loyalties constituted the threshold of an enlightened patriotism that ultimately embraced all freedom-loving Americans across the continent. American nationalism was not predicated on suppressing and supplanting these multiple, overlapping loyalties, but rather on creating a complex constitutional regime that would secure the equal rights of localities as well as individuals." The new constitutional order and the newly emerged national public sphere—especially a rapidly expanding print culture—consolidated the nation imaginatively, as citizens throughout the states and then territories expressed their nationalism locally.[55]

Indeed, in the early republic, national identity, Onuf contends, "depended, not on dissolving preexisting parts in an homogeneous whole, but rather on rationalizing, generalizing, and equalizing the claims of constituent parts—beginning with the irreducible claims of sovereign citizens—in an expansively inclusive, homogenizing whole." But if nationalism was developed and expressed locally, it is not surprising that such nationalism would take various forms. Indeed, different nationalisms emerged as localized articulations were consolidated regionally, sometimes in protest against the perceived regionalism or sectionalism of other Americans. One region's nationalism could be another region's sectionalism. The rhetorical thrust on all sides in the early republic, argues Onuf, was unionist, but although one's own motives were above reproach, opponents were easily painted as disunionists, "whose real, unacknowledged intentions were to promote the interests of specific localities at the expense of others." The South, North, and West discovered themselves as regions, then, as they competed with each other politically to claim the true mantle of nationalism and ungenerously to characterize each other as sectional and partisan.[56]

The Fourth of July as a national and nationalist celebration reflected such complex impulses and developments: it proved an important engine for promoting national feeling throughout the United States, but it did so from dispersed localities, where different versions of nationalism were bred. Like nationalism itself, its national politics were local. Independence Day, then, could bind the nation together as citizens celebrated broadly but in common; it could give vent to oppositional, regionally informed expression of nationalism; or it could be boycotted conspicuously or celebrated on alternate occasions in protest against a perceived corruption of the nation.

The Fourth of July expressed and promoted national feeling and identity. As a nationalizing institution, it was flexible and portable (and reportable), enabling the local performance and articulation of nationalism in a manner that convinced celebrants locally (and through the wide dissemination of newspaper reports) that they were thinking nationally. By mid-nineteenth century, thousands of Fourth of July orations had been delivered throughout the country and the genre had become stale and platitudinous. "The situation of a Fourth of July orator now is like that of a man at the third table of a public dinner, who has left to him little more than scraps and empty dishes," complained one Independence Day speaker in 1854. "The American Eagle . . . has been so plucked and handled that it has become tame as a barnyard fowl. . . . The Stars and Stripes have been so vehemently flourished above admiring crowds of patriotic citizens that there is hardly a rhetorical shred left of them, and even that is somewhat the worse for handling."[57] But before they had become so hackneyed, and even after they had become thoroughly formulaic, Fourth of July orations invariably celebrated national union. As the famed orator Daniel Webster put it,

> This anniversary animates and gladdens and unites all American hearts. On other days of the year we may be party men, indulging in controversies, more or less important to the public good; we may have our likes and dislikes, and we may maintain our political differences, often with warm, and sometimes angry feelings. But today we are Americans all; and nothing but Americans.

Such sentiments were as often expressed in the South as the North. According to the Raleigh, North Carolina, *Star,* for example, the speaker at Raleigh's Independence Day exercises in 1851 chose national union as his theme: he "portrayed in a most impressive and masterly manner its value and importance to the maintenance of our liberties, and the safety, peace and prosperity of the whole country." And in the West, a region unable to claim membership among the thirteen original states formed from the Revolution, inhabitants nonetheless vigorously asserted their American nativity and nationalism in Fourth of July ceremonies, like the one that commenced immediately upon the arrival of Gen. Moses Cleaveland and his party in "New Connecticut" on July 4, 1796. There, in what is today Cleveland, Ohio, the settlers fired a "federal salute," cheered and drank to their enterprise, and christened their new post Fort Independence. As David Waldstreicher has written, "Having left the purview of the official United States, the settlers of the Western Reserve celebrated themselves back into its orbit, by invoking and following its rules for decorous yet innovative festivity."[58]

In the West, American colonizers employed Independence Day rituals as acts of conquest and incorporation, and then, turning back eastward, they performed appropriate Fourth of July ceremonies and festivals to emphasize their claims to equal rights of citizenship and statehood with the East. In 1804, for example, Meriwether Lewis and William Clark embarked on their famous expedition to explore and assert United States control over the vast Louisiana territories recently purchased from France. Like others before them, their efforts to possess the landscape included the practice of renaming its features. On July 4, 1804, the Corps of Discovery welcomed the day with a cannon shot, and later, as they camped, and enjoyed an extra gill of whiskey, they renamed a nearby watercourse Independence Creek, or Fourth of July 1804 Creek. For Clark, such an act was logical, "as this creek has no name, and this being the Fourth of July, the day of the Independence of the United States."[59] Yet the explorers hardly believed the creek was actually nameless; not only were Indians likely to have named it, but so had French voyageurs. Lewis and Clark's efforts to discover such information proved limited. Their disinterest stemmed from their interest in an imperial project—to transform Louisiana into the United States. With nomination, celebration furthered such goals.[60]

These naming practices and festive acts would continue, nowhere more monumentally than at Independence Rock along the Oregon Trail in present-day Wyoming.[61] Designated by an early party of pioneers who spent the Fourth of July there, Independence Rock remained a celebration site and natural monument to American westward expansion and nationalism. In claiming and naming the monolith, Americans possessed the country and proved their nationalism to themselves and those in the East. For these westering settlers, who saw not only their personal destiny but that of the United States itself in the West, western regionalism was a form of nationalism to end all sectionalism.

Expansion into western lands had been a working assumption of white Americans since the colonial period. The success of the American Revolution unleashed migration into the North American interior and helped to make the West a common concern to Americans throughout the thirteen states. If the Confederation government of the 1780s struck many as enfeebled, it proved sufficiently powerful to assume control of the vast territories to the west, which individual states had once claimed but which under the Articles of Confederation were the national trust. Indeed, the Revolution may have severed a common connection among the states to Great Britain, but it soon provided a new common interest in the United States' western lands. For nationalists like James Madison, serving in the first Congress after acting as the chief architect of the United States Constitution, the country's destiny was in the West: "If the calculation be just, that we double [the population] in twenty-five years, we shall speedily behold an astonishing mass of people on the western waters." In 1787, he had written Jefferson, "The people are constantly swarming, from the more to the less populous places—from Europe to Am[eric]a. From the North[er]n. and Middle parts of the U.S. to the Southern and Western." Although northerners and southerners both hoped to replicate their own social, economic, and political patterns in the West—each imagining that their regional offspring would resemble itself rather than its other parent—and although ultimately the West, in places like Bloody Kansas in the 1850s, would become an arena for North-South sectional conflict, for a time many imagined that the West would be a common expression of an undivided American nationalism, an example of the present and future union.[62]

Before Americans projected external, regional rivalries onto the West, they encountered and produced plenty of violence locally in the North American interior. Indeed, military conflict with Native inhabitants, especially during the War of 1812, became a form of nationalist practice; western conquest of people and lands represented a kind of "practical patriotism." Territorial expansion, into an Empire of Liberty in the West, would allow the country to maintain its republican character by offering "free" land, critical both to the economic opportunity and the civic integrity of citizens squeezed by inequality in the older, more densely settled, eastern parts of the country. The term Manifest Destiny was not coined until the 1840s, but its logic appeared earlier, and the celebration of its apparent fulfillment in the West soon became a fixture of Fourth of July orations and toasts. In an 1815 toast issued by easterners but read by westerners, the celebrants proclaimed the realization of American progress in the West, where Indians have been erased (or so the revelers hoped): *"The Western States*—Yesterday a wilderness . . . today cultured and blooming with industry, the *envied home of heroes* and patriots."* On the Fourth of July, American imperial ambitions could be boundless. As the Nashville, Tennessee, *Banner* reported, one toast hailed "The Eagle of the United States— may she extend her wings from the Atlantic to the Pacific; and fixing her talons on the Isthmus of Darien, stretch with her beak to the Northern Pole." For many Americans, then, imperialism was the highest form of nationalism.[63]

We know, however, that the West could not continue to diffuse sectional tensions; indeed the West proved a place to express them. When rivalries between the increasingly self-conscious North and South erupted into war, and ruptured the union, ironically Fourth of July exercises continued to proclaim the authentic nationalism of celebrants both South and North. Clothing one's self in the historical mantle of the nation was easily accomplished in the North, but the task proved surprisingly effortless in the South as well. For much of the South, the Declaration of Independence and the Fourth of July had little to say about slavery. Such questions were less important than union and compromise, which abolitions, in their view, threatened. Following the Compromise of 1850, one North Carolina toast on the Fourth of July praised "The Declaration of Independence, and the Constitution of the United States—Liberty and Union, now and forever, one and inseparable." As the Civil War approached, southerners in North Carolina and elsewhere debated how Independence Day should be observed. Some argued for its abandonment: editors of the Wilmington *Journal* claimed on June 27, 1861, that the day "belongs to the history of a union which no longer exists." But others, like the Raleigh *State Journal,* countered that the South had "as much right to the honors and glories of the first revolution as the North"; indeed, southerners were "obligated to assert the right . . . to . . . share in that . . . common heritage." According to the Raleigh *Register,* on July 3, 1861, there was no reason why the birth of Liberty should be permitted to pass unheeded wherever Liberty has votaries. . . . The conduct of the North in trampling the principles of 1776 under foot and throwing ashes on the memory of its forefathers is no sufficient reason for the failure by the South to recognize and celebrate the Fourth of July as the anniversary of the most glorious human event in the history of mankind.[64]

Despite such sentiments, celebrations of the Fourth of July were dampened considerably by the war, and the holiday remained changed thereafter. While white southerners continued to claim the heritage and heroes of the American Revolution—displaying George Washington on the Confederate national seal, for example—they devoted their energy to prosecuting the war and cultivating their alternate nationalism.[65] After the war, some southern editors saw themselves as victims more entitled than northerners to claim the Declaration of Independence and to apply it in a critique of northern tyranny. Southerners, "whose self-respect has not perished with defeat," a Wilmington, North Carolina, newspaper claimed, cannot embrace "the Fourth of July with senseless uproar and pretended rejoicing. . . . To-day, then, should be passed by our people in dignified silence." "Our people," in such a construction, excluded African Americans, who did celebrate with enthusiasm. According to another North Carolina editor in 1867, "The advent of the anniversary is hailed with feelings of sadness [rather] than with paeans of joy. The Declaration still lives, but its vital ideas are vanquished." Blacks disagreed. "Oh, my, but the Fourth was a big day," recalled Mamie Garvin Fields in her Carolina memoir of her girlhood in the 1890s, "although not for everybody. The oldtime [white] Southerners considered the Fourth of July a Yankee holiday and ignored it. So the white people stayed home and the black people 'took over' the Battery [in Charleston, South Carolina] for a day. . . . I don't think the Battery was ever so alive as on the Fourth." "On the Fourth of July," Mrs. Fields remembered, "many of our parents were actually celebrating their own freedom."[66]

Yet July 4, 1876, was marred by "the massacre of six colored citizens of the United States" at Hamburgh, South Carolina, who had been parading to hail America's Centennial. In the centennial year, larger, more elaborate Independence Day celebrations occurred throughout the country, but the primary focus of nation's festivity was in Philadelphia and centered on its Centennial Exposition, the first international exposition held in the United States. Organized and promoted by a cadre of elite businessmen, manufacturers, politicians, and academics, the exposition ultimately attracted some eight million paying customers, who were regaled with the United States' prospects for unprecedented economic growth—practically synonymous at the fair with nationalism itself. Critical to the success of such plans was the reconstruction of a national community, the integration of disaffected regions—economically as well as politically—especially the American South. While working to reconcile regions, the exposition did little to include women, immigrants, labor, or African Americans and other nonwhites. Indeed, the Centennial Exposition often proved actively hostile. Although Frederick Douglass was a guest at the Fourth of July proceedings, as a black man he was nearly prevented from ascending the official platform. When organizers were not busy imagining a glorious future and ignoring the ongoing problems of racial inequality, they constructed a glorious common past in their Centennial rite of regional reunion. As one North Carolina representative declared, "upon such an occasion the people of all parts of this country can drown out the memories of our late unfortunate struggle with the more glorious memories of the struggle in which our forefathers engaged." This was a forefather clause that excluded African Americans not merely in the South but in the North as well.[67]

Abandoned, then, by white southerners, the Fourth of July became a Republican Party and African American holiday after the Civil War, a contested nationalist celebration in a divided South. The North Carolina historian Fletcher M. Green could write as late as the 1950s, "today little attention is paid to July Fourth by the people of North Carolina." Still, celebrations of American Independence Day returned, at least to some parts of the South, especially after the Centennial as Reconstruction ended, as the issue of slavery was displaced and the agenda of racial justice abandoned, and as white Americans north and south emphasized sectional reconciliation.[68]

In postbellum United States, the West became again a critical site for nationalist expression. In 1893, of course, Frederick Jackson Turner explained American history in terms of its frontier experience, an experience situated fundamentally in "the West." But previous to Turner's formulation, many believed the West to have been critical in the molding of United States identity and national character. More importantly, inhabitants of the West in the last quarter of the nineteenth century sought to prove such a point by placing themselves within the orbit of American political as well as economic and cultural life. In 1864, Nevada entered the troubled Union as the thirty-sixth state. Nine more states—all west of the Mississippi—would join the Union by 1896, having passed their patriotic auditions and achieved the constitutional requirements for statehood. They would be joined by five more in the twentieth century. In each case, the inhabitants of these places used the Fourth of July to demonstrate their patriotic devotion to the nation.[69] Among the most problematic of these prospective states was Utah, which offers a case worth examining briefly.

Fig. 4. Opening ceremonies of the centennial year, midnight on January 1, 1876, Independence Hall, Philadelphia, from *Frank Leslie's Illustrated Newspaper,* January 22, 1876. Courtesy of Knight Library, University of Oregon.

Driven from Missouri and Illinois, members of the Church of Jesus Christ of Latter-Day Saints, or Mormons, migrated to the Great Basin wastelands of Deseret in 1847, arriving on July 24, a date that subsequently would be marked as Pioneer Day. They had escaped the jurisdiction of the United States, but the United States almost immediately claimed their new Canaan, after the Mexican-American War. Soon, the Gold Rush, overland migration to the Pacific Coast, and then the transcontinental railroad linked Deseret to the rest of the United States. The Mormon leader Brigham Young appealed for immediate statehood for his colony, but instead a new, smaller Utah Territory was constructed by Congress in 1850, with Young as its territorial governor. The history of the territory, and its place within the nation, was troubled, as outsiders as well as internal rivals challenged the theocracy of Brigham Young, condemned Mormon religious practices—particularly polygamy, which the church affirmed publicly in 1852—and questioned Mormons' loyalty.[70]

Mormons sought to demonstrate their fealty even during the course of their exodus to Salt Lake. They agreed to supply the United States army with five hundred men—the Mormon Battalion—to march west into Mexican territory, where they celebrated the Fourth of July in Los Angeles in 1847 and helped the United States to establish its control in southern California, before they mustered out and proceeded to the new Mormon settlements in Utah. By 1850, however, President Zachary Taylor had become a severe critic of Brigham Young and his colony, and after Taylor's death (ironically, from a malady caused by overindulgence on the Fourth of July), subsequent administrations would sustain federal hostility toward the territory. In 1857, President James Buchanan sent a military force to chasten Utah, and the territory prepared to repel the "invasion." A more serious crisis was averted when heavy snows blocked the troops' march and when, in return for a general pardon, Young and Utahans accepted the nominal authority of an appointed territorial governor, although not before the infamous Mountain Meadows Massacre occurred in September 1857. The murder of some one hundred members of a wagon train bound for California, by Indians and Mormon militia disguised as Indians, did little to endear Mormons to the federal government or to eastern American "gentiles." Charges of disloyalty continued to circulate, and some Mormons sought to squelch them through festive gestures, like the Fourth of July celebration staged at Salt Lake in 1859, by order of the lieutenant general of the Navoo Legion. "Monday, the 4th, will be the eighty-third anniversary of the birth of American freedom. It is the duty of every American citizen to commemorate the great event," Special Order No. 2 declared. Ceremonies were scripted to include a thirteen-gun salute, the hoisting of the national flag, and the performance of two bands, which were to play the "Star Spangled

Banner," and a public reading of the Declaration of Independence. Late in the day, thirty-three guns saluted the states and five more the territories of the United States.[71]

Yet such efforts could not ameliorate the antagonism toward Mormon religious practice and the frustration among critics that Utah remained a theocracy, despite Brigham Young's shift from the office of territorial governor to that of "president." In 1862 Congress passed the Morrill Act, outlawing polygamy, which the U.S. Supreme Court sustained in 1878. And with the Edmunds Law in 1882, Congress strengthened the legal mechanism to stamp out plural marriage—defined now as a felony—and acted to break the religious monopoly of government in the Utah Territory. The more punitive Edmunds-Tucker Act of 1887 struck Mormons as an attempt to destroy the church itself. By the second half of the 1880s, Utah seemed on the edge of war.[72]

On the morning of July 4, 1885, observers saw the American flag standing at half-mast on a number of public and Mormon-occupied buildings throughout Salt Lake City. When it turned out that neither ex-president Ulysses S. Grant, who was critically ill, nor the Mormon president John Taylor had passed away, this sign of mourning seemed inexplicable, except as a message of Mormon protest against the United States on its day of jubilation. Local gentiles expressed outrage at the disrespect exhibited toward the flag and the nation's natal day, and they again accused the Mormon leadership of treason. The *Salt Lake Tribune* editors questioned, "And this is the loyalty of the Mormon people! . . . Let us hear no more of Mormon love for the Stars and Stripes." The Mormon *Deseret News* defended Mormon Utahans, calling them "the most loyal community within the pale of the Republic of the United States of America." But its editors continued,

> They rejoice when the principles of human liberty upon which the nation was founded are vindicated and maintained.
>
> On the other hand, when these sacred safeguards are trampled in the dust they are striken with sorrow inexpressible.
>
> There are no reason for engaging in expressions of joy under existing circumstances.

In Ogden, Mormon celebrants hailed the Constitution but lamented the perceived abuses Utah suffered under its poor application in the territory. Given the violation of religious freedom, guaranteed in the Constitution, the Mormon apostle and politician Moses R. Thatcher asked, "What blessing, privilege or right extended by human hands can the suffering majority in Utah rejoice over on this our nation's anniversary?" Alarm grew amid suspicions that such acts of mourning and rebellion would be repeated or escalated on July 24, and President Grover Cleveland ordered that all military posts in the West Platte Department remain at full strength and be prepared for a potential Mormon uprising. Of course, that never materialized, and Grant's death on July 23 offered a legitimate occasion for lowering the flag to half-mast on Utah's Pioneer Day.[73]

Mormons felt persecuted by a judicial campaign to imprison their leaders, the most prominent polygamists in Utah. The Church urged victims of these efforts to offer no resistance, which they believed might furnish federal officials an excuse for military intervention in the territory. Some polygamists went underground, but a number of Mormon men—including several bishops— were arrested and confined at the Utah Territorial Penitentiary. Contesting gentile notions of national identity and patriotism, and asserting their own loyalty and citizenship, this "'Pen' Community" staged its own Fourth of July fetes within the prison. George Hamilton Taylor recorded in his diary on Monday July 5, 1886, "This has been a grand galaday." Beginning at 8:30, he and other imprisoned "cohabs" staged an elaborate program with music, dance, and drama, a considerable midday meal of boiled ham, salad, bread, pickles, cake, pie, cheese, butter, lemonade, and ice cream, and in the afternoon races for various prizes.[74]

Partisanship in Utah expressed itself through nationalist language, as both Mormons and their "gentile" opponents sought to define their own positions as loyal and essentially American against the other's acts of particular self-interest, even treason. Non-Mormons, for example, who decried Mormons' rebellious half-masting of the flag on the Fourth of July and denounced their mock funerals for the Constitution, called their own meeting place Independence Hall—a building that served them as a church house, political meetinghouse, businessmen's club, and the caucus site for the Liberal Party of Utah in the 1880s. This invocation of the American sacred site in Philadelphia declared independence from Mormon control locally, while it placed these religious and political dissenters within the narrative of American national history. Mormons themselves, of course, acted similarly. Both sides, then, asserted their nationalism locally, situating local interests and identities within a discourse of nationalism. Partisanism enabled nationalism in Utah, giving it its vitality and peculiar forms; indeed elevation of the territory to statehood—to full membership in the federal system—was the common goal of both Mormons and gentiles as they battled each other for local control and the right to determine the character of Utah. In this contest, the Fourth of July served both parties as an occasion to demonstrate their loyalty, to critique their opponents' versions of nationalist feeling, and to reshape the national political geography by celebrating themselves into the Union on their own terms. Finally, following President Cleveland's January 4 proclamation, in 1896 Utah was able to welcome statehood with parades throughout the state. The festivity, begun in January, continued during the year, especially in midsummer in massive celebrations of localism and nationalism on both July 4 and 24—Independence Day and Pioneer Day.[75]

Declaring Dependence

If the renaming of Deseret to Utah in 1850 recognized that territory as the land of the Utes, it had much less to do with honoring Indians than constraining Mormons. As the conflation of celebrations of American national independence and pioneers in Utah and throughout the West suggests, the place of Indians in the United States, and in the nation's most sacred public festival—Independence Day—was problematic. White Americans had demonstrated their nationalism, identity, and patriotism by conquering the continent's lands and peoples, and the Fourth of July was conventionally an occasion to celebrate their triumph—a triumph based on Native dispossession. Pioneers effected dependency or extinction, not independence, for American Indians. To paraphrase the nineteenth-century black abolitionist Frederick Douglass, we might ask, then, What to the Indian is the Fourth of July?[76]

In the chartering text of the Declaration of Independence, indictments against George III had included the charge that "He . . . has endeavored to bring on the inhabitants of our frontiers the merciless Indian savages, whose known rule of warfare is an undistinguished destruction of all ages, sexes, and conditions." Evaluated historically, such a claim lacks credibility not only because the king had done no such thing but also because of its inaccurate generalization about Native warfare and its failure to place frontier conflict in the context of white expansionism. But the Declaration was a polemical statement, not a dispassionate historical analysis; it told rebellious white Americans what they wanted to hear. Significantly, it defined Indians as savage and placed them in league with the enemy. The American Revolution was most revolutionary, and most violent, when it faced west, where white militia and Continental soldiers confronted Native people, the largest body of "loyalists" in America. George Rogers Clark, for example, whose celebrated capture of Kaskaskia on July 4, 1778, would continue to be celebrated in Illinois, developed a savage reputation as he carried total war to the republic's western borderlands. Forced from their position of neutrality, some tribes like the Oneidas and Tuscaroras supported the new republic, but most Native people in the West maintained loyalty to the Crown, which had protected them better than provincial governments against western white settlers. Yet patriot and loyalist Indians alike saw their positions deteriorate after the Treaty of Paris. In a revolutionary act as radical as any in the French or Russian Revolutions, Native land was expropriated and redistributed to white Americans pushing into the republic's Empire of Liberty. Sacred documents, like the Declaration and the Constitution, had little to say to Native Americans—indeed, they curtailed rather than promised or protected rights—and most Natives sought to avoid the embracing arms of state and federal governments.[77]

It became increasingly difficult, however, for Native people living east, then west, of the Mississippi River to retain their autonomy and lands, and they were forced to find means of accommodation and survival within a republic committed to Native disappearance, either literally through removal or destruction, or culturally through assimilation. This is a complex story, which a generation of historians has worked hard to tell; its contours, barely sketched here, cannot be explored fully. Nonetheless, examination of America's great political festival—Independence Day—and its impact on and invocation by Indians adds nuance to our understanding of both Native history and the complex uses and meanings of the Fourth of July in the United States. How could Indians, cast as villains in America's play of political nativity, find anything to celebrate on Independence Day?

William Apess, a Pequot and a Methodist preacher, published five books between 1829 and 1836, including the first published autobiography of an Indian as well as stingingly critical historical, political, and personal writings on the Native experience in the United States.[78] In his *Eulogy on King Philip, as Pronounced at the Odeon, in Federal Street, Boston* (1836), Apess paired the Wampanoag leader Metacom, or Philip, who died in 1676, with the hero of 1776, George Washington:

> as the immortal Washington lives endeared and engraven on the hearts of every white American, never to be forgotten in time—even such is the immortal Philip honored, as held in memory by the degraded but yet grateful descendants who appreciate his character; so will every patriot, especially in this enlightened age, respect the rude yet all-accomplished son of the forest, that died a martyr to his cause, though unsuccessful, yet as glorious as the *American* Revolution.[79]

Apess's juxtaposition destabilized, even while it appropriated, white patriotic rhetoric. Apess sought to write the elided Indians back into the narrative of American history, and to construct a Native separatism—or Native nationalism—against white assimilationist efforts. Although the Revolution was glorious for whites ("Americans"), for Native people it culminated a destructive process, which continued beyond the 1780s into the nineteenth century. Indian "removal"—the coerced transfer of thousands of Native people to lands west of the Mississippi River—contemporaneously sought to achieve physically what orators like Daniel Webster accomplished rhetorically in Fourth of July speeches—to make Indians disappear. Yet they had not vanished, not even in the East. Like abolitionists, Apess contested the mindless celebration and purposeful amnesia of New Englanders, and of American revelers more generally. Forefathers' Day—when New Englanders commemorated their Pilgrim "Fathers'" mythic landing at Plymouth Rock—and Independence Day—which elevated the Founding Fathers to sainthood—were occasions of Native sorrow: "let every man of color wrap himself in mourning, for the 22nd of December and the 4th of July are days of mourning and not of joy. . . . Let them rather fast and pray to the great Spirit, the Indian's God, who deals out mercy to his red children, and not destruction," Apess declared. That this destruction was a current, not merely a historical, phenomenon added urgency to Apess's words.[80]

Indeed, William Apess, acting as an advisor to the Mashpee tribe in 1834, had been arrested on July 4, prompting the supportive *Boston Daily Advocate* to write:

> Rev. Mr. Apes, who has been conspicuous in the Marshpee [*sic*] nullification, has, we learn, been taken and committed to jail in Barnstable county; upon what process, we are not informed, but we trust, for the honor of the State, that while our mouths are yet full of bitterness against Georgian violence, upon the Indians, we shall not imitate their example.[81]

While decrying the violation of Cherokee sovereignty and the theft of tribal land by whites in the state of Georgia, Massachusetts citizens too often turned a blind eye to local Native rights, their infringement by white neighbors, or efforts toward self-determination by the Mashpees. And Apess's celebrated arrest made it clear that dependency, not independence or the rights of citizenship, was the prescribed status for Indians.

Nonetheless, Apess, himself an American veteran of the War of 1812, and the Mashpees employed the rhetoric of the Revolution and claimed rights they earned as soldiers in the War for Independence. Objecting to their status as wards, overseen by guardians appointed without their consent, the Mashpees asked, "Will the good people of Massachusetts revert back to the days of their fathers, when they were under the galling yoke of the mother country? when they petitioned the government for a redress of grievances, but in vain?"

> And now we ask the good people of Massachusetts, the boasted cradle of independence, whom we have petitioned for a redress of wrongs, more grievous than what your fathers had to bear, and our petitioning was as fruitless as theirs, and there was no other alternative but like theirs, to take our stand.

Was such disregard just? the Mashpees asked their neighbors in the pages of the *Barnstable Journal* on July 25, 1834, especially as the Mashpees themselves had "furnished them with some of her bravest men to fight your battles. Yes, by the side of your fathers they fought and bled, and now their blood cries to you from the ground to restore that liberty so unjustly taken from them by their sons."[82] Here was a double claim for rights and freedoms, which stood both on the principles of Independence Day and on the Mashpee's military service during the Revolution; Apess ambiguously (but effectively) conflated and distinguished white and red Founding Fathers: together they had secured the Revolution, but Natives' continuing struggles predated those of rebellious colonists, and they pit Indians (and Native heroes such as King Philip) against those whites righteously claiming the mantle of liberty.[83]

John Wannuaucon Quinney, a Stockbridge Mahican political leader and diplomat, similarly appropriated and challenged Fourth of July traditions, in ways that approximated black abolitionists' deployment of Independence Day to highlight American hypocrisy. Quinney's Fourth of July speech at Reidsville, New York, in 1854 followed Frederick Douglass's oration at Rochester by only two years. In it, he invoked the heroic traditions of American nationalism but distinguished his own perspective as one of the disinherited who nonetheless, through his educational training, possessed a double knowledge of American history. "I have been taught in the schools," Quinney observed, "and been able to read your histories and accounts of Europeans, yourselves and the Red Men; which instruct me, that while rejoicings to-day are commemorative of the free birth of the giant nation, they simply convey to my mind, the recollection of a transfer of the miserable weakness and dependence of my race from one great power to another."[84]

Using rhetorically the convention of Native Americans as a vanishing race, Quinney asked his white audience to give his words the weight of a deathbed announcement; indeed Quinney himself—referred to at times as one of the "Last of the Mohicans"—would live to see only one more Fourth of July. "In this spirit, . . . standing upon the soil which once was, and now ought to be, the property of this tribe [the Muh-he-con-new, or Mahicans]," he offered a counternarrative of the nation that chronicled the history of his people. This story preceded that of white colonists and failed to appear in schoolbooks: "no mind at this time can conceive, and no pen record, the terrible story of recompense for kindness, which for two hundred years has been paid the simple, trusting, guileless Muh-he-con-new." Broken promises and land theft Quinney decried as a mockery of justice. Comparing the fate of his people with that of African Americans, he declared,

The Indian is said to be the ward of the white man, and the negro his slave. Has it ever occurred to you, my friends, that while the slave is increasing, and increased by every appliance, the Indian is left to rot and die, before the humanities of this model *Republic!* You have your tears, your groans, and mobs, and riots, for individuals of the former, while your indifference of purpose, and vacillation of policy, is hurrying to extinction, whole communities of the latter.[85]

Quinney thus used the occasion of Independence Day to criticize national policy and emphasize the ways that American life departed from the high ideals celebrated on the day. Specifically, the Stockbridge-Mahican leader challenged the pioneer myth itself, which was deeply embedded in conventional Fourth of July rhetoric, and indicted government faithlessness. Despite treaties and promises to protect tribal lands, Quinney charged, "One removal follows another, and thus your sympathies and justice are evinced in speedily *fulfilling the terrible destinies of our race.*" Native disappearance was a self-fulfilling prophecy to which Quinney refused to resign himself or his people. To the residents of Reidsville, he concluded: "For myself and my tribe, I ask for justice— I believe it will sooner or later occur—and may the Great and Good Spirit enable me to die in hope."[86]

Quinney's speech affirmed Americans' faith in the ideals of the Revolution, but it did so through mourning and condemnation. Other Native leaders would follow suit, even when they tried to strike a cheerier note, as in a Fourth of July oration by Allen Wright, governor of the independent Choctaw Nation, whose speech to the people of Fort Smith, Arkansas, in 1878 ended, "Let the strain of music swell. It is neither the time nor place for sorrow. Let us look forward to a happy future—great, happy day for us all—of which this day is but a shadow." To Apess and Quinney such shadowy futures seemed gloomy, and indeed Wright's own rhetoric before a white audience was designed to persuade rather than to reflect his own darker concerns about the fate of Indian people. Speaking in defense of Choctaw sovereignty and land, Governor Wright observed sarcastically that whenever "humane philanthropic congressmen . . . pass a territorial form of government over us, they will cause us to lose a large portion of our common domain."[87]

Yet, ironically, Indians did not merely participate in white-sponsored Fourth of July celebrations; some found occasion to observe their own Independence Day fetes. Alfred Cope, Quaker visitor to the Oneida reservation near Green Bay, Wisconsin, in 1849, reported that "in all respects they [the Oneidas] would bear pretty well to be put in comparison with most communities of whites of as recent date." And like other "pioneers," they made much of the Fourth of July. Independence Day was the climax of Cope's visit.

As had become customary, the entire tribe assembled at their head chief's house for dinner, where they dined at long tables under a bower made from stakes and green boughs. Eating in shifts on white tablecloths and china plates, Oneida celebrants ate a sumptuous meal of venison, pork, beef, beans, and white bread, drank coffee and water, and feasted on desserts of peach pie and rice pudding. The ignition of gunpowder rammed into the hole of an anvil provided explosive salutes in honor of the day, while a lacrosse game added to the festivity.[88]

Remarkably, by 1881 Cherokees were among Native celebrants of the Fourth of July, as an article in the *Cherokee Advocate* attested, despite the bitter history of their removal along the Trail of Tears and their devastating experience in the Civil War. Creek orator G. W. Grayson reminded his Cherokee audience that "we have recent and peculiar reasons for joy"—an all too unusual judicial and military intervention to protect them against local white aggressors—but he added that their joy "in no way relate[d] to the declaration of American Independence." In part, these Oklahoma Indians simply took their own part "in the general feeling" of the nation, "this being a day of general rejoicing in the land."[89] Their commemoration of a moment of survival could not obscure the dangers that remained within a system that often failed them, or the irrelevance on most occasions of the sacred documents of American liberty; on the Fourth of July, their nationalist exercise was decidedly local, alternative if not explicitly oppositional, a celebration of Native nation, community, clan, and family.

As the last of the Indian wars ended late in the nineteenth century, and Native people found themselves confined to reservations and subject to intensified programs of assimilation by white officials and reformers, American Independence Day more often became a central holiday to Indians. Of course, many continued to ignore the day. But in reservation communities, and especially in schools both on and off the reservation, white agents and teachers stressed the "civilizing" effects of national ceremonial observances—in the school calendar, from Columbus Day to the Fourth of July—and they foisted these civic fetes on their wards.

In 1890, United States Commissioner of Indian Affairs Thomas Jefferson Morgan issued instructions for "the appropriate celebration" of various holidays by Indians in government schools, "as a part of their education and a means of preparation and training for civilized home life and American citizenship." Independence Day was a cornerstone in this program of civic indoctrination. "The Indians are destined to become absorbed into the national life, not as Indians, but as Americans," the commissioner wrote to his agents in the field. Indian youth therefore required instruction in "the elements of

American history, acquainting them especially with the leading facts in the lives of the most notable and worthy historical characters," as well as with "the elementary principles of the Government under which they live." Along with "familiar talks," textbooks, debating societies, manuals of rules of order, patriotic songs and symbols, like the "Stars and Stripes," national holidays "should be observed with appropriate exercises in all the Indian schools." "In all proper ways," the commissioner concluded, "teachers in Indian schools should endeavor to appeal to the highest elements of manhood and womanhood in their pupils, exciting in them an ambition after excellence in character and dignity of surroundings, and they should carefully avoid any unnecessary reference to the fact that they are Indians." The Fourth of July and other national holidays were thus enlisted to promote the devastating agenda for Native Americans articulated by men like Richard H. Pratt, the founder of Carlisle Indian School, that is, "to kill the Indian in him and save the man."[90]

Surely these efforts, especially in boarding schools, must have had an impact, but Native people were hardly empty receptacles for patriotic prescriptions. Even the satisfied communications of those encouraging Fourth of July observances in the field betrayed some uncertainty about the nature and content of Native celebrations. In his 1890 report, the commissioner quoted a letter on the subject from the ethnologist and reformer Alice C. Fletcher, among the Nez Percés of Idaho as a special agent: although some five hundred people gathered, a day or two in advance, regaled themselves in "citizens' clothes," and conducted a relatively sedate ceremony, complete with religious services, flag waving, singing, and a procession, something was not quite right. Fletcher did not recognize their song, "We'll Stand, Fourth of July." She found the Nez Percés' salutation odd: "As I walked about I was greeted with a hand-shake, a nod of the head, and smiles, and 'Fourth of July,' much as we say 'Happy New Year.'" And some Indians seemed confused about the holiday: "One man declared that he did not fully understand what we celebrated, but the Fourth of July was to celebrate." Although convinced that festivity was the order of the day, the Nez Percé celebrants exhibited little interest in the official reasons that underpinned the occasion. "Just as a returned student was stepping forth to give the historical data of the day," Fletcher reported, "the crier announced that the people must begin to prepare for dinner, and the audience melted at the summons." Saved from a didactic oration, the crowd promptly commenced their feast of beef, salmon, canned fruit, bread, cake, and wild potatoes, and then they finished their festival with "the business of adopting certain persons into the tribe," some fireworks, and a prayer service.[91]

Alice Fletcher's report poses intriguing questions. The Nez Percé community seems to have expanded the duration and altered the content of its Independence Day celebration. Why did the people gather early and perhaps linger after July 4? What did their song mean, "We'll Stand, Fourth of July"? Was it a simple endorsement of United States nationalism, or did it express Nez Percé endurance and resilience amid the ordeals of reservation life? What, in fact, did Nez Percé people celebrate on Independence Day? Apparently they lacked both knowledge about and interest in the stuff of conventional Fourth of July orations—nationalist myths of pioneers, Founding Fathers, and unlimited possibilities in the pursuit of happiness. What would that Nez Percé orator have said, had he been given the chance to speak? A "returned student" from a boarding school, he might have voiced the standard nationalist clichés. On the other hand, he might have echoed the words of another Native student at Hampton Institute in a Fourth of July speech in 1887: "Then, at the height of this glorious success, a great wrong was done by the American people; this wrong was done to our race. . . . In the eyes of the law and the eyes of the people whose blood . . . was shed for the cause of independence, our race had no protection under the laws of the country. . . . The white man is the Indian's foe."[92]

Yet it is clear that the Nez Percé commemoration expressed genuine festivity: were they celebrating themselves, their own Nez Percé nationalism? Did their adoption ceremony imply such particular nationalist sentiments, in the fashion that ceremonies continue to be staged purposefully by the Immigration and Naturalization Service on the Fourth of July to swear in new citizens of the United States? If, for the Nez Percés in Idaho in 1890, Independence Day was something new, it was a hybrid holiday that cultivated traditions and meanings distinguishing it from the generic, patriotic festival envisioned by T. J. Morgan.

On Indian reservations throughout the West, the Fourth of July developed into a major public festival, despite the holiday's unwelcome ideological goals. While white officials banned Native rituals, they condoned Independence Day gatherings, which could provide cover for continued practice of proscribed rites. As one anthropologist studying a Lakota community reported in the early 1930s, "This is the only time the traditional camp circle is now used. This affair comes near the time of the former Sun Dance and arouses much talk of 'old times.'" The Fourth of July became for Lakotas "Ahn-páy-too wah-káhn táhn-ka, the Great Holy Day," according to an Indian agent.[93]

In 1914 the anthropologist Robert Lowie had hoped that Crows might be allowed to reenact for him their Sun Dance. Agent W. W. Scott refused permission, yet he offered no objections to Crow gatherings that were deemed purely "social." As historian Frederick E. Hoxie has shown, Crow leaders were quick to exploit such opportunities to maintain traditional dances and ceremonies, which they argued were entirely innocent, neither at odds with Christianity nor disloyal to the United States. By the 1890s, white officials sanctioned the Crow celebration of the Fourth of July, which featured large community gatherings over several days, with traditional, although allegedly "secular" dancing. By the early twentieth century, however, such "interesting" Fourth of July activities included the initiation of new members of the Tobacco Society, which organized the most important ritual practiced on the reservation—the local cultivation and harvesting of a rare variety of tobacco—the tribe's "means of living," according to one Crow band leader. Although agents suppressed the winter dances of the Tobacco Society, they inadvertently condoned the society's activities during the Independence Day festival.[94]

Similarly, among Hidatsas living on the Fort Berthold Reservation in North Dakota, the Fourth of July became an important event, a time of joy and celebration, an occasion to nurture traditions new and old. Late in the nineteenth century, white agency staff on the reservation had hoped to transform the congested life of villages, break up tribal organization, and halt traditional dances and ceremonies, all in the interest of "civilization." Allotment in the mid-1880s—pushing villagers out into discrete farmsteads of individually owned parcels across the vast Dakota plains—seemed well designed to accomplish such an objective. In 1886, a few families left their village at Like-a-Fishhook, for example, traveling to lands forty miles up the Missouri River, where a tall hill stood alone above a sharp curve in the river; the Hidatsas called it "Awata-hesh, that is a hill by itself." Ironically, "So considering the character of the people, as well as the landscape, we called the place Independence," wrote a missionary. If officials sought to inculcate independence and individualism, against Native communalism, at the new hamlet of Independence they did not get exactly what they bargained for. The head of one household, Wolf Chief, selected his allotment based not on the sort of rational decision-making reformers anticipated but instead on a dream; following his vision, he built his cabin on the crest of Independence Hill. Wolf Chief and others did assume a certain independence both from old ways and from the prescriptions of missionaries and agency officials, as they forged a new, hybrid way of living in their changed world. Among the most important means they used to cultivate those new traditions while cleaving to some venerable custom was their celebration of Independence Day.[95]

As among the Crows, the Hidatsas, Arikaras, and Mandans at Fort Berthold escaped the suppression of indigenous dances and ceremonies when such exercises were performed on national holidays like the Fourth of July. Superintendent Ernest Jermark, for example, declared in 1922 that "dancing, exchanging of presents, traveling from one dance to another, and dancing feasts were being carried to excess." His January 30 circular therefore conveyed a set of seven special rules to address the problem. Among these, the superintendent ruled that permission "must be obtained in writing" for any dances, and these were "to be limited to legal holidays." Rule 7 stipulated: "Promiscuous running from one dance to another must bee [sic] stopped. Dances are to be conducted during the evening only. No dancing later than 2 A.M. and all Indians to return home not later than the following morning." Jermark's regulations suggest not merely repression by white reformers and agents but the festive means that Native people used to express their resilient cultural identities. It is not clear what effect such rules had on the Native people of Fort Berthold, but it is certain that legal holidays remained havens for traditional practices and that the stipulations of rule 7 had been and continued to be honored in the breach.[96]

In 1907, for example, with the full consent of their agent, Fort Berthold residents congregated at a Mandan village at Elbowoods for a week-long Fourth of July gathering. They camped in tents and tipis in a great circle around a large dancehall and wore traditional clothing. Near sunrise each day the festivities began, sometimes with a church service. But the real action began after noon, with field sports, foot and horse races, and games. At about seven o'clock in the evening things became particularly lively, with music, singing, and alternating men's and women's dancing. About half past ten, according to a white observer, "gifts began to be made. Following old custom, the Indians made presents to visiting friends and societies. . . . As each donor concluded his speech loud applause of '*Hau! hau!*' were heard. Men and women vibrated palm over mouth to express pleasure or joy. Old women chanted and the warriors danced furiously to express their approbation." These were the sorts of festive practices that agents wanted to control or abolish, but under the cover of patriotic celebrations on legal holidays they continued.[97]

Independence Day could even offer a safe, public means of performing more transgressive acts—expressions of Native pride and antigovernment dissent, like the staging of war dances, mock raids, and sham battles. An Indian agent at Klamath in Oregon permitted his charges to engage in such exercises, "dressed in all their barbaric splendor, mounted on fleet horses, filling the welkin with the soul-curdling war whoop." He believed such displays taught schoolboys "the wonderful advancement made in a few years, under reservation training, from active savagery to a position well advanced toward practical civilization." Is this the lesson that Klamaths drew from the demonstration? Did a reenactment of Custer's defeat at Little Bighorn on the Rosebud Reservation in 1900 convey such a "civilizing" message? Indeed, one wonders about the proximity in the calendar between July 4 and June 25, the day in

1876—the United States' centennial—when Custer and his men were destroyed, and whether Cheyennes and Lakotas found a means to merge these two apparently conflicting commemorations.[98]

Among the most public of Indian demonstrations of military prowess and pride were those performed in Buffalo Bill's Wild West and similar shows staged nationally and internationally for white audiences, beginning in the 1880s. Of course, Indians had participated in spectacles in America, as well as in Europe, since the beginning of the colonial period, sometimes as oddities and sometimes, especially after United States independence, to express theatrically American identity and exceptionalism. But Buffalo Bill's Wild West represented an innovation in the popular performance of western and Indian history, legend, and myth. The day of each performance became the Fourth of July, a restaging of William Frederick Cody's first "Old Glory Blow Out" in his hometown of North Platte, Nebraska, on Independence Day in 1882. Building on the Fourth of July prototype, Cody developed a successful formula for his moveable feast; shows began with a grand parade and continued with a series of spectacles typical of Fourth of July celebrations—only better—including races on horse and foot, shooting exhibitions, feats of roping and riding, and—more unusual—dramatic presentations of exciting events, such as an attack on the Deadwood mail coach and the "Grand Hunt—including a battle

Fig. 5. A mock attack on the Rosebud Sioux Agency stockade, South Dakota, July 4, 1897. Photograph by John A. Anderson, courtesy of the Nebraska State Historical Society.

with the Indians." In his first season in 1883, Buffalo Bill employed some thirty-six Pawnees, and in 1885 with great acclaim he hired the famous Hunkpapa leader Sitting Bull and other Lakotas. Sitting Bull's celebrity, which came particularly from his participation in the Battle of the Little Bighorn, helped ensure the financial success of Buffalo Bill's Wild West. Increasingly Lakotas came to dominate the ranks of Cody's show Indians, and Cody added the epoch "Custer's Last Stand" to his show. Although displayed as exotics and deployed to confirm white stereotypes, Native entertainers in the troupe nonetheless found an escape from grim conditions on their reservations and an opportunity to travel and earn money. If their dramatic reenactments of Custer's 1876 defeat and other Native victories signified Indian barbarism and white victimhood to non-Native audiences, such exercises meant something different to the Indians who performed them; winning battles on a nightly basis cultivated feelings of pride among Native actors.[99]

In a fascinating mimetic process, some Native people made "Indian shows" a critical part of their own local celebrations of the Fourth of July, suggesting further the importance of show Indians' performances—at home or on the road—in nurturing and expressing Native nationalism. Historian Richard White has written that the Wild West shows themselves were complex reproductions: "Indians were imitating imitations of themselves. They reenacted white versions of events in which some of them actually participated." Taking this convoluted but meaningful mimesis one step farther, we can see Indians reenacting (and reinterpreting) their own imitations of white imitations of themselves; that is, they used a new conventional form to perform their own sense of Native history and experience. Amos Bad Heart Bull's *Pictographic History of the Oglala Sioux* testifies vividly to the significance of such Independence Day productions at Pine Ridge in South Dakota beginning in 1898. Bad Heart Bull's pictographic record of life at Pine Ridge between 1890 and 1913, the time of his death, included some four hundred drawings and notes in a large ledger book; a great number of these (seventy-two) illustrate two typical Fourth of July celebrations, which Bad Heart Bull called Greater Indian Shows, relating them clearly to the Independence Day extravaganzas of white America and its Wild West.[100]

The Pine Ridge celebrations continued over several days and represented "a return to the old life." They included "give-aways," processionals, various ceremonies, feasting, and courting. To Helen H. Blish, editor of Bad Heart Bull's work, the Greater Indian Shows series suggested "a certain wistfulness." The ceremonies and performances "are distinctly a part of the later reservation life; yet they express a desire for the old-time native manner of living, for they are a temporary return to the older habits of life." One might advance a sim-

Fig. 6. "Preparations for the Oglala Smoothing-the-Place-Dance at Pine Ridge, South Dakota, July 4, 1903," by Amos Bad Heart Bull. Reprinted from *A Pictographic History of the Oglala Sioux* by Amos Bad Heart Bull by permission of the University of Nebraska Press. Copyright © 1967 by the University of Nebraska Press. Copyright © renewed 1995 by the University of Nebraska Press.

ilar claim for historical pageantry among white citizens throughout the United States on the Fourth of July, although Indians and non-Indians did not necessarily share the same "mystic chords of memory," to quote Abraham Lincoln.[101]

Amos Bad Heart Bull himself maintained a critical attitude toward the hybrid Lakota celebrations he observed and joined at Pine Ridge. On one drawing of the camp circle, central dance area, and surrounding arbor of pine boughs at the 1898 Independence Day ceremony, he inscribed comments in Lakota disparaging the traditional give-away practice of his people on the occasion:

> From this kind of Fourth of July celebration the people are getting poorer. Independence Day will keep on getting greater; it will be a thing to remember. But with misunderstanding we Indians celebrate and give away many useful articles unnecessarily. On that account the Indians get poorer. . . . if this kept up, the Indian will give away his last horse; he will go that far to satisfy the demands of a pleasure-seeking people.

For Bad Heart Bull such traditional generosity threatened to be self-destructive, and it seemed to represent a misunderstanding of proper, prescribed Fourth of July conventions. He hoped that the community would regulate itself to prohibit these practices, but at Pine Ridge, give-aways remained a prominent part of the Fourth of July festivals that Lakotas invented for themselves. Bad Heart Bull's powerful drawings similarly show the enduring presence of other new "traditions," such as the Smoothing-the-Place Dance (originally part of the proscribed Sun Dance, adapted for Independence Day), warrior charges and dances, and commemorations of historical events, such as the dance and song memorializing He Dog and a battle on the Powder River, following Col. J. J. Reynolds's attack on a Lakota and Cheyenne village on March 17, 1876.[102]

If Independence Day promoted cultural revival and memory within particular Native communities, it also created opportunities for cultural innovation among Native peoples more generally and supplied a mechanism for forging new, pan-tribal national identities as Indians. In the last two decades of the nineteenth century, relative peace among plains people and their establishment on reservations denied young men the conventional means of achieving recognition and status. Many turned to art and ceremonial activity—including participation in Indian shows—and with cultural exchanges among tribes new rites emerged that transcended old ethnic and political boundaries and established new, broader ways to be and remain "Indian." Among the more significant movements to spread throughout the plains was the Grass Dance. It reached the Hidatsas from the Santee Sioux early in the 1870s, and soon men

Fig. 7. "Omaha social dance, the public portion of the Grass Dance during Fourth of July ceremonies at Pine Ridge, South Dakota, 1903" (detail), by Amos Bad Heart Bull. Reprinted from *A Pictographic History of the Oglala Sioux* by Amos Bad Heart Bull by permission of the University of Nebraska Press. Copyright © 1967 by the University of Nebraska Press. Copyright © renewed 1995 by the University of Nebraska Press.

at Fort Berthold had formed the Big Grass Society. Other societies followed among the Hidatsas, while the dance reached other tribes. The Crows, for example, adopted the Grass Dance from the Pawnees and Omahas by the 1890s; through this ceremony and other activities, Crows similarly found peaceful ways to perpetuate their warrior societies. It became customary to perform the Grass Dance at Fourth of July festivities, which among the Crows, as among the Hidatsas, featured adoption, gift giving, and the distribution of food and clothing.[103]

Such sharing and innovation among Native people, within and across reservation communities, laid the groundwork for development of the modern American Indian powwow, a festive institution that celebrates Native American life, often on the Fourth of July. Today, annual powwows are staged on Independence Day among the Shoshone-Paiutes at the Duck Valley Reservation in Idaho, the Northern Cheyennes at Lame Deer in Montana, the Yakamas at White Swan in Washington, and in numerous other Native communities throughout the West.[104]

In today's powwows—whether held on Independence Day or not—the most stately and spectacular event is the Grand Entry, which begins typically with a flag ceremony, honoring the United States flag along with state banners and Indian staffs. Here, as in the Grass Dance, Native people celebrate and perpetuate their warrior traditions. United States military veterans lead the procession into the dance arena—a considerable honor—wearing war bonnets, dancing regalia, and often military uniforms. In a way that outsiders might find surprising, such acts reflect a deep sense of patriotism among American Indian—a patriotism that finds expression also in Native observances of the Fourth of July. While Indians shaped Independence Day into a Native holiday, in the late nineteenth and early twentieth centuries numerous Indian men enlisted in the United States armed forces to fight for a nation that often failed to extend to them citizenship or the rights that attended such status.[105]

The First World War represented a watershed experience for American Indians. Certainly, Native men had fought for the United States as soldiers and scouts since it had declared independence in 1776. But in response to the challenge of World War I, Indians served in striking numbers. Although most were not subject to the draft, nonetheless more than 17,000 Native men registered and more than 6,000 were inducted into service; only 228 claimed deferment. Thousands more enlisted. Historian Russel L. Barsh has estimated that as many as 30 percent of the Indian adult male population may have served in the military—that is, some 15,000 men. Native soldiers were motivated apparently by a combination of factors—economic opportunity, patriotic feelings that inspired a desire to protect their homelands, and perhaps

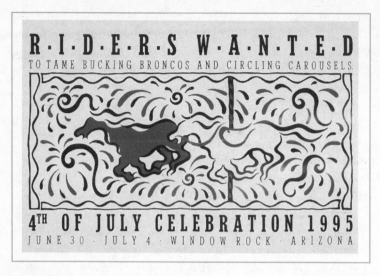

Fig. 8. Navajo Fourth of July rodeo poster, 1995. The Navajos, like other Native people, have used the Fourth of July to stage their own festivals, such as their tribal rodeo. In such events—particularly powwows and rodeos in the West—American Indians assert an ambiguous, complex nationalism. Collection of the author.

the ambition to prove their worthiness for citizenship and their commitment to American ideals (too often unfulfilled) of freedom. Motivation no doubt varied from nation to nation, and according to levels of acculturation. The Seneca anthropologist Arthur C. Parker claimed in 1917 that the "Indian fights because he loves his freedom," while "his country, his liberties, his ideals, his manhood are assailed by the brutal hypocrisy of Prussianism." Others identified that hypocrisy and brutality closer to home; the Yavapai physician and activist Carlos Montezuma, for example, believed the United States' ill treatment of Indians denied the government any legitimate authority to require that they perform military service. Yet few resisted the draft, and Native people served not only in uniform but in striking numbers on the home front as well, with service in the Red Cross and heavy investment in Liberty Bonds. Those nations with strong warrior traditions sent young men who hoped to gain admission to warrior societies upon their return; for some, such service continued a family tradition begun in the Spanish-American War, the earlier plains wars, or even the Civil War or American Revolution.[106]

The Second World War perpetuated this tradition of Native military service and cultivated deeper patriotic sentiments, which continued to grow even through the controversial era of the Vietnam War, when some 42,000 Native

Americans served as advisors or combat troops in Southeast Asia. As one Ute man commented wryly, "We Indians are grateful that the United States became such a militaristic country because it has provided us with an acceptable way to continue our warrior ways."[107] Such comments mixed patriotism with a certain skepticism about the realities beneath the lofty ideals military service was supposed to uphold and protect. Native nationalism was hardly blind. It was born of suffering as well as hope, and military service in a wider world exposed Native people to both new opportunities and fresh prejudices. Fundamentally, Indian patriotism emanated from love of country, veneration literally of the land itself as well as the Native communities it supports. "Although they fought for the nation as a whole," Cherokee-Creek scholar and veteran Tom Holm has written, "Native American veterans identify themselves with a community (tribe) and with that community's specific traditions. Their sense of peoplehood is directly linked to place (homeland / holy land) and a shared sacred history. They tend to think of themselves as warriors of an older, sacred tradition, but placed in a changed set of circumstances." Navajo World War II veteran Albert Smith explained his service in these terms: "What happened to the Navajos in the past were social conflicts. But this conflict involved Mother Earth being dominated by foreign countries. It was our responsibility to defend her." Natives as much as any Americans sought to defend their land and way of life, and even the Stars and Stripes— among the most powerful symbols in Indian country—signifies for many Indians today a particularly local sort of American nationalism.[108]

Independence Day flourished both because the holiday was foisted on Indians and because the fete offered them opportunities to preserve traditions or invent new ways to survive. In Mission, Oregon, as July 4, 1996, approached on the Umatilla Reservation, work crews rushed to complete the Nix-Ya-Wii, or Place of the Quaking Aspens Warrior Memorial, scheduled to be dedicated by the tribal government on Independence Day. On the other hand, in 1987 Onondaga leader Leon Shenandoah, the sachem Tadadaho, had decreed that Fourth of July fireworks would no longer be sold at roadside stands in the New York reservation. "We decided," he said, "that it's not really our way. It's not really independence for us." Such varied responses to the Fourth of July— to express patriotism and particular Native nationalism, to distinguish Indians from whites by avoiding the holiday's rites, or to critique America's record in upholding its principles and promises—all occur without any diminishment of the irony that this holy day continued to celebrate an Empire of Liberty (made possible by the expropriation of Native land) that remained highly colonial and deeply implicated in Indian assimilation and dispossession.[109]

Fireworks

Like millions of other Americans, on July 4, 2000, I watched with amazement and delight as the dark sky exploded with fireworks. I happened to be standing atop a tall building on New York's East Side, a perfect vantage point to witness the spectacle, as barges in the East River sent up volleys of fire, perfectly coordinated with other, duplicate outbursts from similar barges deployed off the tip of lower Manhattan, and on the West Side along the Hudson River. The grand Fourth of July display—the last of the twentieth century and the millennium—was terrific; many declared these fireworks the best they ever saw, and who can argue with such judgments? For a young visitor from Ukraine, Katya Dvornichenko, they were everything she had hoped they would be: "It was my dream to see fireworks above the Statue of Liberty. . . . I saw that. Now since that time I have no more dreams. I do not know what to dream now." But others were more jaded. The *New York Times* art critic Michael Kimmelman recommended the quieter "Fireworks!" exhibition at the Metropolitan Museum of Art over the actual event: "Sure the fireworks tonight will be spectacular. They're spectacular every year, and this time they're supposed to be bigger than ever." But his headline asked, "Why Settle for Real Fireworks?" Indeed, fireworks almost invariably are spectacular, and almost anyone can qualify as a critic in evaluating them, but popular and professional critics alike usually assess fireworks displays in terms of quantity, not quality (or, rather, quality is determined by quantity—bigger is better). How often can we recount in any detail the content of previously witnessed fireworks exhibitions, beyond perhaps recalling how big they were or how long they lasted? We usually say, "they were spectacular." But what do they mean to Americans on the Fourth of July? And what does it say about Independence Day in the late twentieth century if, in order to convenience city officials or fit into citizens' schedules or save money, the day's emblematic fireworks are staged not even on the Fourth of July itself but on other, more expedient and proximate weekend nights before or after the holiday? Has the Fourth of July become a moveable feast? Does it remain a meaningful festival?[110]

As early as the ninth century, the Chinese had discovered the explosive potential in the mixture of sulfur, charcoal, and saltpeter (potassium nitrate). By the fourteenth century—well before the "discovery" of America—knowledge of fireworks had reached Europe, where the concoction was soon redeployed to serve martial purposes. But *feux d'artifice*, or "artificial fireworks," continued to attend festivity in Europe even as gunpowder revolutionized warfare and aided colonial expansion. European fireworks displays marked coronations, royal weddings and births, military victories, saints' days, national commemorations, and similar extraordinary occasions, producing real if fleeting pleasure, wonder, and awe. And they did so for centuries before the United States was born in 1776.[111]

Yet nothing seems as American as fireworks on the Fourth of July. In a sense, "the rockets' red glare, the bombs bursting in air," give proof through the two centuries that the nation is still there, as safe as ever, having withstood military tests since the War of 1812. But mostly, the fiery brilliance of fireworks seems to wash out historical memory, and the ephemeral pyrotechnics themselves leave little lasting impression in the sky, on spectators, or on the future. If viewers are transfixed by the extraordinary presence of the spectacle, such exhibitions have no essential meaning, nor can they bear complicated, partisan messages. They are captivating, thrilling, picturesque, and democratic. Even if sponsored by particular parties, the displays are easily appropriated by the eyes of others in the public space of the night sky. The lightening of fireworks provides no enlightenment; they seldom connect spectators to their historical past or call matters of civic importance to their collective attention. They collect a crowd, direct individual gazes to the same site in the heavens, and amuse many in a vague, mindless, perhaps patriotic joy.

The delightful meaninglessness of fireworks makes them an apt metaphor for American Independence Day in the twentieth century. The holiday came to signify everything and nothing. It could be percussive and startling, as some Americans continued to use the occasion to fight for the rights of first-class citizenship, or in time of war it could be used to mobilize patriotism. But generally the day is more flash than substance, an opportunity for mirth and avoidance of politics, not for redefining political identity, challenging historical memory, or claiming entitlements. A firecracker explodes, sending fire, smoke, noise, and debris in all directions. Like a firecracker, the Fourth of July in the twentieth century exploded with meanings—it became the tool or toy of so many, who have used the day for such disparate purposes, that the total social and political din produced made time stand still and obliterated all particular sounds and significances. The bang itself is an easy affirmation of Americanism—vaguely concocted, fun, "old fashioned," local, and familial—more amusement than political message. To the chagrin of Gene Massey, a forty-one-year-old veteran from Sycamore, Illinois, in 1996, "You ask most kids about Independence Day, and they don't even know what it is. You ask them about the Fourth of July, and they say, 'fireworks.'"[112]

For most Americans, real problems should not intrude on the Fourth of July, although celebrations could prove dangerous, even when filled with good, clean fun. In the previous century, on July 4, 1850, President Zachary Taylor had participated in an Independence Day fete at the yet unfinished

Washington Monument, where he ate uncooked fruit and vegetables and drank large amounts of cold water and milk. On July 9 Taylor died of acute gastroenteritis. More often, however, Fourth of July casualties were related to fireworks mishaps. In the early twentieth century, as injuries climbed (along with fears of "foreigners" and their raucous celebrations of Independence Day), some began to refer to the holiday as the Barbarous Fourth. In 1908, officials recorded some fifty-six hundred casualties; according to one commentator, "During the entire War of the Revolution, . . . the American losses were only slightly more than twice that number in killed, wounded, and missing." In 1903, the *Journal of the American Medical Association* began to compile statistics relating to Fourth of July deaths and injuries; its 1909 report noted that more Americans were killed or injured celebrating Independence Day that year than had suffered similar fates in the Battle of Bunker Hill. Some—mostly "bright, active boys aged from six to eighteen years"—died agonizing deaths, not merely from explosions but from the effects of blood poisoning, or tetanus. "If this annual sacrifice were really necessary, it would be far more merciful to pick out the hundred or more youths each year [afflicted with tetanus in this fashion] and deliberately shoot them," the journal commented. "But this annual outrage is not necessary; it is entirely preventable, and the prevention rests with our city governments," the American Medical Association concluded. That year the Playground Association of America advocated a Safe and Sane Fourth and proposed alternate programs and activities for the day, which emphasized patriotism and Americanization of immigrants, and which, they hoped, might distract celebrants from dangerous mayhem. Communities across the United States began to plan full-day events and ban the sale of fireworks.[113]

Increasingly municipal governments assumed control of Independence Day festivity in the early twentieth century, although they sometimes found they had a tiger by the tail. As individual neighborhood and ethnic celebrations came under the auspices of elite, professional authority, the carnival aspects of traditional fetes could infuse—perhaps corrupt—the orderly, uplifting, and didactic festivals designed by officials. As historian David Glassberg has demonstrated, social elites in the early twentieth century looked upon occasions such as Independence Day as opportunities for reform and revitalization, not merely of the festivals themselves but of American society more broadly. Through a new historical pageantry, artists and social workers could employ holidays or historical anniversaries—particularly by staging historical skits and plays, athletic contests, marching and calisthenic drills, games, and folk dances—to revitalize aesthetics and the emotional basis of American civilization while handing down moral principles and creating new community. In the process, they hoped to tame the vulgar exuberance of ethnic and working-class Americans, counteract the drabness of industrial life and the crudeness of commercial amusements, and build a common civic culture, one that re-worked genteel traditions, making them more democratic and pluralistic. Eventually, however, the new pageantry itself became old, in some cases falling into civic boosterism, becoming mired in antimodernism, failing to accommodate the diverse pasts and experiences of working-class people, and succumbing to commercial and political corruption.[114]

The Progressive reform of Independence Day certainly contributed to its transformation into a more organized, official patriotic occasion, at least in its public guise. But ultimately, the hopes of reformers to use the day as a tool of civic education and social transformation were frustrated. Fireworks became more a spectator sport than previously, but revelers continued to fire them

Fig. 9. "The Fourth of July." Nine sketches of boys celebrating, from *Every Saturday: An Illustrated Weekly Journal,* July 9, 1870. Such antics—loud and dangerous—encouraged some to call the Fourth of July Tetanus Day. The "safe and sane" Fourth of July program sought to curtail this sort of behavior and participated in a broader effort to control public celebration. Courtesy of Knight Library, University of Oregon.

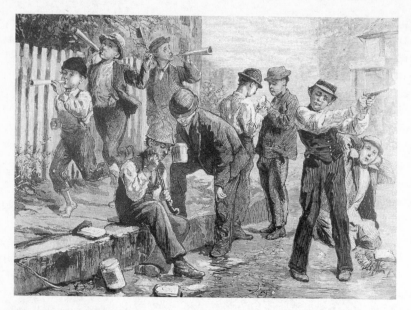

Fig. 10. "The Glorious Fourth—The First Gun (5 A.M.)," from *Harper's Weekly,* July 8, 1871. Courtesy of Knight Library, University of Oregon.

Fig. 11. "The Day after 1878" and "Peace and Quietness," from *Harper's Weekly,* July 13, 1878. These political cartoons commented on the disruption, noise, and danger of public Fourth of July displays, which middle-class civic reformers sought to control. Courtesy of Knight Library, University of Oregon.

off—even when banned by local and state ordinances—exposing themselves and those nearby to danger. Private, unofficial celebration of the Fourth of July continued to emphasize recreation and amusement, which public fireworks programs served by providing apolitical spectacles to complement light diversions such as picnics, concerts, or other popular entertainments.

In Don DeLillo's 1985 novel *White Noise*, Murray—a college professor perversely teaching a seminar on movie car crashes—tells his colleague Jack Lasher, "I see these car crashes as part of a long tradition of American optimism." Murray tells his students to see in the sequences he shows them a certain "innocence," not decay or waste or violence. The car crash is "a celebration," he says. "A reaffirmation of traditional values and beliefs. I connect car crashes to holidays like Thanksgiving and the Fourth. We don't mourn the dead or rejoice in miracles. These are days of secular optimism, of self-celebration. . . . Look past the violence, Jack. There is a wonderful brimming spirit of innocence and fun."[115] In absurd fashion, DeLillo suggests the strange pleasure of modern spectacle, of immersion in the horrible wonder of the technological sublime in which the physical consequences of powerful machines or violent acts can excite but are not really confronted. In films, the crashes are not real, except perhaps to stuntmen who really do risk their lives, but viewers can find them spectacular and awesome, whether at the movies or the motor speedway. Optimism, celebration, innocence, fun: these are not exactly the terms most would use for such acts of destruction. But most would not resist them as adjectives modifying "fireworks," or the day they emblemize, the Fourth of July.

Although more benign and less repulsive than a car crash or (in an earlier era) a public hanging or an auto-da-fé, other sorts of destructive spectacles have been staged since the early nineteenth century in the United States to celebrate Independence Day. Today weird spectacles such as exploding ships, tightrope crossings of Niagara Falls, plummeting over Niagara's abyss in boat or barrel, or shooting off Yosemite firefalls—the practice of dispatching smoldering embers over the cliffs into Yosemite Valley, creating a flaming, thousand-foot cascade—have fallen out of favor, but they suggest the importance of the Fourth of July as a time for indulging in mindless and imprudent activities.[116]

One year in the early 1870s, in anticipation of Independence Day, residents of Yosemite Valley approached one James McCauley, locally famous for pitching things off Yosemite's high canyon walls, to toss fireworks from Glacier Point. McCauley developed his own scheme, which became a fixture of Fourth of July celebrations in Yosemite until 1968—the aforementioned firefall. McCauley would build a large fire, allow it to burn to embers, and then push them over the cliff, creating an astonishing, glowing ribbon of fire. Tourists to the valley delighted in the performance, "shrinking under the ear-splitting detonations of the dynamite that accompanied the fire at intervals," McCauley's son recalled. After McCauley, the firefall survived, more quietly, as a spectacle under David A. Curry, founder of the Yosemite Park and Curry Company, and other proprietors. As the firefall grew in popularity, Curry began to display it nightly during the summer, accompanied now by violins rather than explosions. In 1952, *Collier's* magazine wrote, "for more than half a century, this man-made spectacle has rivaled the natural glories of Yosemite."[117]

In Oregon as well, excited Independence Day revelers sought to make the state's natural wonders even better on the Fourth of July. Mount Hood dominates the eastern skyline of Portland, Oregon, and during the last quarter of the nineteenth century, citizens talked of illuminating the peak as a culmination to their annual fireworks. At 11:30 P.M. on the Fourth of July 1887, the mountaineer and writer William Gladstone Steel succeeded. With a party of fellow mountaineers, he climbed to the summit with a hundred pounds of lycopodium powder, which he exploded into red fire at the appointed moment. According to the *Oregonian*, the bright red light "was greeted with cheers from the thousands congregated on the bridge, wharves, roofs, boats on the river and on the hills back of town, and with vigorous and long-continued whistling from every steamboat on the river." The display lasted exactly fifty-eight seconds and was visible not only from Portland—fifty-one miles as the crow flies—but from even more distant towns in the Willamette Valley and in eastern Oregon. "This was the most novel and the highest illumination ever made, and was seen the farthest and formed a fitting close to the celebration of 1887," the *Oregonian* wrote.[118]

Reports of the event spread even farther, along the West Coast and across the country to New York, with the exploits of Steel even meriting a story in *Frank Leslie's Illustrated Newspaper*. The *Indianapolis News* observed that "the illuminated area was a circle of 150 miles in diameter. We suspect that this was the greatest area ever lighted by artificial means since God spoke light into existence. There is nothing [more] wonderful about it but the daring and endurance of the men who carried their load of show blaze so high." The *New Northwest* declared dramatically that "now the name of Will Steel will be handed down to posterity and future generations will gaze on the slab where he may be laid to rest, and with a long drawn sigh whisper, perhaps for fear of disturbing his ashes, 'He was the one who illuminated Mount Hood on the night of July 4th, 1887.'" From the perspective of those setting the peak aflame, J. M. Baltimore wrote for *Frank Leslie's Illustrated Newspaper*, "a more wonderful, weird and startling effect could not possibly be imagined. The entire western side of the mountain glowed as if covered with a mass of burning, red-hot lava, while stupendous shadows from intervening peaks were projected for miles, far towards the western slopes of the lofty range. . . . The spectacle was one of overwhelming power and brilliancy," but within just over a minute, "the fierce, penetrating flames subsided, and the vast mountain relapsed into its darkness and gloom."[119]

Portland's attempts to boost itself through illumination stunts, to promote economic development and population expansion, coincided with efforts by Steel and others to challenge and perhaps dominate nature, in the interests of adventure, science, and even national defense. Steel and his red fire could convert the dormant Mount Hood into an active volcano, exploding on command, to entertain Oregonians and honor the state and the nation on the Fourth of July. More illumination attempts followed, and some succeeded, like the one arranged for July 4, 1905, in conjunction with Portland's Lewis and Clark Centennial Exposition. But ultimately little scientific value was found in these pyrotechnic experiments, nor was there much practical utility in locating military signal corps on various high Cascade peaks. Sometimes nature defeated illumination expeditions with snows and high winds, but in the early twentieth century no one decried the environmental implications of setting the fragile ecological zones high atop Mount Hood ablaze. Yet the actual or potential destruction here or in Yosemite firefalls was real, even in the absence of expressions of concern. Serious business was seldom allowed to intrude, to kill the joy of the Fourth of July.

Perhaps surprisingly, there remains little concern today for the danger or environmental impact of fireworks—whether the sorts propelled high into the air officially or fired off popularly. In the summer of 2000, however, the Earth Island Institute, an environmental organization in San Francisco, called attention to the toxic particulates blasted about by patriotic fireworks, which have been linked to lung cancer and heart attacks. Fireworks displays, the Institute argued, can generate increased levels of airborne arsenic, cadmium, mercury, lead, copper, zinc, and chromium. In 1976, the United States Environmental Protection Agency studied the effects of a fireworks exhibition in St. Louis, Missouri, on the Fourth of July. The EPA found the concentration of fine particulate matter in the air after the fireworks to be about double its morning reading; arsenic levels had been elevated some twenty-eight times those of twelve hours earlier, and the toxic element antimony was found to be about two hundred times the previous level. The dangers such elevated pollutants pose are not completely clear, with some scientists reserving judgment while others declaring unequivocally, "It's a threat." Fireworks manufacturers, of course, defend their products' safety, and most spectators worry little about such perils.[120]

Still, the horrors of the Barbarous Fourth have not been completely eliminated. In 1993, the National Safety Council reported ten deaths related to fireworks. On July 3, 1996, eight people died in Scottown, Ohio, in a blaze of fire, smoke, whizzing rockets, and exploding firecrackers, which had been ignited in a fireworks store filled with customers. Ironically, although small fireworks could be purchased legally in Ohio, setting them off within the state limits was illegal. Following in the wake of earlier efforts to make Independence Day safe, in 1974 the United States Consumer Products Safety Commission (CPSC) decided to ban all firecrackers and most fireworks. But in the face of opposition, particularly from manufacturers who stood to lose some $50 million in sales that year, the commission outlawed only those larger firecrackers that had already been banned by thirty-two states. With lesser fireworks—including one-inch firecrackers containing no more than fifty milligrams of explosive powder—now declared "safe" by the CPSC, numerous states repealed their fireworks ordinances. By 1988, inhabitants could legally set off fireworks in thirty-two states, sometimes legitimately purchase them in states in which they were proscribed, and often illegally obtain them in states in which they were prohibited, allowing unlawful but seldom prosecuted detonations. A 2000 press release from the CPSC, in anticipation of Independence Day, acknowledged that "fireworks can add fun and excitement to a holiday celebration, but they can also turn a backyard celebration into a rush to the emergency room." In 1999, hospital emergency rooms treated some eighty-five hundred people for fireworks-related injuries, with almost half of the victims children under the age of fifteen. These numbers were down from those recorded earlier in the decade, but few imagine that Fourth of July celebrations will ever be fully "safe and sane." Nothing better demonstrates the unconsciousness of consequences in the pursuit of holiday happiness than the simple sparkler, traditionally placed in the hands of young children even though its tip burns at temperatures of two thousand degrees Fahrenheit.[121]

Political fireworks can still erupt on the Fourth of July, as when the neo-Nazi, white supremacist hate group Aryan Nation marched in Coeur D'Alene, Idaho, in 1997 (attracting more protesters than marchers), but most Americans tolerate only the politics of affirmation on Independence Day—that is, rites that are inclusive and celebratory, not exclusionary and critical. Partisan electioneering speeches are only grudgingly allowed to intrude on celebrations. More characteristic of public programs are naturalization ceremonies, which welcome new United States citizens. During the First World War,

George Creel's Committee on Public Information saw the Fourth of July as the perfect site for promoting Americanism. On July 4, 1918, Creel staged a media event at Mount Vernon in which immigrants paid homage to George Washington. During this period, America was experiencing the "most strenuous nationalism *and* the most pervasive nativism that the United States had ever known," according to the historian John Higham. German Americans were not the only victims of antiforeign feelings; so too were a wide range of hyphenated Americans. It seemed that 100% Americanism demanded loyalty and conformity.[122]

Reformers concerned about the United States' ability to absorb vast numbers of immigrants—even when not questioning their worthiness or loyalty—sought to use patriotic holidays, particularly Independence Day, in their Americanization campaigns. Some even pushed to proclaim the Fourth of July as Americanization Day, and by 1915, cities across the country were using Independence Day as a backdrop for large naturalization ceremonies. Indianapolis, Indiana, staged a massive Americanization Day parade on July 4, 1918. The parade featured immigrants as well as the usual expressions of Americanism and patriotism, and incorporated the immigrants as legitimate citizens. Ethnic marchers carried the flags of their homelands (Germans excepted) and in the process declared that their ethnic heritage was not incompatible with their loyalty to the United States. One speaker declared specifically that foreign-born Americans were needed to maintain the foundations of the republic. Similarly in Cleveland, Ohio, in 1918, some seventy-five thousand immigrants and their children marched in that city's Fourth of July Americanization parade. Here too ethnic Americans, although displaying sashes that read America First, walked in native costumes or built floats recalling their homelands. In short, in Indianapolis, Cleveland, and other cities, Americanization—although assimilationist, and often stifling and repressive—was nonetheless deployed chiefly as a means of incorporation, not exclusion.[123]

The Independence Day naturalization ritual continued well beyond its origins in the First World War era. For example, on July 4, 1996, 713 immigrants in Detroit, Michigan, and 60 in Lincoln, Nebraska, publicly took their oaths of citizenship. Some 75 new citizens participated in a similar ceremony at Thomas Jefferson's home at Monticello in Virginia on the same day, while 4,000 in El Paso, Texas, and 200 in Boston did likewise earlier on July 3. On July 4, 1997, more than 5,000 people from over a hundred countries became new citizens in a sunny football field ceremony on Long Island in New York. Each Independence Day, a favorite feature in American newspapers across the country is the story or picture that shows these acts of naturalization and celebrates the country these freshly minted citizens have chosen. Today such rites carry a greater multicultural tone, but they continue unmistakably to celebrate America through these newly chosen people.[124]

If officials choose the Fourth of July to swear in new citizens, native-born Americans similarly have selected the holiday as a natal day in order to affirm the country and their right to belong. George M. Cohan proclaimed, "I'm a Yankee Doodle Dandy / . . . A real live nephew of my uncle Sam's / Born on the Fourth of July," in the 1904 musical *Little Johnny Jones*. In fact, Cohan took some poetic license, proclaiming a birthday one day later than his actual day of birth, on July 3, 1878. And the great jazz trumpeter Louis Armstrong, although actually born August 4, 1901, always claimed the Fourth of July 1900 as his birthday. The Lincoln Center Jazz Orchestra, in deference to Armstrong, thus chose July 4, 2000, to begin the Armstrong Centennial with its performance at the Music and Heritage Festival at Liberty Park in Jersey City, New Jersey. The Armstrong Centennial celebrated Armstrong as a great American and jazz as an essential American cultural expression. The Liberty Park concert therefore not only adorned the holiday; it implicitly aspired to define the meaning of America. If both the Aryan Nation (and the Ku Klux Klan before them) and the Lincoln Center Jazz Orchestra could use Independence Day to make statements about America at the end of the twentieth century, then the Fourth of July is an untidy festival indeed. Yet the orchestra's approach to the fete is certainly the one more traditional and more popular today—offering a nonpartisan, inclusive, cultural politics, as opposed to a strident, hate-filled politics of exclusion. And trumpeter Clark Terry's decision to showcase the famous Armstrong number "Struttin' with Some Barbecue" seemed to capture the spirit of the day.[125]

Thus the Fourth of July is time for light fare and to express, inadvertently, complex American identities. Picnic patriots often avoid thinking about politics on Independence Day, but they nonetheless act politically, performing a complicated nationalism. Their lack of seriousness or reverence does not necessarily imply disrespect for American principles derived from the Declaration of Independence, the Constitution, or subsequent sacred documents, such as the Gettysburg Address; indeed it may express a certain confidence and satisfaction. For seventy-five-year-old Helen Sondag, of Valmeyer, Illinois, for example, the Fourth of July means having a picnic on her front lawn, from which vantage point she can watch the town parade go by. In 1993 a flood washed out old Valmeyer, forcing residents ultimately to relocate the town in 1996 to ground four hundred feet higher and two miles away. Sondag's major concern in picking out a lot for her new house was to make sure it would be on the parade route. Seemingly a trivial matter, in fact Sondag's successful siting of her soon-to-be-rebuilt house represented an affirmation of tradition, of

American stability, continuity, and community. It simultaneously celebrated local and national affection—a love of country that is broadly conceived, vaguely espousing the nation and more ardently embracing that American country or community closest to home; Helen Sondag's act was political, and her politics was local, expressed through the Fourth of July.[126]

A place on the parade route—in a sense that is all that most Americans want on Independence Day. Most seem disinclined actually to march in the parade themselves, but they are generally happy to allow a diverse array of others—sometimes with more serious agendas—to march as they please. Some Americans continue to use the Fourth of July strategically to make political claims, to influence policy, or to protest failures to realize American dreams and principles. The New Left activist Jeremy Rifkin and the People's Bicentennial Commission he founded, for example, contested the official observances of 1976 by staging demonstrations such as the Boston Oil Party, which protested the actions of major oil companies. In a paraphrase of Paul Revere, the People's Commission warned that "the corporations are coming," and it dismissed the whole extravaganza as the Buy-Centennial. But less criticism emerged than many had expected, in part because official organizers seemed to employ ambiguity as a strategy to preempt dissent and disruption. Without a central focal site—like Philadelphia at the Centennial—but with some three hundred corporate and private sponsors and countless activities across the country, the Bicentennial made vagueness a virtue, cultivated national community without consensus, and embraced nearly any version of Americanism, despite internal contradictions. The nation in 1976 was imagined by promoters as an "aggregate of pleasured spectators," according to sociologist Lyn Spillman, and maximizing participation—pulling off a successful party—was the point. Because of what did not happen—violence or protest that Bicentennial officials could not classify as emblematic of "the inherent right of Americans to disagree"—organizers declared the fete a success. "All of America stood up on the Fourth," which an official spokesman argued, vaguely, implied "a revival of patriotic spirit, the healing of divisive influences, a deeper appreciation of history and the basic principles upon which the nation was founded, a strong impact on young people, and a new cooperative spirit among the nation's community."[127]

Yet some Americans certainly disagreed, dissenting from this "collective effervescence." Ron Kovic's 1976 memoir, *Born on the Fourth of July*, for example, offered a searing indictment of America's war in Vietnam. "For me it began in 1946 when I was born on the Fourth of July. The whole sky lit up in a tremendous fireworks display and my mother told me the doctor said I was a real firecracker. Every birthday after that was something the whole country cel-

Fig. 12. Fourth of July 1986, at the Statue of Liberty Centennial, New York City. Author photograph.

ebrated. It was a proud day to be born on." Kovic's idyllic life was shattered by a barrage of bullets in Vietnam, which Kovic, like many others, came to regard as a senseless war. Returning home permanently disabled, Kovic became an activist against the war and an advocate for veterans. His book's epigraph was a haunting challenge to frivolous Fourth of July celebration in a time of national crisis:

> I am the living death
> the memorial day on wheels
> I am your yankee doodle dandy
> your john wayne come home
> your fourth of july firecracker
> exploding in the grave.[128]

If such indictments have been rare in the last quarter of the twentieth century, Kovic's memoir nonetheless suggests the latent power of Independence Day as a political symbol and as a forum for contesting the status quo as a legitimate embodiment of American ideals.

★ ★ ★ ★ ★ ★ ★ ★ ★ ★ ★ ★ ★ ★ ★ ★ ★ ★ ★ ★

CHAPTER 2

Haven in a Heartless Calendar

America's Thanksgiving, 1621–2000

There were . . . some few national fêtes:—Election day, . . . and one or two training days, . . . sometimes ending in that sublimest of military operations, a sham fight, in which nobody was killed. The Fourth of July took high rank, after the Declaration of Independence; but the king and high priest of all festivals was the autumn Thanksgiving.

Harriet Beecher Stowe, *Oldtown Folks* (1869)

HANKSGIVING is America's most loved holiday. The autumn festival's charm, beauty, and nearly universal appeal come peculiarly from its elasticity and ambiguity, making it the ideal American multicultural ritual. Invented in the seventeenth century, it has been continually reinvented ever since. Although it began as an exclusive tribal rite for white Anglo-Saxon Protestant New Englanders, Thanksgiving has been appropriated generally by Americans of various tribes well beyond the New England Pale. And more successfully than most holidays, Thanksgiving has managed to escape the wanton commercialization that, purists complain, has debauched other sacred calendrical moments. According to the fictitious Irish American character Mr. Dooley, created by Finley Peter Dunne, Thanksgiving "'t was founded be th' Puritans to give thanks f'r bein' presarved fr'm th' Indyans, an' . . . we keep it to give thanks we are presarved fr'm th' Puritans." Some might quibble with Mr. Dooley's historical analysis, but he was surely correct in noticing the value—to immigrants and other marginalized Americans—in the creative recycling of this American tradition.[1]

Because we often expect that holidays should provide a refuge from the turmoil of our regular lives and the whirl of our relentless calendar, we are sometimes shocked that red-letter days can serve as provocations, political and economic, to those who would sell us their ideas and programs, their wares and services. Thanksgiving, like the Fourth of July and other special occasions, has seen its share of political contention. Its erection as an annual, national celebration in the mid-nineteenth century certainly had its political agenda—including the "Puritan," or Victorian, assimilationism that Mr. Dooley feared. And Thanksgiving's history, before and since, has been riddled with controversy. Likewise, Thanksgiving has been the object of promotional efforts by America's mercantile elite, who unsentimentally sought profits by hawking groceries, novelty dinnerware, and greeting cards. But perhaps the most striking thing about Thanksgiving is that today, amid commercial blitzes and multicultural battles, the holiday remains remarkably unpoliticized and uncommercialized.

For a public holiday, Thanksgiving is quite private; for a national holiday, it is distinctively localized and variable. Although for celebrants it is a holiday in which they focus inward, Thanksgiving is also the time when Americans in the largest numbers reach out to the least fortunate in their communities. Without fanfare or manifestoes, Americans collectively shape the meaning of the occasion—and the meaning of America itself as a plural nation—and declare their national identity simply by convening privately and voluntarily and eating turkey. Often religious but not particularly sectarian, the Thanksgiving feast does not exclude non-Christians. Instead, it partakes in the universalism of thanksgiving rituals that cross boundaries of culture, religion, race, and ethnicity. Indeed, even President Ronald Reagan—not renowned as a multiculturalist—deemed it appropriate to observe that "the native American Thanksgiving antedated those of the new Americans" and quoted Seneca tradition in his 1984 presidential Thanksgiving proclamation.[2]

Private celebrations encourage multiple voices and messages, and no central authority, civil or commercial, can dictate their meaning. Even so mercantile an event as the Macy's Thanksgiving Day Parade cannot drown out these disparate voices or subordinate the occasion to the interests of the marketplace. In fact, the Macy's parade is about Christmas, not about Thanksgiving, and the proximity of Christmas and its material extravagance has, in a sense, inoculated the autumn festival against the commercial epidemic. Thanksgiving is a special moment when unity and difference are conflated and negotiated. Without denying the disappointments, the failures, the struggles for economic success or social justice that remain in the United States, and without minimizing the differences among Americans, the Thanksgiving celebration nonetheless focuses attention momentarily on common American beliefs, values, and aspirations. If federal and state governments enable the event by enacting holidays, it is the American people at large who ratify it, overwhelmingly, in their own homes and on their own terms, creating its very significance through their actions. Americans, then, are not mere consumers of a prescribed feast; collectively, they produce the Thanksgiving festival.

So, with apologies to Lydia Marie Child, "over the river and through the wood"—or through the thickets of myth, legend, and lore—we go, not to grandmother's house but on a quick dash through time to assess the history and meaning of American Thanksgiving.

Plymouth Rock

No American holiday is more enshrouded in myth, legend, and lore than Thanksgiving, even though its historical origins can be traced to a real event in autumn 1621 at Plymouth Plantation. Yet we must begin not in 1620 or 1621 but in the nineteenth century, when the national Thanksgiving festival was invented. And we must consider first not Thanksgiving itself—a domestic fete—but a rival Pilgrim pageant, Landing Day or Forefathers' Day, a male-centered celebration of colonization, even conquest, that flourished locally early in the nineteenth century but did not ultimately attain the national prominence of Thanksgiving as an American festive institution. In the late eighteenth and early nineteenth centuries, some Americans reached back self-consciously and designated the so-called Pilgrims, among many potential ancestors, as their sacred progenitors, the particular pioneers who founded America in the moment when they first trod on Plymouth Rock. If these forebears first achieved renown for their landing in 1620, they would secure lasting fame for their act of thanksgiving and hospitality in 1621.[3]

For America's national creation myth, the Jamestown settlers of 1607 were certainly available as a First People, as were those who colonized under the auspices of Spain or Holland. And it is not completely inconceivable that Native people might have been appropriated, as in Canada, as First Nations. The exploits of Capt. John Smith and of the "Indian Princess" Pocahontas occurred earlier than those of Miles Standish, William Bradford, William Brewster, John Carver, and company; the former stood at the heart of a southern regional tradition that, until the Civil War, could challenge the claims of New England tradition as the "national" Genesis. But Virginia cavaliers lost their birthright as founders with the South's defeat in the Civil War. With Pocahontas, or another Native American Abraham or Sarah, white Americans might have acknowledged—after a complicated fashion—that the continent was not an unoccupied, virgin land and that colonization displaced its native inhabitants, who might well retain legitimate claims to the North American landscape. But white Americans generally preferred Indians as a vanishing race, one that European colonists and then United States citizens would replace. In New York, the elite descendants of Dutch colonists celebrated Henry Hudson (although English), Peter Stuyvesant, and (more fantastically, thanks to Washington Irving) Dietrich Knickerbocker. But few New Yorkers pressed the claims of Dutch burghers as American founders. The heirs of Spanish col-

Fig. 13. "Landing of the Forefathers," by Sam Hill, an engraved invitation to an early Forefathers' Day fete, ca. 1798–1800, after a painting by Michel Felice Corné. Courtesy of the American Antiquarian Society.

onists, and boosters living in parts of the United States that had once been part of New Spain, occasionally asserted priority, particularly by challenging Massachusetts's claim to the first Thanksgiving. As a *USA Today* item crowed in 1996, "Move over, Plymouth pilgrims. According to Texas historians, the real first Thanksgiving took place in San Elizario (outside what is now El Paso) when Spanish colonists arrived there in April 1598—a good 22 years before the landing of the *Mayflower*. Under the direction of Don Juan de Oñate, the colonists feasted with the local Manso Indians." Since 1989, the El Paso Mission Trail Association has been celebrating the so-called Texas Thanksgiving—in April. This counterclaim is only one of the most recent in a long string of claims that contest the Pilgrims' priority and primacy.[4]

By the second half of the nineteenth century, to counter nativist attacks, Catholic Americans, especially Irish and Italian ones, sought to upstage the

Pilgrims and claim their own legitimate status as Americans by erecting the Catholic, Italian Christopher Columbus as the first immigrant, the first American hero. Organizations like the Knights of Columbus, founded in 1882, and annual events like Columbus Day, observed widely as a public holiday by the turn of the century, derive from such a motivation. Later, celebration of the Norse "discovery" of North America would be employed similarly by Norwegians and other Scandinavians to assert their legitimate status as hyphenated Americans. Yet despite the priority of these "discoveries" and colonial settlements, the Pilgrims have been enshrined as the nation's Forefathers, and even in the face of revisionist attack they retain their special place today in the popular imagination. An overheard remark on the ferry to Liberty and Ellis Islands in New York Harbor drove this point home to me one day in October 1994. A fellow passenger said to his companion, knowingly placing the massive, late-nineteenth-century immigration experience in its historical context, "Of course, these immigrants were just doing what the *very first Americans*, the Pilgrims, were doing."[5]

Although legend tells us that the Pilgrims gave us our first Thanksgiving, in fact it was really the Victorian Thanksgiving, which became a national holiday only in 1863, that gave us the "capital P" Pilgrims themselves. It is a curious tale. Until late in the eighteenth century, the Separatists who founded Plymouth colony in 1620 were but one marginal group of predecessors, even for most New Englanders. The Separatists had occasionally referred to themselves generically as "pilgrims," identifying themselves in the process with the biblical Chosen People—as in William Bradford's citation of Hebrews 11:13–16 in his classic account of the settlers' ordeal—but only in the late eighteenth century did the pioneers of Plymouth colony become known retrospectively as the Pilgrims. Until then, they were referred to as the Old Comers or First Comers, and later as Forefathers. Plymouth Rock belatedly received its first public recognition (or was invented) as the Pilgrim landing place—according to American Apocrypha—only when Thomas Faunce, third elder in the Plymouth church, assembled his children and grandchildren on the spot and recited the tale in 1742. Faunce was concerned that a proposed wharf would obscure the site. The rock was later fossilized in the historical record by Dr. James Thacher, who learned of the event from witnesses but did not seek corroborating evidence.[6]

The Pilgrims' historical stature grew over time, encouraged by the efforts of local men and their civic organizations, like the Old Colony Club (a group of young men in Plymouth), who in 1769 initiated what they hoped would become an annual commemoration of the Pilgrims, not of their 1621 feast but of their 1620 landing. At Thomas Southworth Howland's inn, on December 22,

1769, Old Colony Club members first hailed the occasion with a dinner of a "large baked Indian whortleberry pudding," dishes of "sauquetach," clams, oysters, and cod fish, a haunch of venison, plates of sea fowl, frost fish and eels, an apple pie, and a course of cranberry tarts and cheese.[7]

Thanksgiving, which this feast resembled, was well established in New England by the time of the Revolution and had its public as well as private dimensions. But the unabashedly public observances of Landing Day, sponsored by men's associations, seemed to absorb most of New England's male energy. Forefathers' Day spread in New England and laterally beyond with the westward migration of Yankees, as nineteenth-century Americans and their leaders sought more consciously to erect a distinctive national identity and cultivate an appropriate collective memory. The holiday, an occasional and moveable feast, was celebrated on December 22 (or, sometimes on December 21), variously with sermons, orations, dinners, balls, processions, concerts, fireworks, and illuminations.[8] Buoyed by special anniversary commemorations, like those observed lavishly in 1820 and 1870 at the holy seat of Plymouth itself, the day secured its prominence on the calendar, and its heroes augmented their place in American popular history.[9]

Daniel Webster's oratory magic highlighted the bicentenary celebration of the landing sponsored by the newly incorporated Pilgrim Society on December 22, 1820. Plymouth's three hotels were bursting, and visitors scrambled to arrange accommodations in private homes. Although it was the beginning of winter, providence blessed the celebrants with a day "as mild as Indian summer." From the platform raised before the high oak pulpit of First Parish Church, Webster linked his age to that of Bradford and Brewster, which he argued inaugurated American progress toward religious liberty, free public education, and representative government. But Webster also lamented the continuity of America's history of slavery and railed, "It is not fit that the land of the Pilgrims should bear the shame longer." Although addressing well-founded rumors that an illegal slave trade still flourished in Bristol, Rhode Island, within the original borders of Plymouth colony, Webster's strong words were not well chosen for promoting the Pilgrims—increasingly represented as northern, middle-class reformers and abolitionists—south of the Mason-Dixon line.[10]

After some twenty-three smaller commemorations in the 1820s, 1830s, and 1840s, in midsummer 1853, on August 1, the Pilgrim Society marked the anniversary of the Forefathers' departure from Delfthaven in the Netherlands with a mammoth procession, speeches, and a banquet. It was Forefathers' Day Thawed Out, as one banner proclaimed. In 1859, the day of embarkation (or, rather, the day after, a Tuesday) was again chosen to commemorate the Pilgrims, this time in a great public ceremony to lay the cornerstones of the new National Monument and the canopy being built to shelter the holy national relic, Plymouth Rock.[11]

In the festivals of the 1850s, orators' messages were mixed, but perhaps with an eye toward the impending crisis of civil war, the issue of slavery seemed to disappear, and organizers and speakers sought to avoid compromising their efforts to construct the Pilgrims as the symbolic embodiment of the virtues of the American union. The Pilgrims' Embarkation Day—August 1—also happened to be West Indian Emancipation Day, an important festive occasion for African Americans, which since 1834 had marked the end of slavery in the British Caribbean. Plymouth celebrants failed to notice or to acknowledge the occasion. Yet if antislavery harangues were missing from these Plymouth Forefathers' Day celebrations, New Englanders were often less circumspect in their sermons and orations marking either Landing Day or Thanksgiving. In the process they antagonized some southerners and tainted Thanksgiving— incurring guilt by association—as a Yankee abolitionist holiday. Joseph Johnson, the governor of Virginia, for example, refused to declare a Thanksgiving in 1853, defending his action as protecting the separation of church and state, in the tradition of native son Thomas Jefferson. But what made the holiday particularly problematic in places like Virginia was its potentially subversive message; here governors sought less the separation of church and state than the separation of their states and abolition. Another Virginia governor, Henry Wise, thus dismissed the national pretensions of the Yankee Thanksgiving as "theatrical national claptrap," notorious for aiding "other causes"— that is, antislavery.[12]

Nonetheless, the festival of Thanksgiving spread throughout the South as well as the West, observed locally and extensively even in the absence of gubernatorial sanction, whereas the commemoration of Forefathers' Day increasingly languished. Following the Civil War, after a decade-long hiatus, Plymouth hosted a major celebration on the occasion of the two hundred and fiftieth anniversary of the Pilgrims' landing on December 21, 1870.[13] But, alas, Landing Day was destined for obscurity if not oblivion. In 1863, six weeks before his Gettysburg Address, President Abraham Lincoln issued a proclamation making the last Thursday in November a national holiday, "a day of Thanksgiving and prayer," honoring all "sufferers in the lamentable civil strife," and attempting to heal the nation's wounds and cultivate a common ground of reconciliation between North and South.[14] Increasingly, Forefathers' Day—a masculine event, with its forthright, sometimes strident speeches and public displays—was replaced nationally by a feminine one: Thanksgiving, a calmer, gentler, domesticated festival. December 21—its patron saints shanghaied by the new November Pilgrim pageant—disappeared, or hung on only in Plymouth and in the memories of scattered New England societies. Forefathers' Day thus returned to its origins, as a peculiar, local, ethnic (that is, Anglo-Protestant) affair without national resonance. The energy behind it was redeployed, especially in the schools, in the promotion of Thanksgiving, a more generic celebration of prescribed middle-class piety, morality, and domesticity. Landing Day was all but forgotten by the time of the Pilgrim Tercentenary, which was celebrated—strikingly—in August 1921 (not 1920), ironically marking less the Pilgrims' debarkation at Plymouth Rock than their "first Thanksgiving"![15]

Thanksgiving Engendered

In his 1835 book *New England and Her Institutions: By One of Her Sons,* Jacob Abbott declared, "blessed *him* who invented the 'Thanksgiving.'"[16] But given New England's celebration of domesticity and the feminization of American culture—at least of white, middle-class, Protestant New England culture—Abbott might have imagined a founding mother. Representing countries and regions as feminine may have been simply conventional, but there was little doubt that at least one prominent New England institution—the church—was highly feminized. Since the late seventeenth century, women had significantly outnumbered men among church members, and revivals and awakenings had not ultimately restored a balance between the sexes. By the nineteenth century, New Englanders and others struggled conceptually to maintain their sense of Protestantism as patriarchal while acknowledging, at least implicitly, its domination by women. Thus, despite standard usage of male pronouns for statements about men and women, and despite representation of New England's founders as generically male—as Forefathers—a minister like John Marsh of Haddam, Connecticut, in a Thanksgiving sermon in 1820, could find himself referring to Pilgrims both as "pious men" and as "*nursing fathers* to the Church" in the very same sentence. And women writers like Lydia Maria Child, in her famous poem "Thanksgiving-Day," talked of rushing to "Grandfather's house," but after the second stanza grandfather was forgotten and in the end, she wrote, "Grandmother sees us come" and brings "a pie for everyone!" Within the patriarchal household on Thanksgiving Day, women presided and, traditionally, performed the domestic work of the feast.[17]

For those in search of a founding mother rather than a grandfather or "nursing father," Sarah Josepha Hale, as the chief inventor of the national Thanksgiving tradition, is the logical choice. Mrs. Hale was the author of *Northwood: A Tale of New England,* first published in 1827, which dramatically described and prescribed the New England Thanksgiving, and subsequently editor of *La-*

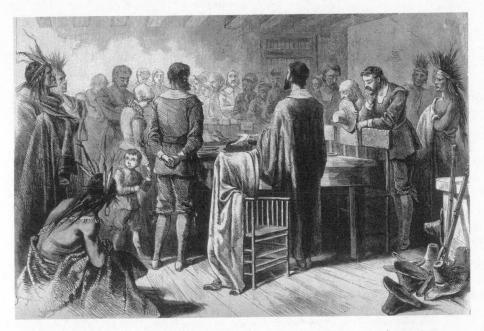

Fig. 14. "Thanksgiving among the Puritan Fathers," from *Harper's Weekly*, December 3, 1870. This idealized, nineteenth-century engraving nonetheless captures the interethnic quality of the First Thanksgiving—a moment of peace, mutual aid, and alliance. Courtesy of Knight Library, University of Oregon.

dies' Magazine and *Godey's Lady Book.* Certainly later commercial promoters would—and did—seize on Mrs. Hale and her tireless efforts to construct Thanksgiving as a national holiday, using her story to promote their own mercantile purposes, as they would later attempt to do with Anna Jarvis, the inventor of Mother's Day.[18] In antebellum America, pious reformers sought to constrain the riotous excesses of male celebration, and capitalists supported efforts to purge the calendar of its "St. Mondays"—unauthorized days of leisure and debauchery—and other occasions violating the new work discipline. In this new industrializing world, public, political holidays became more rigidly managed and even more male-centered in their performance, and celebration in general was increasingly tamed, privatized, and domesticated, especially with the rise of feminized festivals marked by gift giving (like St. Valentine's Day, Easter, and Christmas). The church- and home-centered Thanksgiving emerged as an amphibious occasion, public yet private, and, in the words of one editor, a time "of temperate hilarity and sober joy."[19] Women would come to dominate the calendar, as they did Thanksgiving, despite its apparently patriarchal character, especially through their buying of the holiday-related goods that ever larger numbers of capitalists sought to sell American consumers.[20]

Sarah Josepha Hale had written in 1827, "we have too few holidays. Thanksgiving like the Fourth of July should be a national festival observed by all the people . . . as an exponent of our republican institutions." And in 1863 her political intentions remained clear as she projected a universal Thanksgiving over the entire war-torn nation and asked, "would it not be a great advantage, socially, nationally, religiously, to have the day of our American Thanksgiving positively settled?" Mrs. Hale urged Americans to put aside sectional feelings and challenged them "to become national in unity when we offer to God our tribute of joy and gratitude for the blessings of the year."[21]

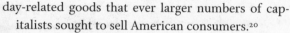

Fig. 15. Sarah Josepha Hale, engraved by W. G. Armstrong for *Godey's Lady's Book*, twentieth-anniversary issue, 1850. Courtesy of Knight Library, University of Oregon.

But Hale's political purpose was to promote a politics to end all politics. National reconciliation might be achieved, she hoped, by bypassing the messy immediate past and instead invoking the common values and heroes that lay, presumably, in America's more remote, shared colonial past. In a preface to the 1852 edition of her book *Northwood*, now with a new subtitle, *Life North and South: Showing the True Character of Both*, she observed that she had set her story in the Granite State—New Hampshire—a place of great men, defenders of the Constitution, "who know no North and no South." She dreamed that the republication of her book might somehow prevent the impending crisis: "the great error of those who would sever the Union rather than see a slave within it borders." These politics of de-politicization, in the 1850s and 1860s, thus depended on emphasizing what Americans supposedly shared and ignoring what tended to separate them. They accented domesticity—the peace and harmony of the ideal home and hearth—over the contentiousness and violence of male-dominated public arenas. What better means of accomplishing such a pacifying (and anesthetizing) task than through a national holiday, centered in the home, and deliberately devoid of any homogenizing or antagonizing national public performance? President Lincoln's 1863 proclamation, which did "fervently implore the interposition of the Almighty Hand to heal the wounds of the nation and to restore it as soon as may be consistent with Divine purposes to full enjoyment of peace, harmony, tranquility and Union," fully endorsed such a project. Lincoln envisioned a time beyond civil war and sectionalism, when God's gifts could be "solemnly, reverently and gratefully acknowledged as with on heart and one voice by the whole American People."[22]

The Politics of Thanksgiving

Although Thanksgiving was being reconstructed as a haven in a heartless calendar, its history shows that it had not always been so isolated from political contention and suggests as well that Thanksgiving might feel the encroachment of politics or commerce in the future. The Plymouth Pilgrims and Massachusetts Bay Puritans did not in fact always resemble those sketched in later mythic renderings. The Separating and Non-Separating Congregationalists who settled in New England in the 1620s and 1630s and maintained their ties with their homeland were hypersensitive to the politics of the calendar. As English historian David Cressy has shown, under Elizabeth I and the early Stuarts, the England that the Pilgrims and Puritans left had developed a relationship to time—current time within the cycle of the year and historical time with reference to the past—that set it apart from the rest of Europe. The new English calendar, founded on Christianity but purged of the "excesses of late-medieval Catholicism," gave expression to a mythic, patriotic sense of national identity and purpose; it was a means of declaring, disseminating, and sometimes contesting a distinctively Protestant national culture. New England Congregationalists, like their radical counterparts in England, believed the calendar should

Fig. 16. "Preparing for Thanksgiving; The First Thanksgiving," from *Harper's Weekly*, November 28, 1868. In this middle-class family, the patriarch lounges while women perform the work preparing the festive meal—the first for the waif being fed at the table as the young children of the family look on. The engraving captures two key ideals of American Thanksgiving—domesticity and charity. Courtesy of Knight Library, University of Oregon.

be cleansed of its corruptions, such as the pagan names of the days of the week and months of the year, or the wanton, anti-Christian bacchanalian celebrations of Christmas, Shrovetide, and May Day. They adopted, at least for a time, a new, numerical system for counting their days, and they used the law to prevent celebrations of supposedly debauched ecclesiastical occasions, or pre-Christian seasonal observances, such as April Fools'.[23]

Even special days sanctioned by English Puritans, like Elizabeth's Crownation Day (November 17) or the Gunpowder Treason Day (also known as Guy Fawkes Day, November 5), often did not translate well to the New World setting, and the extreme Sabbatarian Puritans of New England lived by a spare cyclical calendar.[24] But, as in England, they did punctuate their lives with public days of humiliation and thanksgiving, declared to mark the extraordinary occurrences of their existence. These prescribed fasts and feasts—along with the ancient autumnal festival of the Harvest Home—all contributed, through a strange conflation, to what would become the traditional American Thanksgiving. In the seventeenth century, Puritans saw themselves as denizens of a dynamic world, a "World of Wonder" governed by Providence, and they rejected the routinized relationship with their God that the traditional Christological calendar represented. New England Congregationalists knew, citing their "Confessions," "that nothing can befall us by chance, but by the direction of our most gracious and heavenly Father." All dire happenings were God's punishments, all blessings His approvals; their moral status before God was written out in events. As nineteenth-century historian William DeLoss Love observed, "every event approached them with its shadow before and its sunshine afterward, to be recognized by fasting and thanksgiving."[25]

The public fasts and feasts of New England were designed, in the words of one scholar, "to celebrate and rectify the society's relationship with God, to define and legitimate their social and political order, and to control internal conflict." They were, in short, "solidarity rituals."[26] Within God's covenanted community, contention was a particularly grave danger; fasts might help cure a sickness in the body social and encourage people "to walke in Love & Peace," whereas thanksgivings celebrated not only the saints' compact with God but their covenant with each other. Yet dissension and political controversy proved inescapable in New England, and the manipulation of the calendar by declaring extraordinary days of humiliation or thanksgiving functioned to settle social and political tensions as well as to aggravate them. If Sarah Josepha Hale and Abraham Lincoln looked to the early American past for an institutional means to cultivate solidarity among their own Chosen People, they would nonetheless face the challenge of making it work better in their own time than it often had in the days of the Puritans.

As early as the 1630s, the Rev. John Wheelwright's sharp words during a Massachusetts fast (designed to promote reconciliation amid the rancorous Antinomian crisis) raised a furor, and his disregard for the public thanksgiving of October 12, 1637, helped confirm the ministers and magistrates in their conviction to disenfranchise and banish him. During the English Civil War, although New England affected a neutral posture, its inhabitants clearly favored Parliament, and some imagined they played at least a spiritual and symbolic role in the struggle, especially through their fasts and feasts. In 1642, one Taunton preacher saw the colonists as "bands of souldiers lying in ambush here under the fearn and brushet of the wilderness . . . to come upon the backs of Gods enemies with deadly fastings and prayers, murtherers that will kill point blanke from one end of the world to the other."[27]

Given the colonists' providential worldview, how could fasts and feasts not be highly charged politically, seeing as they appeased God and at least implicitly sought to mobilize His power toward particular, godly ends. Thus, with the rise of the Commonwealth in England, New Englanders like the Rev. John Eliot hailed Cromwell, who had managed "the wars of the Lord against the Antichrist in Great Britain." When seeking a new colonial patent, Massachusetts supported its plea of loyalty by invoking their "fastings and prayers for their good sucesse and thanksgivings after the same was attained." And as the days of the Christian Commonwealth faded in England, New England protected itself politically, because the magistrates allowed churches to observe their own fasts without making them civic and public. Repositioning itself and asserting its loyalty, the Massachusetts General Court sped its petitions to the restored king "by the united fastings and prayers of New England" late in 1660 and, on July 10, 1661, celebrated a thanksgiving for "answer to prayers upon our late addresse or petition made unto ye king, his graciouse acceptance & favorable answer."[28]

By the 1660s, amid controversies over the Halfway Covenant and the province's treatment of Baptists, tensions rose between ministers and magistrates in Massachusetts concerning who possessed the proper authority for proclaiming public fasts and feasts. And the content of the events—that is, the particular objectives behind various public humiliations or celebrations—also became contentious. As King Philip's War—a bloody confrontation between New England's colonists and native people—ended in 1676, for example, the Massachusetts General Court proclaimed a day of thanksgiving, ignoring the preference of ministers James Allen and Increase Mather for renewed fasting.[29]

During the turmoil of the 1680s in New England, fasts and thanksgivings became veritable political footballs. After the death of the Massachusetts charter in 1684, it was unclear who might legitimately authorize such occasions. In 1685, ministers were determined to set December 3 as a thanksgiving, with the sanction of civil authority if possible, if not without it. Indeed, the event was not supported by the governor, and the day was kept by the churches "with unusual interest among such as were disaffected with the government," according to William DeLoss Love. After the formation of a new government in 1686, the old charter party in Massachusetts neglected, as much as it dared, a public fast proclaimed for July 14, and two abstainers were later forced to take an oath of allegiance and "sharply reproved by the Council," according to the magistrate Samuel Sewall, for staying home on a fast day and having a company of men gathered.[30]

With the arrival of Sir Edmund Andros in Massachusetts on December 20, 1686, new controversies seemed certain, and days of humiliation and thanksgiving were at the center of the struggle, reflecting and embodying political contention in the Dominion of New England. Competing factions scrambled to declare fasts and feasts that their rivals would be loath to keep. Soon the "Memorial of the Dissenters of New England" petitioned the king, complaining that inhabitants "are not suffered to set apart dayes of prayer or thanksgiving, no not even for the blessing of your gracious Declaration for Liberty of Conscience. Nor were the people there encouraged to make humble addresses of thanks but ye contrary." Governor Andros's own thanksgiving proclamation (for December 1, 1687), which celebrated an unpopular king, was honored without pleasure and sometimes in the breach. The next spring, Andros audaciously did "appoint, com[m]and & require" New Englanders to keep a more troubling thanksgiving on April 29, 1688—a Sunday, contrary to local will and tradition, and after the manner of the Church of England—to hail the English queen, now with child. And another Sunday thanksgiving was ordered in the dominion after the birth of the unwelcome Catholic heir of James II. Ultimately, this contest was cut short by the Glorious Revolution in New England, and with the continued disintegration of whatever theocratic organization remained, the designation of fasts and feasts became increasingly more centralized and formulaic.[31]

Nonetheless, as long as such civic events required special proclamations, and as long as American subjects or citizens might disagree about what deserved celebration or lamentation, public days of thanksgiving or humiliation would remain the object of politics. Waxing and waning, the political dimensions of Thanksgiving flared up or lay dormant throughout the eighteenth century in New England, as sermons variously struck discordant or harmonious notes, and as events disturbed or conserved the local and regional consensus. In revolutionary and early national America, the politicization of Thanksgiving continued; the ritual was employed to celebrate victories and marshal support for the revolutionary cause in the 1770s and 1780s, and as a forum for bickering between Federalist clergymen and Democratic Republican politicians in the early nineteenth century. After the election of Thomas Jefferson in 1800, for example, a Federalist minister offered a politicized Thanksgiving prayer: "O Lord, endow the President with a goodly portion of Thy grace, for Thou, O Lord, knowest he needs it." In 1811, the Democratic Republican governor of Massachusetts, Elbridge Gerry, accused the largely Federalist clergy of "passion, prejudice, and worldly delusion" in his Thanksgiving proclamation. Numerous ministers refused to read the offensive proclamation, and others who did sometimes had their words obliterated by the "indecent shuffling of . . . feet," as among Federalist-sympathizing Harvard students.[32]

Certainly not every Thanksgiving proclamation, sermon, or prayer became the vehicle for partisan politics in the early republic and antebellum America. The holiday observance seemed to spread easily into the expanding West and even into southern states and the old Southwest. By the 1850s, every northern state, and several southern (including Virginia, Mississippi, Louisiana, Texas, Arkansas, and Missouri), midwestern (including Ohio, Indiana, Illinois, Michigan, Wisconsin, Minnesota, and Iowa) and far western states (including Utah, California, and Oregon), had officially celebrated Thanksgiving, at least sporadically. If, as the Transcendentalist writer and reformer Margaret Fuller proclaimed in the pages of the *New-York Daily Tribune* in 1844, "Thanksgiving is peculiarly the festival day of New-England," she noted its celebration more broadly in the United States as an occasion "for a meeting of families and friends" and "the enjoyment of a good dinner." Yet, despite her appreciation for "the spirit of kindness" and "the instinct of family love" that the holiday promoted, Fuller hoped the holiday might be something more: "How much nobler, more exhilarating and purer would be the atmosphere of that [family] circle if the design of its pious founders were remembered by those who partake this festival!" She prescribed individual and family soul searching and works of charity. "But if charity begin[s] at home," she wrote, "it must not end there." For Fuller, the work of benevolence at Thanksgiving extended even to social action and political reform. "For this present day appointed for Thanksgiving, . . . if we know of so many wrongs, woes, and errors in the world yet unredressed; if in this nation recent decisions have shown a want of moral discrimination . . . , [or if] we know of causes not so loudly proclaimed," Fuller urged, "we must render them for the movement, now sensible in the heart of the civilized world." In this vein, Fuller herself gave thanks for the recent organization of "an Association for the benefit of Prisoners." Thanksgiving thus might be an occasion for reform.[33]

As the impending sectional crisis embroiled the country, Thanksgiving assumed an even larger role as a forum for political messages and contention. In the South, as we have seen, governors sometimes feared the feast as an abolitionist Trojan horse. Certainly the slavery issue entered into Thanksgiving politics. In Texas in 1850, Governor P. Hansborough Bell's proclamation recognized slavery as the most critical among "the vast and perplexing questions which have agitated and divided the public councils." For the governor, such questions were easily answered by the U.S. Constitution, which permitted both slave and free states, and he decried "false interpretations" and "unworthy attacks of ignorance or fanaticism." Yet for committed opponents of slavery in the North, such challenges were neither unworthy nor ignorant. Although not uniform in their condemnation of the "peculiar institution," northern ministers increasingly preached for abolition on Thanksgiving Day.[34]

Among the most troubling events in the escalation of sectional conflict leading up to the Civil War was the crisis following the Kansas-Nebraska Act of 1854, which upended the Missouri Compromise of 1820 barring the spread of slavery into United States territory north of the 36° 30' parallel. The potential admission of Kansas to statehood proved disturbing because its settlers, particularly those from neighboring Missouri, would be permitted (and would be likely) to establish slavery there. The likelihood of Nebraska becoming a free state, although intended as a compromise and a balance to Kansas, was little consolation to opponents of slavery. The region thus became an early battleground in the war between the states over slavery, as pro-slavery settlers moved in and abolitionist settlers joined them in Bloody Kansas. In 1856, when the territory celebrated its first official Thanksgiving, the antislavery Kansas governor, John Geary, offered particularly biting, partisan words in his proclamation: "While insult, outrage, and death has been inflicted upon many of our unoffending citizens by those whom we desire to recognize as brothers, while the attempt is being made to inflict upon us the most galling and debasing slavery, our lives have been spared and a way pointed out by which without imbuing our hands in blood, we can secure the blessings of liberty and good government."[35]

During the Civil War, the Confederacy as well as the Union observed Thanksgiving, although on different days and celebrating different events. A Confederate Thanksgiving on July 28, 1861, for example, expressed gratitude for the South's victory at Bull Run, whereas the North observed Thanksgiving that year in November and celebrated union and its own (limited) military progress. Of course, Lincoln's Thanksgiving Proclamation of 1863, designed to create an annual, national holiday, had no immediate effect on those states that had seceded from the Union. After the war, during the era of Reconstruc-

Fig. 17. "Thanksgiving Day, November 26, 1863," from *Harper's Weekly*, December 5, 1863. The goddess Liberty kneels at the Union altar in the center of this patriotic tableau. In surrounding illustrations, the army and navy, town and country, pray for peace, as do Washington and Lincoln in the top center panel. The lower middle panel celebrates emancipation as a slave breaks his chains. The Emancipation Proclamation took effect on January 1, 1863, with the first national Thanksgiving, proclaimed by President Lincoln, occurring later that year, on the last Thursday in November. Courtesy of Knight Library, University of Oregon.

tion, partisan politics would continue to intervene on Thanksgiving Day. Southern governors sometimes refused to follow northern states in issuing Thanksgiving proclamations. In other cases, Thanksgiving holidays celebrated southern "redemption"—the end of Reconstruction, the restoration of white supremacy, and the abandonment and disenfranchisement of African Americans. Alabama thus proclaimed a special Thanksgiving for December 23, 1875, to hail its new constitution, which restored white rule and constructed barriers to black political participation. Georgia acted similarly, in a petty demonstration of states' rights, defiantly placing its own Thanksgiving a week in advance of the one proclaimed for the entire country by President Ulysses S. Grant. And Louisiana likewise observed an extraordinary Thanksgiving on May 10, 1877.[36]

By the late 1870s, eager to put the loss and chaos of the Civil War behind them, the American public increasingly embraced national reconciliation and indulged in a willful amnesia that represented an implicit national white politics and ignored the lingering problems of racial injustice. A depoliticized Thanksgiving served perfectly as a rite of reunion, and the American holiday achieved unprecedented national stature, particularly because it continued to be prescribed and promoted by newspapers and women's magazines, like *Godey's*, edited by Mrs. Hale until 1877. Americans North and South grieved and remembered personal losses on Memorial Day, and increasingly they staged joint commemorations among veterans of both the Blue and the Gray to promote national as well as local healing. The South also gradually restored celebrations of Independence Day, recognizing the nation's birthday that southerners shared with northerners. If the Fourth of July allowed Americans to bypass troubling recent experiences and focus attention instead on a more distant but glorious and common Revolutionary heritage, Thanksgiving offered the possibility of traveling even farther into a shared, noncontroversial, mythic past. And because Thanksgiving was a home ritual, Americans living in diverse regions and holding different political principles could act in unison—or at least in parallel fashion—as loyal citizens of the nation, without really confronting each other publicly. Segregated within their own households, citizens could define the objects of their own feasts.[37]

Political to Apolitical Football: Thanksgiving in the Late Nineteenth and Early Twentieth Centuries

In the last decades of the nineteenth century, then, Thanksgiving became a relatively comfortable, politically undemanding, popular festival. During these years, the fete became the venue for leisure and popular amusements, which supplemented but hardly replaced the home-centered festive meal. In addition to shooting contests, walking competitions, and bicycle races, baseball became a Thanksgiving tradition in the 1860s and 1870s. America's first automobile race was staged by the Chicago *Times-Herald* on Thanksgiving Day in 1895. The event—won by J. Frank Duryea in ten hours, twenty-three minutes—commenced at Chicago's Jackson Park, ran north to Evanston, Illinois, and then returned, covering a total of just over fifty-two miles. Today, more common are mass foot races, like the New Orleans Athletic Club's annual benefit Turkey Day Race, held on Thanksgiving Day over a five-mile course. These contests trace their origins in part to the traditional turkey trot, in which contestants chased real turkeys on the day before Thanksgiving. Typical was the annual event sponsored by Oliver Hall of Collinsville, Alabama, from 1912 through the 1930s. Each November, Hall attracted large crowds to his Collinsville store on Thanksgiving eve, and as he released turkeys and other fowl from the store's roof, appreciative contestants would scamper to capture the birds that, they hoped, would become their next day's dinner. But more popular than baseball, automobile races, or turkey trots were the "traditional" football games that began to be played on Thanksgiving soon after 1869, when the first college football game matched Princeton against Rutgers.[38]

In 1876, four Ivy League schools formed the Intercollegiate Football Association and instituted a championship game on Thanksgiving Day; within a decade this competition had become the premier athletic event in the country. The annual Thanksgiving Day championship game between the two best college teams, held in New York City and most often featuring Princeton and Yale, marked the beginning of the winter social season. By the 1890s the game attracted as many as forty thousand spectators, some of whom paid as much as $150 for boxes and wagered thousands of dollars on the outcome. In 1893, the *New York Herald* complained, "Thanksgiving Day is no longer a solemn festival to God for mercies given. . . . It is a holiday granted by the State and the Nation to see a game of football." Around the country similar big games were held on Thanksgiving, sometimes to the consternation of local moral guardians, but their disapproval did little to halt the growing tradition. In 1934, in the infancy of professional football, George Richards bought the Spartans football team of Portsmith, Ohio, moved it to Detroit, and renamed it the Lions. Richards scheduled a Lions game against the Chicago Bears for Thanksgiving Day, and using a radio station he owned he arranged to broadcast the contest coast to coast through a radio network of ninety-four stations. Thus, in addition to the twenty-five thousand fans on hand to watch at the University of Detroit, thousands more heard the game, and the Lions' traditional Thanksgiving Day game was born as a sports media event. By the 1950s, when football emerged as a televised sport, even larger numbers of fans could wit-

Fig. 18. "Thanksgiving in New York—As It Is," from *Harper's Weekly,* November 28, 1891. By the 1890s in New York City, where the Intercollegiate Football Association staged its annual championship game on Thanksgiving Day, the contest marked the beginning of the winter social season. In 1893, the New York Herald complained, "Thanksgiving Day is no longer a solemn festival to God for mercies given. . . . It is a holiday granted by the State and the Nation to see a game of football." Courtesy of Knight Library, University of Oregon.

ness the well-established, traditional match. Although late-nineteenth-century traditionalists saw football and tradition at odds with each other, in fact they were easily amalgamated. Indeed, the advent of new electronic media in the twentieth century—radio and then television—conserved and promoted tradition, allowing Thanksgiving to remain a home-centered holiday in which celebrants could act simultaneously as spectators of sporting events and participants in a special family festival.[39]

New forms of consumption accompanied new forms of leisure on Thanksgiving. Following the prescriptions of promoters like Sarah Josepha Hale and good marketing by turkey growers, turkey assumed its preeminent place in the Thanksgiving feast. At the first Thanksgiving, it is unlikely that Plymouth settlers and their native guests ate any turkey; James Deetz, historical archaeologist and a former senior staff member of Plimoth Plantation, a living history museum in Plymouth, Massachusetts, reported that the excavation of some ten sites at Plimoth Plantation yielded only one turkey bone. "We finally found some turkey bone after ten years of digging," he said. "The circumstantial evidence is that it wouldn't be likely [that the colonists ate turkey]. Turkeys are very hard to kill and the matchlocks of the period weren't very good for hunting." Because the 1621 Thanksgiving took the form of a traditional English Harvest Home—a secular harvest festival—the early settlers would have preferred a goose, but they seemed to have settled happily for venison (supplied by Wampanoag hunters), some waterfowl, and perhaps some fish. By the eighteenth century in New England, it had become traditional to serve turkey, but not necessarily as the exclusive main dish; the presence of three or four kinds of meat—in addition to domesticated turkey, goose, chicken, pork, beef, mutton, and venison—signified through quantity, not merely quality, that this was a special occasion.[40]

After the Civil War, according to business historian Thomas DiBacco, turkey won its unique place among celebrants in part because of the marketing efforts of poultry producers in New Jersey, Pennsylvania, and Maryland, who successfully promoted turkey as Thanksgiving's main dish, even though at ten cents per pound, in a time when average wages ran between ten and fifteen cents per hour, turkey was relatively expensive. As illustrators placed turkeys at the center of Pilgrims' tables in their depictions of the mythic First Thanksgiving, consumers increasingly demanded the bird. By 1871, a *Harper's Weekly* Thanksgiving feature could offer a portfolio of pictures of "Our Thanksgiving Bird," which illustrated the entire production process, from buying the birds from local producers, to driving them like cattle to the picking-house, to the culmination with slaughtering and plucking. Here production, not merely consumption, was celebrated. By the late twentieth century, such illustrations of turkey production might be less welcome, as genetically engineered superbirds—now weighing as much as thirty-five pounds and sporting enlarged breasts of white meat that make it difficult for some turkeys to stand and impossible for them to mate naturally—are industrially produced in massive pens. Nonetheless, American consumers successfully bag their low-cholesterol quarry in supermarkets and consume turkey in ever greater amounts. In 1994, an estimated forty-five million turkeys were consumed in the United States on Thanksgiving Day, whereas some three hundred million turkeys were produced during the year, an increase of some 50 percent over the previous decade.[41]

Thanksgiving as a traditional site of American leisure has also influenced consumer patterns in the United States. Ironically, the day's focus on family and home persuades numerous Americans to leave their own households and travel for the holiday—to the hearths of family patriarchs or matriarchs or to neutral locations for family reunions. Such seasonal travel is quite old, dating

Fig. 19. "Turkeys," from *Harper's Weekly,* December 2, 1871. This collage of sketches shows the process of turkey production; thanks to skillful marketing and production, turkey had become the central feature of the festive Thanksgiving meal. Courtesy of Knight Library, University of Oregon.

at least to the early nineteenth century, when Thanksgiving was a time of homecoming for New Englanders and those living in diaspora. By then, migration from New England, into eastern cities and the rural West, had separated extended families, which could be reunited only on special occasions, like Thanksgiving. And Thanksgiving became just such a time of reunion. According to Franklin Benjamin Hough's 1858 history of Thanksgiving proclamations, in that year some ten thousand people from New York City alone left to spend the holiday in New England. Earlier, Horace Greeley, editor of the New York *Herald Tribune* (but a native son of Vermont), recognized the significance of this pilgrimage by publishing an invitation to all New Englanders not to "Go West Young Man" but to go home: "Come home to Thanksgiving! Dear children, come home! / From the Northland and the South, from the West and the East, / Where'er ye are resting, where'er ye roam, / Come back to this sacred and annual feast." The famous Currier and Ives lithograph by George H. Durrie, "Home to Thanksgiving" (1867), depicts an idealized scene of a son stepping from his sleigh at the threshold of his parents' farmstead door on a snowy Thanksgiving Day. Mother and father greet him and wel-

Fig. 20. "Home to Thanksgiving," a Currier and Ives lithograph after a painting by George H. Durrie (1867). This sentimental image—among the most popular ever produced by Currier and Ives—presents the return of scattered family members to kin and hearth, a Thanksgiving ideal. Americans continue to honor the tradition, making the Thanksgiving weekend among the most crowded travel periods in the year. Collection of the author.

come him home for the holiday. Durrie's print caught the day's homing impulse perfectly and became one of the most popular Currier and Ives lithographs of all time.[42]

Those unable to return to New England homes felt a certain loss, like the one expressed by the Rev. R. F. Putnam in his diary in California in 1863: "Thanksgiving, which was here as in Massachusetts, on the 26th of November, was a solemn and unsatisfactory day. . . . We thought of home and longed to be there. . . . Our dinner was plain and simple, for we had no heart for a sumptuous repast. We had been invited to dine out, but declined all such invitations, preferring to remain alone and think of the dear ones who gathered around the Thanksgiving table at home." With the coming of the transcontinental railroad and other transportation links, such distant travel become more feasible, and by the second half of the twentieth century Americans were traveling in record numbers along the nation's highways and through its airports during Thanksgiving. According to a *New York Times* report, an unprecedented 30.4 million Americans traveled at least a hundred miles during the 1994 holiday, "traditionally the busiest travel time of the year." The Automobile Association of America estimated that two-thirds of those travelers stayed with friends or relatives. Although some set off for mini-vacations at tourist destinations, most followed traditional paths to family celebrations.[43]

Yet if American consumers buy more gasoline and airline tickets, more turkeys and other food products at Thanksgiving, as well as flowers, cards, and specialty dinnerware, such purchasing does not compare with that of other holidays, like Christmas, St. Valentine's Day, or Mother's Day.[44] Thanksgiving certainly depends on the mechanism of American commerce, but with its avoidance of gift-giving rites it does so in a more limited and hidden fashion than do other holidays. Indeed, it even conveys aversion to commercialization and capitalist excess. The convention that the Christmas shopping season commences on the day after Thanksgiving only confirms this American tradition.

On the Sunday preceding Thanksgiving in 1994, a business writer for the New Orleans *Times-Picayune* offered a standard refrain, "Due to merchant demand and great shopping expectations for the 1994 holiday shopping season, opportunities for gift-buying have been extended into the month of November." Looking beyond the Thursday holiday, she wrote, "The big kickoff, of course, comes Friday, while many are still full of Thanksgiving cheer. That tradition remains, although merchants are ambitious suitors—they started displaying holiday wares as early as August and shoppers bought." In fact, at one mall, Santa Claus appeared by November 12. But many Americans, even if they sometimes like to get a jump on Christmas shopping, seem to resent this sort of encroachment. If Thanksgiving is a gateway to consumption—many retailers report half of their annual sales during the Christmas season—it is also a time when many Americans hope to keep that gate momentarily shut, at least until the morning of the fourth Friday in November. Thus Thanksgiving itself, even if it plays host to mercantile spectacles like the Macy's Thanksgiving Day Parade in New York City, acts as a sort of sanctuary, a temporal safe house in the calendar before Americans continue on, shopping toward Bethlehem. Recognizing this mood, and hoping to capitalize on it, a group of activists and consumer culture critics in the Pacific Northwest—the Adbusters and the Center for a New American Dream—invented Buy Nothing Day, and in 1999, appropriately, they called for its national observation on the day after Thanksgiving. Whether the public noticed is unclear; many of course were too busy shopping.[45]

If the 1990s saw the advent of a Buy Nothing Day—a political movement to protest commercial excess—in 1939, President Franklin Delano Roosevelt's political manipulation of Thanksgiving stemmed from entirely different motives. The United States, still mired in the Great Depression, would have an exceedingly short holiday shopping season, as only twenty days separated Thanksgiving from Christmas. Following the advice of a consortium of national retail associations—advice he had ignored since 1933—Roosevelt acted, he hoped, to nurture the nation's tender economic recovery by changing the date of Thanksgiving and in the process adding an extra week's worth of shopping days. On August 14, 1939, the president announced that he was moving up the traditional day of Thanksgiving one week, to November 23. A *New York Times* headline the next day read, "Roosevelt to Move Thanksgiving: Retailers For It; Plymouth Not." Roosevelt's tinkering with tradition warmed the hearts of merchants but ignited a firestorm of opposition. One Republican opponent ranted, "Not for revelry and sport, and not for the inauguration of Christmas shopping, is this day set apart," though Democratic governors generally agreed to follow the federally designated date. An Indiana shopkeeper placed a sign in his window, "Do your shopping now. Who knows, tomorrow may be Christmas."[46]

The Thanksgiving festival of 1939 proved chaotic. There were many, in addition to defenders of tradition, who voiced their opposition, including calendar makers, turkey growers worried about filling orders and having to sell premature birds, the American Legion, concerned that the holiday would encroach on Armistice Day, and football fans outraged that their big games might now occur on an ordinary Thursday. A Gallup poll revealed that some 62 percent of the American people disapproved of Roosevelt's action. The president responded by setting a similarly early date for the Thanksgiving of 1940, offering calendar makers some lead time but most opponents little solace. Texas governor W. Lee O'Daniel proclaimed two Thanksgivings for his state in 1939—

one for the president and one for the Texas–Texas A&M football contest. Connecticut commuters to New York stayed home from work on November 23, according to New York State's observation of Roosevelt's day; their children went to school that day but had the following Thursday off as a Connecticut state holiday. Ultimately, Roosevelt's experiment failed, retailers generally reported little change in their sales, and the president admitted his mistake. Franksgiving, the monster created by Roosevelt, was unceremoniously laid to rest by Congress in 1941. This was, of course, hardly the first time that politics had invaded America's cherished festival, but the hubbub confirmed Americans' preference for apolitical over political footballs on Thanksgiving.[47]

Modern and Postmodern Thanksgiving

After 1941, Franklin Roosevelt left Thanksgiving's traditionally official date alone, as have the presidents who followed. What made Roosevelt's Franksgiving ploy so repulsive—if not as serious an offense against American institutions and integrity as Roosevelt's other packing attempt, involving Supreme Court justices rather than shopping days—was that Americans, since at least the 1870s, had cherished Thanksgiving's relative lack of contentious politics. And enmeshed in a mass consumer society, dominated by commercial forces beyond their control, Americans saw in Thanksgiving a sacred refuge from the malevolence of the market place. As cultural historian Leigh Eric Schmidt has argued, in the second half of the nineteenth century, "holidays, instead of being impediments to disciplined economic advancement," were increasingly "geared to retailing, consumption, and profit." If Time is Money, then the commercialization of the calendar gave new meaning to that old Yankee maxim.[48]

But time was not *only* money, and there were limits to Americans' patience with politics and commerce when it violated their traditional calendar. An Oklahoma attorney general, forced to decide between presidentially and gubernatorially appointed holidays in November 1939, for example, opted for Roosevelt's date (the 23rd) but included in his official opinion the following doggerel:

> Thirty days hath September,
> April, June and November;
> All the rest have thirty-one.
> Until we hear from Washington.[49]

In the 1920s, businessmen and industrialists had sought to manipulate and rationalize time in the interest of production and retailing, taking on the "wandering Easter," which could fall anywhere on the calendar between March 22 and April 25. Their defeat, like the defeat of Franksgiving, suggests the strength of religious, folk, and mass culture rhythms in American life, and that Americans at least occasionally found moments to contest commercialization (and politicization), even if they more often seemed to embrace the new consumer culture.[50]

But if Thanksgiving appears unique as a national, civic event isolated from politics—that is, from conspicuous, strident political debate—we should not conclude that it has no political content. The very lack of a public, centralized, homogenizing political voice, emanating from Washington, D.C., or various state capitals, creates the space for real multivocality, and genuine multiculturalism, to operate. The medium of this attenuated Thanksgiving festival is the political message; the ritual is truly federal (in a classic Madisonian sense, emphasizing shared, not centralized national power), and in its decentralization and ambiguity it is perfectly designed for a pluralistic nation. Americans commonly ascribe a vague core of meaning to Thanksgiving, but they variously elaborate the holiday's meaning in the same way that they differentially supplement their turkeys with other, diverse dishes fit for their Thanksgiving feasts.

Plenty of middle-class reformers in the late nineteenth and early twentieth centuries hoped to Americanize newcomers by mechanically remaking them in the image of Pilgrim Olde Comers (or at least in their imagined version of these seventeenth-century forebears), and the Thanksgiving festival could be employed to perform this artifice.[51] But the actual celebration of Thanksgiving was diffuse enough, and its symbols and rituals were universal enough, to allow recent immigrants and other marginalized Americans to commandeer Thanksgiving and use it in their own way. Thanksgiving was repeatedly reinvented, with immigrants from Ireland and Italy, Russia and China, Haiti and the Dominican Republic, transformed into latter-day pilgrims to a golden land. In the 1988 children's book *How Many Days to America? A Thanksgiving Story*, for example, Eve Bunting's words and Beth Peck's illustrations tell a story of the escape of political refugees from an unspecified Caribbean nation (Cuba?) to the United States. Evading soldiers, pirates, hunger, and various dangers of the sea, they arrive in America on Thanksgiving Day and in the process rehearse and embody the Pilgrim story (and conflate Landing Day with Thanksgiving). Asking about the strange new holiday, a small girl learns, "Long ago, unhappy people came here to start new lives. They celebrated by giving thanks."[52]

The odyssey of the five-year-old Cuban boy Elian Gonzalez seemed to imitate Bunting's fiction. Accompanying his mother, who sought to flee Cuba, Elian was shipwrecked off the coast of Florida and pulled from the sea, miraculously, after two days adrift, on Thanksgiving Day 1999. Coast Guard Chief Petty Officer Scott Carr commented, "Here we are on Thanksgiving Day, when most Americans are sitting back and reflecting on what we're thankful for, and these migrants are making a desperate—although illegal—effort to get here." In another interview, noting that several in Elian's party were drowned or lost, Carr said, "It's a very sad and tragic day. . . . Today of all days, Thanksgiving Day, when Americans should be celebrating at home that our forefathers came to America." The Cuban American National Foundation quickly turned Elian into its poster child. According to the Miami talk radio host and spokeswoman for the group, Ninoska Perez-Castellon, "This is a vivid case of the ongoing tragedy of the Cuban people, and this on Thanksgiving, so you can imagine how moved the Cuban American community is." Perez-Castellon compared the voyage of the rafters to that made by the Pilgrims who landed on Plymouth Rock: "They were the first refugees. The Pilgrims would not have survived without the natives' help," she said, ironically naturalizing her own community as Native Americans. "Everyone can identify with this sad story. . . . It's like the Pilgrims. They were coming here to obtain freedom." In this case—unlike the fictional one narrated by Bunting—Elian's mother perished, and Elian himself became the object of virulent political contention between, on the one hand, distant relatives in Miami and supporters in the Cuban-American community, and on the other hand, the United States Immigration and Naturalization Service, the State Department, Elian's father in Cuba, and the Cuban government. If Elian Gonzalez turned out to be a sojourner rather than a new American citizen (when reunited with his father and returned to Cuba), and if his experience did not ultimately conform to the standard pilgrim's story, his Thanksgiving rescue captivated the American public, initially rehearsing and reinforcing a common myth. Elian's story, especially as told by those who sought to keep him in the United States, was shaped by the larger Thanksgiving saga; his Miami relatives' consternation and anguish stemmed, in part, from the fact that this real-life tale was deprived of its conventional ending.[53]

More successful as pilgrims were those described in a 1992 *New York Times* article as an immigrant family squatting or "homesteading" in the "wilderness" of the South Bronx in New York. The writer ironically linked these newcomers with those who had arrived at Plymouth in 1620: "They crossed seas seeking a fresh start in a strange but abundant land. There were people there already, to be sure, sometimes hostile natives with their own customs and language. But much of the land seemed fallow, so the newcomers settled in lonely spaces and scratched out homes, sharing their tools and toil, lugging in fresh water and foraging to meet as many of their needs as they could." In south Florida and the South Bronx, as in southern New England of yesteryear, America became a land of opportunity. The Thanksgiving myth recited that classic narrative of immigration, freedom, possibility, and economic success. And by casting new, non-English, nonwhite players in the roles of pilgrims, the revised play offered legitimacy to ethnically and racially diverse newcomers. The holiday's inclusiveness and spirit of community seemed to cultivate a sense of belonging. Without forfeiting their ethnicity, religion, or individuality, new Americans could use the holiday to craft a legitimately hyphenated identity.[54]

Fig. 21. "Boat People," a cartoon by Paul Conrad, ca. 1974, *Los Angeles Times*. Conrad equates desperate immigrants—in this case, from Southeast Asia—with those Pilgrims who traveled to America in the *Mayflower* in 1620. © Tribune Media Services, Inc. All rights reserved. Reprinted with permission.

Thanksgiving provided a powerful way for immigrant Jews in the nineteenth and early twentieth centuries to become American without abandoning who they were ethnically or religiously, for example, although they did not accept the holiday immediately. In an interesting double mimesis, immigrant Jews reproduced the Puritan pilgrimage to America, which those earlier Pilgrims had imagined reproduced the exodus and pilgrimage of the Israelites into the land of Canaan. We can hear these strains in Anzia Yezierska's story "America and I," first published in 1923. A struggling, embittered Jewish immigrant woman reflects:

> I began to read the American history. I found from the first pages that America started with a band of Courageous Pilgrims. They had left their native country as I had left mine. They had crossed an unknown ocean and landed in an unknown country, as I.
>
>   . . . I read on. I delved deeper. . . . I saw how the Pilgrim Fathers came to a rocky desert country, surrounded by Indian savages on all sides. But undaunted, they pressed on—through danger—through famine, pestilence, and want—they pressed on. They did not ask the Indians for sympathy, for understanding.

The immigrant woman sees latter-day "savage Indian scalpers" all around her, "like the old witch of the sweat-shop, [or] like my 'Americanized' countryman, who cheated me of my wages." She concludes, "There is no America!"

But then she has a revelation, she sees a different America, "a big idea—a deathless hope—a world still in the making."

I saw that it was the glory of America that it was not yet finished. And I, the last comer, had her share to give, small or great, to the making of America, like those Pilgrims who came in the *Mayflower*.[55]

This immigrant, Yezierska suggests, is the embodiment of the Pilgrims; although she is new to the country, she can claim a legitimacy as secure as that of the Pilgrims themselves, as long as she contributes to her new nation—simply by being herself. Such identification was constraining in some ways, but it was also liberating—a way to be American without giving up ethnic or religious identities. America was a story still being written, and Jews as well as other naturalized Americans would be authors.

For some first-generation American Jews, Thanksgiving was something new and strange; some suspected it was a Christian holiday. And it is true that Thanksgiving, like other public holidays, was a tool of Eastern European Jewish Americanization. Commissioners of immigration in New York City, for example, provided turkey dinners for immigrants at Castle Garden and then Ellis Island. And the public school system used the Pilgrims and their feast as a model for teaching Americanism, an assimilationism that had little respect for Judaism. We see this clearly in the short story by Pearl Kazin, "We Gather Together," that appeared originally in the *New Yorker* on November 25, 1955.[56]

The narrator is a Jewish schoolgirl at Brooklyn's P.S. 125, a second-generation American. She reflects on the intense lessons that dominate school days beginning in October about Thanksgiving and Pilgrims. Although they strike her as odd, she is fascinated and hopes for her own Thanksgiving feast at home. But her mother is skeptical and uncooperative. When she hears her daughter singing the hymn "We Gather Together" around the house, she reacts sharply to the lines, "we ask the Lord's blessing." She says, "What kind of a song is this for a Jewish girl to sing! Stop this minute, it's not nice somebody should hear you."

"Why can't we have turkey for Thanksgiving like everybody else?" the girl asks her mother.

"Who's everybody?" My mother would say, without taking her eyes from the sewing machine. "The Feins eat turkey Thanksgiving? Doris Levine's mother goes on the subway to buy a turkey God knows where Thanksgiving?" . . .

"What's the matter, they're giving you a vacation in school all of a sudden? They forgot to give you homework, you have to bother me with stupid things when I'm busy?"

. . . "We don't have enough our holidays for you? Eh, who knows even where to buy a turkey, how much it costs. An arm and a leg it wouldn't surprise me. Go, mamaleh," she would say, with sudden tenderness, . . . "go do your homework, please, do me a favor. Headaches she has to give me with her turkey yet."

The girl imagines nonetheless a grand family Passover seder–like Thanksgiving meal, with Uncle Harry and Uncle Morris, Aunt Frieda, her cousins, and all her family. They sing "We Gather Together" and then watch as an enormous brown turkey is placed on the table. "Then Papa would begin to carve, with magnificent effortless skill, an art taught him by his father, who had learned it from *his* father."

Here, a young Jewish American girl becomes a "real" American by at least imagining a "traditional" Thanksgiving feast, one made temporarily impossible by her mother's suspicion that the holiday is tainted by Christianity, that to observe it would be inappropriate or might cost too much, both materially and culturally.

Gradually, however, most Jews embraced the new American holiday. Its acceptance showed a willingness to fuse Jewish and American ritual, according to historian Andrew R. Heinz. Elizabeth Stern, a social worker whose family had emigrated from Russia to New York in 1892 when she was two years old, remembered how her family adopted Thanksgiving. One Thanksgiving, her father brought home a turkey, not the traditional fowl of the Jews, which her mother sized up as bigger than a duck or chicken. They put out a white tablecloth, "as if it were a holy day," and her father used the occasion to recite tales from the Talmud. Afterward, young Elizabeth explained the meaning of Thanksgiving, which she had learned in school. Her approving mother nonetheless reminded her, "one must not give thanks only on one day and for one bird!"[57]

The playwright Paul Rudnick, who grew up in New Jersey, identified with neither Indians nor Pilgrims as a kid. "The Jews arrived on later boats," he has written. "Rather than cope with the multicultural chaos that surrounds the holiday, my family views Thanksgiving as a time of togetherness and autumn-themed place settings." Rudnick likens his Thanksgiving to his Passover seder, "substituting cranberry sauce for horseradish and King James I for Pharaoh." As religious historian Jenna Weissman Joselit argues, this is the essence of American Jewishness: "Amid the welter of competing and multiple voices, one constant emerged: the centrality of family. Despite the divisiveness and fragmentation that characterized American Jewish life for much of the twentieth century, the community came together and coalesced around the ideal of a domesticated Jewishness in which home and its inhabitants became the core of a modern Jewish identity."[58]

American Thanksgiving is the quintessential domestic holiday—it is home and family centered. It emphasizes precisely those things that American Jews value most: domesticity, thankfulness, generosity, *tzedakah* (charity), justice, tolerance. It is a do-it-yourself means of being an American, which allows you to remain who you are. Lewis Lewisson, a Jewish dry goods merchant who immigrated to Providence, Rhode Island, from Prussian Poland in the late 1840s, exhibited his Jewishness and his American-ness simultaneously each Thanksgiving. Not only did he celebrate the holiday personally, but he offered the *tzedakah* of providing his clientele, primarily the poor living near the harbor, with Thanksgiving dinners. In his first year he distributed some twelve hundred pounds of bread and five hundred pounds of turkey.[59]

If, as one Conservative rabbi commented recently, "for a Jew, every day is a thanksgiving day, every prayer for a Jew is a thanksgiving prayer," then it should not be surprising to see Jews embrace the particular American festival focusing on thankfulness. Howard Zack, a San Francisco Bay Area Orthodox rabbi, observed about Thanksgiving: "Of all the holidays that Americans celebrate, Thanksgiving is the only one that is both non-sectarian and religious. God is recognized but it is a non-denominational holiday, thanking God for what one has. It involves no rituals, which are inevitably essential to one religious group but are anathema to another." Other non-Christians have agreed. Russian immigrant Zhana Vaynshteyn, celebrating Thanksgiving in 1995 even though her Brooklyn apartment had just been destroyed by fire, was typical perhaps: "I am Muslim, but we have adopted all of the American holidays. . . . I never lost faith in this country. If you give more than you expect, you will get more than you could ever have expected."[60]

Thanksgiving celebrates not only diversity and toleration but acceptance and generosity toward others, even those Others native to the North American continent. In 1621, Pilgrims and Wampanoags feasted together, sharing their harvests and cementing their friendship based on a real—if sometimes grudging—mutual respect. The English-Indian relationship in New England and in America in general, of course, would not continue on this basis; indeed, feasts would be celebrated to mark the military destruction of New England's Native people, as in 1637 and 1676. Nonetheless, we might contemplate the contingency of this historical moment in 1621 and its symbolism for later American history, which is being made all the time, especially during holidays like Thanksgiving. Even Native American critics of American society often conclude, like British Columbia Native American Bill Wasden at a protest march in 1991, that "The first Thanksgiving was all right. It started to fall apart after that."[61] Thanksgiving may be employed by Native people as an opportunity to challenge the history of colonialism in America—as at Plymouth in 1997, when an Indian gathering turned violent and resulted in twenty arrests[62]—but more often, unlike Columbus Day, it is the occasion for quiet home or community celebration, or for less confrontational attempts to educate and find new accommodations with non-Native society. The fifth annual A Giving of Thanks in 1992, for example, offered a night of music, dance, ritual, and storytelling to give New York City's 26,272 American Indians "more visibility." Co-chairing the event were Onondaga Nation chief Oren Lyons and Ann Rockefeller Roberts. The latter commented, "Thanksgiving should remind us of how the Pilgrims survived their first winter with help from Native Americans and how the two cultures celebrated the harvest as equals, as peers, and not as conquerors and conquered—at least at that time."[63]

As early as the 1830s, an Indian had criticized the founders of New England publicly, from the rostrum and in print. The Pequot William Apess, in his *Eulogy on King Philip, as Pronounced at the Odeon, in Federal Street, Boston* (1836), called white Americans—and particularly white New Englanders—to task for their ill treatment of Indians, and he chose to do so by challenging the mythology and hagiography of antebellum America, which increasingly lionized the Pilgrims as Founders. Metacom—"King Philip"—was the son of the Wampanoag sachem Massasoit, famous for joining the Pilgrims in their First Thanksgiving and helping them thereafter. Yet King Philip's War in 1675–76 marked the conquest of southern New England's Native people by the expanding English colonists. "Let the children of the Pilgrims blush, while the son of the forest drops a tear and groans over the fate of his murdered and departed fathers," Apess declared.

> He would say to the sons of the Pilgrims (as Job said about his birthday), let the day be dark, the 22nd day of December 1622; let it be forgotten in your celebration, in your speeches, and by the burying of the rock that your fathers first put their foot upon. . . . Let every man of color wrap himself in mourning, for the 22nd of December and the Fourth of July are days of mourning and not of joy. . . . Let them rather fast and pray to the great Spirit, the Indian's God, who deals out mercy to his red children, and not destruction.

It is significant that Apess challenged the patriotic standing of Forefathers' or Landing Day (here misdated by two years and a day)—not Thanksgiving. The former had recently been celebrated with particular patriotic abandon at the bicentennial anniversary at Plymouth in 1820. That legendary colonial act—landing on the rock and claiming the country—offended Apess and other Native people in ways that the equally mythic First Thanksgiving did not. Landing Day—appropriately commemorated by a fast—not Thanksgiving, was a day of mourning for Native Americans.[64]

With the decline of Forefathers' Day and the ascension of the Thanksgiving holiday, however, the latter has devolved into a site of occasional protest—particularly because, as in the aftermath of King Philip's War, a colonial official proclaimed a thanksgiving to mark the English victory and Indian defeat. Beginning in the 1970s, nearly three hundred years after the war's end, Indian mourners peacefully contested the ceremonial space of Plymouth at Thanksgiving, sharing the town with marchers in its Pilgrims' Progress parade. In 1995, Native mourners buried Plymouth Rock, and in 1996 they blocked the traditional parade route. Then, on Thanksgiving Day in 1997, when Indians and their supporters marched through the town's historic center, they found themselves in a confrontation with police that ended with several arrests, charges, and countercharges. Nonetheless, the following year, protesters and Plymouth town officials made their peace, agreeing to share the day; Plymouth committed itself to spend some $100,000 to educate the public about Native American history and to erect in the town's main square a plaque commemorating its Native son, King Philip. Away from the politically charged mythic site of Plymouth, Indians most often celebrated Thanksgiving in the way that other Americans did, by emphasizing family, economic competence, and thankfulness. In an Op-Art Thanksgiving piece in the *New York Times* in 1997—the same year that saw Native arrests at Plymouth—readers could gaze at a montage of photographs depicting "Thanksgiving Day with San Juan Indians in New Mexico, 1996." The Garcia clan "opened with prayer, first in their Tewa language, then in English." After dinner, in another picture, "the Denipah clan crowded onto the couch to watch football on television." What could be more typically American on Thanksgiving Day?[65]

The mythic First Thanksgiving represents generosity. And if Americans see themselves as a generous people, Thanksgiving is the time when they can most persuasively make such a case. Although home centered, the festival is the occasion for reaching out and displaying concern for one's community. Since the early seventeenth century, thanksgivings were moments for sharing the bounty of life, as at Scituate, Massachusetts, in 1636, when the morning church service was followed by merrymaking, "the poorer sort beeing invited of the richer."[66] Such charitable practices continued during the eighteenth and nineteenth centuries, and indeed persist into our own time. In Houston in 1993, for example, the city's tenth annual Thanksgiving Superfeast served Thanksgiving meals to some fifteen thousand to twenty thousand needy people. Yet the *Houston Post* reported that volunteers outnumbered hungry people, who streamed in throughout the day and received an abundance of blankets, coats, and clothes in addition to a turkey dinner.[67]

Americans seem to match their enthusiasm for charity at Thanksgiving time with at least a momentary aversion to commercialism, which at this feast they strive to keep at arm's length. Even if most Americans do not duplicate the New England country home Thanksgivings prescribed by Sarah Josepha Hale or Harriet Beecher Stowe, and memorialized by countless others, they see their own Thanksgivings as homemade, traditional, and authentic. No gifts cloud the social atmosphere and complicate the semiotics of the festival. The marketplace does not mediate their observance, as it seems to at Christmas. In this modern American potlatch, hosts and hostesses offer family and guests all the food that their stomachs can hold (and as leftovers, all that can be crimped into aluminum foil packages), while partakers fully reward this generosity simply by taking part.

Not all family Thanksgiving gatherings leave such a rosy glow, of course. Few families avoid at least some sort of strife, and Thanksgiving can sometimes provide a recipe for disaster. Even when all appears to go well, some participants in the feast can harbor resentments and bear the fatigue of performing all the work. If Thanksgiving is a domestic festival, with women at its center, all too often women are left with the prodigious tasks of arranging the meal, inviting the guests, shopping, cleaning, cooking, and washing mountains of dishes. The science fiction writer Suzette Haden Elgin, in conjunction with her novel *Native Tongue*, published a companion volume, *A First Dictionary and Grammar of Láadan*. Among the dictionary's entries is the word *radíidin*, which she defines as an occasion, allegedly a holiday, that in actuality is so much of a burden because of the amount of work and preparation it requires that it is a dreaded occasion, especially when there are too many guests and none of them helps. Did Elgin have Thanksgiving in mind? In an analysis of consumption rituals associated with Thanksgiving, scholars Melanie Wallendorf and Eric Arnould found that their surveyors often overlooked or underreported the fact that the meal's female host—often the presiding mother—seldom sat down. Numerous photographs nonetheless documented (by her absence) the missing matriarch. Moreover, recorded comments like, "we all sat around [after the meal] and talked," did not always reflect the fact that some sat and talked more than others, or that such conversation and relaxation was gendered. Wallendorf and Arnould's data demonstrate a point obvious to many women: "Although regarded as a day of rest by men, in most households Thanksgiving Day is a day of both ritual and physical labor for women." One female participant-observer wrote, "By the end of our meal I was completely exhausted and full of thoughts and ideas. . . . I wish I could be like my brothers. They don't have a care in the world today. They haven't done a thing all day long and I resent that." The researchers observed that differences in men's and women's labor in producing the feast are representative of distinctions that exist throughout the year. On Thanksgiving, however, "on this one day, women's domestic labor, taken for granted most of the time, is celebrated." Perhaps. Yet clearly Thanksgiving, even when offering women recognition for their uncompensated household and family labor, is seldom a feminist festival, one in which liberation of women is heralded or promoted. Thanksgiving, like other American holidays, is a work in progress; in the future, should women's rights continue to expand, and should domestic work be more broadly shared among women and men, then we may see the considerable work of preparing a Thanksgiving meal embraced more enthusiastically and self-consciously by women as "women's work," a ritual throwback to yesteryear when, remarkably, women fixed the whole feast.[68]

If Thanksgiving is defined by the domestic feast, it is also distinguished by and loved for what it is not—and especially, it is not Christmas. The sometimes crass, overblown, expensive extravaganza of Christmas today simultaneously repels and attracts Americans. Even Christians—to say nothing of Jews and Muslims—embrace Christmas as the holiday they love to hate. By

Fig. 22. Thanksgiving parade, Durham, North Carolina, November 28, 1957. This Thanksgiving parade, like so many others in the United States, gives Santa Claus a place of honor; indeed Thanksgiving, as Franklin Delano Roosevelt well knew, inaugurated the Christmas shopping season. Wyatt T. Dixon Papers, Rare Book, Manuscript, and Special Collections Library, Duke University.

the fourth Thursday in November, the Christmas avalanche has begun, and Americans collectively pause at Thanksgiving to gather their powers of endurance. Seeing their immediate future clearly, they attempt to stop the clock momentarily and relish the present of Thanksgiving simplicity. Even Thanksgiving parades, in New York, Detroit, St. Louis, and elsewhere, serve not to commemorate this moment but to herald the Christmas frenzy. In the New York City Macy's parade, Santa Claus always culminates the procession of massive balloons, for example, and in Detroit three dozen mail carriers troop through the annual Michigan Thanksgiving Day Parade to collect children's letters to the North Pole. In Atlanta, on Thanksgiving night, Rich's Great Tree is lit in front of thousands of spectators.[69] These flamboyant events, on but not of Thanksgiving, collectively vaccinate the American Thanksgiving festival

Fig. 23. Advertisement for the 68th Annual Macy's Thanksgiving Day Parade, *New York Times*, November 23, 1994. Published by permission. Macy's Thanksgiving Day Parade™ and copyright notice © Macy's East, Inc. A subsidiary of Federated Department Stores. All rights reserved

against the contagion of commercialization. More often observed on television than in person, mercantile parades and big money football games do not displace the home-centered, family traditions of Thanksgiving, against which they stand in such stark contrast.[70]

In early November, Americans go to the polls in a public rite to buy or reject political candidates and their ideas. At the month's end, they abandon themselves to the frenzy of Christmas shopping. In between, they celebrate Thanksgiving as a sacred moment when they need not engage politics or the marketplace. Individually, and amid family and friends, they give thanks for whatever advantages they enjoy and seek authenticity as people and as Americans. Like the so-called Pilgrims and their Wampanoag allies at the First

Fig. 24. "Uncle Sam's Thanksgiving Dinner," by Thomas Nast, from *Harper's Weekly*, November 20, 1869. Nast's diverse feast seems to capture the essence of the multicultural Thanksgiving, more than one hundred years before the term was invented. It emphasizes the inclusiveness and benevolence of American Thanksgiving. Sitting in portraits on the back wall, the two great American heroes—Washington and Lincoln—preside. Courtesy of Knight Library, University of Oregon.

Thanksgiving in 1621, Americans are still struggling to learn the lessons of survival—how to cultivate alliances and a sense of common purpose that might integrate people without obliterating their distinctiveness. Thanksgiving is a uniquely quiet, privatized negotiation of American-ness, while it is simultaneously a time of reflection on the possibilities of American life—abundance (too often inequitably shared), pluralism (although cacophonous), and democracy (however imperfect). Thanksgiving, in all its complexity, indeterminacy, and multivocality, is at once America's oldest and most modern —even postmodern—national holiday. As such, it begs a question each November that most Americans care not to address on this day of sanctuary from politics: does it reflect the worst fears of the critics of multiculturalism and postmodernity—a declining America, increasingly divided, fragmented, and chaotic? For me, the Thanksgiving cup is not half empty but more than half full; indeed, it runneth over. In its de-centered, ambiguous celebration of America, Thanksgiving nonetheless incorporates and unifies the nation's diverse inhabitants like no other American festival.[71]

★　★　★　★　★　★　★　★　★　★　★　★　★　★　★　★　★　★

CHAPTER 3

Reinventing America

Columbus Day and Centenary Celebrations
of His Voyage of "Discovery," 1792–1992

For 499 years he's the dullest man in second-grade history, and then all of sudden we decide he's controversial.

Joe Bob Briggs (1991)

---

*T*HE PUBLIC quincentenary commemorations of Columbus's voyage of "discovery," recently observed in 1992, made history. They did not alter social, economic, or political life, nor did they re-create the past. Yet the various events shaped public memory and subjected America's past to popular interpretation. This recent episode in the history of American commemoration may challenge us to consider Columbus's place in earlier historical moments when identity and historical meaning were contested and shaped in the United States.

In fact Columbus has been at the center of American history-making and mythmaking for at least two hundred years, since the critical period after the American Revolution, as the new republic searched for its national identity. Christopher Columbus has been, perhaps, the emptiest—if among the most priceless—of American historical vessels, somehow available to be filled with a stunning variety of facts and interpretations, meanings and moral lessons. This chapter examines the history of Columbus, not simply the man and his accomplishments or misdeeds, but the public history of Columbus the hero and symbol, especially as the Columbian icon has been made and deployed through centenary celebrations and annual Columbus Day holidays over the past two hundred years.

As eighteenth-century Americans sought to define themselves as a people, the figure of Columbus—and, more abstractly, "Columbia"—allowed them to represent their unique American national identity and purpose, which included territorial expansion and the creation of an Empire of Liberty. And as waves of immigration challenged and remade America in the nineteenth century, Columbus again presented himself as a new champion for ethnic Americans—especially Irish, Italian, and (later) Hispanic Catholics—who could bypass the United States' Anglo past as they raised up their patron Columbus, an ethnic founding father, indeed America's first immigrant. The cacophony of celebration in 1892–93 would be followed by slumbering interest in Columbus until the 1990s and the quincentenary, in which Columbus faced unprecedented challenges to his heroic stature. In essentially the same way as those who preceded them, however, Native Americans (and other dissidents) found in Columbus—now an antihero and foil—a tool to establish their own identity, a means to challenge traditional ethnocentric narratives of American history and to assert their legitimate, prior place in America, past, present, and future. In tracing America's love-hate relationship with Christopher Columbus, I am chronicling and critiquing, paradoxically, America's long-term attempt to "predict the past." Although the events of 1492 are now five hundred years old and unalterable, Americans will continue to refashion that history. Here we look back to see how the history of Columbus and America has been made, in books, classrooms, advertisements, speeches, parades, and counterdemonstrations; and, reflecting on the recent quincentenary, we contemplate how the meaning of Columbus will be reshaped in the years following 1992 and into the twenty-first century.

Columbus and the Utility of Mystery

Who was Christopher Columbus, or Christoforo Colombo, or Cristóbal Colón? And what do we really know about him? Perhaps surprisingly, given that this is the man at the center of what the Spanish historian Francisco Lopez de Gomara called in 1552 "the greatest event since the creation of the world (excluding the incarnation and death of Him who created it)," there are substantial gaps in our knowledge.[1] Columbus remains a man of some mystery, with a variety of names, with a strange, enigmatic cipher for a signature, without a single portrait done from life; we cannot even be sure where the bones of the Admiral of the Ocean Sea now rest.[2]

Given his humble beginnings, there is no reason to expect that Columbus's early life would have been chronicled at all. His date of birth is usually given as 1451 (although alternate dates are often reported), and most historians accept, although they cannot be certain, that he was born into an unremarkable family of weavers in Genoa. His youth and early adulthood can be traced superficially, although even many modern accounts disagree about his experiences: was he shipwrecked off the coast of Portugal by pirates, for example, and was this the event that landed Columbus in the leading maritime nation in the world? Did Columbus visit Bristol and learn of new lands to the west from

Fig. 25. "Landing of Columbus," engraving by H. B. Hall (1874), after John Vanderlyn's painting installed in the United States Capitol Rotunda in 1847. Collection of the author.

its merchants and fishermen? Did Columbus travel to Iceland, as some claim, or even to Greenland?

We do know that Columbus developed a plan—was it brilliant or insane? prescient or ill-informed?—of sailing west to reach the East, and that he presented it to the crowns of Portugal, Spain, France, and England. It was rejected, for various reasons, by all but Isabella and Ferdinand, after they reconsidered, and in August 1492 Columbus departed from Palos with three ships. After several weeks, on October 12 (old style), Columbus or his crew sighted land; moments later Columbus stepped ashore and claimed this New World for Christendom and his Spanish monarchs. Where precisely was Columbus's landfall? We do not know for sure, but certainly it was somewhere in the present-day Bahamas. Columbus had "discovered" a new world.

But in what sense was it new? Students of this history differ, often dramatically, in their answers to such a question. This world was new to most Europeans (if we exclude the Norse explorers and settlers of Greenland and, most likely, North America, as well as a number of fishermen of the Northern Atlantic), and Columbus's deed revealed it to them.[3] After Columbus, never again would the Americas be unlinked continents. On the other hand, of course, the New World was not new to its longtime inhabitants, nor—if Columbus's claims about an Asian landfall had been correct—was it new to much of the world beyond Europe, that is, to the East. Although historians disagree on the matter of what Columbus himself believed about the *otro mundo* he found, and although many contemporary Americans fail to question the nature of his "discovery" at all, the Admiral apparently continued to maintain to his dying day that he had reached Asia and its offshore islands, never admitting that he had, in fact, run aground on a completely new, previously unknown landmass. Thus Columbus, by his own logic, had discovered nothing more than a new route to an old world.

Early in 1493, Columbus returned to Spain, found Isabella and Ferdinand in Barcelona, and informed them, and all of Europe, of his remarkable achievement. We might conclude here, as so many have in their invocation of the Columbus story, that "the rest is history." This conventional sign-off has proven convenient for mythmakers, crafters of a heroic Columbus. It suggests that what follows—all "the rest"—are unimportant or irrelevant details, in other words, "history," the trivia that occupies historians. We might assume that later aspects of Columbus's life and colonial career are without interest or importance, or at least that they do not in any way contradict our sense of the man and his reputation. Yet, as we have known all along, this was hardly the case. Columbus's later endeavors as an explorer and especially as a colonial administrator were little short of disastrous, leaving him, in his own view, unappreciated, under-rewarded, indeed subject to humiliation and abuse.

As for those New World peoples encountered by the Admiral and his men, the consequences of the 1492 "discovery" were infinitely more grim. It is now clear that the Columbian voyages commenced (inadvertently) a process of demographic catastrophe—some call it genocide—that decimated the indigenous inhabitants of the New World during the colonial period by the introduction of Old World disease. Within fifty years of 1492, for example, the Greater Antilles and Bahamas saw their population reduced from an estimated million people to about five hundred. Spurred by his quest for wealth, or in response to conditions that his own incompetence as a colonial governor had created, Columbus initiated or tolerated acts of real brutality (even by standards of the day). After the bloody pacification campaigns he led in 1495, which according to sixteenth-century historian Gonzalo Fernandez de Oviedo claimed victims without number (Peter Martyr estimated fifty thousand native deaths), Columbus himself boasted that he had "conquered" Hispaniola.[4]

Finally, the conquistador Columbus can be credited with inaugurating the

New World slave trade. As his journals indicate, as early as October 14, 1492, the Admiral had begun to kidnap native people, as curiosities and translators and, potentially, as slaves. "Should your Highnesses command it," he wrote to Ferdinand and Isabella, "all the inhabitants could be taken away to Castile or held as slaves on the island, for with fifty men we could subjugate them all and make them do whatever we wish."[5] In the absence of gold, and other valuable commodities, Columbus discovered natives as a source of wealth; he systematically enslaved Indians and transported them to Spain beginning in 1494 or 1495, only to have them freed and the practice condemned by his monarchs. Nonetheless, as late as October 1498, after being warned repeatedly that enslavement of natives violated not only natural and cannon law but his instructions as governor and viceroy, Columbus wrote to Ferdinand and Isabella that "as many slaves as can be sold" could be dispatched from Hispaniola "in the name of the Holy Trinity," producing some twenty million *maravedis* in income if but four thousand slaves could be sold "at a modest price." He continued: "And although at present they die on shipment, this will not always be the case, for the Negroes and Canary Islanders reacted in the same way at first."[6] Thus Columbus the hero might be recast as villain, if not the devil himself, as the result of a closer and more critical examination of his postdiscovery career.

How is it that one man could be invested with such diverse and contradictory meanings? Not only are facts sometimes scarce in the Columbus story, but those that are widely accepted are nonetheless interpreted in strikingly varied ways. More importantly, why do we care so much about a single man who died some five hundred years ago? Why did eighteenth- and nineteenth-century Americans care? Clearly, Columbus is conspicuous—famous or notorious—because the Columbian voyage of 1492 was a seminal event in the history of the world. Yet Columbus continues to command our attention and remains uniquely useful to us, not as a real, living and breathing, human actor on the historical stage but instead as a symbolic figure; indeed, that symbol is more important than the man himself. Since the era of the American Revolution, Americans have invested so much in the symbolic Columbus—in a variety of personas—that to challenge any of the particular Columbuses they have constructed is to despoil the constructors, to question their identity as Americans.[7]

Columbus has thus been too important a figure to be left to professional historians, notoriously a troublesome bunch, who display annoying tendencies to debunk, deflate, and ruin the carefully constructed edifices of popular meaning. As Washington Irving, the Columbus biographer most responsible for establishing the Admiral as a great American hero, wrote in 1828:

There is a certain meddlesome spirit, which, in the garb of learned research, goes prying about the traces of history, casting down its monuments, and marring and mutilating its fairest trophies. Care should be taken to vindicate great names from such pernicious erudition. It defeats one of the most salutary purposes of history, that of furnishing examples of what human genius and laudable enterprise may accomplish.[8]

If the purpose of history—as opposed to "pernicious erudition"—was, as Irving suggested, to supply models and moral lessons, then Columbus was indeed uniquely useful. Because so little was known of Columbus the man, he could be represented in a vast variety of ways and constrained only by the bare consensus that existed about his life and by an author's imagination. The blank spaces in Columbus's biography allowed purposeful writers unusual flexibility in drawing out their prescriptive tales. Professional historians, who claim simply to tell the truth, revoking the poetic license of popular writers and orators, miss the point; not only do facts get in the way, but they do not speak for themselves, nor do they express all that so many Americans feel compelled to say about their past and future. Moreover, the circumspect, factual approach of historians has more recently appeared as a threat to Columbus's detractors, potentially denying them the opportunities enjoyed for so long by the creators and conservators of the heroic Columbus myth. If protestors are permitted to confront only Columbus the man, whose narrow shoulders cannot possibly bear all the sins of Western civilization—capitalism, imperialism, racism, sexism, environmental degradation—then they are denied a certain flexibility in molding and presenting their own sinister Columbus, Columbus the antihero. Conventionally, then, Christopher Columbus has been significant to Americans as a totem, an emblem to represent and personify America, its past and future, and through him Americans can work out crucial social and cultural problems facing the nation—the meaning of nationalism, of American expansionism, of immigration and ethnic diversity, and of multiculturalism. Columbus is "Columbia," that is—with apologies to Amerigo Vespucci—America. And so we must turn to common or public history and the shifting meaning of the past as it is remembered, invoked, reshaped, celebrated, decried, indeed as it is "made," popularly over time.

Columbianism in Colonial and Revolutionary America

Among Americans, appreciation of Columbus's voyage of discovery predated the foundation of the United States itself. The prominent Massachusetts Puritan merchant, judge, and diarist Samuel Sewall was among the first English residents to designate the New World as Columbina, a form of Columbia, the land of Columbus. In his *Phaenomena qaedam Apocalyptica* (1697), Sewall endorsed the English cleric Nicolas Fuller's endeavors "to do *Columbus* the Justice, as to eternalize his Honour, by engraving his Name upon the World of his Discovery." Sewall argued, "It is every where called America: but according to Truth, and Desert, men should rather call it *Columbina*, from the magnanimous Heroe *Christopher Columbus a Genuese*, who was manifestly appointed of GOD to be the Finder out of these Lands."[9]

For Puritans who conceived of their American settlements in eschatological terms, as forming a New Jerusalem in which God's plan would be made manifest on earth, Columbus, rather vaguely at first, could fill the role of Moses, the divinely selected "Finder out of these Lands." America as Columbina linked New England directly to Columbus's discovery, making it the culmination of the providential process commenced by the Admiral, even if Columbus, Moses-like, could never himself enter the Puritans' New English Canaan. Few American colonists matched Sewall's modest interest in Columbus, however; they ignored not only the bicentenary in 1692 (the year of Salem's witch trials) but also the two hundred and fiftieth anniversary that fell in 1742. Few besides Samuel Sewall noticed the yearly anniversary of the discovery that occurred each October 12.[10]

Not until the era of the American Revolution did Americans invoke Columbus with any frequency. By then, Columbus's part in the drama of American millennialism was expanding, both in its religious and secular—or rather civic—versions. In midcentury, for example, Jonathan Edwards, the great Puritan minister, theologian, and philosopher, developed the millennialist theme of Sewall and others as he made sense of the Great Awakening and prophesied America's future amid the turmoil of the times: "This new world is probably now discovered, that the new and most glorious state of God's church on earth might commence there; that God might in it begin a new world in spiritual respect, when he creates the *new heavens and new earth*."[11]

Others would secularize this vision, and, employing the historic and symbolic Columbus, they would advance the same sense of America as a new land of opportunity, possibility, and progress.

Significantly, this project would be conducted in an emerging public sphere, especially through the act of publication. Print not only enlarged the audience for news, information, and ideas expressed by men (and sometimes women) of letters in America; it largely constituted that audience as public and autonomous (relative to the state). In contrast to "traditional cultures of print," the new republican print discourse "made it possible to imagine a people that could act as a people and in distinction from the state," argues literary critic Michael Warner. Such a reading public understood itself to be nearly limitless, yet, although individuals within this public could never actually assemble and encounter each other physically all at once, they could imagine a vital connection through the common act of reading. Moreover, publication could reproduce and thus extend and allow the appropriation of experience itself. The reported public activities of subjects and then citizens—whether riots, parades, orations, banquets, or toasts—which spoke to Americans' search for a national identity, could be read by others without direct involvement and incorporated as collective memories, vicarious but critical contributions to a developing American national consciousness.[12]

Thus we can see a semipublic ceremonial act—a commencement address—reproduced and enlarged through publication, helping to constitute the American public it addressed on America's identity and destiny. And playing a prominent role in this cultural and political work was Christopher Columbus. In *A Poem, on the Rising Glory of America* (1772), by Philip Freneau and Hugh Henry Brackenridge, first delivered by Freneau to the College of New Jersey's graduating class, the progress of civilization began with Columbus and ended with colonial Anglo-America and its utopian future. It was "the last, the best / Of countries," representing the cumulative improvement of humanity. Although still "sons of Britain," the poets nonetheless gave voice to a rising sense of American nationalism, and sense of mission, which would help fuel the colonial revolt against Great Britain and, later, American expansionism to the Pacific and beyond.[13]

The Columbus myth would continue to forge a sense of nationalism or peoplehood, as it cast the Admiral as a latter-day American Moses. Joel Barlow, the American poet, patriot, and politician, who returned often to the Columbus story, wrote in his *Columbiad* (1807):

> The bliss of unborn nations warm'd his breast,
> Repaid his toils, and sooth'd his soul to rest;
> Thus o'er thy subject wave shall thou behold
> Far happier realms their future charms unfold,
> In nobler pomp another Pisgah rise,
> Beneath whose foot thy new-found Canaan lies.
> There, rapt in vision, hail my favorite clime.
> And taste the blessings of remotest time.[14]

Yet ironically, before the 1770s, a mythic Columbus could as easily have figured as a symbol of British Empire as opposed to the American nationalism he would later represent. Philip Freneau's vision of Columbus hardly differed from that of James Kirkpatrick (d. 1770), the Anglo-Irish doctor, writer, and poet laureate of Britain's commercial empire. For Kirkpatrick, whether on the

Atlantic or in Charleston, South Carolina, he was in Britain. In Kirkpatrick's *The Sea-Piece; A Narrative, Philosophical and Descriptive Poem* (1750), Columbus stands as a heroic visionary: "Bold was the Man, who dar'd at first to shew / From the old World the Passage to a new" (5:29–30). And given Columbus's achievements, which somehow redounded to the credit of the British Empire, Kirkpatrick advocated (like others before him) the renaming of the continent for the American Aeneas, recommending the nominative Columbona. Similarly, and ironically, Columbus's difficulties with his Spanish Catholic monarchs qualified him as an opponent of superstition and a representative of Reformed Christianity and its imperial mission, despite the Admiral's clear Italian origins, not to mention his mysticism and faith in Catholicism. Kirkpatrick knew that Britain's present and future greatness depended on the seas, and he naturalized Columbus, as a companion to Britannia, to represent the ancient origins of Britain's imperial, mercantile triumph.[15]

Although Kirkpatrick lionized the mythic Columbus and incorporated him into the narrative of British imperial progress, some American writers initially found it more difficult to naturalize him. In 1758, in Sylvanus Americus (aka Samuel Nevill)'s "The History of the Northern Continent of *America*," the first extended account of Columbus published in the colonies, the author associated Columbus with Spain and its Black Legend—that is, Spain's reputation for colonial brutality. Yet in contrast to this and later nationalist treatments, and congruent with Kirkpatrick's heroic Columbus, the figure Columbia appeared regularly in American loyalist verse as late as 1761, as, for example, in a poem attributed to Thomas Hutchinson, lieutenant governor of Massachusetts, which celebrated the marriage and accession of George III: "Behold, Britannia! in thy favour'd Isle; / At distance, thou, Columbia! view thy Prince."[16]

During the revolutionary protests, and especially after Independence was achieved, the use of Columbus's name proliferated as Americans fashioned his persona to fulfill the needs of an emerging new republic in search of a national identity. In the process, as they molded the Admiral into a national hero, Americans would conserve some of the imperial connotations of Kirkpatrick's Columbus and ultimately transform him into a patron of their own new Empire of Liberty.

All the while, references to Columbus became increasingly frequent. In the late 1760s, as colonists decried the tyranny of the Townsend Acts, Columbus began to appear in their liberty songs and liberty poems. "Rusticus," in his long poem *Liberty* (1768), had Columbus warn the colonists of George Grenville's plans to invade their freedom; "On *Care* and *Union* your *Success* depends," the Mariner advised, and as their guardian and patron he took their case to the king. In *America. A Poem*, by Alexander Martin (1769), Columbus's discovery—so pregnant with promise—was compared with the hated Townsend duties, with the question posed, "Was it for this?"[17] Among the reasons for the growing appeal of Columbus as an American patron saint, of course, was the fact that the Italian discoverer, who sailed for the Spanish crown, was not British, despite the poetically licensed attempts by some British imperial writers to naturalize him. In Columbus, Americans found "a past that bypassed England," as historian Claudia Bushman has so aptly put it.[18]

By the 1770s, the colonies were more frequently being referred to as Columba or Columbia, as in Mercy Otis Warren's "Poetical Reverie," published in the *Boston Gazette* of February 13, 1775; in Philip Freneau's *American Liberty, A Poem*, which appeared in April; or in a Phillis Wheatley poem addressed to "His Excellency, Gen. Washington" in October of the same year. Freneau was among the first literary figures to emerge in the cultural ferment of the revolutionary period, which began to produce, for the first time in America, a modern, Western, but nationally distinct cultural life. Like many of his contemporaries, Freneau turned to Columbus as a worthy American subject, beginning, as we have seen, with *The Rising Glory of America*. His 1772 poem "Discovery" celebrated the Mariner and his accomplishments, although not without a measure of doubt about the cost of colonization, anticipating the harsher criticisms that would emerge in the nineteenth and twentieth centuries:

> Alas! how few of all that daring train
> That seek new worlds embosomed in the main,
> How few have sailed on virtue's nobler plan,
> How few with motives worthy of a man!

For the moment, however, Columbus seemed to escape the stain of the Spanish Black Legend and represented the nobility of the American nation.[19]

By the 1780s, America as Columbia had become thoroughly conventional. New York City's institution of higher learning could not remain King's College after the Revolution and in 1784 became instead Columbia.[20] The allegorical, classical female figure Columbia—replacing the rude, unclothed, and uncultured Indian maiden as the symbolic representation of America—adorned coins struck by the Congress in 1785 and 1786. In 1786, Columbia became the new capital of South Carolina, and in Philadelphia the *Columbian Magazine* began publication; in 1787, it printed Timothy Dwight's song "Columbia," which served as an unofficial national anthem into the nineteenth century. Within fifty years of the American Revolution, versions of Columbus's name graced the titles of some sixteen periodicals, eighteen books, and a half dozen scholarly societies.[21]

By 1789, the New York Tammany Society had diversified its name, becoming the Saint Tammany Society, or Columbian Order. Through the mythical Delaware sagamore Tammany and Christopher Columbus, the society could identify itself with the best of both Europe and America yet avoid any reference to British forebears. In 1791, Americans decided to seat their national capital on the Potomac River and to call it the Territory of Columbia. Washington, D.C., conjoined in its name the two greatest deities in America's republican pantheon. And in 1792, in the year of the tercentenary, Capt. Robert Gray discovered and named the great river of the American Northwest, the Columbia, after his ship the *Columbia Rediviva*. The powerful course of the mighty Columbia seemed to embody the vision of westward expansion proclaimed in the works of nationalist poets Philip Freneau, Timothy Dwight, and Joel Barlow. Through such representations of Columbia, Americans sought to define their place in history, subdue the North American landscape, situate their republic in the world, and distinguish their nation from its tainted British origins.[22]

In short, Columbus proved central to Americans' practice of nationalism. Although intricately related, two facets of American Columbianism might be distinguished to illuminate the particular cultural and political work that the myth, image, and symbol of Columbus performed in changing revolutionary and early national America: Columbus as symbol of a republican national destiny, and Columbus as symbol of a rising American continental empire. Since the early eighteenth century, in the religious writing of Samuel Sewall, Cotton Mather, and then Jonathan Edwards, Columbus had symbolized American destiny. By the period of the American Revolution, that destiny seemed to entail the emergence of an independent republic in North America.

Fig. 26. Columbia-Washington medal. Design attributed to Joseph Barrell. Copper. Boston, 1787. MHS image nos. 1892, 1893. Courtesy of the Massachusetts Historical Society.

Columbus, abstracted and feminized as Columbia, vaguely represented that Promised Land. Like other European symbols of sovereign lands, the goddess Columbia was depicted as feminine. Lands—homelands—were conventionally feminized (that is, as Mother Earth and Motherlands), whereas political states were more often (although not always) represented as masculine (that is, Fatherlands). In the early American republic, this female symbolism—imbued with notions of Republican motherhood—achieved a particular potency. Columbia suggested more than the nation; it signified the subdued, domesticated space of the continent that had become, or was destined to become, part of the United States. More than the masculine figure Columbus, Columbia expressed the dignity and gentility of an emerging American civilization.[23] But the symbolic hero / heroine had little specific to say about the particular social and political arrangements that would develop in the new United States. In its vagueness, Columbianism promoted consensus among disparate Americans joined in coalitions to effect their independence from Great Britain. By the 1790s, amid the partisan battles that emerged to confound the republic, Columbus was sometimes reinvented and enlisted in factional struggles. But the abstractness and antiquity of Columbus, in contrast to the living, breathing Washington or Jefferson, made the hero less useful in partisan debate.

More important, Columbus proved a perfect symbol for America, not merely as a discrete republic but as an expanding continental empire. A crisis of the West in the 1780s challenged the very notion and destiny of the union achieved by the Revolution. Western lands, placed under the control of Congress in the Articles of Confederation, were among the very few common possessions of United States citizens, most of whom were arrayed in separate states along the Atlantic coast. Yet the fate of these lands remained ambiguous. Expansion of white Americans into such regions was a foregone conclusion, but would westerners' interests diverge from those of eastern Americans and create conflict and disunion? On what basis would such lands be incorporated into the Union? Indeed, could they be protected from the grasp of imperial powers with footholds in the American interior? Could political integration be effected without creating a new colonialism that re-created the evils of the British colonial system so recently rejected? Was it possible to maintain liberty and republicanism under the sort of centralized, energetic regime apparently required to govern so extensive a nation? If the Northwest Ordinance of 1787 was the practical solution offered to these problems, Columbianism was the cultural and symbolic response. By facilitating the peaceful incorporation of new states in the West, not as colonies but as full members of the Union on a par with the original thirteen states, Congress avoided the mistakes of British imperial policy and designed an expansionism that was understood to be not colonial. Of course, the policy was both colonial and imperial, but Columbianism helped Americans justify the latter and ignore the former. Through Columbus imagery and place-names, America could imagine what at one time might have seemed oxymoronic: an Empire of Liberty. In a sense, the common reading of the West as America's destiny helped constitute the readers—that is, United States citizens, otherwise divided by different regional or class interests—as a nation, Columbia.[24]

Columbianism and the Tercentenary

While an imperial Columbianism was taking shape, Columbus in his vaguer manifestation, as a symbol of American destiny and the beginning point for national history, was appearing prominently in public, celebratory, and political demonstrations on the streets of the new republic. After the drafting of the Constitution in Philadelphia in 1787, the symbolic Columbus was enlisted in the ratification debates. In New York in April 1788, for example, the American Company—a theatrical group—promoted "A Serious Pastoral . . . by Citizens of the United States, called The Convention, or the Columbian Fathers," joining the Constitution with Columbus, and suggesting implicitly that this frame of government was the natural culmination of America's founding process, which had begun in 1492. As state after state adopted the Constitution, citizens celebrated with public festivals—parades, public banquets, orations, poetry readings, concerts, and plays. After Congress's official announcement on July 2, 1788, that the Constitution had garnered the approval of the requisite nine states and was therefore enacted, spectacular demonstrations erupted both to toast the new nation and to prod those states that had not yet ratified. In New York, a grand procession was held on July 23, while upstate in Poughkeepsie, men still heatedly debated the Constitution; within three days New Yorkers joined the new union as the eleventh state to ratify.[25]

These events were designed to "make history," to shape the direction of the new nation, and to interpret actively the meaning of America. As James Wilson noted explicitly in his oration following Philadelphia's Grand Federal Procession on July 4, 1788, such public actions,

> may *instruct* and *improve*, while they *entertain* and *please*. . . . They may preserve the *memory*, and engrave the *importance* of great *political events*. They may *represent*, with peculiar felicity and force, the *operation* and *effects* of great *political truths*. The *picturesque* and *splendid decorations around me*, furnish the most *beautiful* and most *brilliant* proofs, that these remarks are FAR FROM BEING IMAGINARY.[26]

Among the national heroes displayed as portraits or effigies, along with Washington, was Christopher Columbus. Pictures, floats, and costumed figures were carefully arranged to form a long historical chain linking Columbus ultimately to the new federal Constitution and to the future. Citizens were the producers as well as the consumers of such events; they were participants as well as observers. As they made history, they made themselves as Americans. In imagining—and publishing—their local festival as the celebration of an extralocal community, they encouraged others to conclude as well that the nationalist sentiments expressed by men like Wilson were indeed "far from being [merely] imaginary."[27]

The year 1792 offered Americans a rare opportunity to develop the Columbian theme, to define themselves, as all centenary years since have emerged as invitations to employ the symbolic Columbus in the service of particular notions of Americanism. A number of celebrations occurred throughout the republic, in Philadelphia and Baltimore, Providence and Richmond, and in smaller communities like Windsborough, South Carolina, marked typically with military parades, dinners, and toasts.[28] In Boston on October 23, in the first public lecture sponsored by the newly formed Massachusetts Historical Society, its founder the Rev. Dr. Jeremy Belknap provided an oration, subsequently published as *A Discourse Intended to Commemorate the Discovery of America by Christopher Columbus* (1792), which served as the centerpiece of a major civic event attended by Governor John Hancock, Lieutenant Governor Samuel Adams, and numerous other dignitaries. After their quarterly meeting, the society proceeded, accompanied by music, to the Brattle Street Church, where they heard Belknap's address as well as prayers and an ode written for the occasion. Members and honored guests then adjourned to a lavish feast at the house of the Hon. James Sullivan, the society's president, where, according to newspaper reports, "the memory of Columbus was toasted in convivial enjoyment, and the warmest wishes were expressed that the blessings now distinguishing the United States might be extended to every part of the world he has discovered."[29]

Although organized by Boston's elite, the tercentenary celebration was intended nonetheless to have a wider impact. Attendance at the lecture and banquet was limited to society members and notables, but the procession invited popular attention and at least vicarious participation. The vagueness and venerability of Columbus promoted such goals. As a newly constructed but ancient American hero, he was a bipartisan champion in an era of vicious partisan contention. Belknap's, and the society's, intention was not to function merely for their own edification. They sought to disseminate historical information broadly, to promote "useful knowledge," and in general to cultivate a learned, virtuous, patriotic American citizenry. The society therefore published Belknap's "public discourse" for popular consumption and advertised its sale in the *American Apollo*, the society's magazine.[30]

The New York City tercentenary celebration preceded and exceeded the events in Boston. As one contemporary newspaper reported, "The 12th inst., being the commencement of the IV. COLUMBIAN CENTURY, was observed as a Century Festival by the Tammany Society, and celebrated in the style of sentiment which distinguishes this social and patriotic institution."[31] John Pintard, sagamore of the Tammany Society or Columbian Order in New York City, had been in correspondence with Jeremy Belknap on a number of matters and may well have been the first to suggest that the Massachusetts Historical Society celebrate the three hundredth anniversary of Columbus's voyage. In New York, Pintard's Tammany Society staged a larger, less sedate, and more popular festival, the first ever held exclusively for Columbus in the Americas. In addition to their customary "Long Talk" and banquet, members erected an illuminated shaft or monument to the memory of Columbus, "ornamented by transparency with a variety of suitable devices."[32]

In the shape of an obelisk, the monument stood upward of fourteen feet in height and could be moved from place to place. From its base—a globe emerging out of clouds and chaos—an elongated pyramid arose, depicting on its four sides mythologized scenes from the Admiral's life and emphasizing the themes of progress, science, commerce, the ingratitude and abuse of monarchs, and the ultimate triumph of freedom over despotism and knowledge over superstition. The Genius of Liberty ultimately appears before the dejected Columbus and cheers him, pointing to the Tammany monument itself, "sacred to his memory, reared by the Columbian Order," and allowing him to see the glorious legacy of his discovery, which America now embodied. The obelisk was exhibited "for the gratification of the public curiosity" prior to the tercentenary program, and at the close of the celebration it was placed in the Tammany Society's museum in a large room in the Exchange on Broad Street, where it attracted considerable attention. Thereafter, it was illuminated annually each October 12, a day sacred to the society's second patron, Columbus. The unusual monument figured prominently in the advertisements of the Tammany Museum, until the collection was sold, ultimately finding its way into the hands of P. T. Barnum. Like many of the museum's objects, the obelisk slipped into oblivion.[33]

The Tammany Society in New York, like those elsewhere, was "conceived in a spirit of festival and celebration," the movement's historian has observed; its purpose was both patriotic and recreational. Although its leader John Pintard shared many of the same aspirations that inspired Jeremy Belknap and the members of the Massachusetts Historical Society—indeed, Pintard was instrumental in founding the New-York Historical Society and was the driving force behind the Tammany Museum—the New York Tammany Society had more populist inclinations. And along with other Tammany Societies in Pennsylvania, New Jersey, Maryland, Virginia, the Carolinas, and Georgia, it exhibited a strong social and nationalistic character. Their principal holiday, St. Tammany Day, fell traditionally on May 1, the beginning of the sporting season, which clubs would inaugurate with raucous celebrations and plenty of strong drink. In the context of American opposition to Britain, the societies had become more clearly political—and they would remain so after Independence—but they refused to abandon their commitment to frivolity and amusement, even when they aspired to greater gentility and respectability.[34]

Early Tammany spokesmen committed the society to nationalism, patriotism, liberty, charity, and brotherly love. It came out against local and class prejudices; its membership was not based, at least theoretically, on caste, wealth, or ethnicity. Like the plebian society that apparently supplied much of its membership and enjoyed its festivals, it embraced a democratic vision.[35] In the Columbian tercentenary celebration—its impact magnified by its popular and festive appeal—we see the Tammany Society in the act of making history, inventing traditions that would define and promote the new American republic as a nation dedicated to liberty, equality, fraternity. Through direct participation, as they viewed the society's portable monument or took part in its parades, illuminations, and songs, its Columbian odes, feasts, and toasts, celebrants helped to constitute an American people, while they shaped popular perceptions of America's national identity and destiny.

Amid the "rational amusements" that filled up the evening's entertainment, members of the Tammany Society toasted "the discoverer of *this* new world" and "the United *Columbian* States." Revelers expressed the dream that their world would forever enjoy peace and liberty, escape "the vices and miseries of the old," and provide "a happy asylum for the oppressed of all nations and of all religions." They raised their cups hoping that this might "be the last Century Festival of the Columbian Order that finds a slave on this globe." They toasted George Washington, Thomas Paine, the Rights of Man, Lafayette, and the French nation.[36] Through the mythic persona of Columbus, constructed in their own image, these patriots found a means to legitimize their particular national vision and supply it with an ancient, sacred pedigree. They imbued the Great Mariner and his exploits with meaning—he stood for bold independence, initiative and persistence, triumph over Old World tyranny and oppression, freedom, and economic, political, and religious liberty, their odes and speeches tell us—and then they, as the American sons of Columbia, enlisted the Columbus they had made as their direct ancestor, patron, and inspiration. For neither the first time nor the last, the malleable Columbus proved useful as Americans fashioned their identity and crafted a national purpose.

Only in retrospect, perhaps, is it ironic that orations and toasts, in Boston as well as in New York, would read Columbus out of the Black Legend of Spanish colonization, dissociating the Admiral from slavery and the slave trade.[37] Almost immediately after the tercentenary, such indiscrete mixing in toasts—to Washington and to Paine, the Rights of Man, or the French nation—would become impossible in the charged partisan climate that pitted Jeffersonians against Hamiltonians, and enthusiastic supporters against alarmed critics of the French Revolution in the United States.[38] Nonetheless, Columbus somehow remained an untarnished, popular hero.

Later in the 1790s, the Tammany Society became involved in other festive promotions of Columbus, as in its sponsorship of the opera written by Mrs. Anne Julia Hatton, titled *Tammany, or the Indian Chief,* which somehow managed to feature Columbus in a prominent role. Little remains of the opera; apparently only the prologue was printed, and the plot is only barely sketched in the hostile reviews by the Federalist dramatist William Dunlap, who called the opera "a mélange of bombast," "seasoned high with spices hot from Paris, and swelling with rhodomontade for the sonorous voice of Hodgkinson." Dunlap admitted that the performance was "received with unbounded applause" but denigrated the audience as composed of "the poorer class of mechanics and clerks." Columbus shared with Tammany the audience's acclaim. The opera subsequently played successfully in Philadelphia and Boston. In September 1797, the English playwright Thomas Morton's *Columbus, or the World Discovered,* first acted at London's Covent Garden in 1792, ran successfully in New York and later at the Boston Haymarket, where it was the hit of the season, further attesting to the popularity of the hero Columbus. In 1798, William Dunlap put on his play *Andre,* a sympathetic treatment of the British major John Andre hanged in 1780 for his part in the conspiracy arranged by Benedict Arnold to hand over West Point to the British. Andre himself was an engaging sort who played a prominent role in British military theatricals during the war. But American audiences apparently were disappointed by the play's "lack of patriotic fervor," according to historian Jared Brown, and the Federalist Dunlap "was forced to rewrite his play as a patriotic pageant entitled *The Glory of Columbia* in order to attract audiences."[39]

In the 1790s, Columbus became increasing important as a Tammany Society patron; as Tammany members deemphasized their Indian saint and elevated Columbus, their actions mirrored those occurring nationally in the iconography of the United States. As early as July 4, 1782, a Philadelphia Tammany Society poem had remarked, "While mimic Saints a transient joy impart, / That strikes the sense but reaches not the heart, / Arise Columbia!—nobler themes await." These sentiments seemed designed to denigrate not just the Indian "St. Tammany" but his newest, immigrant rival, St. Patrick.[40]

But Indians as symbols proved to be a growing liability for the society and

Fig. 27. Columbus at the head of a pillar of American heroes, from Washington Irving's *The Life of George Washington*, vol. 15 (1857). Columbus occupies a critical place as the first American hero, linked with Founding Fathers Washington, Franklin, Jefferson, Adams, and Lafayette. Courtesy of Knight Library, University of Oregon.

the nation. As historian John Higham has suggested, after the Revolution, the conventional Indian maiden as a symbol for America seemed to concede "the cultural inferiority of the New World." Americans needed symbols that would connect them with the civilized world while yet declaring their separation. Perfectly suited to the task was the new spirit of America, the goddess Liberty, or Columbia, a reworking of the Roman goddess Britannia. If the patronage of the ancient sagamore Tammany, safely buried, helped assert white Americans' claims to the North American landscape, the memory of real Indians, like those who mauled Generals Harmar and St. Clair in the Ohio Country before their defeat at Fallen Timbers, undermined the effectiveness of such "savage" Native people as legitimate American icons. The broadside "The Columbian Tragedy," for example, which appeared late in 1791, depicted two rows of coffins above its headlines, pictures of a "BLOODY INDIAN BATTLE" and the slain Maj. Gen. Richard Butler, and "A PARTICULAR AND OFFICIAL ACCOUNT Of the Brave and Unfortunate Officers and Soldiers, who were Slain and Wounded in the Ever-Memorable and BLOODY INDIAN BATTLE." When the broadside called the battle "Perhaps the most shocking that has happened in AMERICA since its first Discovery," it menacingly linked Columbus to an unacceptable American destiny.[41]

To the extent that Indians could be naturalized as American Ancients and assigned a place among the American natural antiquities, which some argued rivaled those of Greece or Rome, they could be useful components in the new republic's nationalism. Imposing classical names on the landscape (and later building Greek and Roman revival structures) similarly might assert an American nationalism based simultaneously on distinction from Europe (at least from Great Britain) and identity with Western civilization. Another effective means was to Columbianize the American landscape. Referring to the continent as Columbia at least discursively claimed and subdued it and legitimated white possession in the present and future. Faulting the goddess symbol Americans created for her remoteness and abstraction, historian John Higham has written, "naming her Columbia scarcely began to bring her down to earth." Yet, in a sense, it did precisely that. Columbia, not simply the goddess but the place, *was* the American earth, and the hero Columbus had given it to Americans. The mythic Columbus discovered the New World, and unlike the conquistadors of the Black Legend, he "endeavored as far as possible to treat [the natives] with justice and gentleness," Jeremy Belknap told his compatriots. Columbus's example seemed to promise, as did the vanishing of the sagamore Tammany and the appropriation of his legacy by Tammany Society members who dressed up like Indians, an American expansion with honor.[42]

In 1790, addressing a visiting Creek delegation, New York Tammany Grand Sachem Dr. William Pitt Smith informed his guests that

> Although the hand of death is cold upon their bodies, yet the spirits of two great Chiefs are supposed to walk backwards and forwards in this great wigwam and to direct our proceedings—Tammany and Columbus. Tradition has brought to us the memory of the first. He was a great and good Indian chief, a strong warrior, a swift hunter, but what is greater than all, he loved his country. We call ourselves his sons. Columbus was a famous traveller and discoverer . . ., the first white man that ever visited this western world. But history makes it known that because he wished to treat the Indians with kindness, friendship, and justice, he was cruelly used. Brothers—Tammany and Columbus live together in the world of spirits in great harmony, and they teach us to cultivate like friendship and reciprocal good offices with you and all Indians.[43]

The spirits of Tammany and Columbus together, as lovers of the American land and as fathers, peacefully consigned the American landscape to the early republic's white citizens, and, having made his bequest, the sagamore faded into the shadows.

Philip Freneau's important poem "The Indian Burying Ground" (1787) can be read as just such an expression of the Vanishing Indian myth and the ways that the Indian past could be imagined (simultaneously with conquest) and naturalized. Whereas Freneau interred Indians, Tammany Society members such as New York's John Pintard helped to transform Native subjects into objects of antiquarian interest through their efforts to found and maintain museums. Yet Ignoble Savages continued to exist in tandem with Noble Savages, the latter treated nostalgically because they were gone, and the former treated with disdain as all too alive and threatening. Nonetheless, white Americans seemed prepared to claim their continental legacy and domesticate the landscape, whether through peaceful means or warfare. With the War of 1812, playing Indian became untenable; both western Indians and Great Britain merited American wrath, as each failed to yield gracefully. Thus an anti-British cartoon linked evil Britain—again threatening the republic—with malignant Indians, who were depicted scalping American soldiers and being paid for the trophies by a British officer. Rhyming lines provided the following caption:

> Arise Columbia's Sons and forward press,
> Your Country's wrongs call loudly for redress,
> The savage Indian with his scalping knife
> Or tomahawk may seek to take your life.
>
> By bravery aw'd, they'll in a dreadful fright

Shrink back for refuge to the woods of flight.
Their British leaders then will quickly shake
And for those wrongs shall restitution make.[44]

As the American landscape was cleared of Indians and classicized, it was Columbianized. In New York State alone rose the new cities of Troy, Utica, Ithaca, Sparta, Syracuse, and Rome. Yet Columbus would give his name to more places in the United States than anyone except Washington himself, a heroic figure often paired with the goddess Columbia. In the old Northwest, in the process of being tamed, Cincinnati, Ohio, so named by Governor Arthur St. Clair in 1788, incorporated an earlier town named Columbia. In 1812, after the initial conquest but in a time imperiled by new threats from the British and Indians, the Ohio state legislature sought to reimpose the heroic eponym on their landscape and directed Joel Wright to plan a new capital city on the bend of the Scioto River named Columbus. Columbus's name thus marked conquest but represented that aggrandizement as legitimate and benevolent. Western Columbias and Columbuses, whether new towns or counties or rivers, represented the triumph of an expanding American republic. Such place-names implicitly linked the rising glory of America with the intrepid explorer Columbus, who had ventured west to find new lands and claim them for Christendom. In some cases, latter-day explorers, like those reconnoitering the Columbia River, would carry Columbia-Washington medals west to distribute to Native peoples. Such medals, literally representing the currency of Columbus and the potency of his symbolism when paired with Washington, depicted the ships of discovery named after the two great American heroes, minted to celebrate the opening of trade with Canton and the Pacific Northwest.[45]

Expansion itself became a national ritual, a means of constituting the nation (literally and imaginatively) and celebrating it through westward movement. These events and experiences were marked and reproduced in texts and illustrations—not just in the published accounts of explorers and travelers but in maps. Place-names themselves, then, could function as national monuments for residents, local expressions of national history and identity. And when read on maps, such names could encourage those in other parts of the United States to imagine that they, along with others throughout their far-flung republic, shared a single national community and identity as Americans. If this was the case, the practice of expansion, inscribed in text and disseminated through publication, could in turn produce national thought and practice. Geographical description became national prescription. The land Columbia became a monument to the nation itself, a place inspired and guided by its eponymous hero Columbus.

The Ethnic, Catholic Columbus: The First American Immigrant

During the tercentenary in the 1790s, Columbus had yet to achieve his greatest stature as an American mythic hero. Indeed, apart from Tammany Society observances, which continued, the American public did little to keep October 12 holy in the decades following the 1792 anniversary. Even the Tammany Society or Columbian Order began to lose some of its interest in Columbus in the 1820s, as the organization became increasingly dominated by the Irish and St. Patrick assumed the role of the society's second patron. Ignoring the Admiral in 1831, members attending an anniversary banquet toasted instead "St. Patrick and St. Tammany—Both purified their respective countries,—the first from poisonous reptiles, the other from the tools of tyranny and despotism. Heaven grant that they may soon exchange great works."[46]

The work of Washington Irving—appearing in some 175 editions—and the growing presence of the brave, moral, hard-working, and persistent Admiral in the schoolbooks of American children would maintain Columbus's place in America's mythology and civic religion. But ironically, given the advent of the Tammany Irish and their substitution of St. Patrick for St. Columbus, the Admiral would make a glorious return, thanks to the efforts of American Catholic immigrants, Irish, Italian, and later Hispanic. If Columbus could help a new nation find its identity as the United States of America in the late-eighteenth century, he could prove invaluable as well to the immigrants who were remaking the nation in the second half of the nineteenth century. Through Columbus—the Italian Catholic explorer sailing for Spain and Christendom—these new Americans would declare their long-standing American identity, asserting and laying claim to their rightful place in Columbia.[47]

In the decades following the Civil War, rapid economic development and the promise of America as a Golden Land attracted thousands of immigrants from Europe each year. Between 1881 and 1884, well over 2.5 million entered the country; in 1882, more immigrants arrived than in any of the succeeding twenty years. Increasingly, the source of such immigration was shifting from northern to southern and eastern Europe, and the influx included an ever-growing proportion of Italians, Poles, Lithuanians, and Russians—mostly Catholics and Jews. Between 1830 and 1860, the United States Catholic population grew more than tenfold, from approximately three hundred thousand to over three million. From 1880 to 1924, some four million immigrants from southern Italy came to America, joining an earlier group of Italian immigrants, mainly from the northern peninsula. These "new" immigrants, who often clustered more conspicuously in America's large, industrialized, chaotic cities, alarmed some Americans of older, Protestant stock. Ironically, the descendants of those who had labored to shed their British past in the 1780s and 1790s had by now reconstructed themselves exclusively as Anglo-Saxon Protestants, and they feared that foreigners among them might destroy the middle-class, Christian, civic culture that they controlled and identified simply as American. As the industrialist and United States senator Chauncey Depew illiberally declared in his oration at the dedication of the Chicago World's Columbian Exposition in October 1892, "Unwatched and unhealthy immigration can no longer be permitted to our shores. We must have a national quarantine against disease, pauperism, and crime. . . . We cannot admit those who come to undermine our institutions, and subvert our laws."[48]

Since the 1850s, the United States had endured waves of nativism and anti-Catholicism, first directed at the Irish. In 1854, the American Party—popularly known as the Know-Nothings because members committed themselves to secrecy and would reply to probing questions that they "knew nothing"— emerged in the political turmoil of the antebellum period and achieved national cohesion and prominence on the basis of its anti-immigrant, anti-Catholic programs. Party stalwarts pledged never to vote for Irish Catholic candidates, who, Know-Nothings argued, pledged allegiance to the pope in Rome and slavishly followed the orders of their local priests. After the Civil War, in the 1870s, 1880s, and 1890s, new forms of bigotry and discrimination threatened to erupt, including the anti-Catholic crusade of the American Protective Association, founded in the 1880s, and various efforts to restrict immigration, which first succeeded in 1882 with the Chinese Exclusion Act. In the same year, Congress passed the first comprehensive federal immigration law, denying admission to those labeled criminals, lunatics, idiots, or others who might become public charges. And such efforts continued, culminating in 1924 with passage of the National Origins Act, which completely prohibited "Oriental" immigration and limited the total number of European immigrants to 2 percent of each nationality's United States population as of 1890—a measure that severely restricted entry from those regions that had contributed most heavily to the new waves of immigration.[49]

In the context of such nativism, in New Haven, Connecticut, in 1882, a small group of Irish American men, led by their parish priest, Father Michael J. McGivney, founded an organization that they determined to call the Knights of Columbus.[50] Although some members were Civil War veterans, these men and other parishioners were not fully accepted in their community. As a hostile 1879 headline in the *New York Times* concerning their parish church suggested—"Roman Catholic Troubles in New-Haven; How an Aristocratic Avenue was Blemished by a Roman Church Edifice"—the Catholic Irish, although "old immigrants," faced nativist prejudices and remained second-class citizens.[51] In response to such attitudes, founders of the Knights carefully considered names for their organization. As one recalled, "I suggested the name of the Columbian Order having in view the name of Columbus, the great Catholic discoverer of America whose name would be a token of strength as showing we Catholics were no aliens to this country, but were entitled to all rights and privileges due to such Discovery by one of our faith."[52] Quickly, the Columbian Order became the Knights of Columbus, thereby linking itself directly to the Catholic founder of America, cloaking itself in the nobility and romance of the chivalrous, crusading knights of medieval Europe, while bypassing the more recent English colonial past being revived by elite guardians of American culture and society.

Celebrations of the ethnic hero Columbus provide a telling comparison with those surrounding that other patron of Irish Americans, St. Patrick. As early as the 1740s in New York City and elsewhere in colonial America—for example, in Savannah, Georgia—by the 1760s, Irish inhabitants (Protestant as well as Catholic) boisterously marked St. Patrick's Day on March 17. Societies of St. Patrick emerged before the American Revolution—like the Ancient and Most Benevolent Order of the Friendly Brothers of St. Patrick in New York, beginning in 1769—as nonsectarian benevolent associations to aid poor countrymen, providing assistance with food or firewood, or redeeming them from debtors' prison. But like other, similar fraternal organizations—such as the St. Andrew Society, which staged annual dinners on November 30 to honor the patron saint of Scotland, or the English St. George Society, known for its special events in April, heralding England's patron saint—the St. Patrick societies were largely male eating and drinking clubs that celebrated their national and ethnic origins, cultivated pride, and provided themselves with diversions and amusement.[53]

During the American Revolution, one of the first St. Patrick's Day parades in New York City was organized in 1779 by a British regiment, the Volunteers of Ireland, who sought to recruit soldiers among New York's Irish community. Here, ethnically Irish inhabitants were mobilized for a nonsectarian purpose, ironically to defend the British Empire. After the Revolution, Irish American leaders, and the mixed Protestant and Catholic Irish community generally, continued to oppose religious sectarianism, while they organized to support civil rights movements in Ireland and aid emancipation efforts for British Catholics. The Friends of Ireland and the Shamrock Friendly Association of New York, as well as the *Shamrock, or Hibernian Chronicle,* from 1810 to 1817 New York's first Irish American newspaper, were committed to ecumenicalism and to the creation of a united Protestant and Catholic Irish American community based on republican values. Yet St. Patrick's Day soon became an occasion to compete for Irish support; by the second decade of the nineteenth century, the Tammany Society, not yet an Irish political machine, confronted its political rival, DeWitt Clinton, who had allied himself with Irish immigrants, by becoming more staunchly nativist—or rather, anti-Catholic—ironically by wooing the Protestant Irish on St. Patrick's Day. Increasingly in the 1820s, working-class Irish Americans began to reject the nonsectarian, integrationist program of earlier Irish immigrants and, in reaction to discrimination and growing nativist threats, to adopt a defensive ethnic separatism. The Hibernian Universal Benevolent Society expressed these ethnic interests best, boldly parading on the Fourth of July and celebrating St. Patrick's Day with annual processions through Irish neighborhoods. In the late 1820s and early 1830s, Irish ranks increased dramatically; by 1835 more than thirty thousand Irish immigrants arrived in New York each year, most of them young, poor, unskilled, male, and—for the first time—overwhelmingly Catholic. St. Patrick's Day parades and celebrations became tools to demonstrate not only Irish pride and solidarity but, increasingly, Irish power in the face of discrimination.[54]

If March 17 processions had been small affairs in New York City through the 1840s, in the 1850s they became massive. In 1851, seventeen organizations came together to form the Convention of Irish Societies, which assumed control of the annual St. Patrick's Day parade and made it into an event that commanded the full attention of the city, shutting down businesses and meriting the ceremonial review of the mayor and city officials. The New York Irish participated in Independence Day events too, to the consternation of nativists—as in 1853 when some five hundred Irish marchers, wearing the green and carrying a banner of George Washington shaking hands with the Irish patriot Daniel O'Connell, took the streets and ultimately battled nativist mobs. In this appropriation of the United States' sacred national holiday, the Irish declared the legitimacy of their American citizenship. On St. Patrick's Day, by contrast, their patriotism was more local, ethnic, and religious—it celebrated an ethnic Irish nationalism and emphasized distinctiveness and separatism, not integration (let alone disintegration) in an American melting pot. As historian Timothy J. Meagher has argued in his study of Worcester, Massachusetts, St. Patrick's Day parades in America—characteristic of Irish communities in the United States but not in Ireland itself—were less about paying homage to St. Patrick than about declaring allegiance to Irish nationality, demonstrating Irish patriotism, and resisting threats to Irish ethnic interests, particularly by giving the appearance of strength and solidarity.[55]

Worcester's St. Patrick's Day parade tradition began in 1847, and it grew as Worcester's Irish burgeoned. Yet, surprisingly, by the 1880s some Irish American citizens began to doubt the parade's utility in promoting the community's interest or its reputation. Like many ethnic communities, the Worcester Irish were divided, with some committed to integration into the American mainstream and cooperation with Yankee Protestants and others suspicious of such cooperation and convinced that Worcester's leadership would never promote working-class Irish interests. The former group—more often young, American born, and organized into Catholic temperance associations—often voted in the Convention of United Irish Societies (charged with staging the St. Patrick's Day parade) against holding the parade, and when they participated they treated the procession as a means of acquiring respectability and furthering Irish integration. One Irish American temperance orator, Richard H. Mooney, urged his audience on St. Patrick's Day in 1886 to become "more American than the Americans themselves"; in 1888 he hoped St. Patrick's Day might become "almost an American day." On the other hand, the latter group—more often working class and recent immigrants, some of whom considered themselves exiles—tended to support the annual parade and participate enthusiastically to demonstrate their Irish patriotism, manhood, solidarity, and ethnic power. The economic traumas and the shifting political and religious climate of the 1890s worked to the advantage of this Irish nationalist group and convinced most Worcester Irish Americans of the importance of solidarity and more aggressive demonstration of ethnic unity and power.[56]

Yet by the early twentieth century, some in the Worcester Irish community became concerned about ethnic isolation and sought to promote upward economic mobility and respectability, even if they remained circumspect about achieving full acceptance. Like other Catholic Americans in New Haven and elsewhere in the United States, they sought to use the new Catholic American hero, Columbus, to promote their objectives. Uniting with other Catholics in the now more ethnically diverse city—including new immigrant communities from Lithuania, Poland, and Italy, as well as French Canada—Irish Americans adopted a broader, more inclusive self-definition as patriotic American Catholics. Epitomizing this new identity were members of Worcester's new chapters of the Knights of Columbus, and at the forefront of their efforts was their sponsorship of a new Columbus Day parade beginning in 1910. Through "St. Columbus," Irish Americans not only built a larger and more powerful ethnic coalition among co-religionists, but they found a potent champion who could represent them locally and nationally as legitimately American, because, not in spite, of their Catholicism. After 1913, the Knights gave up responsibility for the annual Columbus Day parade to the city. In part, this resignation resulted from the Knights' difficulties in negotiating between various ethnic enclaves and in handling the fund-raising and logistics of the parade, but as municipal authorities assumed responsibility for the Columbus Day program, they also ascribed official sanction to the parade, a celebration of ethnicity as Americanism.[57]

The symbolic Columbus, then, has been a powerful talisman for Catholics, and other ethnic Americans, for more than a hundred years.[58] In claiming the mantle of a sacred American hero, who had lent his name to more places in the United States than anyone save George Washington himself, the Knights of Columbus—and the ethnic communities from which they drew their membership—disarmed nativists and thrust themselves into the mainstream of American society. Although St. Patrick was more than a religious figure to the Irish and remained significant as their chief political emblem, Columbus was an American hero.

If Irish Americans in New Haven and Worcester could be reborn as Americans through the patronage of Columbus, Italian Americans could lay an even stronger claim to the Genovese explorer as their American patron saint. By the middle of the nineteenth century, Italian immigrants, united in American cities from coast to coast, had formed themselves into Columbus societies, social and fraternal organizations that served their communities through self-help and benevolent efforts, and diligently observed Columbus's landing day on October 12. In Boston, New York, San Francisco, and Philadelphia, in St. Louis, Cincinnati, and New Orleans, wherever Italian immigrants congregated in the United States, they found in Columbus a source of ethnic pride and a means of claiming their place in American society. Ironically, immigrants from the Italian peninsula, given their localized identification with native villages and towns, often became "Italian" only in America, as they were lumped together by others and found social and political reasons to construct more consciously a sense of themselves as Italian Americans. Columbus mutual aid societies and festivities surrounding Columbus Day helped to effect this ethnic metamorphosis. Today, in cities across the country—most notably New York, Boston, and San Francisco—parades, banquets, and pageantry continue to mark Columbus Day as an Italian American festival, a living legacy of nineteenth-century (although not particularly fifteenth-century) America.[59]

The Quatercentenary and the Confused Columbian Discourse

These ethnic celebrations, and the occasional Columbus orations and memorials that occurred irregularly throughout the nineteenth century, were dwarfed in 1892 by the massive commemorations surrounding the four hundredth anniversary of Columbus's landing. Americans marked the quatercentenary grandly, with a weeklong Columbian festival in New York, with the opening of the World's Columbian Exposition in Chicago, and with unprece-

dented pageantry in cities across the United States.[60] Rising out of the swamp-
lands on the shores of Lake Michigan, seven miles south of Chicago's Loop,
the great Columbian fair covered some seven hundred acres, filled with four
hundred buildings—some of colossal dimensions—and landscaped with ca-
nals, lagoons, plazas, and promenades. Balancing the imperial White City was
the Midway Plaisance, its anthropological exhibits mixed in with a hodge-
podge of popular amusements. In the months that it was open during 1893, the
fair collected more than twenty-seven million admissions. The World's Columbian Exposition and other events sprang from the efforts of a diverse array
of organizers, representing different interests and assumptions, and promoting different messages. And the results, as experienced by ordinary participants and spectators, may have been as confused as they were spectacular.

In New York, too, Columbian spectacles marked the four hundredth Columbian anniversary, even though the city had lost out to Chicago as the con-
gressionally sponsored site of commemoration. A monumental pageant lasting five days in October 1892 enveloped New York, which seemed to use
Columbus as a vehicle to honor itself. The city, elaborately decorated for the
occasion, hosted a commemorative opera, opened Columbus Circle, staged a
massive parade on city streets (as well as a grand naval review in 1893, in conjunction with the opening of Chicago's Columbian Exposition), and held various receptions, banquets, and balls.[61]

Among the many voices in 1892–93, Irish American and Italian American
Catholics, often organized in associations like the Knights of Columbus, promoted quatercentenary events, and lobbied to make Columbus Day an annual
state or national holiday, all in the interest of solidifying their place in American society and supporting their vision of American pluralism. America's
business leaders saw the quatercentenary, especially the Columbian Exposition in Chicago, as their chance to celebrate themselves as latter-day Columbuses, bringing progress to the world through industry and commerce; in various celebrations they sought to strengthen and legitimate their position as an
American elite, and at the World's Fair they laid claim to a larger role in the
world, as did American imperialists in general. Middle-class guardians of
American culture saw in the quatercentenary an opportunity to provide
wholesome civic instruction, lessons in Americanization, for the American
masses; through carefully managed programs and events, especially in the
schools, they hoped to regain their grip on the nation—a grip that seemed to
be slipping away from them as a result of unbridled industrialization and an
unrestrained plutocracy, massive immigration, political corruption, and other
plagues. Among the most important efforts to use the quatercentenary ped-
agogically was the plan developed by Francis C. Bellamy, an editor of the

Fig. 28. "The Modern Heirs of Columbus—European Immigrants Saluting the Bertholdi Statue of Liberty, in New York Harbor," from *Frank Leslie's Popular Monthly,* January 1893. Through commemoration, Columbus became, retroactively, the first American immigrant, an American hero and symbol for Catholic—especially Italian—newcomers. Courtesy of Knight Library, University of Oregon.

Youth's Companion, to observe the dedication day of the World's Columbian Exposition as a national holiday, with children congregating in schools across the country and carrying out a set program celebrating Columbus, America, and the great fair in Chicago. In conjunction with this observance, endorsed by President Benjamin Harrison, Bellamy's Pledge of Allegiance—still today a fixture in schools, public and private—was distributed by the Federal Bureau of Education to teachers nationwide.[62]

Whereas middle-class custodians of American piety, purity, and patriotism acted out of concern, if not fear, social scientists at the quatercentenary's main stage at Chicago's World's Fair, through exhibits and professional meetings, like the International Congress of Anthropology, hailed the civilization of the United States as the height of evolution. This was the triumphant end of history, or at least of the frontier and the "first period of American history," as Frederick Jackson Turner argued at the American Historical Association convention held at the exposition. The fair introduced millions to ideas that combined evolution and race—a pseudoscientific racism—by functioning as a peculiar, "illustrated encyclopedia of civilization." The display of relics—living "primitive" people and their curiosities, modern machines, and the grand edifices of the White City, all ordered spatially or by the recommendation of guide books—was designed to illustrate the march of progress, from savagery to civilization over time and space, east to west, culminating of course in the utopian United States, present and future.[63]

Such an evolutionary approach could ultimately justify even the most unpleasant chapters in the nation's past. The fair opened only three years after the tragic massacre of some two hundred Miniconjou-Lakota people at Wounded Knee in 1890, which marked the end of an era. In 1892, both "wild" and "civilized" Indians (from Carlyle Indian School) had marched down Columbus Avenue in New York City's quatercentenary parade, the latter group representing the salutary results of Americanization, the former appearing as feather-clad avatars of a primitive past. And on the fairgrounds in Chicago, living Lakota people appeared as human exhibits, less-evolved oddities providing a contrast to the civilized heights of white America. Africans and African Americans similarly found themselves assigned low places in the evolutionary hierarchy. Commenting on the juxtaposition at the fair of blacks from Africa and those living in the United States, one souvenir book commented, outrageously, "Perhaps one of the most striking lessons which the Columbian Exposition taught was the fact that African slavery in America had not, after all, been an unmixed evil, for of a truth, the advanced social conditions of American Africans over that of the barbarous countrymen is most encouraging and wonderful."[64]

Meanwhile, some—especially African Americans—began to contest the Columbian celebrations, challenging not so much the accepted view of Columbus the Man but rather the image of Columbia as a land of freedom, opportunity, and progress. African American newspapers urged their readers to boycott the exposition, after black petitions to include exhibitions documenting three decades of African American freedom since the Civil War were rejected. Frederick Douglass, representing the Republic of Haiti, was the only black official at the fair, and the Haiti Building was the only place on the fair-ground where restrooms were made available to the few African Americans who visited on the special Colored People's Day.[65] Finally, the Admiral himself, lionized by most, nonetheless came under fire in the works of some historians. To the aggravation of patricians and plebeians, capitalists and ethnic workers, if not African Americans and Indians, historian Justin Winsor wrote of Columbus, for example, "the age created him and the age left him. There is no more conspicuous example in history of a man showing the path and losing it." Summing up the Admiral's record, Winsor concluded,

> Hardly a name in profane history is more august than his. Hardly another character in the world's record has made so little of its opportunities. His discovery was a blunder; his blunder was a new world; the New World is his monument! Its discoverer might have been its father; he proved to be its despoiler. He might have given its young days such a benignity as the world likes to associate with a maker; he left it a legacy of devastation and crime.[66]

In the end, though, Winsor's point was irrelevant. His harsh judgment was not so much refuted as simply lost in the din of celebration. In fact, did Americans really care about Columbus at all? What, really, did Chicago's great World's Columbian Exposition have to do with the man himself, the mariner who actually had sailed the ocean blue in 1492? Models of the *Niña*, *Pinta*, and *Santa María* rode in the White City's lagoon (along with a Viking ship), and a statue of Columbus stood above the throngs. Yet for most Americans, the mammoth parades, festivals, and World's Fair that marked the quatercentenary hailed America, or Columbia perhaps; the "discover" Christopher Columbus was merely the excuse, the vaguest of patrons for a grand, ambiguous barbeque. The Chicago Exposition's first board president, Lyman Gage, observed that visitors "beyond all, will behold the boundless waters of Lake Michigan, linking the beautiful with the sublime, the present with the past, the finite with the infinite,"[67] and, he might have added, "history with myth." In the present of the 1890s, Americans created a past; they "made history" or rather myth, and they rejected the less useful, disturbing accounts drawn by some professional historians like Justin Winsor. Despite historical revisionism and popular protests, history records the quatercentenary as the last great, uncontroversial celebration of Christopher Columbus.

Goodbye Columbus? The Contest to Define Columbus and the Nation in Modern America

After the hubbub of the quatercentenary, Columbus settled back into his place as a Catholic Italian American (and increasingly, an Hispanic American) hero and continued to function as a moral exemplar for schoolchildren. In 1905, Colorado observed the first official state Columbus Day in a noncentenary year; two years later, after the persistent lobbying of Italian American Angelo Noce, new legislation made Columbus Day an annual state holiday in Colorado. Throughout the United States, Italian Americans, led by the Knights of Columbus, which had grown from eight men in 1882 to a membership of some forty thousand by the end of the century, pressed for such official endorsement of Columbus Day. By 1910, it was an annual holiday in fifteen states, and the inaugural state observances were commemorated with huge parades in Boston and Providence. By 1938, thirty-four states celebrated Columbus Day officially, when President Franklin Roosevelt's proclamation made it a national holiday, but it was not until 1971 that it became an official federal holiday, set annually for the second Monday in October.[68]

One index of the vigor and potency of Columbus as a useful American icon in the twentieth century was the ongoing tendency of various ethnic and religious groups to appropriate the Admiral as their particular American hero or to offer up a reasonable facsimile, that is, someone who might represent a better claim to the title of American Discover and ethnic Founding Father. And vice versa: the erection of Columbus Day and its success as a public holiday—not only among certain ethnic communities but nationally, at least in urban arenas—marked the political arrival and strength of ethnic Americans in the United States. As Italians and Hispanics made their cases, and as the Irish, Poles, and other Catholics joined them (or confounded them) with their claims based on the Mariner's Catholicism, Greeks stepped forward to assert that Columbus was actually their countryman. Others contended that Columbus was Portuguese, while still others argued that Columbus was, in fact, a Jew. Few were ready to claim a Norse ancestry for the Admiral, but the eleventh-century Norse explorer Leif Eriksson, who traveled to North America nearly five hundred years before Columbus, could supplant the "discoverer" of 1492 and supply Scandinavians with their own ethnic founder. Similarly, cases continue to be made that others ventured to America first, as in a recent hypothesis that a Chinese explorer, Xiu Fu, anticipated Columbus by some seventeen hundred years.[69]

Because Columbus sailed under the flag of Spain, Columbus Day has also become an Hispanic celebration, designated in some places as El Día de la Raza (the Day of the Race, suggesting the ethnic and racial mixing that has been Columbus's legacy), but the Spanish-speaking peoples of the United States have been divided in their assessment of the Discoverer. Generally, those of mixed Spanish-Indian or Spanish-African descent, and who tend to define themselves as Latinos, have been much less enthusiastic about Columbus's deeds or eager to celebrate his legacy than those who identify themselves strongly (and often exclusively) with Spain. Nonetheless, when the *New York Times* Weekender Guide described an upcoming Italian American community Columbus Day parade in 1989 but neglected to mention an Hispanic Columbus Day parade occurring in Manhattan two days later, a letter to the editor complained, "while Italian-American people may choose to celebrate Columbus as a national hero (. . . many historians believe he was of Spanish-Jewish origins), his accomplishments were made in the name of Spain. . . . The impact he made on the New World was wholly Iberian in character; it had nothing to do with Italy, which did not even exist as a nation at the time." A year later, one Jose Gonzalez wrote, "I, as a descendant of the conquistadors, am proud and thankful for their having come. The Spaniards left a legacy of culture and decency that still pervades all of Latin America. So, I will certainly be celebrating the quincentenary in 1992."[70]

But if Columbus maintained his place in the hearts of urban Italian Americans and some Hispanics, if not Latinos, as well as ethnic Catholics and other ethnically and religiously defined claimants, who hailed their patron each year in parades and pageants, for many Americans he was simply a ticket to a paid holiday, or a favorite gimmick of merchants who hoped to move their wares in Columbus Day sales. How many citizens actually reflected on the life and legacy of Columbus as they enjoyed their three-day weekends or carried home their discounted purchases? As recently as 1990, *Five Hundred*, the official magazine of the United States Quincentenary Jubilee Commission, could promote the quincentenary as "a unique opportunity for the private sector to band together in support of a cause which is noncontroversial and universally appealing."[71] That cause, of course, was celebrating America and making money; it had very little to do with the historic Columbus. Americans therefore experienced a bit of a shock when their amorphous benefactor and national hero began to come under attack. As the self-described drive-in movie critic of Grapevine, Texas, Joe Bob Briggs, aptly, if crassly, put it, "for 499 years he's the dullest man in second-grade history, and then all of sudden we decide he's controversial."[72]

Of course, the intervening years had not been completely without storm. Like most previous Columbus controversies, the one that erupted in New Haven, Connecticut, on October 12, 1965, centered on the Admiral's priority in voyaging to America; it did not necessarily challenge the concept of discovery itself or the notion of America as a New World. Yale University Press dropped a bombshell with its landmark publication—on Columbus Day no less—of a volume detailing the Vinland Map, which had been "authenticated," at least for the moment, as a genuine pre-Columbian map of the New World lands discovered by Leif Eriksson in the eleventh century. The event generated a tremendous commotion. Getting off a quick salvo at a rally in Brooklyn, New York, the Italian Historical Society announced its intention to defend Columbus and declared that it would enlist the help of the Vatican and others to disprove the disturbing new revelation. Quickly the dispute spread to Spain, Italy, and Norway, and then to Canada, Bolivia, Iceland, and no doubt other places as well, encouraging new claims and counterclaims about the "real" discoverer of America. Meanwhile, as Yale University remained silent on the controversy, and the university press enjoyed heavy sales, Scandinavian Airlines used the map in its window displays and advertisements. In this moment, then, we can see many of the elements that would be reconvened in the new controversy of 1992—ethnic pride, cultural politics, nationalism, troublesome historical revisionism, and commercialism. Rather quickly, though—at least for outsiders—this controversy receded into the background, scholarly opinion on the Vinland Map's authenticity was later reversed, and the Admiral was able to hold his ground, although not for long in the emerging brave new postcolonial world.[73] As 1992 approached, Columbus began to encounter the worst squalls of his strange career as an American hero.

Fig. 29. "Norse Discoverers," from *Frank Leslie's Popular Monthly*, January 1893. This engraving illustrates, ironically, a story titled, "America Before and Since Columbus," published on the occasion of the four hundredth anniversary of Columbus's 1492 voyage and celebrating the great international Chicago Exposition in 1893. Courtesy of Knight Library, University of Oregon.

What had happened? Even at his vaguest, Columbus the Hero symbolized America. In the early republic, he proved useful to white Americans attempting to forge a new postcolonial national identity against Britain. Then, in the nineteenth century, Columbus served immigrant and ethnic Americans who sought to escape the discrimination they endured and to achieve legitimacy as first-class citizens of the United States. It should not be a complete surprise, therefore, that Columbus—as antihero, if not as hero—would figure prominently in another, late-twentieth-century postcolonial moment, when other ethnic, racial, class, and gender subalterns would similarly seek liberation and the redefinition of America. (Nor is it surprising that the latest successful revisionists would be opposed by those who continued to embrace an older version of the hero and the nation for which he stands). As America has changed and remade itself, so has its history been remade, even as the historical "facts" remain constant.[74] Thus Columbus, somehow entangled in the meaning of America, himself underwent a makeover. If the image of the new Columbus was fractured, it is because Americans themselves proved divided, uncertain, or disagreeable about their national identity and direction; in the 1990s, they grappled anew with the challenges of American pluralism, attempting to work out who they were as a nation. Did the United States constitute a single people defined by a core experience and set of values? If so, what was that experience? What were those values, and according to whom? Or were Americans simply a collection of individuals and groups hemmed in by arbitrary geopolitical boundaries, or wandering through that terrain, North American sojourners in a transnational world? Perhaps the most striking characteristic of the quincentenary, then, was its squabbling; it became a contest in the culture wars, which some entered more consciously and enthusiastically than others, to define America, past, present, and future. In the process, combatants acted politically and practiced nationalism, each putting their group's distinctive stamp on the meaning of America, as they imagined the national community in sometimes more, sometimes less inclusive fashion and dismissed alternate images as naïve, corrupt, or mendacious. If many quincentenary promoters of the heroic Columbus failed to forecast this brewing storm, they soon discovered that others hoped to rain on—and reign in—their parades.

From the very start, the United States Columbus Quincentenary Jubilee Commission, created in 1985 to preside over the official celebration, foundered in its own ineptitude, if not malfeasance. By the time its chairman, Cuban immigrant, real estate developer, and Republican Party fund-raiser John Goudie, resigned in disgrace, the commission was on the rocks and its new chair, Frank Donatelli, found himself engaged in a salvage operation to save the quincentenary. Although some public and private quincentenary projects, programs, and events proved to have real educational and entertainment value, many (even when free of mismanagement or fraud) seemed silly, as in the commission's support for the Columbus Bowl—showcasing American football in Genoa, Barcelona, and Seville—or crassly commercial, as in the licensing of virtually any product to display the official Quincentenary Jubilee logo.[75]

Whether regarded as a fun, harmless, perhaps even inspiring celebration or as an unsavory commercial venture that trivialized important, often tragic, historical events, the official quincentenary focused unprecedented attention on Columbus the Man and the five-hundred-year legacy of his first landing in 1492. While some decried the work of the Quincentenary Commission as incompetent and scandalous, the new Columbus controversy was not really about mismanagement and waste. Instead, it was about the way that Americans make and remake history. The hoopla of the quincentenary raised the stakes, making an apparently tired historical event important again. As in 1792 or 1892, Americans were invited implicitly or provoked to interpret the event and themselves through their participation in the observance of its anniversary. But in 1992 a differently constituted, more diverse public confronted the Discovery.

If the quincentenary offered corporate America new prospects through public-private partnerships, it presented even greater opportunities for dissidents to challenge the Columbus myth and to promote their counternarrative. In a 1989 interview, Rayna Green, director of the American Indian Program for the Smithsonian's Museum of Natural History, saw the quincentenary as a chance to raise issues. "This is an extraordinary opportunity to talk about the invasion of North America and the things we are still living with. I keep telling people that it is not over. This is an ongoing story. We've got to take this occasion to talk about what is affecting our people even today."[76] Because advertising executives and public relations officers had based their calculations on the old Columbian verities, they often failed to anticipate, even to imagine, the bitterness and anger of those groups that had emerged politically only within the last thirty years. Native Americans, and to a lesser degree African Americans, not only held an opposing view of Columbus and Columbia, but they did so with a passion and conviction unmatched by their opponents.

Native American artist Jimmie Durham's poem "Columbus Day" (1983), for example, could not be farther removed in tone and sensibility from Winifred Sackville Stoner Jr.'s "The History of the United States" (1919), which contains the immortal lines, "In fourteen-hundred and ninety-two / Columbus sailed the ocean blue." Durham conveyed some of the pain and rage felt by American Indians, when he wrote,

In school I was taught the names
Columbus, Cortez, and Pizzaro and
A dozen other filthy murderers.

. . . .

No one mentions the names
Of even a few of the victims.

. . . .

In school I learned of heroic discoveries
Made by liars and crooks. The courage
Of millions of sweet and true people
Was not commemorated.

Let us then declare a holiday
For ourselves, and make a parade that begins
With Columbus' victims and continues
Even to our grandchildren who will be named
In their honor.[77]

With even greater iconoclasm, Russell Means, Lakota (Sioux) activist and a founder of the American Indian Movement (AIM), confronted the heroic Columbus by pouring blood on the Columbus statue in Denver, Colorado, and declaring, "Columbus makes Hitler look like a juvenile delinquent." In October 1992, the Treaty Council, an arm of AIM, staged various protests as media events, including mock trials of Columbus and Spanish conquistadores Hernán Cortés and Hernando de Soto. Russell Means more than any other American Indian attracted the attention of the national media, which loves the stereotype of the Angry Indian. Although some Native people questioned Means's tactics, most shared his distaste for Columbus and a celebratory quincentenary. In a variety of ways, both calm and strident—from sunrise prayer ceremonies to guerrilla theater—American Indians protested. Suzan Shown Harjo, national coordinator of the 1992 Alliance, a coalition of Native groups opposing the holiday, explained, "for us, Columbus is no hero. For us, Western civilization was no gift. We urge all people of conscience to forgo celebration of five centuries of genocide. We urge all to listen to our voices and to join us now to make the next 500 years different from the past 500 years."[78] Like Rayna Green and Jimmie Durham, Harjo thus criticized Columbus and considered the painful past but focused on the American present and future. Yet no matter how critical, they all took Columbus with them, using the Admiral as an antihero against whom to define themselves, and to ensure that America would never forget.[79]

Other critics of American society and its political and economic system,

Fig. 30. A political button and sign of the times during the quin- centenary in the United States, 1992. Collection of the author.

especially those associated with environmental causes, also raised their voices to protest Columbus and his conventional heroic representation. Again, the quincentenary emerged as a chance to challenge the system and refashion it. As Kyle Kajihiro wrote in the leftist newspaper the *Portland Alliance* in October 1991, "ironically, the high profile of the Quincentenary makes this an important opportunity for us to advance our work for social and environmental justice. 1992 will be a 'teachable moment,' a rare occasion to build alliances, draw historical links between our different struggles, and . . . to frame the issues of contemporary political discourse."[80] Indeed, in some places—like Eugene, Oregon—the results of such efforts were to produce a counter-quincentenary, which existed almost exclusively, with barely an official, conventional celebration or "dominant" narrative for it to critique, except perhaps as the quincentenary appeared in national media and advertising.[81] Environmental activists, like Native Americans, focused less on the man than the colonial and environmental implications of Columbus's voyage and of those who followed. Charges of ecocide against the Admiral himself are much weaker than those of genocide, but for green activists it hardly mattered. They too confronted the symbolic Columbus, the mythic figure who inaugurated and now represented for them the devastating ecological revolution that followed 1492.[82]

But the real irony of 1992 was not so much that an opportunity arose amid the quincentenary tumult to contest conventional, popular views of America's past and present. Most public celebrations or commemorations have been contested in some way or another. Instead, the irony was that the loose anti-Columbus coalition—American Indians, some religious groups, environmentalists, peace activists, political protesters, and others—often used Columbus in essentially the same way as did those whom they opposed. Like their opponents, through the construction of a particular symbolic Columbus, they attempted to establish their ethnic or political group identity, history, and solidarity—in this case in opposition to Columbus—to advance their own claims to legitimacy, to contribute their voices to the debate over the meaning and purpose of America, and to promote their own vision for America's future. Did such critics of Columbus merit reproach for indulging in such license? for doing what virtually everyone has done with Columbus for some two hundred years? Hardly. Professional historians, more comfortable with complexity and contradiction, and more prepared to sort through masses of historical documents and the tomes of their colleagues, might prefer that the public leave history to them. But that wish is unlikely to come true. Nor should it. When academic and popular history collide, things can get messy, but the quincentenary seemed to demonstrate at least that history—even at a distance of half a millennium—still matters.[83]

Where does that leave us as we try to discover Columbus—and the meaning of Columbus Day—following the occasion of the five hundredth anniversary of his voyage? More the villain than standard accounts claim but less the war criminal of his most strident critics, and less responsible for both the good and evil of the last five hundred years, Columbus is still a man we hardly know. But he is a man Americans generally do not seek to know; so much more useful are the personas they make for him. As never before, the recent centenary was a conflicted fete, based on the multiple personalities Americans assigned to their schizophrenic hero.

The conflict can be painful, as in Denver's confrontation between American Indians and Italian Americans during Columbus Day 1991 and its aborted celebration in 1992. While Indian protesters blocked a downtown parade in 1991, chanting "No parades for murderers," and poured two gallons of blood-colored water on the street, Frank Busnardo, the beleaguered president of Italian-American Organizations of Denver, desperately argued that Columbus Day, as they conceived it, honored all people: "the theme for our parade is that Columbus is a bridge between two worlds. . . . The Italian community has gotten a bad deal out of this. It's supposed to be for all ethnic groups, including the Indians." To Busnardo's chagrin, while trying to reconcile Indian groups to his cause, he was confronted by the equally unappreciated offers of assistance from the Ku Klux Klan, which vowed to protect the city's Columbus plaque. Has Columbus outlived his usefulness to Italian Americans?[84] Even some voices within the Catholic Church (although not that of Pope John Paul II), like the bishop of Gallup, New Mexico, Donald Pelotte, have urged the Knights of Columbus to change its name. "If the Russians can become democratic, it's possible the Knights can become the Knights of Christ," he told the Tekakwitha Conference, a Catholic organization for Indians, in August 1991.[85]

Urban Italian Americans seemed unprepared to abandon their hero. Large crowds turned out for the annual Columbus Day parade along Manhattan's Fifth Avenue in 1992, with Italian American politicians, including Governor Mario M. Cuomo, Geraldine A. Ferraro, and Senator Alfonse M. D'Amato, joining the African American mayor David N. Dinkins. Protesters too were active but unable to waylay the proceedings. Defending Columbus against the negativity of his detractors, Cuomo said, "It's like talking about Abe Lincoln's constipation or Thomas Moore's occasional moods of despondency. . . . It is not Abe Lincoln, Thomas Moore or Christopher Columbus. It is what they began. Christopher Columbus pushed open the door to 500 years of progress. What we're celebrating today is 500 years of the American experience." Another Italian American, the poet Robert Viscusi, like Cuomo, refused to desert Columbus, not because he failed to understand Columbus's critics but because he comprehended both their arguments and the perspective of Italian immigrants, who made their own voyages of discovery a mere hundred years ago and built a new world in America for themselves and their children. If Italian American celebrants in places like Denver felt ambushed, at least one Italian American community anticipated the reactions of American Indians and other dissenters and with sensitivity reached out to them, explaining their own affections and listening to Native critiques.[86]

This uniquely successful Indian–Italian rapprochement occurred in Chicago, where the headline of the Italian American newspaper *Fra Noi* proclaimed in September 1991, "Italian and Native Americans Forge Historic Link." Working to assuage mutual feelings of mistrust, representatives of the

Fig. 31. A reconstruction of Columbus's *Santa Maria* in Op-Sail 1992, New York Harbor. Although dissenters against the Columbus myth used the quincentenary as a teaching moment, the show went on. Author photo.

two communities met more than a year in advance of the quincentenary. James Yellowbank, coordinator for the Indian Treaty Rights Committee, concluded, "the Italian American community is a minority community that has gone through many problems. They have deeply rooted religious connections similar to ours and we don't want to take a similar pride from people." Dominic DiFrisco, president of the Joint Civic Committee of Italian Americans, commented after the July 1991 meeting, "We asked them to understand that Columbus is an ethnic hero to us. . . . We have a great deal of compassion for Native Americans. Now, we have to put our sentiment where our mouth is and lend a hand to our Native American brothers and sisters." More meetings followed, as did invitations of Italian American leaders to attend a powwow and of Native American leaders to participate in the Columbus Day parade. "The solution is toleration and respect," Yellowbank remarked, and Fred Gardaphe agreed: "We have come together to learn about each other's culture, and to learn to live together. . . . This is not just about working together toward 1992, but about working from now into the future."[87]

Subsequently, the two communities made good on their entente and cultivated their friendship. In April 1992, the Italian Travel Commission sponsored the travel of a delegation of Chicago Indians to Sicily. Although Columbus came from Genoa in northern Italy, more Italian Americans trace their ancestry to southern Italy, and according to Dominic DiFrisco, "Sicily has always been oppressed by outside forces, . . . so they feel an affinity (toward Native Americans)." According to a report in *Fra Noi*, the Native American delegation received "the sort of reception that Italy generally reserves for sports stars and world leaders." Accompanied by Italian government officials and a group of local Chicago Italian Americans, they heard the cheers of Sicilian high school students, received gifts from Genoa merchants, and signed autographs in the streets wherever they went, while the Italian press followed their every move. Indian delegation member Sam Keahna said, "I was really moved by the response of all the people in Sicily and of course all of Italy. . . . And they were very astute on Indian concerns." DiFrisco vowed to "keep building on our new-found friendship": "We will have more cultural exchanges, always remembering that our two groups have both been victimized by ugly stereotyping."[88]

This preparatory work produced a harmonious quincentenary at Chicago's fortieth annual Columbus Day festivities in 1992; members of the Native American, Spanish, Puerto Rican, Norwegian, Polish, and Lithuanian communities joined together to make the event "a true celebration of unity within diversity," according to a *Fra Noi* reporter. A mass at Holy Name Cathedral began the fete, and a buffet and an evening of entertainment ended it, but the day's most important, public event was the parade of some 180 floats and marching units along Dearborn Street. In addition to a large cast of local, national, and international officials, among the marchers was a contingent from Chicago's American Indian Center, under the leadership of Sam Keahna, assigned the place of honor as the first entry in the parade. Elsewhere, parades were halted by Indian protests or festivity was tempered by comments such as those from Stephanie Betancourt, the Seneca tribal coordinator of the Native American Education Program, who said, "For Native Americans, every Columbus Day is like salt in our wounds. These are days of mourning." The Columbianism of the 1990s proved as inconclusive as it was contested. The experience in Chicago suggested the possibilities of a multicultural practice in which real people work with each other—not relying on stereotypes—to understand their differences and their interests, search for common ground and practical solutions, and accept the historical complexities of their world. But on the basis of these events alone, we cannot yet confidently proclaim the discovery of a New World of political and cultural harmony.[89]

Columbus Day continues, institutionalized on the United States calendar as the second Monday in October. For some it remains a day to celebrate ethnic heritage and cultivate pride, and for some it represents an affront, a day of mourning. Most Americans, perhaps, wishfully and willfully treat it mindlessly as, simply, a day off, perhaps an occasion to shop. Certainly times have changed—merchants, in the light spirit of the day, now advertise presumably feminine-friendly "Queen Isabella sales" along with Columbus Day sales, and President Bill Clinton in 1996 found a way in his Columbus Day radio address to use the explorer and his holiday to promote an environmental message: "Today is Columbus Day, marking the day an Italian explorer came upon a new world. . . . We can only imagine the beauty of the land explorers found. In the centuries since, as we grew, our environment and resource often paid a price. Some have been depleted, destroyed, endangered. And some, thankfully, have been preserved, restored and replenished." Leading up to his signing of the Water Resources Development Act and announcing his commitment to sign a National Parks bill passed by Congress, Clinton continued, "This doesn't just happen. Every generation must work to insure that the next generations can enjoy the blessings of America and clean air and pure water." On the other hand, in 1993 even Columbus, Ohio, could not quite find a way to accept a five-hundred-ton, 311-foot statue of Columbus, six feet taller than the Statue of Liberty, the gift of a prominent Russian sculptor, Zurab K. Tsereteli, who sought to present it as a token of friendship between Russia and the United States. Dubbed Chris Kong by opponents, the statue predictably provoked controversy. "To Native American people, Christopher Columbus represents 500 years of genocide," said Mark Welsh of the Native American Indian Center in Columbus. "Plus, the statue is ugly and the whole country will be laughing at us if we put that thing up." Columbus, Ohio, thus said "Goodbye Columbus" to the Tsereteli monument.[90]

A 1998 Mercedes-Benz advertisement suggests how far Columbus has fallen as a hero: "Everyone Knows . . . Columbus discovered America, . . . [and that] a Mercedes is prohibitively expensive to own." The advertiser rejected both propositions, dismissing Columbus's discovery as mere myth and hoping readers would agree that the common knowledge that its automobiles were too costly was a similarly unfounded belief. "Rethink your perceptions," the ad suggests, but of course it was the advertiser who had determined how popular perceptions had changed and crafted an ad accordingly. Thus advertisers have played both sides of the street, appropriating Columbus's mantle when the hero's reputation was bright and mocking him cleverly when the climate of opinion had shifted. Such shifts were perceived well by an S. Gross cartoon that appeared in the early 1990s. It depicts Columbus landing on an island and encountering three native inhabitants. The Admiral flashes not a sword or banner but a credit card, and his surprised hosts declare, "We no longer accept the Discover card." Few Americans wish to give Columbus much credit these days. Not only is the idea of discovery now often discarded, but so is the Admiral's association—typical of the late nineteenth century especially—with commerce, entrepreneurial vision, and economic development. The Natives' words strike us as funny, not only because they are anachronistic in a time before plastic and modern instruments of credit but also because they knowingly suggest an impossible prescience of how badly things worked out for Native people, many of whom had greeted European newcomers, beginning with Columbus, with striking hospitality. Finally, their rejection of the Discover Card is darkly comic because, of course, Native people were not able to rebuff the European intrusion. The cartoonist coaxes readers to identify not with Columbus but with the Indians, perhaps because of an implicit awareness of our own dependency in a fast-paced, complex world. Perhaps with a tinge of schadenfreude—because we are bound in webs of credit and debt and economic forces beyond our control—we laugh at these Indians who absurdly (but wisely) issue an edict they cannot enforce.[91]

Predicting the past—in this case, how American understanding and regard for the Ancient Mariner Columbus will evolve in the future—is a difficult business. But it seems likely that Columbus is too important and useful a figure for Americans to forget. In 2092, as in 1992, and on the second Monday of every October, Columbus will have his day.

★ ★ ★ ★ ★ ★ ★ ★ ★ ★ ★ ★ ★ ★ ★ ★ ★ ★

CHAPTER 4

Washington, Lincoln, and the Unheroic Presidents' Day

For 30 years, the days commemorating our two greatest presidents have been kind of squished together into one more Monday holiday designed to give Americans a chance to do what they do best: sleep late and prowl the malls. . . . Why not celebrate the birthdays of every man who has been president? There are only 42. We can handle the load. True, some of those men were mediocrities . . . [but] they are entitled to a little representation, aren't they?

Clyde Haberman, columnist for the *New York Times*, February 14, 2001

ABOUT 1881, Erastus Salisbury Field painted one of the strangest presidential portraits in American history, *Lincoln with Washington and His Generals.* Not only are George Washington (1732–99) and Abraham Lincoln (1809–65) shown incongruously side by side, left hands clasped, but they are surrounded by four of Lincoln's (not Washington's) generals, three of whom became unmemorable United States presidents.

The fantasy and comedy of Field's nineteenth-century portrait is perhaps more apt today than it was more than a hundred years ago. We live in a postheroic age, in which memories of the Father of His Country and the Union's savior and Great Emancipator are threadbare. February 12 and 22 still merit red letters on some calendars, but the holidays of Lincoln's and Washington's Birthday are eclipsed by the intervening Valentine's Day card and candy extravaganza of February 14, and by the day of leisure and consumption mandated for federal employees since passage of the Monday Holiday Act of 1968, Presidents' Day.[1]

Presidents' Day is as unheroic as it gets. It is a time for forgetting, not remembering—an antimemorial moment. We can forgive the artist Field for his playful, anachronistic pairing of the two great men who lived in different centuries but who shared a single birth month as well as the highest place in Americans' pantheon of heroes. Indeed, he seemed to suggest in his collapse of time, as had other artists and orators, that Lincoln preserved the Union, which Washington created. Still, when we see these demigods enveloped by Ulysses S. Grant, Rutherford B. Hayes, and Chester A. Arthur—mediocre, almost accidental presidents all—we cannot help but ask, "What is wrong with this picture?"[2] In a sense, Field's painting is the perfect illustration for our contemporary holiday, with its parody of history and its dilution of the heroic. It is an anti–Mount Rushmore, like Presidents' Day itself. Are we celebrating Clinton, Bush, Reagan, and Carter, along with Grant, Hayes, Garfield, and Arthur, when we commemorate the births of Washington and Lincoln? Generic presidents do not seem worth the trouble of a parade or a banquet, and pity the poor schoolchildren who might be asked to cut out silhouettes of some forty unprepossessing heads, instead of those heroic two whose outline the penny and quarter, the five and one dollar bills, have already made familiar.

This chapter traces the origins of Presidents' Day, or rather it analyzes its prehistory in the rise of George Washington and Abraham Lincoln as heroes and in the public celebrations of their natal days. The holidays of Washing-

Fig. 32. *Lincoln with Washington and His Generals*, ca. 1881, oil on canvas by Erastus Salisbury Field. The Morgan Wessen Memorial Collection, Museum of Fine Arts, Springfield, Massachusetts.

ton's Birthday and later Lincoln's Birthday offered Americans annual moments to express thanksgiving and gratitude to their favorite pair of American heroes and in the process to lionize the American nation, its foundation and its preservation. Both men merit their unique acclaim in American history, but our focus here is less on them as historical persons than as personas. Washington in his lifetime, and both in their deaths and apotheoses, came to personify the nation. The Continental Congress appointed George Washington commander in chief on June 16, 1775—before the creation of the Continental Army itself, even before the United States existed as a nation to fight for. Washington thus became the standard for the revolutionary movement toward Independence, a living symbol of that national effort. And he remained a totemic figure for the nation throughout the war, during his graceful departure to private life as citizen-farmer, during his return to public service when recalled as the nation's first president, and in his final retirement and internment at Mount Vernon. Lincoln too would come to represent the nation, as its savior and martyr following his assassination on April 14, 1865, Good Friday. In death, the hero Lincoln, alone or paired with George Washington, came to symbolize the righteousness of the Union, African American liberation, the tragic cost of the Civil War, and the reconciliation and fire-tested strength of the United States.[3]

If particular causes and abstract ideals were made concrete and persuasive through their embodiment in the figures of George Washington or Abraham Lincoln, then public celebration of these men—particularly on the occasions of their birthdays—provided Americans a popular and regular means to broadcast their ideas, feelings, and programs widely. Citizens' heartfelt gratitude to their heroes, which they expressed in banquets and toasts, parades and performances, did more—they helped to create, not merely to recognize, the mythic figures they hailed. And in the process these celebrations molded American identities in the style of the sculpted heroes they raised on pedestals.

If Washington and Lincoln initially represented particular political programs—war, Independence, and national consolidation; war, emancipation, and the Union—the success of their causes and their virtual deification transformed them into potent nonpartisan symbols for most Americans.[4] As such, these symbolic heroes became touchstones of United States identity, supreme moral exemplars, and forces for nationalism as well as social and political unity. Association with Washington or Lincoln offered Americans and their causes legitimacy and could sanctify various political agendas if imagined, posthumous endorsements by these heroes could be made to seem likely or plausible. The images of Washington and Lincoln, then, became political resources and were therefore contested among those with different views, visions, and interests. The Father of His Country and the country's Savior were not completely protean figures, available for just any cause—their utility as nonpartisan symbols could actually enhance their value in partisan politics—but the range of people and purposes enlisting the two heroes suggests both the power of their personas and the frontiers of American creativity.

Washington and Lincoln were not sexless heroes but mythic patriarchs, and as such they spoke to citizens about the proper ways that Americans should be men and fathers. Representations of both figures reflected critical shifts in the understanding and practices of gender in American life, and both figures—as heroes and as objects of public celebration—offer us opportunities to assess the changing lives, expectations, and public roles of women and men in American history. If Washington and Lincoln are now sometimes dismissed by impertinent critics as just two more dead, white males, we can nonetheless reconstruct how these men in their own times represented innovation in gender and race relations—not simply reaction—while we can also appreciate how their demise as American icons is an index of the diversification of American society in the last half of the twentieth century, particularly following the civil rights and feminist movements.[5]

The power of Washington's or Lincoln's posthumous sanction and support remains important even in the post-heroic era, in an ironic, complicated way that acknowledges their greatness on the one hand yet employs their images to challenge the very idea of the hero, to poke fun, and often to sell consumer products and services—from beer to pizza to electronic equipment to life insurance—through light-hearted mockery. The Washington or Lincoln figure in American advertising suggests a negative answer to the question, Is nothing sacred? The authors of this anti-veneration clearly regarded profits as divine, yet they nonetheless understood something important about the American public in the late twentieth century. Americans, it is generally believed, no longer need exemplary men such as Washington or Lincoln to define them, unite them, or teach them lessons, and they display a deep suspicion of all public figures. Such misgivings are hardly new; indeed, feelings of ambivalence toward powerful men—objects of both esteem and suspicion—were expressed even as the cult of Washington was taking shape in revolutionary America. Samuel Adams warned, "Let us beware of continental and state great men," and John Adams, though he was prepared to "honor him for his good qualities," voiced concern about "the superstitious veneration which is paid to General Washington." Whether the emergence of mass culture, the worldwide web, multiculturalism, feminism, and transnationalism has written the obituary of the traditional American hero is a question beyond the scope of this chapter to determine. It seems clear, however, that the stars of Washington and Lincoln are dimmer now, obscured by the blinding glare of our complex world, and that the ambiguous Presidents' Day is an apt reflection of a postmodern United States.[6]

Washington's Birthday

George Washington was first called the Father of His Country in 1778 by the *Lancaster Almanack* even before it was fully clear that such a country existed at all. In the same year, army officers celebrated Washington's birthday at Valley Forge, and by February 1779 civilian celebrations of the general's birthday had commenced in at least two communities, at Williamsburg, Virginia, and Milton, Connecticut. As historian Paul K. Longmore writes, "Within a few years, the Twenty-second of February had become an important patriotic holiday. In the early nineteenth century, it would be second only to the Fourth of July."[7]

Barry Schwartz, in his revealing analysis of Washington's transformation into a living monument, argues that Washington's personal qualities or accomplishments are insufficient to explain his emergence as the great American hero. Moments of crisis produce great leaders, Schwartz contends, and George Washington quickly emerged as the best available man.[8] Certainly, Washington represented a plausible, unifying figure, with noble bearing and military experience. After the fact, and on the eve of another war with Great Britain, John Adams recalled somewhat bitterly, "The great character [Washington] *was a Character of Convention.* His first appointment was a magnanimous sacrifice of the north to the south, to the base jealousy, sordid envy, and ignorant prejudices of the southern and middle states against New England." Adams recognized clearly, as he had in 1777, both the constructed nature and symbolic quality of Washington's status as the nation's champion:

> I mention a *Character of Convention.* There was a time when northern, middle, and southern statesmen and northern, middle, and southern officers of the army expressly agreed to blow the trumpet of panegyric in concert, to cover and dissemble all faults and errors, to represent every defeat as a victory and every retreat as an advancement, to make that Character popular and fashionable with all parties in all places and with all persons, as a center of union, as the central stone in the geometric arch.[9]

Adams's correspondent here was the famous patriot, politician, and physician Benjamin Rush of Philadelphia, a man whom George Washington apparently hated and whom he allegedly called "the most black-hearted scoundrel he had ever known." Rush well knew of Washington's animosity, but in a letter to Adams he imagined his own discreet response, which nonetheless failed to credit Washington for personal talents or great military or political actions:

"In answer to the epithet which G. Washington has applied to me, I will as cooly reply, 'He was the highly favored instrument whose patriotism and name contributed greatly to the establishment of the independence of the United States.'" Rush confided to Adams about Washington, "At no time after the year 1777 . . . did I believe him to be the 'first in war' in our country." Later in life both men would find Washington's beatification repugnant. With sarcasm, Adams wrote Rush after Washington's Birthday in 1808, "Sancte Washington, ora pro nobis"—that is, St. Washington, pray for us.[10]

We need not accept the opinions of Adams and Rush concerning Washington's limitations, any more than we need to endorse the panegyrics of Parson Weems, Washington Irving, or other admirers, to acknowledge

Fig. 33. "General Washington at Trenton, 1777," a popular nineteenth-century engraving by A. Dagget, after a painting by John Trumbull. Collection of the author.

that George Washington indeed became the nation's totem. According to a French observer in 1781, even before the victory at Yorktown,

> Through all the land he appears like a benevolent god; old men, women, children they all flock eagerly to catch a glimpse of him when he travels and congratulate themselves because they have seen him. People carrying torches follow him through the cities; his arrival is marked by public illuminations; the Americans, though a cold people who even in the midst of troubles have always sought the dictates of methodical reasoning, have waxed enthusiastic about him and their first songs inspired by spontaneous sentiments have been consecrated to the glorification of Washington.[11]

Such festivity could be spontaneous, but it took on a greater, more purposeful regularity as February 22 became a holy day to celebrate the nation through Washington, the living man not merely the marble monument.

Fig. 34. *The Return of Rip Van Winkle,* 1849, by John Quidor. When Rip awoke from his fateful slumber, he re-entered a confusing world that was strangely familiar yet changed, a scene that the artist suggests brilliantly. On the tavern sign, one George had replaced another. George Washington, his birthday celebrated like those of kings, was nonetheless a republican hero, an emblem of both revolution and national order. Andrew W. Mellon Collection, Photograph © 2001 Board of Trustees, National Gallery of Art, Washington, D.C.

Not surprisingly, though with its own ironic twists, commemoration of Washington's birthday built on the conventions and traditions of English celebrations of the king's birthday. Conveniently, as patriots toppled one George from his pedestal—as they did literally in New York City's Bowling Green in 1776—they erected another George on a national pedestal—again, literally, as Americans placed Washington's statue on the very same base in 1792. The song "God Save the King" became "God Save Great Washington! God Damn the King," and Washington's face replaced the profile of George III on coins circulating in the republic. If one awoke suddenly after a lengthy slumber—having missed the American Revolution altogether—as did Washington Irving's character Rip Van Winkle, the world would look very different, yet with the pre-Revolutionary milieu. Disoriented by the changes he encountered as he reentered his Hudson River village, now with a liberty pole planted where a great tree had stood and a strange flag—"a singular assemblage of stars and stripes"—fluttering above, Rip found something he did recognize in the sign above the old tavern: "the ruby face of King George under which he had smoked so many a peaceful pipe." But "even this was singularly metamorphosed. The red coat was changed for one of blue and buff; a sword was held in the hand instead of a sceptre; the head was decorated with a cocked hat, and underneath was printed in large characters GENERAL WASHINGTON." Rip's bewilderment—the dissonance experienced in the juxtaposed familiarity and innovation of the tavern's eponym—proved amusing yet comically plausible to American readers of the story when it was first published in 1819 or 1820 and suggests the ways that Washington functioned as a foundational but transitional figure for America's former British subjects who themselves had metamorphosed into republican citizens.[12]

Thomas Jefferson dismissed the popular coronation of Washington easily: "We were educated in royalism; no wonder if some of us retain that idolatry still." And he remained convinced throughout his life that Washington was a true republican, as were the vast majority of Americans.[13] For all his efforts to craft his own persona, Washington was decidedly a republican hero, not a new American monarch. As historian David Waldstreicher writes, "Self-effacing yet ever forthcoming when called upon in the name of the public weal, a military and civic leader who voluntarily relinquished authority," Washington "was precisely the kind of political father required by those of a rebellious generation." Washington represented both resistance to authority and popular political participation, as well as order, deference, and obedience. As Americans tried to imagine themselves as a new nation, as a republic, Washington's persona aided them in that imaginative political work. Linking constituent parts of the country was a growing print culture and emerging national political institutions, but Washington's person—the great man himself, a living hero, not merely an emblem—seemed to make the nation real.[14]

Citizens of the United States sought to discover and define themselves as a political and moral community. As historian Andrew Burstein has demonstrated, "the most distinctive emotional force of those early national years was sentiment and sympathy." Americans' sense of superiority over the British resided in their belief in their own virtuous simplicity and sensibility, in contrast to Great Britain's unfeeling, authoritarian king and parliament. The Declaration of Independence, and the American Revolution itself, made literal, physiological "sense" to the nation's citizens; that is, the Declaration, the

Glorious Cause, and their military champion had a kind of sensory power, provoking noble feelings that coursed like blood through the patriotic body as well as the body politic. The Revolution released Americans from the constraints of artificial and arbitrary bonds to the British king, liberating them to create a rational yet passionate republic governed by moderated sensibility, to borrow Adam Smith's term. In an independent America, authenticity, natural feeling, social obligation, and disinterested virtue would reign. Such virtue depended on public spiritedness and fellow feeling, which could be easily traced on the faces of one's countrymen at public events. Against base self-interest, faction, and calculation, Americans sought to cultivate a law of the heart and a nation of benevolence, balancing reason, principle, and conscience.[15]

Washington was America's sentimental hero, embodying these virtues and inspiring in his countrymen not merely rational respect and admiration but feelings of love. The great general's appearances, during his tours, at civic ceremonies, or (directly or indirectly) at public celebrations of his birthday, offered Americans an opportunity to express and strengthen their bonds of love with Washington, their fellow citizens, and their new country. If the George Washington of his biographers is "a rather cold fish," Waldstreicher writes, "those who met him . . . told a different story." Countless reminiscences testify to the emotion, even ecstasy, experienced by women and men in Washington's presence, as they gazed at the face of "the man who unites all hearts." The face of Washington—like all faces, according to contemporary understanding—reflected his character, his virtues (and vices). To look upon it, and to do so collectively, according to contemporary testimony, was to see and feel an emotional connection to the new republican state. At Trenton, as Washington rode toward his inauguration in New York as the country's first president in 1789, his reception by the ladies of Trenton moved him visibly, according to the Fourth of July oration of Samuel Stillman: "His soul was in his eyes,—and the silent tear stole down his venerable cheek." Such tears—his and those of his fellow Americans—melted the hearts of the republic's citizens, and helped to meld them into a nation.[16]

In the 1790s, observance of Washington's birthday assumed a greater regularity, and the hero's continued acclaim—amid the factional conflicts pitting Hamiltonians against Jeffersonians, Federalists against Democratic Republicans, and in the context of the international crisis provoked by the French Revolution—made Washington's birthday an event worth celebrating and contesting.[17] By mid-decade, the holiday took on a familiarity in its celebration, pomp, and circumstance, almost like an additional Fourth of July, conveniently spaced a half year away from Independence Day in the nation's calendar. John Fenno's *Gazette of the United States* reported from Philadelphia on February 22, 1796, for example,

> This being the anniversary of the President's Birth day, the dawn was ushered in with a salute of fifteen cannon, and a joyful peal from the bells of Christ's Church. At noon, the Members of both Houses of Congress, heads of Departments, Foreign Ministries, The Reverend Clergy of all denominations, The Cincinnati, Civil and Military Officers of the Union and State, and many other respectable Citizens and Foreigners, waited on the President at his House to congratulate him on the occasion. The military companies in uniform paraded in honor of the Day—and this evening there will be the most splendid Ball ever given in the United States at the Amphitheatre, which has been prepared with a rich variety of emblematic devices, and every requisite accommodation.[18]

If these events were designed for society's elite, those at Rickett's New Amphitheatre the following night, including equestrian and stage performances and an opportunity for the public to view the splendid scenery, painting, and illuminations left in place after the festivities, were more plebian. Soon thereafter, members of the public could view Washington himself at Ricketts and offer him great acclaim, if a "letter from a gentleman in Philadelphia" printed by the Federalist publisher Fenno can be believed:

> as he [the president] came forward [to take his seat], an instantaneous loud and general plaudit took place—a second—and a third, still louder: when these were over, an honest sailor, in the sincerity of a generous full heart, called out, "Damn me if that is enough for the Old Fellow, let's give him three cheers." In which the whole audience, gentle and simple, old and young, most heartily joined. It must have given the President pleasure; his benign countenance and graceful demeanor shewed his sensibility and the goodness of his heart. I verily believe he is more sincerely admired and beloved at this moment than he ever was.[19]

The celebration extended beyond Philadelphia, through similar if less distinguished fetes in other parts of the country, and vicariously as Americans read about—and thus indirectly experienced—such events through ubiquitous newspaper reports. In the days after February 22, the Federalist *Gazette of the United States* reported celebrations near and far, from the Pennsylvania town of Lansingburgh, to New York City, to Providence and Newport in Rhode Island, to Boston, Cambridge, Roxbury, Salem, Newburyport, Worcester, and Petersham in Massachusetts, and to Richmond, Winchester, and Norfolk in Virginia. According to a report reprinted from Worcester,

The celebration of the birth day of our beloved President has been so general throughout the States as leaves not the shadow of a doubt that he continues to be "THE MAN OF THE PEOPLE." To give particular accounts of the festivity of the day, from the numerous places from whence they arise, would more than fill the columns of our paper: Suffice it to mention, that gratitude for past services, and love and affection for recent ones, were expressed on that day, in all parts of the Union, from which we have heard, with that peculiar animation, and "flow of soul," which discovered the sincerity of the hearts from whence they sprung.[20]

Washington's birthday festivity, the descriptions of which threatened to overflow newspaper columns throughout the republic, included cannon and bells, processions and parades, orations and sermons, odes and songs, banquets and balls, toasts and cheers. Some even suggested that Americans indulged themselves too intemperately in their honoring of Washington. Though filled "with emotion, both pleasant and painful" and though full of veneration of Washington on "this auspicious day," James Miltimore, the pastor at a church in Stratham, New Hampshire, speaking at a birthday celebration in 1794, sought "to direct the rapture of our hearts, to that *indulgent Power,* who has destined him for just such a period, country[,] and cause as ours"— that is, he asked his listeners to contemplate God first before His instrument, the illustrious Washington. "While some are celebrating the event in view, by the unmeaning roar of cannon—the sprightliness of balls—the splendor of assemblies or the circulation of the sparkling glass and sentimental toast—I am happy to signify approbation of the method you have chosen," that is, a sermon and religious observation.[21]

More serious contestation of Washington's birthday celebration emerged in the criticisms and actions of Democratic Republican opponents of the Washington administration, particularly as they observed their rivals the Federalists erecting Washington as a decidedly Federalist hero. The Democratic Republicans found themselves disadvantaged by Washington's own statements decrying the dangers of faction and the illegitimacy of political opposition, and by the stature of the president himself as a man above party, despite his appropriation by Federalists as their particular hero. Washington's potency as a political emblem and shield could not be dismissed and demanded a response, especially because Federalists aggressively linked praise for Washington and his administration's policies with attacks on Democratic Republican ideas, positions, and personalities. Yet faced with ever-grander Washington's birthday fetes, Democratic Republicans had limited options to criticize, subvert, or appropriate the holiday for their purposes—all difficult or dangerous strategies.[22]

In Boston in 1790, in response to an elite banquet honoring Washington's birthday, more humble citizens at Boston's Coffee House countered the lionization of the president with their toast to "the Fourth of July, 1776," purposefully placing this popular, radical moment in opposition to celebration of a single personage, the commander in chief. In December 1792, an article in Benjamin Franklin Bache's Philadelphia *Aurora*, the leading Democratic Republican newspaper and rival of John Fenno's Federalist *Gazette of the United States*, identified as a threat to American republicanism, among other things, "Keeping the birth days of the Servants of the public," which inappropriately elevated the officers of the government above the people. In the following year, another correspondent who signed himself "Democrat" wrote the *Aurora* approving the New City Dancing Assembly's decision not to stage a ball in honor of Washington's birthday and seconding its judgment that "a celebration of this sort" was "incompatible with their republican character." In an unusually extreme reaction to a Washington's birthday affair sponsored by Federalists, Democratic Republicans in Roxbury, Massachusetts, sabotaged their town's cannon on February 21, 1796, a blast from which would commence the festivities on the following morning.[23]

The *Gazette of the United States*'s diatribe against the *Aurora* on February 29, 1796, for its criticism of Washington's birthday celebrations illustrates the nature of the contest as well as its stakes. It took Bache to task for republishing "a tiresome essay, reprobating the celebration of the President's birth-day." The *Gazette* critic asked, "Would he gag the mouths of *patriots*, and restrain them from huzzaing at a civic feast?"

The *Gazette* writer rejected the charge that the celebration represented "*servile adulation*" simply because "kings and despots cause their birth days to be celebrated." He asked, "Is more [confidence] reposed in him than he is worthy of? . . . Is any one in America compelled to join in the rejoicings of the 22d February? And are the *free* and *sincere* effusions of respect and gratitude in this country to be restrained by the sons of omnipotent reason . . . ?" He charged that critics of the festivity themselves "fear that the people are children and fools, and soon to become slaves, because they voluntarily, and even unasked, express the true and warm sentiments of their hearts towards the President!" Claiming the moral high ground and relegating his opponents to base, unfeeling partisanism, the *Gazette* writer concluded,

> The voluntary and cordial affection of a nation toward WASHINGTON exalts the character of our country: The constancy of the sentiment, in spite of wicked arts to extinguish it, evinces patriotism and good sense— It is the best reward

of virtue, and by being liberally bestowed, it tends not to debase men, not to en-
slave them, but to awaken emulation, and to rise up future Washingtons.

The following year the *Gazette of the United States* pronounced against Bache
simply, "That a man who was born in America, and is now one of the great
family of the United States, should thus basely aim his poisoned dagger at the
'FATHER OF HIS COUNTRY' is sorely to be lamented."[24]

Because criticism of Washington's birthday celebration, even when it exhibited clear Federalist partisanship, was easily cast as ingratitude, even disloyalty, Republicans typically accepted the inevitability (and legitimacy, even the
desirability) of February 22 festivities and worked to shape them to their own
principles and proposals, through sometimes more raucous but peaceful
counterdemonstrations, alternative suppers, and toasts respectful to Washington but emphasizing their own interests. With Washington's much celebrated voluntary retirement from the presidency, and then his death on December 14, 1799, the nation's admiration and celebration of the hero only
soared. So although his apotheosis seemed to strengthen the value of St.
Washington to the Federalists as a symbol, it functioned ultimately to make
him America's common—not the Federalists' exclusive—property. And Federalists proved unable to transfer the adulation of Washington to his successor
as president, John Adams.

It would be hard—even in our own age of hyperbole—to overstate the impact of George Washington's death on the young nation. The republic's citizens poured out their hearts in grief for the ex-president, in thanksgiving for
his life and concern for the future. Throughout the country, leading citizens
delivered eulogies, people wore crape, and many towns staged mock funerals
and planned memorials and monuments to honor their deceased champion.
According to one lay preacher from Pennsylvania writing in the Worcester,
Massachusetts, *Independent Gazette*, the death of Washington was

> an occurrence not less interesting than extraordinary, that the departure of a
> single man should command the unaffected and indiscriminate lamentation of
> five millions of people. It is an event, the like of which the world has never
> witnessed, that the death of an individual should so touch a whole nation, that
> "the joy of the heart should cease, and the dance be turned into mourning."

The elegist, quoting the words of other American eulogies, declared, "His
deeds exceed all speech.' His fame is 'written with a pen of iron with the point
of a diamond.' His deeds, his fame, and his counsel will endure, till 'the great
globe itself; yea, all which inherit it shall dissolve.' "[25] The nation's newspapers
reported its citizens' rites of mourning far and wide, expanding the scope of

Fig. 35. Detail from "The Apotheosis of George Washington," on the cover of *Harper's Weekly*, December 15, 1866, after the fresco on the Capitol Rotunda by Constantino Brumidi (1865). Courtesy of Knight Library, University of Oregon.

the national funeral and uniting mourners in a common national community in grief.

In Oxford, Massachusetts, for example, a military observance included a ceremonial bier and a mock internment by his "Masonic Brethren," featuring "an elegant urn, covered with black and an obelisk, on which was drawn a striking likeness of President WASHINGTON," which citizens placed over a symbolic grave. In the next several weeks, the *Independent Gazette,* and virtually every other newspaper in the country, followed such events with headlines like "Continued Testimonies of National Sorrow!" The culmination of this national funeral came on February 22, 1800, following the recommendation of Congress that the day be set aside "as a day of mourning for the loss of our illustrious chief, Gen. *George Washington.*" Orators typically commiserated,

> Yes, the *princely* soul of our beloved WASHINGTON has taken its flight! The heavens open wide their huge portals to receive his pure and ennobled spirit; angels hail him welcome to his native feat; the immense temple of God becomes the place of his residence forever. He has ceased from his labours, but

his works will long live. The inscription on the lofty marble will for a long time inform the inquisitive traveller—*Here lies the venerable chief*—"*First in war, first in peace, and first in the hearts of his countrymen.*" The monumental inscription shall mouldering time efface; but his heroic and benevolent deeds are recorded on the tablet of the heart. . . . Yea, his justly acquired fame shall survive the wreck of nature; and wreaths of glory crown his head, when time shall be no more.

Following these rites, advertisements for countless pamphlets of printed eulogies and orations crowded the pages of newspapers nationwide, and February 22 stamped itself more firmly on the nation's calendar as the day to remember the Father of His Country.[26]

A decade later John Adams would complain of such political performances. "Our citizens in our great commercial cities, if they are not the greatest politicians that ever lived, are great masters of the theatrical exhibitions of politics. Were there ever more striking *Coups de Théâtre* than mock funerals?" he asked. "We never instituted mock funerals for Warren, Montgomery, Mercer, Hancock, Franklin, or Sam Adams. . . . This is a more modern discovery and improvement of the great art of aristocratical trick, intrigue, manoeuvre or what you please to call it." Indeed, after Washington's death, Federalists in particular would find in the passing of their heroes new opportunities to trumpet their cause, under the cover provided by the supposedly nonpartisan displays of gratitude represented by real and mock funerals. But as David Waldstreicher has written, "Unfortunately for Federalists," men like Alexander Hamilton and Fisher Ames "were not George Washington. . . . While Federalists might have wished for more entombments, the party needed something more regular than the all-too-occasional funeral of a passing hero." Washington's fame and political influence were not transferable.[27]

John Adams was not a popular president, and no one at the time would have considered celebrating his birthday—October 19—as a national holiday, or even integrating celebration of the second president into a generic Presidents' Day. That Adams was no Washington became painfully clear in the pathetic prosecution of Luther Baldwin in 1798 under the Alien and Sedition Laws for insulting the second president during a Federalist welcome in Newark, New Jersey. The Republican Baldwin, tipsy after exiting a dram shop, heard a ceremonial cannon shot and disdainfully remarked that "he did not care if they fired thro' his a—." If Baldwin's subsequent imprisonment and fine displayed federal power, it also exhibited Adams's deficiency in charisma or popularity.[28] With the election of Thomas Jefferson in 1800, however, a new American hero ascended to the presidency, although not one who could rival the wide acclaim enjoyed by Washington. Jefferson himself was critical of Washington's imperial style, "his ceremonies of levees, birth-days, pompous meetings with Congress, and other forms of the same character."[29] "The Revolution of 1800" began with Jefferson's inauguration on March 4, 1801, according to his supporters, which they would mark like another Fourth of July, although Jefferson's inauguration—with its modest procession, and Jefferson on foot, wearing plain clothing—consciously eschewed the pomp and pageantry of earlier presidential installations. According to Jefferson, that day "buried levees, birthdays, royal parades, and the arrogation of precedence in society by certain self-stiled friends of order, but truly stiled friends of privileged orders."[30]

Jefferson and his supporters observed March 4—not the third president's birthday, April 13—as an antibirthday and counterholiday, a gesture against the cult of an individual, however great, which they found inconsistent with republicanism. Ironically, celebration of the president's inauguration seemed to imitate the English practice of hailing monarchs on the anniversaries of their accessions to the throne—as with November 17, Queen Elizabeth I's Accession Day—and Jefferson certainly became the preeminent republican champion, not merely because he presently occupied the office of the presidency but because he was Thomas Jefferson the man and persona.[31] Nonetheless, a cult of Jefferson did not emerge, although March 4 did offer the Republicans a late winter opportunity to celebrate their hero, show their strength, and make political hay. A disgruntled Federalist observer in Leicester, Massachusetts, complained of such festivity in her diary on March 16, 1803, "The re[p]ublicans, or Democrats, or Jacobins celebrated the birthday of Jefferson's." Ruth Henshaw Bascom's remarks—mistaking Jefferson's inauguration day for his birthday—suggests the effectiveness of the political fete and the confusion about shifting political symbolism and tactics.[32]

Inauguration day demonstrations, political birthday celebrations, and the theater of mock funerals—if annoying to John Adams and Ruth Henshaw Bascom—proved significant in forming and expressing local and national political identities, and they signaled a transition toward a new sort of American politics, more often associated with the rough-and-tumble world of popular electioneering in the Age of Jackson. These early-nineteenth-century political events and performances helped Americans not only to imagine themselves as a national community but to act as such—that is, they constituted physical, not merely imaginary or vicarious, political participation.[33]

Federalists themselves continued to employ Washington's birthday as a nonpartisan means to partisan ends, and perhaps in response to Republican tactics they enlisted April 30 as an additional red-letter day on their political calendar. Washington had been inaugurated as the nation's first president in New York City on April 30, 1789. Celebration of the day trumped Jefferson's inauguration and sandwiched the March 4 event between February 22 and the late-April commemoration of Washington.

As Federalism shrunk from a national to a regional party, and then disintegrated altogether, newly formed voluntary organizations often assumed control of Washington's birthday commemorations. In fact, the chapters of the Washington Benevolent Society—founded in Alexandria, Virginia, in 1801 and spreading widely in the first decade of the nineteenth century—were typically composed of Federalists who imagined themselves above party but who nonetheless promoted their particular political agenda through what they claimed were thoroughly respectable, nonpartisan means. In addition to parades and orations on February 22 and the Fourth of July, and various meetings (often including an annual meeting on the April 30), local Washington Benevolent Societies practiced acts of charity. Initially, they performed enough charitable work to maintain at least the façade of an authentic philanthropic purpose, in a way similar to the Jeffersonian clubs and Tammany Society chapters, which had similarly spread throughout the new nation. The Worcester, Massachusetts, chapter, for example, made five donations of between $10 and $150 to the needy (mostly victims of fires) between February 1814 and March 1815. Yet such beneficence was suspect and challenged by the Washingtonians' rivals, who knew firsthand (although they would not admit it) that "some acts of charity are undoubtedly performed to blind the eye of deluded followers." A Republican newspaper critic charged in 1814, "It is as evident as the sun at midday that their objects are not only political, but intended to overthrow the present republican administration." It soon became clear that these Washington Benevolent Societies (as well as Republican Tammany Societies) were political associations more committed to self-service than charity.[34]

Despite the efforts of these Washingtonians, claims to the Washington name did not go uncontested. Indeed, George Washington remained a popular, available, and valuable icon in nineteenth-century America. In Boston, Republican rivals to the dominant Federalists formed their own Washington Society, adopting the name in 1811. In an 1806 Fourth of July toast, the young Republicans had said of Washington: "May his worth be always duly estimated, and may his name never be used to cover the crimes of aristocrats and Juntos." In 1809, the third toast during their annual Independence Day gala challenged their rivals' possession of the great hero: "WASHINGTON—We are all his friends; we are all his disciples; and they who deny us our claim have none of his manners, feelings, or principles." An ode marking the society's new organization and name in 1811 repeated in its chorus, "To grace our social joys, we claim / COLUMBIA'S sainted HERO'S name." And in 1812, a "volunteer" toast (that is, one not previously scripted and approved) aggressively challenged their rival Washingtonians, "While federal *old* men use the name of Washington with hypocrisy, may republican young men follow his principles with sincerity." A representative from the Bunker Hill Association similarly distinguished among those claiming Washington's mantle, hailing his hosts as "The genuine Washingtonians assembled at the Exchange Coffee House—we trust they will support the glorious heritage of their immortal ancestry." In 1816, a letter from Thomas Jefferson himself distinguished the society's annual Fourth of July celebration; Jefferson expressed his pleasure "to see the revered name they have chosen for their designation, restored to its genuine principles of union and independence; to no other than which, was its authority or countenance ever lent."[35]

As the nineteenth century progressed, Washington's revered name—and its authority or countenance—would be lent repeatedly to (or appropriated by) numerous causes, political, social, and economic. The orator Thomas A. Budd told a Philadelphia Washington's Birthday audience in 1828, for example, that Washington was essentially the father of "that system of Internal Improvements, by which the prosperity of the country has been so much increased"— that is, that Washington, although departed, nonetheless foresaw and sanctioned the canal-building mania of Budd's time. The scheme of internal navigation being constructed was a system "worthy of the gigantic intellect, and patriotic heart of Washington." From the grave, Washington seemed to throw his weight behind such efforts: "Had it been the will of Providence to prolong his life . . . , with what admiration would he have beheld the wonders of unrivalled improvement springing up, as if by magic, around him." Those with a different view of the wonders of economic development— laborers in an increasingly industrialized America—similarly invoked Washington. The great shoemakers' strike of 1860 in Lynn, Massachusetts, which strikers called "sacred to the memory of one of the greatest men the world has ever produced," began on Washington's birthday, tying the event significantly to America's great champion and his celebration.[36]

The Washington Benevolent Societies' interest in philanthropy may have been limited, even disingenuous, and its discussion of Washington's likely nineteenth-century political positions self-serving, but the Washington Temperance Society (founded in Baltimore in 1840) committed itself sincerely and selflessly to reviving the temperance movement. In contrast to other such reform associations (like the American Temperance Union), the Washington Temperance Society adopted a nonpartisan, nondenominational, and nonpolitical approach and sought to reform all drinkers, in a sense applying to its

Fig. 36. Newspaper illustration tribute for Washington's Birthday, ca. 1857. By the late 1850s, Mount Vernon—where Washington was buried—had become a national pilgrimage site; the view of the Washington Monument is purely conjectural here—its cornerstone was laid on July 4, 1848, but the monument was not completed until 1884. In 1857, the monument was a 155-foot stump. Collection of the author.

efforts the prescriptions of Washington's Farewell Address (September 17, 1796), which in the nineteenth century held a distinguished place among the sacred texts of the United States, next to the Declaration of Independence and the Constitution. These cold-water Washingtonians resolved "to recognize no creed of religion, nor party in politics; . . . neither political nor religious action of any kind, should ever be introduced into the society's operations." Personal abstinence from all intoxicating drink was the only basis for membership. "All this neutrality is necessary in order to combine the heterogeneous elements, that make up the Washington Society. The object is not only to avoid all sectarianism, but even the appearance or suspicion of sectarianism."[37]

Yet temperance was often yoked to other reform causes, even among the Washingtonians, as Abraham Lincoln's address to the Springfield, Illinois, chapter on Washington's birthday in 1842 illustrates. Praising the new society for its "enlarged philanthropy," its message of hope, and its unprecedented successes, Lincoln compared the temperance revolution to the nation's political one. Concluding the speech, he imagined the completion of each, "when there shall be neither a slave nor a drunkard on the earth. . . . How nobly distinguished that People who shall have planted, and nurtured to maturity, both the political and moral freedom of their species." Lincoln ended in praise of Washington but pleaded inadequacy: "To add brightness to the sun, or glory to the name of Washington, is alike impossible. . . . In solemn awe pronounce the name, and in its naked deathless splendor, leave it shining on."[38]

As Lincoln's words suggest, antislavery activists also found power in the image of the nation's founder. If the stipulation in Washington's will—that those whom he personally held in slavery were to be emancipated following Martha Washington's death—made him a hero to many African Americans and antislavery advocates, here the Washington name would not prove equal to the task of bringing all Americans together in the interest of the abolition of slavery. Washington's record on slavery was mixed. Some have claimed he treated his slaves harshly, while others argue that he was a benign master. Even if the latter case were proved, the fact remains that he did own, rigorously manage, and profit from the labor of slaves. Yet he resolved ultimately to buy no more slaves "unless some particular circumstances should compel me to it." During the American Revolution, Washington first prohibited, then accepted, the enlistment of black soldiers. Yet at the war's denouement, he feuded with the British commander in chief, Guy Carleton, regarding the return of nearly four thousand African Americans in New York City claimed by former masters. When Carleton decided to honor black loyalty, protect African Americans from masters seeking to re-enslave them, and facilitate transportation to Nova Scotia when the British evacuated the city in November 1783, Washington expressed his displeasure and demanded an inventory to assist in later compensation cases. Washington himself had lost from his farms at Mount Vernon at least seventeen slaves after a British raid in 1781. By 1786, he expressed his hope that the legislature might find a means to abolish slavery "by slow, sure, & imperceptible degrees," yet he never publicly challenged the institution or worked for its systematic abolition. And while he contributed to the Philadelphia Free African Society's fund to secure a site for a black church, he disparaged a modest Quaker memorial against the slave trade in 1790 and became annoyed when the Pennsylvania Abolition Society sought to bring the slaves of government officials under the protection of Pennsylvania law, which had legislated gradual emancipation in 1780.[39]

Washington's personal, human ordeal with the institution of slavery notwithstanding, he earned the reputation as a liberator and became the Father of His Country for African Americans as well as for white citizens. When the nation's capital shifted from New York to Philadelphia, President Washington freed Mary Simpson Washington, well known as a street vendor and aid to the unfortunate, such as those afflicted in the yellow fever epidemic in the city in 1793. New York knew no greater admirer of the president than the freed-woman Washington, who prepared and sold Washington cakes in her small shop on Chatham Street on Washington's birthday. Her table on the street, from which she sold hot corn, featured a picture of her hero, a leather trunk marked with the initials G.W., and a bible inscribed by Washington. Upon his demise, Washington freed his enslaved companion William Lee, and after the death of his widow Martha, he manumitted some 150 African Americans who had toiled at Mount Vernon in bondage.[40]

Such actions inspired Richard Allen—with Absalom Jones, leader of the postrevolutionary black community in Philadelphia and founder of the African Methodist Episcopal Church—to eulogize Washington on Sunday, December 29, 1799. Allen saw the hero's death as "an event in which we participate in common with the feelings of a grateful people—an event which causes 'the land to mourn' in a season of festivity. Our father and friend is taken from us." Deacon Allen called Washington a "sympathising friend and tender father," a man of "compassion" whose heart "was not insensible to our suffering." "He whose wisdom the nations revered thought we had a right to liberty. . . . He dared to do his duty, and wipe off the only stain with which man could ever reproach him"—that is, through the manumission of his own slaves. Washington "became to them a father, and gave them an inheritance!" "The name of Washington will live when the sculptured marble and statue of bronze shall be crumbled into dust—for it is the decree of the eternal God that 'the righteous shall be had in everlasting remembrance, but the memorial of the wicked shall rot.'" Washington not only "broke the yoke of British burdens 'from the neck of the people'" but "emancipated his 'bondsmen and bondswomen.'" For this uncommon act, in Allen's opinion, Washington had earned his extraordinary fame as "his country's deliverer." In death, would the name of Washington lend its prestige to African American liberation?[41]

The Rev. Lemuel Haynes believed it should. In his February 22, 1813, sermon before the Washington Benevolent Society of Brandon, Vermont, the African American Revolutionary War veteran and Congregational minister declared, "The society this day convened have attached great responsibility, by the name they have assumed." During the unsettlement of the War of 1812, when currents of disunion circulated in New England, the Federalist Haynes urged his listeners to remain loyal and true to the spirit of Washington, particularly as espoused in the Farewell Address, even though he remained critical of Madison's war. But his antiwar sermon also lashed out against slavery and linked that cause to Washington. Haynes found it hypocritical for Republicans to lament the impressments of seamen—despite his sympathy for "our [white] brethren in slavery"—when in President Madison's own state there were hundreds of thousands of "humans beings holden in bondage for life!" Of Madison's fellow Virginian, the great Washington, Haynes said, "He was an enemy to slave-holding, and gave his dying testimony against it, by emancipating, and providing for those under his care. O that his jealous surviving neighbors would prove themselves to be his legitimate children, and go and do likewise."[42]

By the 1830s, after the emergence of radical abolitionism, which rejected gradualism and sought an immediate end to slavery, antislavery societies used the occasion of Washington's birthday to promote their cause and enlisted the mythic Washington as their champion. The February 22 orator William Dexter Wilson told his audience, the Anti-Slavery Society in Littleton, New Hampshire, in 1839, for example, that "the birth-day of Washington brings with it, to every lover of freedom, and especially every freeman in America, associations calculated to awaken in his bosom the noblest and holiest emotions." Recollection of the great man, "almost beyond human weakness, a nation's father and idol," Wilson hoped, could awaken the country to its sins.

> It cannot be that a nation, before whose eyes has been displayed so much greatness, such purity, such devotion to the cause of man, should still rob three millions of their fellow-men of their dearest rights. It cannot be that men made of the same clay, and in the same image with Washington, can be so unlike him as to hear calmly the chains of the slave clank upon their native soil, and in their own dwellings; the bread of the soil watered by the tears and blood of slaves cannot be sweet to their mouths; the shrieks and groans of the chain-galled African cannot be music to their ears. But, alas! it is so; it is no dream.

Wilson reasoned,

> It does seem that the mention of human slavery in connection with the name of Washington would be enough to make any man an abolitionist, . . . that the thought of three millions of slaves in our own country, occurring amidst the thoughts and feelings inspired by this day and occasion, would be enough to call every heart and hand to the assistance of the oppressed.

Imagining "a bloody sweat roll down" the marble face of Washington's statue, sadly witnessing the country's perpetuation of slavery, Wilson called for the immediate abolition of slavery in the District of Columbia, an end to the internal slave trade, and interference however possible with the institution in southern states.[43]

As the impending crisis over slavery escalated, George Washington remained an important idol to African Americans and the antislavery movement, as in his invocation in the haunting Fourth of July oration delivered by Frederick Douglass at Rochester, New York, in 1852. Equating Washington with the biblical patriarch Abraham, Douglass observed that "people contented themselves under the shadow of Abraham's great name, while they repudiated the deeds which made his name great." For Douglass, inherent to Washington's greatness was his last act of manumission. "Washington could not die till he had broken the chains of his slaves. Yet his monument [that is, the United States itself] is built up by the price of human blood, and the traders in the bodies and souls of men shout—'We have Washington to our father.'—Alas! That it should be so; yet so it is." Quoting Shakespeare's *Julius Caesar* (III, ii), Douglass lamented that Washington's fame could not have had a more positive effect: "The evil that men do, lives after them, / The good is oft interred with their bones."[44]

Washington as the nation's patriarch, as the virtual patron saint of the United States, significantly defined the meaning of the republic. The nation, it seemed, was created in his image, and to imitate his example or obtain his (even posthumous) approval or endorsement was to achieve legitimacy. Washington, from Virginia but a champion of antislavery (at least according to the myth), had freed his own slaves, removing all moral stain and offering actual deeds in the place of others' mere words. Washington's example suggested to some that slavery could be extinguished and, given Washington's many pronouncements against party and in support of national unity, particularly in the Farewell Address, that America could enjoy both real liberty and union.

The year of Douglass's famous Fourth of July oration was the same year that Harriet Beecher Stowe's *Uncle Tom's Cabin* first appeared in book form. Significantly, in Tom's cabin itself, on the wall above the fireplace along with some scriptural prints, hung the portrait of another saint, sacred to blacks as well as whites, that of "General Washington, drawn and colored in a manner which would certainly have astonished the hero, if ever he had happened to meet with its like."[45] Did Tom thus display an African American Washington? Indeed, Washington might have been amazed to see himself transformed into a black man, but such a metamorphosis testifies to the power of Washington's persona, the malleable nature of the Washington symbol, and the significance (despite his mixed legacy on slavery) of the mythic figure to African Americans. Tom's portrait literally made Washington the father of all his countrymen.

Perhaps surprisingly, Washington could be adopted as a hero by other nonwhite, noncitizens of the United States, as we see among some American Indians who appropriated the Washington name and incorporated the great man into their cosmology. The Rev. Jacob Cram, a missionary touring western New York in 1805, might have been startled to encounter the son of Black Chief, a leader of the Allegany Seneca community, who was named George Washington. This Seneca G.W. knew some English and helped Cram with translation and provided an escort.[46] Why would a Seneca man take or accept the name of Washington? We cannot know for sure how this George Washington got his name, but we do know that George Washington, the general and United States president, earned a respected place among Senecas, despite his role in initiating the most devastating invasion of Seneca territory in history. In 1779, in an effort to bring total war to Indian country, end Indian and British attacks on western settlements, and secure the western theater (significant not just militarily but economically for the grain produced there), Washington commanded Gen. John Sullivan to march on the Iroquois homeland, "cut off their settlements, destroy their next Years [sic] crops, and do them every other mischief which time and circumstances will permit." By the end of their campaign, Sullivan and his soldiers had destroyed some forty Indian towns and 160,000 bushels of corn; by the end of the war, Iroquoia was in ruins and its Native people, while not destroyed, were divided and demoralized. These actions earned Washington the name Town Destroyer.[47]

Yet Washington seems not to have been hated by the Senecas and their Iroquois kin. Indeed, they established good relations with Washington and the new national government—particularly because their survival depended on their ability to counterpose the federal government's jurisdiction against state governments and private land companies. As Washington wrote to the Seneca chiefs as president in December 1790, "it is my desire, and the desire of the United States that all the miseries of the late war should be forgotten and buried forever. That in the future the United States and the six Nations should be truly brothers, promoting each other's prosperity by acts of mutual friendship and justice." Negotiations at Tioga Point in 1790 and the Treaty of Canandaigua in 1794, which recognized existing reservations, ensured peace, and even restored land that Senecas had previously lost, established President Washington as the Senecas' friend, benefactor, even father.[48]

It is nonetheless striking to see Washington's appearance within the cosmology of the new, revitalized Iroquois religion introduced by the Seneca prophet Handsome Lake after a series of revelations beginning in 1799, just at the moment of Washington's death and apotheosis. According to Handsome Lake—and the regularly recited accounts of his experiences and teachings, which have been incorporated into the liturgy of the Longhouse Faith—four messengers of the Great Spirit visited him and conducted him on a tour of hell and heaven. The latter was a place of dazzling light, sweet fragrance, and material abundance. In heaven, families reunited and enjoyed perfect harmony and the absence of all evil. "But no white man ever entered heaven." Just outside its boundaries, however, in a comfortable mansion or fort, lived the Destroyer of Villages, that is, Washington, "of whom you have so frequently heard." According to Handsome Lake, who had met Washington in person, "his countenance indicated a great and good man." The angel-like messengers told the prophet,

> The man you see is the only pale-face who ever left the earth. He was kind to you, when on the settlement of the great difficulty between the American and the Great Crown, . . . you were abandoned to the mercy of your enemies. . . . The great American judged that this would be cruel and unjust. He believed they were made by the Great Spirit, and were entitled to the enjoyment of life. He was kind to you, and extended over you his protection. For this reason he has been allowed to leave the earth. But he is never permitted to go into the presence of the Great Spirit. Although alone, he is perfectly happy. All faithful Indians pass by him as they go to heaven. They see him, and recognize him, but pass on in silence. No word ever passes his lips.

Handsome Lake declared, "It was by the influence of this great man, that we were spared as a people, and yet live. Had he not granted us his protection, where would we have been? Perished, all perished."[49] Washington thus became a peculiarly Seneca Moses, a man who helped deliver his Indian people from danger but who could never reach the promised land himself. In this Seneca scripture, Washington seemed to play both Pharaoh and Moses, and his greatest accomplishment was preventing—not leading—a Seneca exodus from their homelands in New York.

The Seneca relationship with the hero Washington grew out of personal experience and real service to Seneca survival. Today it is difficult to determine how other Native people regarded Washington, although Indians continued to be named for him, as was the nineteenth-century mixed blood Creek nationalist leader George Washington Grayson (1843–1920).[50] And the Cherokee Nation was among those who contributed an inscribed stone block to embellish the interior of the Washington Monument, which rose gradually between 1848 and 1855, then languished as a stump for twenty years, before its eventual completion in 1884. In 1836, the mixed-blood Pequot orator William Apess used Washington as a touchstone of greatness to eulogize and lionize the seventeenth-century Wampanoag leader Metacom, or King Philip: "as the immortal Washington lives endeared and engraven on the hearts of every white in America, never to be forgotten in time—even such is the immortal Philip honored." In this fashion Apess came not to bury Washington but to borrow him, and to construct a separate if comparable Indian nationalism. And in this sense, so did Crow Indians of Montana in the late nineteenth and early twentieth centuries, when they used Washington's Birthday as a sanctioned holiday to stage traditional dances, which were otherwise proscribed under the surveillance of U.S. Indian agents. Here the celebration of Washington—on the surface an act of assimilation—in fact provided cover for the conservation of tradition and ethnic identity. Whether Crows actually formed any opinions on the relevance or meaning of the hero to them is unclear, although it is possible that Washington's reputation as a soldier and his image on purple heart medals, issued for wounds suffered in combat, permitted his appropriation by Native warriors—not only Crows but men from numerous other tribes—who (ironically) served proudly in the United States armed forces.[51]

In Indian boarding schools, the introduction of a new ritual calendar functioned along with other assimilationist tactics, reformers hoped, to transform Native students into new Americans. As one of the United States' oldest holidays, Washington's Birthday took its place among other annual events, which included Columbus Day, Thanksgiving, Christmas and New Year's, Indian Citizenship Day (commemorating passage of the Dawes Act on February 8, 1887), Arbor Day, Memorial Day, and Independence Day. A letter home, written in fractured English by an Indian student at Haskell Institute in Lawrence, Kansas, in 1911 suggests both the ways that teachers sought to use the hero's biography to offer moral lessons and the manner in which such instruction in Americanization could be assimilated by Native students:

> We had a holiday yesterday and a social last night. George Washington was old yesterday and next year day, February 22, 1912, George Washington be old again. He left a good house and mother and father to see Washington. George Washington liked to work and he liked to go to school. He went to study books. He liked to play soldier. And Washington love country. He have wagon and horse, one horse Washington.

Confusion about Washington—his identity and meaning to American Indians—became clear as well at a Phoenix Indian School ceremony in 1909, which featured a visit from President William Howard Taft. One student, spying Taft on the reviewing stand, is said to have commented in surprise, "Gee, George Washington is fat."[52]

By the mid-1990s, an Oglala man from the Pine Ridge reservation in South Dakota could tell an interviewer, "I'm not too high into . . . how Washington chopped the cherry tree. I'm not too much into that. . . . I don't think my kids are into it either. They have to study it but they're not much into it." But by that time, of course, most other Americans were not much into it either—

neither the history nor the Parson Weems's legend of George Washington—and those on Pine Ridge would best signify their commonality with other Americans by virtually ignoring Washington on Presidents' Day. Earlier, however, the outward acceptance of Washington as father offered a means of Native acculturation and accommodation, although not uncritically. In commemorating Washington and his birthday, then, American Indians acted politically, acknowledging the power of a dominant social and political system and encouraging it to accept them, or affecting such an embrace and using demonstrations of patriotism as a cover for their resistance to assimilation and their cultivation of tradition, proscribed by federal Indian policy and local Indian agents. For Indians, Washington's Birthday was a rite of belonging—to a nation they could not avoid.[53]

In antebellum United States, the memory of George Washington functioned largely as a force for unity, a common symbol for Americans North and South, East and West, even for Americans of different ethnicities and races. As early as the Revolutionary War, and subsequently as the new federal union took shape, Americans marked the national landscape with Washington's name, beginning with Washington Heights, which appeared in Manhattan in 1776. Thereafter, Washington counties emerged in North Carolina, Maryland, Virginia, and Pennsylvania; towns bearing Washington's name materialized all over the map; by 1782, a Washington College appeared in Chestertown, Maryland. Soon the nation's capital itself, the District of Columbia, was named Washington, followed by streams, lakes, and mountains, and additional counties, cities, and towns, especially in the new territories and states of the West. Each site or topographical feature paid tribute to the Father of His Country and inscribed the nation onto that local landscape.[54]

On the centennial of Washington's birth, citizens in Lexington, Kentucky (named after the town in Massachusetts, a "place stained and consecrated by the first blood of our revolutionary struggle"), heard an ode that equated Washington with the westward-moving American empire. February 22, 1832, was not merely Washington's birthday but " 'Tis an empire's jubilee." As Lexingtonians assembled "in sentiment, with millions of our fellow-citizens, in a festive act," "pledged to perform our part, however humble," their celebration of Washington both signaled their own nationalism and ensconced their western town firmly within the national community. Both imitating and cultivating emulation among their countrymen, their ode urged, "Annual raise the grateful paean, / Sainted Washington, for thee!" The great orator Daniel Webster echoed such sentiments at a celebration that year in Washington, D.C., as he hailed the "voluntary outpouring of the public feeling . . . from the north to the south, and from the east to the west. . . . In the cities and in the villages, in the public temples and in the family circles, among all ages and sexes, gladdened voices, to-day, bespeak grateful hearts, and a freshened recollection of the virtues of the father of his country." Webster asked, "If we might regard our country as personated in the spirit of Washington, . . . how should he answer him, who would array state against state, interest against interest, and party against party, careless of the continuance of that *unity of government which constitutes us one people?*"[55]

Although Washington could be used divisively when claimed as an exclusive hero—by Federalists, by abolitionists, or by those promoting particular policies, such as canal building and other internal improvements—more often he was deployed as an emblem of American unity and consensus, as the patron saint who anchored the "mystic chords of memory" (in Lincoln's later phrase) in a glorious past, tethering all Americans and sections to a common hero, history, and heritage. Henry Adams, from the distinguished line that included two presidents, illustrated this characteristic of the heroic Washington in *The Education of Henry Adams* (1918), as he recalled his visit to Mount Vernon in the early 1850s with his father, the diplomat Charles Francis Adams. Although an antislavery New Englander, conscious of the "wickedness" and "social crime" of slavery, which he could see all around him as he traveled the poor-quality rural roads toward the shrine, Adams wrote, "yet, at the end of the road and product of the crime stood Mount Vernon and George Washington." Despite his aversion to slavery and his knowledge of Washington's complicity, he nonetheless accepted Washington—as so many other Americans did—as "an ultimate relation, like the Pole Star . . . ; he alone remained steady, in the mind of Henry Adams, to the end." The young man "never thought to ask himself or his father how to deal with the moral problem that deduced George Washington from the sum of all wickedness." Charles Francis Adams let his son "satisfy himself with the simple elementary fact that George Washington stood alone."[56]

The world little noted, nor long remembered, that at the November 19, 1863, dedication of the Gettysburg Cemetery the Massachusetts statesman Edward Everett gave the main oration, which ran to some two hours, in contrast to Abraham Lincoln's two-minute address. Everett spoke especially of the causes, course, and consequences of the war, of the three days of the battle at Gettysburg in July, and of a Union victory. But he also talked of reconciliation that would follow.[57] Edward Everett, who had made a second career of oratory after service as a United States senator, secretary of state, and Harvard University president, focused most of his speechifying on George Washington. Everett, with the Mount Vernon Ladies' Association, led efforts to save Washington's home and grave site, which had fallen into disrepair and had become a national embarrassment. In the 1850s, Washington's heirs, unable to maintain it any longer, placed Mount Vernon up for sale. "Old Silver Tongue" Everett crafted an oration titled "The Character of Washington" and delivered it some 129 times between 1856 and 1860 in front of paying audiences at venues spread from Massachusetts to Mississippi. In celebrating Washington, Everett's purpose was to preserve the Union itself: "O, that his pure example, his potent influence, his parting counsels, could bring us back the blessings of national harmony! O, that from the heavens to which he has ascended, his voice might even now be heard and teach us to unite again in the brotherhood of love." Invoking Washington, Everett inveighed against disunion: "the Father of his Country cries aloud to us from the sods of Mount Vernon, and calls upon us, East and West, North and South, as the brethren of one great household, to be faithful to the dear-bought inheritance which he did so much to secure to us." Thanks in part to Everett's donation of the proceeds of these speeches—totaling nearly $70,000 (one-third the purchase price)—Mount Vernon was saved.[58]

Everett hoped that once restored, Mount Vernon would become a national shrine, a place of patriotic pilgrimage. Henry T. Tuckerman imagined it as the sacred spatial complement to the temporal site of Washington's birthday in the national calendar:

> Around the tomb let us annually gather; let eloquence and song, leisure and remembrance, trophies of art, ceremonies of piety, and sentiments of gratitude and admiration, consecrate that day with a unanimity of feeling and of rites, which shall fuse and mould into one pervasive emotion the divided hearts of the country, until the discordant cries of faction are lost in the anthems of benediction and of love, and, before the august spirit of a people's homage, sectional animosity is awed into universal reverence.[59]

Ultimately, although Mount Vernon could be saved, the nation could not. The common memory of Washington proved insufficient medicine for the United States' sectional ills. On February 22, 1860, John Washington transferred the hallowed property to the Mount Vernon Ladies' Association. Within the year, on December 20, South Carolina seceded from the Union, with other southern states following; on February 7, 1861, they organized the Confederate States of America and elected Jefferson Davis as their president. On April 12, the Civil War began with the shelling of Fort Sumter.

Although the South abandoned the Union, it nonetheless claimed for itself the legacy of the American Revolution and represented itself as the rightful heir to George Washington. Frederick Douglass had been correct in 1852: even "the traders in the bodies and souls of men shout—'We have Washington to our father.'" The great Virginian became an icon of Confederate nationalism. An image of Washington graced one of its first postage stamps, and a mounted Washington appeared on the Confederate national seal, dated February 22, 1862. It was on this date that Jefferson Davis chose to be inaugurated in Richmond, at the base of its statue of Washington, ironically the same sculpture that had been dedicated on Washington's birthday only four years earlier by Edward Everett and one of his ubiquitous speeches. A southern ballad optimistically acclaimed the Confederate president as "our second Washington," and a southern songster included lines appropriating Washington as the Confederacy's own particular champion:

> *Rebels* before,
> Our fathers of yore,
> *Rebel*'s the righteous name
> *Washington* bore.
> Why, then, be ours the same.[60]

Northerners, of course, found such claims unconvincing and maintained their own grip on the father of their country, whom they continued to see as the emblem of union. Meanwhile, both sides treated Mount Vernon as neutral ground. The Union victory seemed to substantiate northerners' assertions. According to a Washington's birthday piece in the *New York Times* in 1865,

> Ever since WASHINGTON's day, secession has been trying to show its head, but it has always been put down in his name. WASHINGTON is completing a second cycle. . . . [H]e put that old flag on fort Sumter once more. He has been with ABRAHAM LINCOLN, and has gone with us through the war. . . . His spirit leads us in this second war of the Constitution, and if the rebellion should cease, he would still guide us in peaceful enterprises.[61]

On April 9, 1865, Gen. Robert E. Lee surrendered, ending the bloody war. Just five days later, on April 14—Good Friday—John Wilkes Booth assassinated President Lincoln, sending the martyred president, many believed, to be with Washington in heaven. Thereafter, Washington the national deity, and Washington's birthday as a national celebration, would share the highest place in the American pantheon and in the national calendar with Abraham Lincoln.

Washington, Lincoln, and "Somewhat of a Festival of Patriotism"

In his proclamation sanctifying the semicentennial of Lincoln's assassination on April 14, 1915, Illinois governor E. F. Dunne declared, "Both Washington and Lincoln are our first Americans. They will shine forever as twin stars of

Fig. 37. "National Picture. Behold Oh! America, Your Sons the Greatest Among Men," a popular lithograph of 1865 eulogizing Lincoln by enthroning him with Washington in this patriotic apotheosis. The two champions stand, heads in the clouds, astride the continent, holding sacred documents—Washington holds the Constitution, Lincoln the Emancipation Proclamation. A heavenly banner proclaims, "Under Providence Washington Made and Lincoln Saved Our Country." Library of Congress, Prints and Photographs Division, LC-USZ62-90652. Reproduced from the Collections of the Library of Congress.

the first magnitude in our political firmament." Indeed, Lincoln would continue to be paired with the Father of His Country, as he was on Mount Rushmore. That shrine's design originally called for but two figures—Washington and Lincoln—but was later enlarged to include the heads of Thomas Jefferson and Theodore Roosevelt as well, a move that presaged the eventual devaluation of the two heroes. It was as if Trustbuster Roosevelt began the assault on Washington and Lincoln's monopolistic hold on the month of February, which culminated in the two heroes' dilution when mixed with the rest of the United States presidents (not to mention with their February colleagues, St. Valentine and the ground hog Punxsutawney Phil) in the strange, generic concoction of Presidents' Day after 1971. Yet as recently as the 1940s, a commentator in the magazine *Lincoln Lore* could observe, "The period between February 12 and February 22 has now become somewhat of a Festival of Patriotism, and more emphasis is being placed on the interval each year." How did this Festival of Patriotism emerge in the postbellum period and continue into the twentieth century (even as a "somewhat" festival), and what were its effects and implications?[62]

In a sense, the pairing of Lincoln with Washington provided a means not to diminish the luster of the latter but, with the help of the former, to reshape the great American hero to address the needs of an altered and rapidly changing American political landscape. Lincoln, with Washington, proved indispensable when deployed in both long and short annual cycles of memory. Personifying America, the divine dyad—if still available to be used by those cultivating exclusivity—represented Union, national reconciliation, liberty, republicanism (in both its upper- and lowercase forms), democracy, and equality. And the holidays of Washington's and Lincoln's Birthday provided occasions for Americans to imagine, reinvent, and represent themselves, their nation, and their history.

Abraham Lincoln's assassination on Good Friday and his death on Easter Saturday—even if he did not rise from his tomb on Black Easter—"transported him to immortality." Lincoln's burial at Springfield, Illinois, after twenty days of funerary events culminated "the grandest funeral spectacle in the history of the world."[63] President Andrew Johnson set aside June 1, 1865, as a national day of fasting and prayer, the first such national event in the United States since February 22, 1800, when the nation mourned George Washington's passing. Under the extraordinary circumstances of the Civil War, of Lincoln's accomplishments and public esteem, and of his shocking murder, Lincoln was immediately elevated by many to a status more lofty than mere martyr: he was deified as a Christlike figure. Memorial banners read, "Washington the Father, Lincoln the Savior," a lithograph of the two, shown astride the continent, proclaimed "Under Providence: Washington Made and Lincoln Saved," and a popular print of Lincoln's apotheosis depicted Washington, assisted by angels, receiving Lincoln into heaven.[64]

June 1 was an arbitrary date; Americans could hardly be expected to wait for their great national funeral honoring the fallen hero until the next February 12. Within two years, however, some began to celebrate Lincoln's birthday annually, and by 1896, five states officially commemorated the day. Increasingly, Republican Party clubs used February 12 as a traditional occasion to host festive banquets to celebrate their sainted patron. In 1891, the partisan nature of these fetes drove an embarrassed Hannibal Hamlin, Lincoln's first vice president, to urge Congress to make Lincoln's natal day a national holiday. Although Congress had received petitions in favor of such legislation since 1875, it failed to act, blocked by the reluctance of southern representatives and by the proximity of Washington's Birthday on the national calendar. By the centennial of Lincoln's birth in 1909, three more states had joined the ranks of Illinois, Minnesota, Washington, New York, and New Jersey in their annual observance of Lincoln's birthday. Nationally, Congregationalists set aside the Sunday nearest February 12 for their Lincoln Memorial Sabbath. Meanwhile, on a more occasional basis, special events, such as the 1901 Carnegie Hall benefit for Lincoln Memorial University, founded at Cumberland Gap, Tennessee, in 1897, made February 12 a red-letter day on the country's calendar. In the same year, even Democratic Party organizations began to celebrate Lincoln annually, appropriating him to their own causes, in a Lincoln's birthday gala sponsored by the newly formed Jefferson-Jackson-Lincoln League. As early as 1884, the Democratic Party candidate for president, Grover Cleveland, had claimed Lincoln as an inspiration and guiding spirit. The year 1909—the Lincoln Centennial year—heralded massive, new commemorations not merely in the United States but worldwide, the most dramatic occurring on February 12.[65]

The Lincoln Centennial Association, created by an Illinois state commission to promote the Lincoln commemoration of 1909, continued to function after the centennial year, mostly to honor Lincoln each February 12 and to push for holiday status. In mid-1920, the association was reorganized and in 1929 renamed the Abraham Lincoln Association, dedicated "to observe each anniversary of the birth of Abraham Lincoln; to preserve and make more readily accessible the landmarks associated with his life; and to actively encourage, promote and aid the collection and dissemination of authentic information regarding all phases of his life and career."[66] Such annual and occasional anniversaries honoring Lincoln—not just in Illinois, "the Land of Lincoln," but nationally—culminated finally in 1959 with the sesquicentennial of the Great Emancipator's birth, overseen by a U.S. congressional commission. With his profile already on the penny (since 1909), his name on the map designating countless United States counties, cities, and towns, East and West, North and even South, and honored with a grand memorial on the Capitol Mall in Washington, D.C. (dedicated in 1922), Lincoln was celebrated annually on his birthday in more than thirty states but not yet by an official annual national holiday. Only in 1971 would the day become a national legal holiday, after a fashion, enveloped as it was in Presidents' Day, observed on the third Monday in February. Theodore Roosevelt, at Arlington National Cemetery on Decoration Day in 1902, had linked Washington and Lincoln and praised them above all other Americans. Although both heroes' birthdays deserved to be marked publicly, he argued, there should be "few such holidays. To increase their number is to cheapen them." Strangely, Presidents' Day proved both to decrease the number of holidays and to devalue the holiday.[67]

Before this post-heroic age, what sort of political, social, and cultural work did Americans perform on Lincoln's birthday, and in the larger patriotic festival running from February 12 to 22? If Radical Republicans could use the memory of Lincoln the liberator to promote Reconstruction in the South, deploying a retributive, Unionist Lincoln against the traitorous South, more often Lincoln appeared as a force for reconciliation, particularly by the late 1870s, after northerners and the Republican Party had abandoned Reconstruction—and African Americans—in a "redeemed" South.

In a sense this made Lincoln, like Washington, an emblem of nationalism and antisectionalism. Despite his status as patron saint of the Republican Party, Lincoln belonged to all Americans, at least those who wanted him, which was virtually everyone living outside of the former Confederate States of America (and many—particularly African Americans—who resided in the region). Lincoln seemed to uphold the sentiments expressed so compellingly in Washington's Farewell Address. If Washington's concerns about "the baneful effects of the Spirit of Party" no longer seemed so relevant, his warnings against the dangers of disunion had proved all too prophetic:

> The Unity of Government which constitutes you one people . . . is the main Pillar in the Edifice of your real independence. . . . You should properly estimate the immense value of your national Union to your collective and individual happiness, . . . indignantly frowning upon the first dawning of every attempt to alienate any portion of our Country from the rest, or to enfeeble the sacred ties which now link together the various parts.
>
> The name of AMERICAN, which belongs to you, in your national capacity, must always exalt the just pride of Patriotism, more than any appellation derived from local discriminations. . . . The independence and liberty you possess are the work of joint councils, and joint efforts; of common dangers, sufferings and successes. . . .
>
> . . . While then every part of our country thus feels an immediate and particular Interest in Union, all the parts combined cannot fail to find in the united mass of means and efforts greater strength, greater resource, proportionably greater security from external danger, . . . and, what is of inestimable value! they must derive from Union an exemption from those broils and Wars between themselves, which so frequently afflict neighboring countries.
> . . .
>
> In contemplating the causes which may disturb our Union, it occurs as a matter of serious concern, that any ground should have been furnished for

characterizing parties by *Geographical* discriminations—*Northern* and *Southern*—*Atlantic* and *Western;* whence designing men may endeavor to excite a belief, that there is a real difference of local interests and views.[68]

If Washington saw "the continuance of the UNION as a primary object of Patriotic desire," so did Lincoln. After Lincoln withstood the nation's greatest challenge in the Civil War, his presidency and his life ended, but only after the Union had been saved. As Lincoln recalled in his Second Inaugural Address, remembering the dark days when he assumed office in 1861, he had been "devoted altogether to *saving* the Union without war," while others had been "seeking to destroy it. . . . Both parties deprecated war; but one of them would *make* war rather than let the nation survive; and the other would *accept* war rather than let it perish. And the war came." In 1862, President Lincoln had written Horace Greeley, in an often-quoted passage, "My paramount objective in this struggle *is* to save the Union. . . . If I could save the Union without freeing *any* slave I would do it, and if I could save it freeing *all* the slaves I would do it; and if I could save it by freeing some and leaving others alone I would also do that."[69]

Yet as early as March 1860, in a long speech at New Haven, Connecticut, Lincoln had suggested his commitment both to the Union and against slavery and linked that dual commitment to George Washington himself. Citing Washington's Farewell Address specifically, and its denunciation of sectional parties—which some had used to attack Lincoln's Republican Party—he shifted the ground of the argument by citing President Washington's own stand against the spread of slavery, which Lincoln derived from Washington's approval of a provision enforcing the prohibition of slavery in the Northwest Territory. Lincoln asked rhetorically of his detractors, "Could Washington himself speak, would he cast the blame of that sectionalism upon us, who sustain his policy, or upon you who repudiate it?" In his Second Inaugural Address, Lincoln clearly identified the cause of Civil War with the problem of slavery and represented that terrible war as God's will and punishment. Yet he emphasized the similarities between North and South ("Both read the same Bible, and pray to the same God"), seemed to counsel against harsh judgment ("judge not that we be not judged"), and, looking to the future, preached mercy and reconciliation in the interest of a new, kind nationalism:

> With malice toward none; with charity for all; with firmness in the right, as God gives us to see the right, let us strive on to finish the work we are in; to bind up the nation's wounds; to care for him who shall have borne the battle, and for his widow, and his orphan—to do all which may achieve and cherish a just, and a lasting peace, among ourselves, and with all nations.[70]

The ambiguity of Lincoln's address—which juxtaposed charity and firmness, mercy and completion "of the work we are in"—as well as the hero's premature departure from the historical stage allowed Americans to mobilize Lincoln posthumously behind both the liberation of blacks and retribution, on the one hand, and reconciliation during Reconstruction, on the other. In the political turmoil following the war, many lamented the loss of Lincoln and his political gifts as a president who might have guided the nation through the shoals of Reconstruction more gracefully and successfully. The words of the Second Inaugural Address notwithstanding, the leader of the Union was not easily embraced by postbellum white southerners. Nonetheless, Lincoln's spirit reigned over the national rites of reconciliation, which sought to "bind the nation's wounds" and mend the national fabric after 1877.

Lincoln himself—as the rail-splitter from the prairies of Illinois—embodied the transcontinental connections between the West and East. The poet James Russell Lowell, in his "Ode Recited at Harvard Commemoration in July 1865," called Lincoln a "New birth of our new soil, the FIRST AMERICAN":

For him her Old-World moulds aside she threw,
And choosing sweet clay from the breast
Of the unexhausted West,
With stuff untainted shaped a hero new.[71]

Places such as Lincoln, Nebraska, nominated themselves as a part of the nation through their heroic namesake Lincoln, representing the state of Nebraska, the West, and the United States simultaneously.[72] In 1862, Lincoln had signed into existence the Union Pacific Railroad, which would truly link the country from coast to coast when it met the Central Pacific Railroad somewhere between Omaha, Nebraska, and Sacramento, California, and Lincoln's signature on the Homestead Act (1862) also marked him, symbolically, as a hero not only of the West but of the dynamic nation itself expanding into that westward territory. Testimonials to Lincoln in countless odes, orations, and editorials on his birthday or on other commemorative occasions portrayed Lincoln as the very embodiment of the nation, as a man molded from the very earth—the "sweet clay"—of the West. If Washington was the Father of His Country, Lincoln's humble western origins made him almost literally the mother earth of a vaster, continental United States.[73]

Lincoln as the symbolic link between a reconciled North and South proved a harder sell, however. Only black southerners mourned Lincoln's death, and whites continued to disdain Lincoln during Reconstruction.[74] With the rise of the New South, southern voices began to join with those of the North in their appreciation of Lincoln. Maurice Thompson's Phi Beta Kappa poem "Lincoln's Grave," delivered at Harvard in 1894, offered a paean from a native of Georgia who had fought for the Confederacy: "He was the North, the South, the East and West, / The thrall, the master, all of us in one." On the other hand, as late as the 1909 Centennial of Lincoln's birth, Lyon G. Tyler, president of the College of William and Mary, refused to say what "Southern People Think of Lincoln Today," out of politeness. "In due frankness," he did respond to a newspaper query, "the mass of Southern people can never be brought to see Lincoln in any other light than that of a representative of a section of the country."[75]

According to the historian Merrill D. Peterson, "Many southerners felt diminished and threatened by the apotheosis of Lincoln. They might utter regrets over his loss, but after that found no good reason to remember him. He was neither a symbol of reconciliation nor a historical character worthy of emulation. Southern children grew up knowing almost nothing about him." Postbellum white southerners erected their own heroes, particularly Gen. Robert E. Lee, whose January 19 birthday became a sectional holiday (and later would rival the birthday of Martin Luther King Jr. for a place in the national commemorative calendar). The centennial of Lee's birth occurred in 1907 and drew southern attention away from Lincoln, toward their Lost Cause and their tragic, indigenous champion. But George Washington remained an important, untainted national figure in the South (as he did throughout the United States) and was commemorated in February without competition from Lincoln. As a northern visitor to New Orleans in 1897 commented, "Certainly as far as honoring Washington's birthday is concerned, the people of New Orleans are more patriotic than [those] in many Northern cities." In the South in fact, the heroes Washington and Lee were often linked together, as they were in the renamed Washington and Lee College in Lexington, Virginia, where Lee himself had served as president. If Lincoln thus failed in the nineteenth century to realize reunion between North and South (at least from a white southern perspective), Washington's memory could be used to reknit the nation together, as in the New York Southern Society's invitations to Yankees to address the organization at its Waldorf-Astoria annual Washington's Birthday fete. Although Decoration Day (Memorial Day) was increasingly observed nationally after the war—to honor fallen soldiers of the Blue and the Gray by decorating their graves, North and South—and although Lincoln's spirit often presided in the North, he had no place in the South. In fact, Confederate Memorial Day, an unofficial holiday throughout the South, shadowed but did not exactly coincide with the national day of mourning; it occurred in many places on June 3, Jefferson Davis's birthday. In any case, men of great fame—

whether Lincoln or Lee or Davis—were less the focus on Decoration Day or Memorial Day than were the Civil War's common soldiers.[76]

Nonetheless, some southerners, particularly those such as Henry W. Grady, editor of the *Atlantia Constitution*, who advocated the transformation of the South, began to praise Lincoln, if not observe his birthday. A northern venue for such accolades often proved accommodating. In 1886, Grady found himself in New York at the New England Society's annual gala, commemorating the 266th anniversary of the Pilgrims' landing at Plymouth Rock. There he called Lincoln "the first typical American, the first who comprehended within himself all the strength and gentleness, all the majesty and grace of this republic. . . . He was the sum of Puritan and Cavalier, for in his ardent nature were fused the virtues of both, and in the depths of his great soul the faults of both were lost." By the early twentieth century, particularly after the Lincoln Centennial, more southern words of praise began to be heard, as in the remarks of the U.S. senator from Arkansas, Joseph T. Robinson, which he offered at the 105th birthday celebration of Lincoln at Springfield, Illinois, and later published as "Lincoln—A Tribute from the South." In proximity to Lincoln's Springfield tomb, Robinson began, "Here lie his remains, his memory cherished by old friends, his fame secure in the love and gratitude of a reunited country. May I assume to contribute to these proceedings a message from the present-day South, the heartfelt tribute of all her people?" Praising Lincoln's "resolute mercy," in contrast to others' spirit of revenge, Robinson observed (perhaps too optimistically),

> It is for this magnanimous service that the South reverently joins the North in celebrating this occasion; commissions me to bring a white rose plucked by the daughter of a Confederate soldier from a garden blooming in the heart of Dixie. If Mr. Lincoln were now alive there is not a home in all the South that would not give him joyous welcome. The surviving followers of the dauntless Lee, untitled knights in grey, would combine with the scattered fragments of Grant's legion to form his guard of honor.[77]

Senator Robinson commended Lincoln both for his "reestablishment of the Union on a permanent basis" and for Emancipation, not only (or primarily) for what it had done for former slaves but because "if it had continued, it would have made the poor white man's condition intolerable." In a unique twist, Robinson saw reconciliation of North and South as marked symbolically by two new white marble figures in the statuary hall of the nation's capitol—not of Washington and Lincoln but rather of Lincoln and Lee! Citing Lincoln's First Inaugural Address, Robinson believed that Lincoln's prayers had been answered: "The mystic chords of memory" now did stretch from a common patriotic past "to every living heart and hearthstone all over this broad land."[78]

Although many represented the mythic Lincoln as nonpartisan—as a man above section and party, a man for the ages—Lincoln was in fact employed in partisan fashion and remained a thoroughly political force. Indeed, even his apparent separation from the tumult of partisan politics had its political implications. Lincoln was, like Washington, a vital political resource, someone who could legitimate, even sanctify, initiatives from the grave, depending on the answer given to the often-asked question, "What would Lincoln have done?" Carl Schurz linked the departed Lincoln with civil service reform; others resourcefully found evidence that Lincoln favored the protective tariff. Still others enlisted Lincoln's support against American imperialism, particularly as it was reflected in the undertaking of the Spanish-American War and the United States' efforts to dominate the Philippines. In Chicago, Lincoln became a guiding presence behind Jane Addams's settlement house movement; in his presidential campaigns in 1896 and 1900, William Jennings Bryan invoked Lincoln as an advocate of bimetallism and, more importantly, as a supporter of the rights of labor. We have already seen how Senator Robinson could tether Lincoln to a sort of white populism. Others, urban and agrarian radicals alike, saw Lincoln enrolled in their campaigns. The socialist William J. Ghent called Lincoln "fundamentally a Jeffersonian," but nonetheless "his Jeffersonianism was qualified by a good deal of what today would be called socialism." By the 1930s, even the American Communist Party would appropriate Lincoln and offer its own version of who he was and what he stood for; for its leader Earl Browder, Lincoln was "the single-minded son of the working class." Along the way, Lincoln could be made (with varying degrees of success) an advocate of women's rights, of temperance or prohibition, and of most other causes that appeared on the American political scene. Herbert Hoover summoned Lincoln repeatedly during the early days of the Depression, found him an inspiration, and hoped his example might be deployed—especially on Lincoln Day in 1930, 1931, and 1932—in Hoover's efforts to avoid the perils of big government and encroachments on individual liberty in that time of crisis. On the other hand, Franklin Roosevelt and other Democrats adopted Lincoln as a patron saint. "It is not easy," conceded the U.S. senator Arthur Vandenberg, "to pursue political genealogy in this puzzling, volatile age." By the 1960s, not surprisingly, Lincoln supported the civil rights movement, while also backing, less plausibly, the war in Vietnam, according to President Lyndon Baines Johnson.[79] On the American Mount Olympus, Lincoln seemed most akin to the Greek god Proteus.

But not exactly. Most often, Lincoln represented the expansion of American democracy, inclusiveness, liberty, and equality. He was posthumously the champion of African Americans, of women, workers, immigrants, and others left out or left behind in the march toward greater democracy and the American Dream. As Garry Wills and Pauline Maier have incisively argued, Lincoln made the Declaration of Independence "the moral text of his politics." If the nation's founders were unable to abolish practices at odds with their articulated principles, that did not "destroy the principle that is the charter of our liberties," Lincoln asserted in the context of his famous debates with Illinois senator Stephen A. Douglas. According to Lincoln, the authors of the Declaration meant

> simply to declare the *right,* so that the *enforcement* of it might follow as fast as circumstances should permit. They meant to set up a standard maxim for free society, which should be familiar to all, and revered by all; constantly looked to, and constantly labored for, and even though never perfectly attained, constantly approximated and thereby constantly spreading and deepening in influence, and augmenting the happiness and value of life to all people of all colors everywhere. The assertion that "all men are created equal" was of no practical use in effecting our separation from Great Britain; and it was placed in the Declaration, not for that, but for future use.

Lincoln thus offered a powerful rereading of the Declaration of Independence. It was not merely a revolutionary decree, announcing independence from Great Britain; in 1859 Lincoln wrote in admiration, "All honor to Jefferson," who "had the coolness, forecast, and capacity to introduce into a merely revolutionary document, an abstract truth, applicable to all men and all times, and so to embalm it there, that to-day, and in all coming days, it shall be a rebuke and a stumbling block to the very harbingers of re-appearing tyranny and oppression." In a speech at Chicago in July 1858, Lincoln emphasized the breadth of the Declaration's promise: even those not descended from its signers "have a right to claim it as though they were blood of the blood, and flesh of the flesh, of the men who wrote that Declaration."[80]

Lincoln thus served as an appropriate champion for the slaves he had freed, African Americans he had abandoned unwillingly, only in death; for women who sought greater political rights, particularly the vote; and for immigrants from Europe, Catholics and Jews as well as Protestants. Freedmen and freedwomen after the Civil War, for example, named a new town Lincolnville in honor of the Great Emancipator. Frederick Douglass dedicated much of his oration at the unveiling of the Freedman's Monument, on April 14, 1876—the anniversary of Lincoln's assassination—to Lincoln's memory, recognizing "the vast, high and preeminent services rendered by Abraham Lincoln to ourselves, to our race, to our country and to the whole world." Although insisting that Lincoln was "the white man's President" and that blacks were "at best only his step-children," Douglass nonetheless urged his audience "to build high his monuments," for "while Abraham Lincoln saved for you a country," he told whites, "he delivered us from bondage." "No man can say anything that is new of Abraham Lincoln," Douglass observed, but his honest and heartfelt tribute eloquently summed up the hero by calling him "our friend and liberator." "Because of his fidelity to union and liberty, he is doubly dear to us, and his memory will be precious forever." In the 1920s, W. E. B. Du Bois, a founder of the National Association for the Advancement of Colored People and editor of its monthly magazine *The Crisis*, wrote tributes to Abraham Lincoln, whom he called a "big, inconsistent, brave man." Although flawed, as even great men were, Lincoln was "the greatest figure of the nineteenth century," according to Du Bois. He explained, "I love him not because he was perfect but because he was not and yet triumphed. . . . It was the bloody sweat that proved the human Christ divine; it was his true history and antecedents that proved Abraham Lincoln a Prince of Men."[81]

The Great Emancipator would continue to inspire African Americans in their quest for equality through the civil rights era, although not without the strains of ambivalence, which Douglass introduced in 1876 and Du Bois echoed. In 1962, the U.S. Civil War Centennial Commission sponsored a small commemoration of the fiftieth anniversary of the Emancipation Proclamation on September 22 (the date of preliminary proclamation) at the Lincoln Memorial, and the NAACP held its own commemorative events in 1963 on dates of particular significance to African Americans—January 1 (when the emancipation decree took effect in 1863), February 12, and July 4. Civil rights leaders wished for more from President John F. Kennedy and his administration; indeed they hoped that he might imitate Lincoln more literally and issue a Second Emancipation Proclamation. In response to Kennedy's reluctance, Martin Luther King Jr. boycotted a reception the president proposed for the next Lincoln's Birthday; instead, civil rights leaders organized the March on Washington for Jobs and Freedom, and staged their massive event at the Lincoln Memorial itself, on August 28, 1963, filling the plaza and beyond with some two hundred thousand people. Times had changed, and many blacks, although still appreciative of Lincoln, increasingly had outgrown their need or desire to revere Lincoln as their particular hero. African Americans could be their own heroes: "Exactly one hundred years after Abraham Lincoln wrote the Emancipation Proclamation *for them*, Negroes wrote their own document of freedom in their *own* way," King declared.[82]

By the 1960s, Americans generally shared a sense of ambivalence, or estrangement, toward familiar American icons, even ones like Lincoln so clearly associated with equality and justice. But earlier in the century, such reticence was uncommon. The reformer and founder of the Free Synagogue in New York, Rabbi Stephen S. Wise, himself an immigrant from Budapest, called Lincoln "God's choicest gift to the American nation, America's first commoner." In his Lincoln's Birthday address in 1914, Wise celebrated American pluralism through the memory of Lincoln: "This day every American citizen, every American man and woman and child has in spirit brought a petal to the grave of Lincoln, who sleeps tonight beneath a wilderness of love-tokens from men of all faiths and tongues and races and backgrounds,—who become one and indivisible in their love and honor for the memory of Abraham Lincoln."[83]

Lincoln the commoner, the typical American, a plebian rather than an aristocrat, a man who worked with his hands, represented a democratization of the American hero. George Washington may have been fully committed to republicanism, but Lincoln, himself a Republican, unlike Washington was a thoroughgoing democrat. If, ironically, Lincoln's assumption of great war powers would provide a model for the strong presidency of the twentieth century, he—like Washington—served the country not out of ambition, self-interest, and thirst for power but because of his sense of duty, sacrifice, and disinterestedness. In short, Lincoln measured up to the heroic standard set by the Father of His Country, and shared or assumed Washington's mantle, even as he revised the image. As a composite hero, Washington-Lincoln could be both father and brother, or even father and mother, or parent and grandparent to the nation (to some children, the bewigged Washington looks like a grandmother); the doubled hero could be both old and young, traditional and modern, solemn and light, high born and low, a native son of the South and the North and the West. Eulogies delivered for Washington could be recycled for Lincoln, and both could be called the First American. Pushed to choose between the two heroes, one orator resorted to a story of a small boy who was asked, "Do you love your father best or your mother best?" and who replied, "I love both best." America loved both best.[84]

Considered together, as they were (and are) so often, Lincoln and Washington worked in tandem as a heroic pair, with Lincoln not only extending or revising Washington's symbolic reach but even tempering or militating against more outlandish uses of the original United States hero. An orator could claim, for example, that Lincoln's Emancipation Proclamation "was the finishing touch upon the work of Washington." But by the 1880s and 1890s, as Karal Ann Marling has demonstrated, celebration of Washington became a means through which "the best people" could signal and cultivate their own elitist

Fig. 38. Washington's Birthday card, early twentieth century. Collection of the author.

Fig. 39. Lincoln's Birthday card, early twentieth century. Collection of the author.

pretensions, and as Michael Kammen has shown, this era—roughly the last quarter of the nineteenth century—initiated an unprecedented surge of patriotism, religious nationalism, filiopiety and hero worship, nostalgia, and the cultivation of heritage. Most of the familiar lineage-based patriotic societies—such as the Daughters of the American Revolution, the Society of Colonial Wars, or the Society of Mayflower Descendants—emerged during the 1890s. In an age that took Social Darwinism seriously, genealogy mattered not only to elites but to common people, even to hyphenated Americans. Often many hereditary patriotic organizations worshipped ancestors in order to celebrate themselves, to practice exclusivity and promote social hierarchy, and to gain or consolidate social power. As early as the Centennial in 1876, the hero Washington—or rather his consort—served such an agenda through elaborate Martha Washington teas as well as costumed pageants, receptions, and balls. Socially prominent women staged such affairs in imagined imitation of those held by the first First Lady during Washington's presidency. These pretentious fetes, fitting moments for conspicuous consumption and display, and serving to demonstrate aristocratic lineage, culminated in the festival commemorating the centennial of George Washington's inauguration in April 1889.[85]

The 1889 centennial became a major society event in Chicago and New York. In New York City, most attention focused on the grand Centennial Ball staged at the Metropolitan Opera House as well as on an elite banquet with President Benjamin Harrison as the guest of honor. "The best people," according to Marling—that is, New York society as defined almost single-handedly by Ward McAllister, the social arbiter of the so-called Four Hundred, the city's social crème de la crème—"would be the custodians of George Washington's public persona in 1889." The festivity extended over three days and included, along with the ball, a range of activities and spectacles: an exhibition of historical relics; the progress of Washington in 1789 from Mount Vernon to the national capital, then New York City, re-created by President Harrison, including a naval parade in New York harbor to accompany the landing of Harrison's boat—like Washington's—at the foot of Wall Street; a reception and lunch hosted by the city's business community; a public reception at city hall; a reenactment of Washington's inauguration day by President Harrison; a parade of fifty thousand marchers, composed of several state militias; the elite banquet (like the ball at the Metropolitan Opera House, with galleries above admitting viewers for a fee); fireworks; and a "pageant of peace," a parade organizers claimed would be the largest ever staged. These performances constituted a veritable "serial masquerade ball," with President Harrison in the main role as Washington, "a kind of antique millionaire in the velvet and lace of fancy dress." In 1889, Washington became "another robber baron with a houseful of tasteful possessions and an aristocratic bearing," like the Astors, Vanderbilts, and Gilders. This blue-blooded Washington was hardly a man of the people.[86]

Yet a concerted campaign by civic elites in Chicago in the late 1880s sought to remake Washington into a hero and example for the people—to instill good citizenship, establish law and order, breed patriotism among the masses, and turn them against labor radicalism. These business leaders and professionals, especially those in the Union League Club—founded in 1879 "to encourage and promote . . . unconditional loyalty to the Federal Government, and . . . to inculcate a higher appreciation of the value and sacred obligations of American citizenship"—initiated annual public exercises for Washington's birthday and staged a massive celebration of the Washington inauguration centennial in 1889. Their efforts were inspired by a perceived social and political threat, felt especially in Chicago in the wake of an unprecedented wave of strikes and the Haymarket incident of 1886—when a bomb exploded as police broke up a strikers' rally in Chicago's Haymarket Square, where a riot erupted that killed seven policemen and two demonstrators. Consciously, the Union League Club and other backers emphasized the Constitution, and Washington's 1789 inauguration to commence that new government, over the radical Declaration of Independence, which had initiated a political revolt. As a spokesman for the Chicago festivities' executive committee observed, the Fourth of July "is a day calculated to arouse enthusiasm for independence . . . , a day for the removing of barriers"; Constitution Day and the Washington Inauguration Centennial, on the other hand, were not occasions "for license, freedom from law and restriction" but moments to stress "creation rather than destruction, . . . to rejoice not that we have thrown off the yoke of England, but that we are a nation with national ideas and a history." In these events, patriotism would be defined for the masses, stressing duties rather than rights and a universal Americanism that transcended ethnic distinctiveness.[87]

The masses could draw their own lessons as they enjoyed the displays but crafted their own meanings and implications. In Chicago in 1867, in an eight-hour-day rally, the Journeymen Stone Cutters Association had claimed George Washington as a patron of trade unionism, displaying "The Father of Our Country" on its banner and joining him in declaring, "In Union There Is Strength." Contesting the Union League Club and similar organizations, Washington's Birthday rallies became key moments in building solidarity and support for the American Federation of Labor's renewed campaign for the eight-hour day in 1889 and 1890. In New York, the Civil, Industrial, and Commercial Parade on the last day of that city's Washington Inauguration Centennial festival was an opportunity for common folks. The *New York Tribune* called it "the people's day," and some seventy-five thousand marched in loose order, the former spectators to elite events finally becoming the spectacle itself. One chronicler wrote, "Few parades . . . have seen so large a body of foreign-born citizens in the ranks." Ethnic societies, bands, and floats led the way, demonstrating that the nation founded by Washington was a land of immigrants. Ensconced among the people was their more familiar hero, Lincoln, who seemed to balance or mitigate the elite version of Washington. Flags of German regiments that had fought in the Civil War surrounded a bust of Lincoln on one float. On another, constructed by the Plasterers' Society, workman crafted small busts of both Washington and Lincoln and passed them out to the crowd lining the route. After this division featuring tradesmen and workers, the parade concluded with numerous floats depicting the life of Washington and the history of New York. These final moving displays reasserted the elite representation of Washington as refined, aristocratic, even regal. What ordinary New Yorkers thought about all this is unclear, but their parade seems to suggest that they could still embrace Washington on his own terms, partly as a result of Lincoln's compelling reinterpretation of the nation's founding and his own presence as Washington's heroic partner.[88]

But Washington continued to be deployed by some Americans in ways that belied his status as republican hero. Somehow, he could stand for causes whose adherents would never conceive of using Lincoln as their emblem. Lincoln symbolized inclusiveness, not exclusivity, and he challenged ancestor worship. The great commoner had said, allegedly, "a man who boasts only of ancestors confesses that he belongs to a family that is better dead than alive." And as we have seen, Lincoln's rereading of the Declaration of Independence offered the legacy of the nation's founders to all, whether native or naturalized. Washington, on the other hand, seemed to some Americans to offer the cachet of high birth and privilege. In New York City, for example, where Washington's birthday celebrations continued to be held annually in February by social elites, New Yorkers had another holiday in which Washington figured prominently—Evacuation Day (November 25), commemorating the evacuation of the city by British troops in 1783 and the town's liberation by Washington's army. After falling into decline, the occasion was revived and celebrated with an elaborate dinner by the local branch of the hereditary patriotic society, the Sons of the Revolution, founded in 1883. Dining in splendor at Delmonico's in 1892, the society's president, Frederick S. Tallmadge, told the two hundred celebrants that Evacuation Day was "the real American Thanksgiving." The day "meant bringing order out of chaos." Tallmadge equated order with "the purity and patriotism of the American citizen," whereas chaos seemed to reside now in the unsettling presence of immigrants.

Fig. 40. Invitation to a Washington's Birthday banquet, the Sons of the Revolution, New York City, 1894. In 1889, the centennial of Washington's 1789 inauguration was celebrated grandly in the United States, especially by civic elites hoping to use the Father of His Country to instill good citizenship, establish law and order, and breed patriotism among the masses. Washington remained an essential icon, particularly among the hereditary, patriotic societies—such as the Daughters and the Sons of the Revolution—which emerged during this era. American Antiquarian Society, Bowen Family Papers. Courtesy of the American Antiquarian Society.

"We have asylums for the insane and hospitals for the sick, but we have no schools where those who come to our shores without money and without price, without principles and with cholera, can be educated in Americanism." Despite naturalization laws, Tallmadge complained, the mayor's office "turned out citizens at so many a minute." Quoting *Hamlet*, Talmadge said, "those citizens do imitate humanity so abominably." The Sons of the Revolution cheered in 1892, but were these in fact, as the newspaper headline declared, "the Themes to which Washington listened 100 Years Ago"?[89]

Americans celebrated the centennial of Washington's inauguration in other parts of the United States as well, and they continued to mark Washington's birthday. In no place, however, did such festivities emerge in a more bizarre, antirepublican fashion than they did in Laredo, Texas, in 1898. Sponsored by the local chapter of the Improved Order of Red Men—a club of ambitious, middle-class white men, which had adopted elaborate, pseudo-Indian rituals—the 1898 inaugural Washington's birthday celebration featured a strange pageant designed to naturalize the South Texas borderland town as Anglo-American and to assert white social, political, economic, and cultural dominance. These white fathers of Laredo (like Chicago's civic elite) found Washington's birthday a more suitable occasion than the Fourth of July to promote United States identity, nationalism, and their own hegemony. Independence Day's association with the Declaration of Independence—an anti-

Fig. 41. *The Apotheosis of Suffrage,* by George Yost Coffin, 1896. Washington is here flanked by Susan B. Anthony and Elizabeth Cady Stanton at the twenty-eighth annual convention of the National American Woman Suffrage Association, in a cartoon that plays off of the famous fresco by Brumidi in the United States Capitol Rotunda. Library of Congress, Prints and Photographs Division, LC-USZ62–10862. Reproduced from the Collections of the Library of Congress.

colonial document—was as unwelcome as July's heat. For Laredo's white leaders, February was a more pleasant month, as was Washington's stature as Father of His Country. Linking themselves with Washington and claiming him as their patron saint, on February 21 and 22, 1898, they sought to make Washington into a symbol of their racial and ethnic superiority (as neo-feudal patrons) and their benevolent, paternalistic rule, over the more numerous poor Mexicans in the population. In an odd mélange of ritual and pageantry, and amid confusing symbolism, the festival continues to be celebrated in Laredo to the present day, now including, among other events over ten days, various luncheons, dances, parades, a carnival, fun run, golf tournament, jalapeño festival, and pageant celebrating Princess Pocahontas, as well as a ball sponsored by the Society of Martha Washington.[90]

Perhaps the worst example of all for its manipulation of the Father of His

Country occurred in 1939 at a rally of the German-American Bund in Madison Square Garden, which featured a thirty-foot banner of General Washington at the very center of the stage, flanked by the American stars and stripes as well as Nazi swastikas, and capped with the American eagle. A banner suspended from a balcony read "Stop Jewish Domination of Christian America." Clearly this was not the Washington of unity, liberty, and toleration, not the Washington who had written to the Hebrew Congregation of Newport, Rhode Island, in 1790 that "All possess alike the liberty of conscience and immunities of citizenship," that "the government of the United States . . . gives to bigotry no sanction, to persecution no assistance"; President Washington in fact had been an ardent advocate of religious liberty and a protector of the rights of religious minorities.[91]

The German-American Bund's inappropriate use of Washington testifies to the continuing power of the Washington symbol in twentieth-century American life. Could Washington—at least as manipulated by admirers—sanctify anything? While some attempted (unsuccessfully) to transform Washington into a Nazi, others mobilized Lincoln (as well as Washington) as an antifascist. During the Spanish Civil War, from 1937 to 1938 nearly 3,000 American volunteers fought with some 35,000 others from fifty-two countries for the Spanish republicans against Franco's fascists. They organized themselves into the Abraham Lincoln Battalion, the George Washington Battalion, and the John Brown Battery, but they became known collectively as the Abraham Lincoln Brigade, actually a misnomer originating in the name of a United States support group, Friends of the Abraham Lincoln Brigade. If a misnomer, the name of Lincoln, the crusader for equality and justice, nonetheless had an appropriate ring for most Americans.[92]

By the time of the centennial of Lincoln's birth in 1909, Washington had become a remote if still significant presence in the United States patriotic firmament. In 1922, writing in *Crisis*, W. E. B. Du Bois expressed his preference for Lincoln as the great American hero, dismissing Washington altogether: "I care more for Lincoln's great toe than for the whole body of the perfect George Washington, of spotless ancestry, who 'never told a lie' and never did anything interesting." Washington's Birthday cards could offer humorous quips and images, often centering on cherry trees and cherries, and sometimes Manhattan cocktails, which featured cherries, whereas Lincoln's treatment on such cards remained reverential. As late as the 1970s, according to late night entertainer Johnny Carson, Lincoln remained uniquely off limits to comics, despite Lincoln's own reputation as a humorist.[93]

The two hundredth anniversary of Washington's birth in 1932 refocused attention on the great American hero, but it was no longer clear exactly what

had been founded as a nation. The infant republic could utter no cry of joy over its rending deliverance before it had been delivered. Thus the days of the year were but the days of the year—a parity of days. They were to it the small, moving measurements of astronomy; none had yet been set apart by it as great fixed landmarks on the plains of its history.

After one century, and nearly twoscore years of another, this nation still has no national holiday. It may surprise one-half the nation to encounter such a statement, but the statement is true. The nation has never instituted an American holiday. There is no Federal statute to authorize and embody one in the republic's laws. Congress may sit on every day of the year; the government has never legislated itself out of the right to do business for the space of any twenty-four hours.

This fact may be interpreted according to the fancy of the interpreter. He may regard it humorously as a characteristic oversight of the nation, which in this respect would be typical of the ordinary American citizen. Both nation and citizen have never during their lifetimes remembered to grant themselves a holiday! Or he may consider the fact gravely, as showing the deliberate purpose of the government to reserve for itself the right of convening at any moment to meet any sudden na-   tional crisis. The fact may be

LINCOLN'S BIRTHDAY.

Fig. 42. "Lincoln's Birthday," from *Munsey's Magazine,* November 1911.
Courtesy of Knight Library, University of Oregon.

Washington meant. During the 1930s, Franklin Delano Roosevelt invoked Washington (as well as Jefferson and Lincoln) to cultivate a presidential heroism consistent with his own aspirations as the country's leader and architect of the New Deal during the Great Depression. But the Father of His Country seemed all too available to others of his twentieth-century children. As anti-Semites called Washington "the first Fascist" in 1938, America's leading communist, Earl Browder (having already recruited Lincoln), called Washington a homegrown radical, commander in chief of a workers' Continental army, one in which his own ancestor, "Littleberry Browder" of Dinwiddie County, Virginia, had served. Representing capitalism, advertising executives increasingly signed on Washington as a shill for their products. William E. Woodward's debunking biography, *George Washington: The Image and the Man* (1926), presented Washington as an antihero, all too like the businessmen of the 1920s whom Woodward loathed. Here Washington became, in retrospect, the embodiment of a captain of industry, a fiscal conservative, a shallow, self-interested and self-satisfied George Babbitt of the eighteenth century. By the late 1930s, according to Karal Ann Marling, Washington "had been too popular for too long. His popularity had finally blunted all sense of what that large and lonely figure stood for. Worse still, from sheer overexposure, Washington had come to be a bore."[94]

Although the festivities commemorating the 150th anniversary of Lincoln's birth in 1959 revivified the memory and heroic stature of the nation's Savior, and although Lincoln avoided becoming a prop for cartoonists and comedians longer than Washington had, he too faded and became indistinct or ambiguous as an iconic force. Perhaps it was simply impossible for any United States hero, even ones as lofty as Washington and Lincoln, to sustain such fame and the respectful adulation of Americans. Although their sacred quality made them attractive as totems for various causes and concerns, prolonged, inflated use of Washington and Lincoln seemed to devalue their currency as idols. Commercial exploitation of the heroes began early and certainly contributed to this debasement. In Washington's lifetime, promises of portraits, illuminations, or plays about the president's life were used to entice audiences to attend February 22 theatrical performances. Washington's image or name adorned tavern signs and helped proprietors solicit customers. Soon George Washington was featured by tobacconists, druggists, salt manufacturers, brewers, cotton and woolen producers, and makers of crockery and china. By the late nineteenth century, one advertiser could write, "The centennial of Washington's inauguration, which has been celebrated in regal style . . . recalls another event for which all our loyal citizens should be thankful, viz.— the invention of Pear's Soap." From there to the use of Washington to promote tourism, or to sell cigarettes, coffee, furniture, insurance, soft drinks, biscuits, electronic products, pizza, and even underwear, was a short step. The artist Alfred Maurer, whose cubist portrait of Washington sought to honor the hero through its stylistic transgression, complained that the hucksterism of the 1932 Bicentennial treated the Father of His Country as "a commodity sold over the counter, like a pound of sausage."[95]

Yet the contours of Washington's career as a commercial hero—his appropriation, celebration, and apparent debasement—and Lincoln's similar, if less comic deployment, present a complicated story. Commercialization is not the primary explanation for these champions' decline; irreverent commercial employment was a symptom as much as a cause of their recession in popular historic stature. Indeed, department store magnates and show window designers had been among those most involved in staging public holiday memorials to these heroes, often to the delight of their audiences and customers. Stores and shop windows became another stage for enacting and shaping the heroic memory of Washington and Lincoln and other luminaries (such as Columbus). As historian Leigh Schmidt has argued, "consumer culture—more than folk tradition, local custom, or religious community—increasingly provided the common forms and materials for American celebrations." In this sense, commercialization has been a force for nationalism and patriotism, working through its promotion of heroes, red-letter days, and consumer products. A trade journal's self-serving contention in 1914 that "the American people are money-making people, and it does not detract from the sacredness of an occasion for them to make money out of it" is hard to simply dismiss; jeremiads against the commercialization of the calendar seemed to express an elite, minority opinion, with the refrain so often repeated because so little seemed to change.[96]

Lincoln's commercial exploitation began with the tasteful deployment of his name and likeness by the Lincoln National Life Insurance Company of Fort Wayne, Indiana, in 1905. Lincoln Logs, the children's building toys, traded on the Lincoln log cabin myth, and the Lincoln Motor Company offered a positively presidential automobile, bizarrely at odds with Lincoln's common man persona as typified by his profile on the humble penny. In a devolution of reverence, by 1996 a "Washington Week in Review" advertisement could cleverly but not disrespectfully place a television in front of Lincoln's great statue in the Lincoln Memorial to make the point that its program was "television to sit still for." "Every Friday night, you'll be glued to your seat." Still, Lincoln's most important attribute here was that he was inanimate, even more sedentary than the average television viewer. In 1998, two side-by-side sketches of the seated Lincoln in the Memorial—one with a tie and the other clad in loud golfing attire—advertised lower weekend rates at a Washington, D.C., hotel. Such treatment would have been inconceivable in an earlier, pre-television era, as would similar handling of more recent martyrs, such as Martin Luther King Jr.[97]

Commercialization of famous figures and the holidays that commemorate them in the United States stems logically from the country's contemporary capitalist mode, which is dependent on consumption and commercialized leisure. Holidays linked superficially to men such as Washington and Lincoln but emphasizing Presidents' Day sales and three-day weekends filled with recreation, not civic or historical contemplation, reflect well the general state of late-twentieth-century economic abundance, faith in the future—particularly through technological innovation—and disinterest in the past. That some Americans do not share in that abundance or blind faith (even if tempered with de rigueur cynicism) does not seem to alter the equation. Paradoxically, those marginalized by race and ethnicity tend to be the most historically aware and committed to historical memory. Historians Roy Rosenzweig and David Thelen argue, for example, in their study of popular historical consciousness in the United States, that African Americans are more apt than whites to venerate particular historical figures, although Washington and Lincoln are no longer likely to be prominent among them. One man from suburban Maryland rejected Washington as "the father of the country. . . . Being black, he is no father to me . . . , that has no meaning to me," he said. Discussing Lincoln, the man dismissed his Emancipation Proclamation as expediency: "[it] was only done to win the war." Since 1968, celebrations of Washington and Lincoln must compete with the commemoration of Black History Month in February. Originating in 1926 as Negro History Week, created by Carter G. Woodson (founder of the *Journal of Negro History*), Black History Month situated itself in the calendar's second month, ironically, because it contained the birthday of Abraham Lincoln as well as that of Frederick Douglass.[98]

In contrast to African Americans or other marginalized Americans, who have developed counternarratives of famous figures and events, according to Rosenzweig and Thelen, white Americans today have virtually no common narrative or set of shared, revered public figures. Historical amnesia and simple-minded heritage are privileged indulgences exercised by Americans who are able to claim habitation in the mainstream, and they only occasionally express reservations about their light dismissal of American heroes, heroines, or the collective past. Indeed, the occasional cri de coeur about the declension of historical memory and ingratitude toward dead heroes simply lends what limited authenticity events such as Presidents' Day have as days of actual remembrance and thanksgiving. Such critiques, which consider heroes and historical events as if they mattered, tend to heighten awareness, refresh memory, and—mostly—assuage whatever collective guilt Americans feel about their neglect. One suspects that for some time the discourse of condemnation of America's failure to remember, to praise its heroes, or to appreciate the transcendent meaning of anniversary events *is* the dominant political holiday discourse, the chief way that the American political nation celebrates its past and that past's great champions.

In the 1990s, visits to the Lincoln Memorial dropped off, and the Disney Corporation unveiled plans to replace its southern California Disneyland attraction, "Great Moments with Mr. Lincoln"—an animated, electronic, and rather stiff Lincoln, programmed to deliver excerpts from key speeches—with a new one starring Kermit the Frog (too sacrilegious even for the late twentieth century, the decision was reversed). In Washington, D.C., interest in the Washington Monument was piqued only mildly in 1998 when, in order to clean and repair the obelisk, it was artistically draped with scaffolding and blue screen netting designed by Michael Graves. Mount Vernon commemorated the two hundredth anniversary of Washington's death and attracted additional tourists, but things quickly returned to normal—that is, to a state of bland, superficial interest in the two great American heroes. Writing about Washington in 1987, the historical sociologist Barry Schwartz found such declension unsurprising: "As the years go by, the past becomes more crowded; heroes and events accumulate and compete with one another for the present generation's attention. Memorial sentiments and ritual energies, apportioned among more, and increasingly remote, objects, become cooler, less intense." Schwartz reasoned, "To expect that a nation should turn out, year after year, in heartfelt veneration for a man who died many generations ago is to make unrealistic demands on its capacity for emotional attachment."[99]

If Washington and Lincoln could signify anything and everything, they meant very little. Yet their lack of particular meaning, paradoxically, gave these figures a certain value and antiheroic significance well suited to a joking, iconoclastic culture that trades on irreverence in the carnival of the American economic and cultural marketplace. Americans have in common their ability to mock the same former heroes; if irreverent treatment is no longer shocking, at least it remains amusing. In 1995, John F. Kennedy Jr. unveiled a new magazine he called *George*, a "post-partisan" fan magazine about politics, named for the first president. The name was a sort of hip joke, and to make sure that the American public got it, the first issue's cover featured the model Cindy Crawford, bewigged and partially clad in a tight-fitting, buff and blue Continental army officer's uniform. A photo caption in *Time* magazine, which covered the major media event, read "Buy George." Like the *Mona Lisa*, Leonardo da Vinci's masterpiece dating from the early sixteenth century, Washington's and Lincoln's visages became famous for being famous. Today the two may be better known as resident figures on the one and five dollar bills, and the quarter and penny, than for their real deeds, in a way not dissimilar to the popular understanding of the twentieth-century sports hero Joe DiMaggio as the guy who sold Mr. Coffee machines. The recent advertising campaign in print and on television for the new gold-colored dollar coin, with an imagined ren-

Fig. 43. "They Just Don't Make Presidents Like They Used To," a cartoon by Paul Conrad, *Los Angeles Times*, 1989. © Tribune Media Services, Inc. All rights reserved. Reprinted with permission.

dering of Sacagawea, the Shoshone woman who aided Lewis and Clark, features the head of Washington—taken from the Gilbert Stuart portrait that is etched on the paper dollar—attached to a funny, animated cartoon body. The strange juxtaposition, which catches our attention and makes us smile or wince, is a sign of the times.[100]

With the natural diminishment of our passion for the heroes Washington and Lincoln over time, with their limited ability to speak to pressing concerns such as environmental pollution, worldwide public health crises, or transnational economic challenges, and with their devaluation through sheer overexposure, the two champions have lost a measure of their importance in American life. Presidents' Day did not precipitate such decline; it expresses it. The progression from the sublime to the ridiculous was marked nowhere more starkly than in the front-page story and photograph in the *New York Times* on February 22, 1996, Washington's birthday. Presidential hopeful Patrick J. Buchanan, following up on his primary election victory in New Hampshire, had himself photographed in South Dakota (one of the next states to hold a primary), inserting his own face to the right of Lincoln's on Mount Rushmore. Hoping to join these immortals in the presidency, if not in massive stone, Buchanan claimed their endorsement: "All four of these gentlemen up here on Mount Rushmore agreed with Pat Buchanan," the candidate declared.[101] Buchanan's campaign for the White House failed in 1996 and is unlikely ever to prevail, yet on Presidents' Day Americans nonetheless celebrate a Buchanan (James Buchanan, president 1857–61) every year on the third Monday in February, along with a host of other undistinguished chief executives of the United States. In his 1999 book *I'm a Stranger Here Myself: Notes on Returning to America after Twenty Years Away*, Bill Bryson summed up well this nonevent well suited to our post-heroic time: "It's Presidents Day tomorrow. I know. I can hardly stand the excitement either."[102]

★ ★ ★ ★ ★ ★ ★ ★ ★ ★ ★ ★ ★ ★ ★ ★ ★ ★ ★

CHAPTER 5

St. Monday

Memorial Day, Labor Day, and the Celebration of Leisure

Saint *Monday* is as duly kept by our working people as *Sunday;* the only difference is that instead of employing their time cheaply at church they are wasting it expensively at the ale house.

Benjamin Franklin (1768)

ENJAMIN FRANKLIN, America's Poor Richard, could not condone loose habits among American working people, whose virtue and success depended on good, honest toil. Indeed, many would argue—from Alexander Hamilton, the promoter of manufacturing, to the agrarian Thomas Jefferson—that the new American nation could not endure and prosper—become "healthy, wealthy, and wise"—without hard, regular, orderly work. If some initially saw the New World as a terrestrial paradise, where wealth could be gained without effort, it soon became clear that only work—laborious work—would transform the continent into farms, plantations, shops, and manufactories. In the southern colonies and states, slave labor produced wealth and enabled southern white leisure, at least among elites. In the North, particularly in New England, Americans celebrated "free labor," not only because it cultivated economic competence and comfort but for its own sake. The Puritan idea of "calling" suggested that God beckoned every man and woman to right action, to salvation, and—most practically—to a particular, personal occupation. One's work, then—whether as farmer, shoemaker, goodwife, minister, or magistrate—was "the work of Christ." According to the seventeenth-century minister Thomas Shepard, "Seeing yourself thus working in worldly employments for him [God], you may easily apprehend that for that time God calls you to them, and you attend upon the work of Jesus Christ in them, that you honor God as much, nay, more, by the meanest servile worldly act, than if you should have spent all that time in meditation, prayer, or any other spiritual employment, to which you had no call at that time." Puritans and their American descendants thus yoked the practical work of making a living to religious expression, in the process emphasizing the sacredness of labor itself.[1]

One of those Puritan legatees, born in Boston and self-made in Philadelphia, Benjamin Franklin complained not that Americans idled their time away with meditation, prayer, or other spiritual employments but that they did so with frivolous dissipation. For Franklin, time was money. "He that idly loses 5 s. worth of time, loses 5 s. & might as prudently throw 5 s. in the River," wrote Poor Richard in 1737. In 1758, *Poor Richard Improved* observed,

> It would be thought a hard Government that should tax its People one tenth Part of their *Time*, to be employed in its Service. But *Idleness* taxes many of us much more, if we reckon all that is spent in absolute *Sloth*, or doing of nothing, with that which is spent in idle Employment or Amusements that amount to nothing. . . . *Sloth, like Rust, consumes faster than Labour wears; while the used Key is always bright,* as *Poor Richard* says.

Writing the second part of his *Autobiography* in the 1780s, Franklin outlined thirteen moral virtues, among them Temperance ("Eat not to Dulness / Drink not to Elevation"), Order ("Let all your Things have their Place. Let each Part of your Business have its Time"), Frugality ("Make no Expence but to do good to others or yourself: i.e. Waste nothing"), Industry ("Lose no Time.—Be always employ'd in something useful.—Cut off all unnecessary Actions"), and Moderation ("Avoid Extremes"). Saint Monday—a popularly extorted day of rest (and too often of debauchery, its critic claimed)—seemed to Franklin to violate all these virtues.[2] St. Monday was the colonial and early national version of our own three-day weekend.

Puritans in old and New England loathed the cluttered and (they believed) debased calendar bequeathed to them by Christendom before the Reformation, filled as it was with more holy days than profane; from their perspective, the former had become the latter. According to Martin Luther himself, "With our present abuses of drinking, gambling, idling, and all manner of sin, we vex God more on holy days than on others." "Besides these spiritual evils," Luther observed, "these saints' days inflict bodily injury on the common man in two ways: he loses a day's work and he spends more than usual, besides weakening his body and making himself unfit for labor, as we see every day." As historian Leigh Schmidt has written, "In Sabbatarian ardor, New England set a mean standard." Its liturgical calendar was remade in the interest of austerity and discipline, with the Sabbath as its main, regular focus. Special days were appointed as required by God for fasting or thanksgiving, not assigned permanent places in the calendar. Banished were the festivals of Christmas, Easter, and Whitsuntide, as well as other popular occasions in the English liturgical calendar. Thus in Plymouth colony in 1621, just after the first Thanks-giving, Governor Bradford called his people out to work on "Chrismasday." Some—the non-Puritan "strangers" among them—excused themselves from regular work out of conscience, but when Bradford at noon "found them in the streete at play, openly; some pitching the barr, & some at stoole-ball, and shuch like sport," he confiscated their equipment, admonished them, and told them to "kepe their houses, but ther should be no gameing or reveling in the streets." Today it may strike us as odd that Christmas would come in for par-ticular criticism by Puritan reformers. But like Bradford, they saw the day filled with idleness, mad mirth, and worse; in response, and in their own good conscience, they piously profaned it with work. As late as 1883, a latter-day Pu-ritan such as Austin Dickinson, brother of the famous poet Emily, could write in a December 24 letter, "A lonesome Sunday gone, and tomorrow Christmas. What of it! The day I was brought up to believe was a joint device of the Devil and the Romish Church for the overthrow of true religion."[3]

Of course, even Puritans found sleep and some "seasonable recreation" ac-ceptable, and in the next century Franklin himself could honor his own stric-tures in the breach. Yet the complex of ideas commonly known as the work ethic endured and ensconced itself in American life in the nineteenth century, with a particular emphasis on republican usefulness, improvement, and duty, along with a continuing, pervasive, nervous fear among the middle classes of idleness. The work ethic served American industrialization well, and with the phenomenal success of United States manufacturing in producing an aston-ishing output of goods, businessmen were forced to confront the possibility that their factories could produce more than consumers could buy. What would happen to the intense faith in labor when too much labor produced too much, causing turmoil in the larger economy? And did factory labor actually produce economic success for workers? Did it cultivate feelings of pride, self-worth, or actual republican independence? Did it make workers healthy, wealthy, and wise? In the United States (and in other industrialized econ-omies), the changing needs of the industrial and postindustrial economy, and of its workers, precipitated an erosion in the older commitment to work for its own sake and increasingly validated, even valorized, leisure. In the early twentieth century, Americans increasingly focused on consumption—not merely on ways to produce more and more quickly—and with the help of a re-markable new advertising "industry," Americans found new ways to define themselves, less through work than leisure, less through production than con-sumption.[4]

Although we continue to hear complaints that new holidays cost American business and government needless millions in paid days off, undermine the productivity of workers, and provide an excuse for idle recreation (rather than appropriate civic acts of veneration)—controversies over the birthday of Martin Luther King Jr. are a case in point—the twentieth-century American calendar can easily bear (indeed, it may require) a range of public holidays spread throughout the year. What Memorial Day would be complete, for example, without its traditional admonishments to put down the barbecue and put the "memorial" back into the holiday? By now, public holidays have become essential to American commerce, providing a regular cycle of marketing opportunities and organizing popular consumption, just as the liturgical cycle of holy days arranged time and experience in an earlier era. The systematic ordering of the United States calendar mandated by the Monday Holiday Act of 1968, creating new holidays and making others into moveable three-day-weekend feasts, thus recognized the modern economic and social imperative of leisure and consumption. Today this imperative has become a transnational liability and opportunity, as different parts of the world seek to do business with each other without a synchronized calendar. As a recent article in the *New York Times* proclaimed, "For the financial services industry, the emergence of global capitalism has unleashed a new horror: global holiday schedules." In response, financial publisher Paul Spraos, reported the *Times*, has produced an international holiday calendar, "which heroically tries to identify all the holidays—'bad business days,' he calls them—that will occur in more than 100 countries over the next 100 years." If time is money, so is leisure in transnational business. Ironically, Spraos invested so much work in assembling so complex a financial calendar that he concluded, ultimately, "that it would be foolish to give it away."[5]

That some commemorative occasions in the United States are more than mere "bad business days," that they carry real meaning for some Americans, prevents them from becoming irreducibly capitalist fetes or safety valves and offers them a legitimacy and authenticity critical to their persistence. Such holidays' original meanings—themselves highly contested and negotiable—linger and can be deployed to support contemporary social and political agendas (sometimes at odds with corporate America), to cultivate a more informed and nuanced sense of the United States' past, and to help preserve the holidays themselves from (and for) American business. Like our currency, public holidays are legal tender—we consume them and accept them while assuming that they have meaning, that something valuable stands behind them, even if we seldom (or never) bother to examine what that might be. Our Monday holidays, our St. Mondays—Martin Luther King Jr. Day, Presidents' Day, Memorial Day, Labor Day, and Columbus Day—are diverse in their origins, meanings, and implications, even as they all cap three-day weekends, sanctifying

American consumption and leisure. Like weathered (or weathering) statues in the park, they have become part of the landscape, lurking as commemorative sites while fading into the background as Americans unselfconsciously re-create, forget, and occasionally remember their past.[6]

We have already examined two St. Mondays, but what of these other two, Memorial Day and Labor Day? Both are products of the nineteenth century and at one time meant more to Americans than simply the commencement and termination of summer. For some these days continue to evoke strong feelings and stir them to ceremonial action. The history of each can tell us about shifting American identities (national, regional, local, ethnic or racial, and class based) and the popular deployment of the past in the United States during the previous century and a half.

Memorial Day: From Decoration to Recreation Day

What could be sadder, more disturbing, or offer a more powerful supplication for personal and national remembrance and reconciliation than the massive death toll exacted by America's Civil War, which cost the lives of some 620,000 soldiers North and South? The origins of Memorial Day are obscure but begin with vernacular acts of mourning. Southern legend tells us that women of the South expressed their grief and honored their fallen husbands, sons, and brothers by strewing flowers on their graves. Late in the war, in April and May 1865, Union soldiers in the South themselves observed this customary act, and some began to imitate it, decorating the graves of their comrades who had died far from home. The idea of Memorial Day caught the attention of northerners when the northern abolitionist James Redpath, in Charleston, South Carolina, to organize schools for freed slaves, led a group of African American children in May 1865 to adorn the graves of several hundred Union soldiers buried nearby.[7]

Soon these memorial rites—featuring particularly the decoration of graves with spring flowers—spread North and South. Among those somber ceremonies, one organized by veterans in Waterloo, New York, on May 5, 1866, was recognized by Congress as the first Memorial Day. But certainly hundreds of others occurred unofficially before, during, and immediately after the Waterloo commemoration. Many of these were held under the auspices of a new, politically powerful veterans' organization in the North, the Grand Army of the Republic, founded in 1866 by Gen. John A. Logan of Illinois. On May 5, 1868, GAR commander in chief Logan—apparently influenced by his wife, who had seen such ceremonies on her tour of southern battlefields in spring 1868—issued a general order that designated May 30 as a national Memorial Day, "for the purpose of strewing with flowers the graves of comrades who

Fig. 44. "Honoring Our Dead Heroes," from *Harper's Weekly*, June 6, 1868. In this symbolic scene, an obelisk dedicated to the Union dead is surrounded by mourning women and grave markers, each labeled with the name of a key Civil War battle. In this image, the Union is honored, and the South is unforgiven. Courtesy of Knight Library, University of Oregon.

died in defense of their country during the late war of rebellion, and whose bodies lie in almost every city, village, hamlet church-yard in the land." In that year, local GAR chapters held more than a hundred such ceremonies, and in 1869 some 336 Memorial Day observances occurred throughout the North. Quickly this new tradition became obligatory for every post and veteran, making the failure to remember fallen comrades on the day sacrilegious if not unimaginable. In 1873 New York became the first state to make May 30 a legal holiday, and by 1881 it had been followed by Rhode Island, Vermont, New Hampshire, Wisconsin, Massachusetts, and Ohio. Within another decade, every northern state had designated Memorial Day as an official holiday.[8]

The South, of course, forwarded its own claims as inventor of Memorial Day. Southern women had scattered flowers over the graves of fallen Confederate soldiers during the war, and in Georgia in 1866 Mrs. Charles J. Williams, a Confederate widow, published an appeal for southerners to designate a day "to be handed down through time as a religious custom of the South to wreathe the graves of our martyred dead with flowers." Southern states observed Decoration Day on various dates, from April in the deep South (April 26, the date of Gen. Joseph E. Johnson's surrender) to late May or early June in Virginia, which corresponded to the height of the local flower season. In the Carolinas, celebrants selected May 10, the anniversary of Thomas Stonewall Jackson's death. By 1916, ten southern states had set June 3—Jefferson Davis's birthday—as their Confederate Memorial Day. If men dominated the proceedings in the North, women took the lead in the South, forming Ladies Memo-

Fig. 45. "Decoration Day, May 30, 1871," by W. J. Hennessy, from *Every Saturday: An Illustrated Weekly Journal*, May 30, 1871. Hennessy's engraving captures the sense of loss and sorrow of the Decoration Day rite—but not the sectional reconciliation that would emerge later in the decade. The shield reading *pro patria* reminds mourners that northern troops fought for *their* country—the Union. Courtesy of Knight Library, University of Oregon.

rial Associations to care for graves and to disinter the remains of soldiers killed in distant locales and rebury them locally with honor. In the 1890s, southern women organized themselves into chapters of the United Daughters of the Confederacy to oversee rites of remembrance.[9]

In 1866, Congress created an extensive system of national military cemeteries for the Union war dead. Across the Potomac River from Washington, D.C., on Robert E. Lee's former estate, Arlington National Cemetery emerged, in part as an act of vengeance, as a sacred site of patriotic mourning and memory. Decoration Day at Arlington both reflected and helped to prescribe appropriate memorial rites for the nation. In 1868, some five thousand attended (including future presidents Ulysses S. Grant and James Garfield), amid the twelve thousand soldiers' graves decorated with small United States flags. Patriotic speeches, the dirges of a band, a procession, hymns and prayers, the firing of a cannon, and the broadcast of flowers by children orphaned by the war over the graves of the war dead composed the ceremonial event.[10]

In towns across the northern American landscape, similar scenes unfolded each year. Typically such remembrances would include the advance work of the boys from the Grand Army of the Republic, who would construct a platform and drape it with bunting; the early arrival of farmers and their families in their four-seated hacks; the lining of main street with the local populace; and a parade, complete with grand marshal on horseback, the colors and color guard, a military band, the GAR, the fire department, and perhaps troops of Boy Scouts marching toward the cemetery, which had been decorated with flags earlier in the day. A solemn memorial ceremony at the graveyard commanded the attention of all, before the congregants moved to adorn the tombstones of their own kin with flowers. The melancholy of the mortuary rites then would give way to the lighter moments of picnicking, visiting, play, and perhaps some tippling, followed by a band concert from the platform, words from the mayor, a reading of Logan's General Orders, which mandated the holiday observance, a recitation of the Gettysburg Address, and a long-winded, tear-jerking, and flag-waving oration. Taps and a benediction ended the affair officially, and celebrants drifted home.[11]

Romanticized reminiscences about such rites, set in the golden glow of a late-nineteenth- or early-twentieth-century yesteryear, typically suggest a unified, consensual, and patriotic world in which North and South no longer disagreed—indeed, in which the sections could hardly recall what they had been quarreling about. But the United States in the years immediately following the war was a nation still rent. Gen. Logan's request to Congress on June 22, 1868, to make Memorial Day a national "commemoration of the gallant heroes who have sacracficed [sic] their lives in defence of the Republic," was a sectional,

Union appeal, for only one side had defended the Republic against the other, which had sought to destroy it. At a Memorial Day service at Arlington National Cemetery in 1869, although the day's orator pleaded for brotherly union between the sections, Union veterans patrolled the graves of Confederate soldiers to prevent their decoration with flowers. Meanwhile southern states disparaged May 30 as a Yankee holiday and accused the GAR of deploying Memorial Day cynically for its own partisan purposes. Such attitudes help to explain the 1876 defeat of a bill in the U.S. Senate that would have erected May 30 as a national holiday.[12]

The animosity that divided North and South, and that separate sectional Memorial Days might have exacerbated, however, began to fade, and Decoration Day became a rite of national reconciliation. Even if some GAR and Republican Party orators continued to waive the bloody shirt, and even if white southerners cultivated nostalgia for their Lost Cause, Memorial Day increasingly served reunion rather than contention and vindictiveness. By the mid-1870s, joint Decoration Day ceremonies emerged, and federal troops stationed in the South joined ceremonies honoring the southern dead, while southern women scattered flowers on Union as well as Confederate graves. In the North too, as in the Memorial Day observance in Cincinnati in 1875, officers of the southern army along with those of the North marked the day

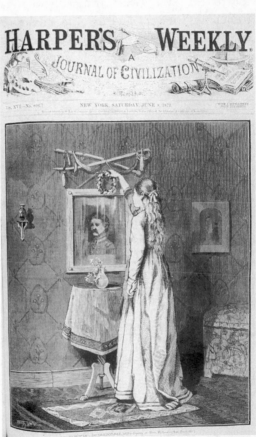

Fig. 46. "Decoration Day 1872," cover of *Harper's Weekly*, June 8, 1872. Memorial Days, North and South, were gendered female; grieving girls and women played a central role in these rites of loss and mourning. Courtesy of Knight Library, University of Oregon.

jointly with a "fraternal and charitable spirit." As early as Memorial Day 1869, the mayor of Charleston, South Carolina, emphasized the similarity of the sacrifice in the North and South. Gazing over graves of both Union and Confederate soldiers, he asked, "cannot we who survive catch the inspiration which swells the chorus of these who, once estranged, are now forever glorified?" In northern and southern towns alike, virtually indistinguishable statues arose—cast by the same foundries and sold in the same mail-order catalogs—typically depicting an erect, white common soldier, dedicated generically to "the cause" (whether it be the Union or state sovereignty), and commemorating bravery and heroism in the defense of one's country (itself ambiguous in its signification of local community or particular homeland as well as nation). These vernacular tributes created a standardized memory locally, which ironically, on a national scale, Americans both North and South could share. "The essence of Memorial Day in relation to reconciliation was its appeal to sympathy," wrote the historian Paul H. Buck in 1937. "North and South the sacrifice of war had led to a common meeting place, the cemetery, where strife and bitterness were hushed in death."[13]

But the strife endured by African Americans and the bitterness of their experience after the Civil War were also hushed in these rites of reunion. Memorial Day helped to construct through celebration "a policy of historical amnesia," as the Republican Party, and northerners generally, abandoned their program of Reconstruction in the South and deserted African Americans there. After 1877, Memorial Day activities sometimes lagged in northern communities, becoming more fully the property of the Grand Army of the Republic in their public celebration, or less overtly political and more focused on individual remembrance and on leisure. Working people enjoyed a late spring holiday, which they could fill with baseball games, horse (later bicycle) races, picnics, and ice cream festivals. In 1888, President Grover Cleveland allegedly went fishing on Memorial Day, which did not help him in his unsuccessful bid for reelection that year, but his action expressed a growing national mood. The Grand Army of the Republic condemned "indulgences in public sports, pastimes and all amusements on Memorial Day," an occasion that should inspire piety, not play. Whether indulging themselves in relatively mindless pursuits of recreation or committing themselves to a program of national and international economic development, which could not tolerate sectional divisions, white Americans purposefully forgot black contributions to the Union victory in the Civil War—some two hundred thousand blacks fought—and neglected the current dilemmas and dangers that faced African Americans in the South and made the United States a flawed republic. A Confederate monument in Columbia, South Carolina, carried an inscription, "Let their virtues

Fig. 47. "Decoration Day," by Thomas Nast, from *Every Saturday: An Illustrated Weekly Journal,* May 30, 1871. Nast anticipates here the romance of reconciliation that would emerge especially on Memorial Day later in the decade, as a single, grieving female figure kneels at two graves—those of a Union and a Confederate soldier—while their specters float in the background, locked in a haunting, conciliatory handshake. Courtesy of Knight Library, University of Oregon.

plead for the just judgment of the cause in which they perished." If the virtues or the gallantry of these Confederate dead could be acknowledged, did that alone grant legitimacy to the southern cause? GAR members might dispute this, but most white Americans simply chose not to remember.[14]

African Americans, however, could not forget. If white Americans shunted the issue of slavery and redefined the war "as a struggle between two ulti-

mately compatible 'principles' of union and state sovereignty," as the art historian Kirk Savage argues, "the four years of the worst bloodshed in American
history seem to be an inexplicable, Job-like test. And the local monuments
that help recast the war in this light tell us in effect that neither side lost." Yet
the North did win, and the South lost; the war was fought for a reason and carried important messages, blacks argued. A poem published in the Kansas *State
Ledger* in honor of Decoration Day in 1893 asked, for example,

> Why should we praise the gray, and blue,
> And honor them alike?
> The one was false, the other true—
> One wrong, the other right.

Frederick Douglass and other black leaders argued against oblivious reunion,
sometimes using Memorial Day to link reconciliation to real southern repentance and reform. In 1871, Douglass was invited to speak at Arlington on Decoration Day and addressed a great multitude including President Grant and
his cabinet near the monument honoring the Unknown Loyal Dead. Like
other orators, he praised "those unknown heroes whose whitened bones have
been piously gathered here, and whose green graves we now strew with sweet
and beautiful flowers, choice emblems alike of pure hearts and brave spirits."
And Douglass assured his audience, "I am no minister of malice. I would not
strike the fallen. I would not repel the repentant." But if the South was fallen,
was it repentant? "May my 'right hand forget her cunning and my tongue
cleave to the roof of my mouth,' if I forget the difference between the parties
to that terrible, protracted, and bloody conflict," the orator proclaimed, quoting Psalms 137:5–6. Douglass preached informed remembrance. "I say, if this
war is to be forgotten, ... in the name of all things sacred, what shall men remember?" Memorial Day, in his view, did not simply honor bravery, which
"marked the rebel not less than the loyal soldier." Douglass argued, "we are
not here to applaud manly courage, save as it has been displayed in a noble
cause. We must never forget that victory to the rebellion meant death to the
republic." His praise and gratitude showered exclusively on the loyal Union
dead, those who saved the nation, reunited it, and banished "the hell-black
system of human bondage."[15]

On a rainy, windy May 30, 1878, Frederick Douglass addressed the Grand
Army of the Republic in New York City in a Memorial Day speech in which he
denounced the violations of the Constitution in the South and urged listeners
to remember the justice of the Union cause. Douglass again told his audience
he came not "to fan the flames of sectional animosity, to revive old issues, or to
stir up strife between the races." But he insisted—in the face of the nation's ab-

sent-minded reconciliation—that "we are still afflicted by the painful sequences both of slavery and of the late rebellion." Quoting Ulysses S. Grant's famous phrase, "Let us have peace," Douglass added, "but let us have liberty, law, and justice first. Let us have the Constitution, with its thirteenth, fourteenth, and fifteenth amendments, fairly interpreted, faithfully executed, and cheerfully obeyed."[16]

"We must not be asked to say that the South was right in the rebellion, or to say the North was wrong." Douglass reiterated that there *was* a "difference between those who fought for the Union and those who fought against it, . . . between loyalty and treason." The Civil War "was a war of ideas, a battle of principles," which opposed "the old and the new, slavery and freedom, barbarism and civilization." If the Civil War was a war of liberation, why did African Americans in the South remain oppressed, denied their rights as citizens? As historian Alessandra Lorini has written, "the road to national reconciliation was paved only for

Fig. 48. "Decoration-Day. U.S.A. (*to his Grave-Diggers*): 'Not just yet,'" by Thomas Nast, from *Harper's Weekly*, June 15, 1878. This political cartoon uses the occasion of Memorial Day—and the ghostly skeleton figure of a Union soldier—to criticize President Rutherford B. Hayes (recently elected in a disputed contest) and congressional supporters for abandoning not merely Reconstruction and African Americans but the military as well. Nast and *Harper's Weekly* editorialized against proposals to reduce the army and navy. The shovels burying the armed services bear the names of Hayes's "collaborators," including Senator Benjamin Butler, who stands behind Hayes. Courtesy of Knight Library, University of Oregon.

whites," something Frederick Douglass well knew. Douglass continued to speak out, on Memorial Day as on other occasions, even addressing a May 30 audience at Storer College in Harper's Ferry in 1881 in an oration "not merely defending John Brown"—who just twenty years earlier had led a raid on the armory there as the first step in igniting a rebellion that would destroy slavery—

"but extolling him as a hero and martyr to the cause of liberty." Douglass's words, however, were often drowned out by the increasingly boisterous rites of reconciliation and collective amnesia that decorated Memorial Day. In 1889, Congress made Memorial Day a national holiday; in the 1890s Arlington National Cemetery created a special Confederate burial area, and in the next decade legislation committed the federal government to the care of Confederate graves in the North. In Chicago on Memorial Day in 1895, some five thousand people turned out to dedicate a monument to Confederate prisoners who had died at nearby Fort Douglas and were interred at Oak Woods Cemetery. Ultimately, President William Howard Taft approved a bill permitting the United Daughters of the Confederacy themselves to erect a Confederate memorial at Arlington. In a strange coda to Frederick Douglass's Memorial Day address on John Brown in 1881, the United Daughters of the Confederacy marked Harper's Ferry in 1937 with a stone dedicated to Heywood Shepherd, a slave who refused to join the raid, symbolic of those loyal slaves who faithfully remained with their benevolent masters during the Civil War. For white Americans, faithful remembrance of the war, and of black history during this period, seemed gone with the wind.[17]

Memorial Day thus proved to be a profoundly conservative occasion, with a radical content not frequently or easily tapped, even by those who suffered most from the national amnesia. Decoration Day among African Americans in South Carolina remained vital, as the annual observances at Beaufort illustrate. In 1897, for example, excursion trains brought black celebrants from as far away as Greenville until some ten to twelve thousand filled the streets to hail the black regiments whose members had fought and died both for the Union and to free themselves in the Civil War; the celebration continues today. This Decoration Day commemoration represented a counterweight to Confederate Memorial Day as well as to the national one. But its impact remained local or segregated within the African American community.[18]

If African Americans could remember their own contributions to the Union victory in the Civil War, recognize the courage of black troops, and mildly contest mindless reconciliation through localized celebration of Memorial Day, Native Americans in their own way could highlight their own patriotism and defense of country (that is, their particular homeland if not the American nation-state) on Decoration Day. Adopting white custom in the early twentieth century, for example, Hidatsas in North Dakota celebrated the day (as they celebrated other patriotic holidays, such as the Fourth of July) by gathering wildflowers when available or, if the season did not allow it, buying silk flowers to decorate their graves. Memorial Day could also be the occasion of imposed, heavy-handed reeducation. T. J. Morgan, the commissioner of Indian affairs, in his instruction to Indian agents and superintendents of Indian schools in 1890, included Decoration Day among those holidays to be inculcated among Native students "as a part of their education and a means of preparation and training for civilized home life and American citizenship." In the commissioner's annual report, Morgan claimed that "both teachers and pupils entered heartily into the spirit of various occasions." Even some "adult Indians took active part, . . . and for the time being, at least, identifying themselves with the new ideas brought forward." "On a few of the reservations," Morgan noted, "Memorial Day could be as fittingly observed as elsewhere, by the decoration of graves of Indians who enlisted in the United States Army and lost their lives during the war."[19]

At Haskell Institute in Lawrence, Kansas, and at other Indian boarding schools, Native students continued to be taught the rites of Memorial Day, which promoted patriotism and Americanization, but which also provided an opportunity to mourn the loss of those classmates who had died amid the difficult conditions of the schools themselves. School officials orchestrated the rites to conform to preferred gender arrangements in their own society, requiring Native girls to wear white dresses and designating them as the ones who would place flowers on the graves. In some instances, the rites could be cruelly colonial, forcing Native students to decorate the graves of traditional enemies or white conquerors. After visiting the Lapwai boarding school in Idaho in 1890, Alice Fletcher wrote a friend, "On Decoration Day we happened to see the procession of [Nez Percé] school children going to decorate the graves of the soldiers who slew their fathers in the [Chief] Joseph war." As with black Americans, Indians remembered a past at odds with the one preferred by whites; for Native people, Memorial Day rites of reconciliation (following a different domestic conflict—the Indian wars) ignored and insulted their plight.[20]

Such practices among African and Native Americans, at least when voluntarily adopted, nonetheless suggest the effort to cultivate ethnic or racial pride, identity, and solidarity more than to challenge publicly mainstream white interpretations of the past or current social and political arrangements. American Indians have served in the United States military in numbers disproportionate to the size of their population, commencing in the American Revolution and continuing in virtually every war in United States history, including the Civil War (fighting for both the Union and the Confederacy). They did so for their own reasons, within the context of their own social structures, beliefs, customs, and interests. The Cherokee-Creek historian and Vietnam veteran Tom Holm found that many Native people viewed military service as a family or tribal tradition and that some 75 percent of Native Vietnam veterans had volunteered or submitted to conscription for this reason. After a war, most Native societies honored their warriors and performed ceremonies to cleanse and reintegrate them into their peaceful communities. Native people continue to honor military service in their own ways—even when not compelled to do so by white authorities—sometimes commemorating the national Memorial Day, as well as the new holiday that appeared after the First World War, Armistice Day (later Veterans Day). Powerful images in photographs by Eugene Buechel from the 1920s and 1930s and by Don Doll from the 1970s of Lakota people at the Rosebud Sioux Reservation honoring their dead, particularly veterans, on Memorial Day and Armistice Day testify to the naturalized significance of these solemn holidays for Native people. Rites like those at Rosebud were primarily nonpolitical (or only implicitly political), designed not to comment on the meaning of particular wars, or to criticize or promote particular policy, but to restore the community and its members, who had faced horror and death.[21]

Likewise, other groups prominent in late-nineteenth- and early-twentieth-century social and political protest—women's rights advocates or labor activists—found little ground or inclination to mount their challenges on Memorial Day. Labor, of course, would have its own day, and feminists too looked elsewhere in the calendar for politically useful moments. Indeed, as Memorial Day became an occasion of national reconciliation, one that required as much forgetting as remembering, it was cordoned off from conventional politics, especially from the partisan wrangling of Reconstruction that so many whites sought to bury after 1877. As a nonpartisan festival, Memorial Day went further than depoliticizing (or rather, altering the political meaning of) the war; its white supporters North and South at times seemed to demonize politics and politicians, particularly the Radical Republicans who had engineered Reconstruction. Meanwhile, they lionized veterans, focusing on their manly valor, heroism, and fellow feeling.[22]

Decoration Day rites reinforced traditional gender notions and arrangements. As historian Nina Silber has shown, Memorial Day ceremonies in the North—organized largely by the Grand Army of the Republic—cultivated veterans' image of manly heroism. Union veterans affirmed their manhood particularly through their concern for the protection and advocacy of widows and orphans, and in general women played a supporting, silent, and passive role in Decoration Day events. The adulation of women helped mark and elevate men as society's public protectors, preservers of home and hearth, where women and children—real or potential victims—properly took refuge. Women's sentimental floral tributes placed on male graves recognized masculine courage, duty, and sacrifice and represented a continuation of the secondary, nurturing role played by women during the Civil War itself. As on other holiday occasions, male orators spoke and male marchers paraded while mixed audiences listened and watched. But in contrast to Independence Day or even Washington's or Lincoln's Birthday, on Memorial Day one was unlikely to hear calls for women's suffrage.[23]

In the South, Ladies Memorial Associations dominated Decoration Day rites. Fulfilling culturally prescribed roles as remembrancers and mourners, southern women reclaimed the dead bodies of their sons, husbands, and brothers and shed tears and flowers over their graves. Confederate Memorial Day became "the Sabbath of the South," and flowers that wreathed the mortuary sites of gray soldiers offered, according to one southern woman, an aroma "like incense burning in golden censers to the memory of the saints." Although leading the way in sentimental commemoration, southern white women still adopted a subordinate role to men, through fulsome expressions of gratitude for male heroic efforts, through their pains to relieve male anxieties and reconstruct defeated soldiers' sense of their manhood, through loving welcomes to returned boys in gray and snubs to Yankees, and through a shared, racist fear of newly freed black men. In fact, men were more prominent in the southern Ladies Memorial Associations than the name suggests; they helped in local organization, offered aid and advice, gave financial assistance, performed manual labor in cemetery projects, sometimes presided at meetings, and became honorary members. In short, in the South, memorial projects belonged in the realm of women, and although they were gendered female, such ritual activity did little to upset the South's traditional patriarchal order. Southern white women's organizations proved uninterested in political or historical discussions or in social reform; if speeches accompanied decoration rites, the mixed audiences listened to male orators. Like their counterparts in the North, southern women embraced a politically passive, supporting role; unlike northern women, however, women in the South raised and managed the funds required to care for graves, which the federal government refused to support, and presided at sentimental Memorial Day services, permitting those rites to avoid confrontation with the difficult political and ideological implications of southern defeat.[24]

In the South as well as the North, Decoration Day—though it commemorated a national event—was a local affair, promoting localism itself within a nationalist context. Observers of Confederate Memorial Day, as we have seen, insisted on their own dates for local celebration, and southern women worked tirelessly to repatriate the remains of their dead and inter them in local cemeteries. Ladies Memorial Associations were not closely affiliated in a larger regional organization but were distinctly local institutions. Northern communities too put a local stamp on their commemorations, celebrating common soldiers as never before and emphasizing the particular contributions of their own towns and villages to the Union victory. Reconciliation between North and South emerged in the United States—symbolized and rehearsed through joint, intersectional Memorial Day rites—as northern politicians abandoned Reconstruction and removed troops from the South, returning the region to local rule. After 1877, such autonomy bred, in addition to a great deal of mischief, a more ambiguous patriotic holiday on May 30.

Increasingly devoid of sectional, partisan content, Memorial Day grew as a simple day of leisure. The new patriotism of the late nineteenth century lacked a clearly defined set of values and principles, instead cultivating an almost mindless devotion to country. On Memorial Day 1895, Oliver Wendell Holmes could declare, "The faith is true and adorable, which leads a soldier to throw away his life in obedience to a blindly accepted duty, in a cause which he little understands." Given the character of this patriotic content, it is not surprising that so many Americans would prefer to commemorate Memorial Day with amusements. In 1887 in New York, the old Dutch carnivalesque holiday of Pinkster (Pentecost or Whitsuntide) and Barnum's Circus Day were made to coincide with Memorial Day. Elsewhere, even if Decoration Day was no circus, it was frequently a lively parade, a picnic, or an excuse for athletic competition. Beginning in 1911, Memorial Day became the traditional date of the Indianapolis 500, today America's oldest automobile race. Or the day became an occasion for more general expressions of memory, as ordinary people visited the graves of their deceased relatives, whether they had served as soldiers or not. With the Spanish-American War at the end of the nineteenth century, and then the First World War in the twentieth century's second decade, Americans had new soldiers to honor and military dead to remember. Often, memories of recent conflicts obscured older ones, as in Memorial Day exercises in Indianapolis after 1918, which focused attention on the recent international conflict, even as they continued with respectful seriousness to center on the Civil War Soldiers and Sailors Monument, erected in 1902. In Cleveland, the obliteration of memory was even more literal, as its Soldiers and Sailors Monument was constructed on the very site—and with the destruction—of the city's most important previous memorial, one commemorating Oliver Hazard Perry's victory in the Battle of Lake Erie during the War of 1812. The new Civil War monument was dedicated on July 4, 1894; within another generation, however, it would serve other political agendas, as historian John Bodnar has shown.[25]

After the First World War, the United States inaugurated a new memorial holiday, Armistice Day (later Veterans Day), which unlike the Soldiers and Sailors monument in Cleveland, found a separate site in American culture, on the calendar (November 11), even though its purpose seemed to duplicate Decoration Day. Armistice Day won acceptance through the lobbying of the American Legion, the largest veterans' organization to appear in the United States after the Great War in 1919. The Legion participated actively with Civil War and Spanish-American War veterans in Memorial Day rites, even establishing an endowment fund to ensure the decoration of American graves on foreign soil. But it sought the creation of a memorial day dedicated exclusively to those who served in the First World War. The nation's first Armistice Day observance occurred on November 11, 1919, in conformity with President Woodrow Wilson's proclamation, which emphasized peace: "A year ago our enemies laid down their arms in accordance with an armistice which rendered them impotent to renew hostilities, and gave to the world an assured opportunity to reconstruct its shattered order and to work out in peace a new and juster set of international relations." Armistice Day, for Wilson, celebrated the end of "the war to end all wars" and the new possibilities of international peace: "To us in America the reflections of Armistice Day will be filled with solemn pride in the heroism of those who died in the country's service and with gratitude for the victory, both because of the thing from which it has freed us and because of the opportunity it has given America to show her sympathy with peace and justice in the councils of nations." At the eleventh hour of the eleventh day of the eleventh month, American citizens were instructed to observe two minutes of silence to honor the war dead and promote the cause of peace.[26]

Yet despite its apparent erection as a holiday to advance peace, Armistice Day took on a militaristic character; its chief promoter, the American Legion, denounced pacifism and radicalism and vigorously joined efforts to destroy leftist activity in the Red Scare of 1919 and 1920. In the small logging community of Centralia, Washington, on a cold, gray November 11, 1919, the Grant Hodge Post of the American Legion sponsored an Armistice Day parade that erupted in riot and resulted in three deaths, the destruction of the town's International Workers of the World (IWW) offices, and the arrest of all available Wobblies. That night, Britt Smith, secretary of Centralia's IWW, was lynched —taken from his cell, castrated, hanged, and repeatedly shot on a nearby bridge over the Chehalis River, where his body remained for days.[27] Such despicable acts were not repeated elsewhere—indeed, the day's ceremonies could be inclusive of America's diverse ethnic, racial, and religious, if not its labor and political, groups—but Armistice Day retained its martial character and typically featured less solemn parades and more celebratory events. Rather quickly by the 1930s, although Armistice Day continued as an annual observance, its intensity and seriousness eroded, and like Memorial Day, its celebrants turned their attention increasingly to leisure and amusement when the nation was not actually at war.[28]

Why did Americans need another memorial day when they had one already, observed annually on May 30? Some believed they did not. Congressman Hamilton Fish Jr., who authored legislation to create a memorial to an unknown soldier in Arlington National Cemetery in 1920, believed that Memorial Day would serve best as the occasion for the dedication ceremony. Fish and others hoped to further national unity, make Decoration Day a truly cross-sectional observance, and encourage recent veterans of the First World War to adopt Memorial Day as their own. But instead President Warren G. Harding chose to re-inter the Unknown at Arlington on November 11, 1921, giving additional support to the separate existence of Armistice Day.[29]

Armistice Day faced the same problems that Memorial Day encountered as memory faded and its veteran constituency passed away. In the 1940s and 1950s, new military conflicts—a Second World War and the Korean War—blocked out remembrance of the First World War, and some campaigned to broaden the meaning of Armistice Day to honor the dead who had fallen in all American wars, just as Memorial Day increasingly also commemorated those who had died in conflicts following the Civil War. In June 1954, President Dwight D. Eisenhower signed into law a bill officially renaming the November 11th holiday as Veterans Day, now honoring all United States veterans living as well as deceased, and in the process perhaps better distinguishing the occasion from Memorial Day. (Ironically, Decoration Day itself had become a day of advocacy for veterans under the auspices of the GAR by the late 1870s.) On Memorial Day in 1958, two more bodies of unknown soldiers, representing the previous two wars, were buried with honor at Arlington in the expanded Tomb of the Unknown. Maintaining the ambiguity surrounding the meaning of the two public holidays of mourning in the United States, the president each year participates in a service at the memorial, on the third Monday in May—Memorial Day—and at eleven o'clock on the morning of November 11, Veterans Day.[30]

The renomination of Armistice Day to Veterans Day, like the name change to Presidents' Day, did not prevent the holiday's deflation as a meaningful event in American life. Included in the 1968 Monday Holiday Bill, Veterans Day became a moveable feast and part of a three-day weekend in November, beginning in 1971. But in 1978, Congress returned Veterans Day to its original November 11 spot, in deference to the complaints of veterans' organizations that such tampering had devalued or profaned the holiday. If veterans groups were assuaged, the public was unmoved. By 1974, a year after the United States' withdrawal from Vietnam, the annual Veterans Day ceremony at Arlington, over which President Gerald R. Ford presided on a mild, sunny day, drew but three thousand people and merited only a short article (and no picture) on page twenty-nine of the *New York Times,* whereas in 1921, the original dedication of the Tomb of the Unknown Soldier on Armistice Day had attracted some hundred thousand people; in 1975, the *Times* did not cover the Arlington event at all.[31]

In contrast, on a gray, cold Veterans Day (actually November 13) 1982, thousands turned up in Washington, D.C., to dedicate a new Vietnam Veterans Memorial. The event was hugely successful, uniting physically if not politically and ideologically, a wide range of Americans with varying interpretations of the late war but with a common commitment to honor those men and women who served. The memorial itself became the most visited monument in the capital, a city of monuments. The procession preceding the dedication ceremony was peaceful but disorderly, containing an array of marchers, from polished troops to disgruntled veterans protesting their exposure to the chemical defoliant Agent Orange. The memorial itself challenged traditional expressions of the heroism and glory of war, with its sunken, gravelike placement of a black marble wall of names of those Americans killed in Vietnam. Later additional statues were added—of common soldiers representing different races, and in 1993 of army nurses—compromising the integrity of Maya Lin's original design, perhaps, but representing the groping, inconclusive efforts of Americans to find clear meaning in the history of the Vietnam War. This dedication did not commence a renewed commitment to serious commemoration of Veterans Day (let alone Memorial Day) in the United States, except perhaps among a minority of veterans themselves, organized into posts of the American Legion, the Veterans of Foreign Wars, and other associations. If Memorial Day remains a St. Monday—as the patron saint of summer's inauguration—the other memorial holiday, Veterans Day, has been decanonized, remaining pure but often forgotten every November 11.[32]

At any rate, massive, national observations of Memorial Day or Veterans Day are exceptional. Such rites, most often and most effectively observed locally, asserted a local identity and projected it onto the nation. Americans have rehearsed nationalism on these days, but as in Fourth of July celebrations, they did so in particular local settings and in a particularly local fashion. Nonetheless, for celebrants, these local and localized commemorations embodied nationalism and national patriotism. In a sense, as during Independence Day, all politics—all national commemoration—was local. Ironically, localized rites of remembrance, in both the nineteenth-century North and South, provided a means of effecting national reconciliation between the sections in postbellum America. Narrowing one's vision to the particular duties fulfilled by soldiers

Fig. 49. Native veterans of the Vietnam War march in regalia—in the Veterans Day parade held in 1982 for the official dedication of the Vietnam Memorial in Washington, D.C.—exhibiting pride in their service to their nations, both the United States and their tribe. Such pride did not preclude criticism of the United States and ambivalence toward its treatment of American Indians. Author photo.

Fig. 50. Veterans Day parade, official dedication of the Vietnam Memorial, Washington, D.C., November 1982. The procession preceding the dedication ceremony was peaceful but disorderly, containing an array of marchers, from polished troops to discontented veterans protesting their exposure to the chemical defoliant Agent Orange. Author photo.

clad in both gray and blue—protection of family, home, community—and focusing on the common tragedy suffered by fellow Americans North and South, who had lost sons, brothers, and husbands alike, Americans could use a common rite of mourning to reimagine themselves as a single nation. To remember their mutual national affinity, however, Americans had to forget their animosity and the chief cause of their Civil War—the conflict over slavery and the place of African Americans in the United States (white Americans were even less conscious of Native Americans). The war between the states over the institution of slavery did not resolve the question. And Memorial Day, as a day of national reconciliation, colluded in the nation's purposeful amnesia by ignoring black contributions toward the Union victory as well as the continuing failure to achieve social, political, or economic justice for African Americans. Real remembrance and reconciliation were at odds, and the United States seemed to choose the latter over the former, opting for forgetting over historical memory and racial justice. Ultimately, as Civil War veterans died, and as new wars created new veterans and different memories, Memorial Day commemoration evolved (some would say devolved) and even spawned another memorial holiday to serve its new constituencies, often supplying Americans simply with a day of unselfconscious leisure. Today most Americans have forgotten even those things that the original Memorial Day as a day of forgetting was designed to remember.

Fig. 51. Memorial Day parade, Orange, Connecticut, ca. 1971. Memorial Day evolved into an occasion for the expression of more generalized mourning for deceased family and friends. Even this generic grieving has played an ever decreasing role in Memorial Day events, as the holiday has become a St. Monday, part of a three-day weekend marking the beginning of summer, a time for leisure activities, and, as in this parade, a moment to cultivate a sense of community. Author photo.

American Labor Day

If on Memorial Day we often choose not to remember, on Labor Day today we seldom commemorate American labor or perform much ourselves. Rest and relaxation—of the mind as well as the body—dominate the day, marking the end of summer, and of the vacation season, with another celebration of St. Monday. But American Labor Day was not always devoid of meaning or political import, and it retains a latent potency as an occasion when, if necessary, organized labor in the United States can mobilize union members, build solidarity internally, intimidate foes, and press its interests in public.[33]

America's Labor Day began dramatically on Tuesday, September 5, 1882, with a parade in New York City. Earlier, on May 14, in the midst of a resurgent labor movement, the newly formed Central Labor Union—an umbrella organization composed of a range of labor activists, from Marxian radicals to conservative craftsmen and their unions, and including a heterogeneous religious and ethnic mix—proposed a "monster labor festival" for all workers in early September. On August 6, the Central Labor Union set the date, resolving "that the 5th of September be proclaimed a general holiday for the workingmen of this city," which would coincide with the national Knights of Labor general assembly scheduled to meet then in New York City. The Central Labor Union hoped to exhibit labor's militancy and to promote solidarity among its diverse working-class constituency. A massive demonstration in the city's streets would "show the strength and esprit de corps of the trade and Labor organizations" and "warn politicians that they shall go no farther in pandering to the greed of monopoly and reducing the condition of the masses." On the appointed day, a parade of laboring men assembled at City Hall Park and set off up Broadway to Union Square, then made its way across 17th Street and up 5th Avenue, finally ending at 42nd Street and 6th Avenue, where the marchers boarded the Metropolitan Elevated Railway to travel to a picnic grounds hired for the day, at Wendel's Elm Park. Over the course of their more than three-mile procession, union members were led by Grand Marshal William G. McCabe, delegate from Local No. 6 of the International Typographers. At the parade's start, McCabe could muster only about eighty men, and he despaired that the grand demonstration would be a miserable failure. But they were soon joined by some two hundred members of the jewelers union and Voss's Military Band from Newark, New Jersey, and along the way hundreds, then thousands more joined the procession. At Union Square, they passed a grandstand, where Terence Powderly, among the most important labor figures in America and leader of the Knights of Labor, formally reviewed the marchers, who ultimately numbered between ten and twenty thousand. On the stand, Robert

Washington's Birthday! Your thoughts go back to the period when the foot of the throne of England rested on her American colonies scattered along the fringe of the Atlantic—rested on a republic which did not yet know that with the birth of a child it also had been born and was singing in its cradle—in its cradle under the throne, the throne which it was destined to shake. You look back in the history of the nation to the Day of Revolt.

Lincoln's Birthday! Your thoughts come down to the time when the people of those colonies had grown into an irresistibly expanding nation, had crossed the eastern mountain range of the continent, and swept through a wilderness toward the Pacific. This day compels the thoughts of all people to center upon one man of that time — as upon a towering piece of com- mon rock, still in its place

LABOR DAY.

Fig. 52. "Labor Day," from *Munsey's Magazine,* November 1911. Courtesy of Knight Library, University of Oregon.

Price allegedly turned to Gen. Worthy Foreman of the Knights of Labor and said, "This is Labor Day in earnest, Uncle Dick."[34]

At Wendel's Elm Park, the massive picnic attracted between fifteen thousand and twenty thousand revelers, including women and children, who were admitted free, as well as union men. Each union chose a picnic area, which it marked with colorful banners, placards, and flags. At a large pavilion, a band played waltzes and polkas, and other musicians and singers performed for the crowds, while celebrants ate, danced, played, and at least some drank heavily. The *New York Herald* reported, "Fellow-workers and their families sat together, joked together and caroused together. . . . American and English, Irish and Germans, they all hobnobbed and seemed on a friendly footing, as though the common cause had established a closer sense of brotherhood." According to Grand Marshal McCabe, "Our parade had awakened the city. . . . What a brotherhood was formed that day! The young people danced and sang, the old people smilingly looked on, and augured on the grand future of labor as the outcome of the day's good work!"[35]

It was an auspicious beginning, which the Central Labor Union in New York followed with another on Wednesday, September 5, 1883. In 1884, George K. Lloyd, the union secretary, resolved that "the Central Labor Union does hereby declare and will observe the first Monday [in September] in each year as Labor Day," and at the Knights of Labor convention that year Lloyd introduced a similar resolution. The national Federation of Organized Trades and Labor Unions (predecessor of the American Federation of Labor) determined as well in 1884 to mark the first Monday in September annually as Labor's National Holiday. By 1889, the holiday had spread beyond New York City to four hundred cities, where parades and especially picnics, oratory, sporting events, dancing, and games quickly became traditional.[36]

As early as 1885 and 1886, some municipal authorities recognized the new holiday, and legislation to make Labor Day a state holiday was first introduced in 1885 in New York. In 1887, Oregon became the first state to pass such legislation and make Labor Day an official state holiday; other states soon followed, recognizing that labor organizations increasingly wielded significant power on election days. In 1887, five states passed Labor Day laws; some twenty-four states had sanctioned the event as a public holiday by 1894, the year that Labor Day became a national holiday. Nonetheless, the rapid ascent of the new holiday, and the apparent assent of the state to celebrate it, can obscure the continuing struggle—both internal and external—that working-class activists faced as they sought to secure Labor Day's place in the calendar. Few businesses voluntarily gave employees the day off, and government officials proved unprepared to enforce their holiday measures. As historians Michael Kazin and Steven J. Ross have noted, "for nearly two decades [after its origin] Labor Day was a virtual one-day general strike in many cities."[37]

Kazin and Ross, Labor Day's most perceptive historians, argue that from the start the holiday operated in a complex, perhaps even contradictory fashion, expressing both discontent and satisfaction, conflict and consensus, particular class interests and classless American loyalty, seriousness and amusement, even frivolity. According to Kazin and Ross, union leaders continue to wrestle with a dilemma—"how to build a class-conscious movement while also affirming their loyalty to conceptions of American citizenship that muted class distinctions"—while pursuing two distinctive goals simultaneously: "building, inspiring, and mobilizing a labor movement and courting a mass public whose opinion about that movement could help legitimize and advance its reputation and power." Could labor activists on Labor Day be both "proud, militant workers" and "loyal, unthreatening Americans"? And could they pursue both a serious political agenda and celebration, through leisure activities, of the achievements of American labor?[38]

Activists on Labor Day walked a fine line between cultivating internal solidarity and militancy for their cause, on the one hand, and on the other hand developing legitimacy externally with a mass public and the state, which was often suspicious of particular, class-based rhetoric, especially when it emanated from hyphenated Americans, relatively recent immigrants often demeaned as un-American foreigners. Radicalism, whether promoted by native-born Americans or newcomers, drew public distrust as well as repression by powerful business interests and their allies in government. Given the two audiences—one internal and one external—on Labor Day, leaders faced difficult decisions in defining and presenting their messages. Internal divisions within the labor movement only compounded their problems. In some instances, in fact, a single Labor Day witnessed alternate, competing demonstrations in the same cities. Such was the case in Chicago in 1885, when that city's first Labor Day celebration actually produced two contesting demonstrations. One, sponsored by the craft union–oriented Trades and Labor Assembly, sought moderation and cooperation with capitalists, banning, for example, any displays of the socialist red flag; another more radical observance, spawned by such prohibitions, emerged under the guidance of the Central Labor Union, which embraced an array of socialist and anarchist unions. Whereas the trade unionists invited civic elites to review their parade and speak at their rally, and featured pragmatic goals, such as the eight-hour day, the Central Labor Union's procession featured militant placards, with mottoes designed to galvanize: "Hail to the social revolution!" for example, or "Down with government, God, and gold!" The *Chicago Tribune*'s reporting of these Labor Day events illustrated not only its own conservative bias but the real differences in approach and agendas between the two groups. While praising the Trades and Labor Assembly's exercises, it derided the radicals of the Central Labor Union as wild-eyed fanatics and ignorant, un-American foreigners: "With the smell of gin and beer, with blood-red flags and redder noses, and with banners inscribed with revolutionary mottoes, the anarchists inaugurated their grand parade and picnic yesterday morning." Although solidarity was sometimes possible, such divisions would fester and intensify into the next century, until in the late 1930s and early 1940s, the rivalry between the American Federation of Labor (AFL) and the new Congress of Industrial Organizations (CIO) reached its height. Such competition within the labor movement also played itself out through alternate and competing celebrations of labor's day, on May 1—May Day—as well as on the first Monday in September.[39]

Further, as the *Chicago Tribune*'s reportage suggests, labor could not necessarily control the meaning of Labor Day in the larger public arena, where the sense of events was construed more broadly by individuals, by the press, and by business, especially through advertising; that is, the "true" meaning of Labor Day would be determined not merely by organized labor but by others as well, both supporters and those hostile to labor's cause. Did Labor Day honor all those who labored—that is, nearly all Americans—or did it single out for commemoration particularly the working class engaged in industrial work and organized in unions? The United States Department of Labor declares definitively on its website, "Labor Day, the first Monday in September, is a creation of the labor movement and is dedicated to the social and economic achievements of American workers. It constitutes a yearly national tribute to the contributions workers have made to the strength, prosperity and well-being of our country." But such clarity is challenged by works like *Celebrations: The Complete Book of American Holidays,* written with the editors of Hallmark Cards, which concluded in 1972 that the holiday was once "tied to the militancy of the Labor movement," but today "Labor Day honors all who work—laborers and skilled workers in steel mills and coal mines; technical and professional people in offices, hospitals, and schools; wives and mothers at home. . . . It has become one of the great holidays for all Americans."[40]

Promoters of Labor Day thus confronted a challenge similar to the one facing advocates of the United States' newest public holiday, the birthday of Martin Luther King Jr.: how to negotiate between particularity and universalism in the American public sphere. Does the new holiday (whether Labor Day or Martin Luther King Jr. Day) justly honor and celebrate the particular contributions of a segment of the American public—the American working class or African Americans—or does it appeal more generally to that larger American public, commemorating universal principles or values—the nobility of all labor, or the foundational ideal that "all men are created equal"? Emphasis on the former can place the holiday's greater legitimacy at risk, but emphasis on the latter, although it might help legitimate the group's place in American society and polity, threatens to dilute the holiday's message and appeal to its core constituency, while it can undermine the festive occasion's utility as a tool for radical transformation or reform. By trying to mean too much, a holiday like Labor Day can come to mean too little.

America's Labor Day emerged from no sacred event such as the American Revolution or the mythical founding of America at Plymouth Rock (St. Augustine, Jamestown, or previous Native American sites notwithstanding); nor does it celebrate a holy figure in American history, such as Christopher Columbus, George Washington, or Abraham Lincoln. The Haymarket Massacre of 1886—when a bomb exploded after an anarchist rally in Chicago and police fired indiscriminately into crowds of demonstrators—does not have the hallowed status of the Boston Massacre of 1770, nor does the visage of Samuel Gompers or Walter Reuther grace Mount Rushmore. Lacking a secure place in American origin myth, and wanting an appropriate American demigod as a totem, Labor Day cannot fully transcend its status as a partisan fete, except when it is divested of its original meanings and political implications. Unlike other holidays, it never approached the status of a general American holy day, even at the moment of its inception. If occasions such as the Fourth of July, George Washington's Birthday, or even Memorial Day permitted Americans locally and arrayed in special interests groups to assert their own particular agendas as if they were nonpartisan—the embodiment of nationalism and patriotism—Labor Day promoters found it difficult to assert convincingly that their interests were in fact those of the entire country or sanctified by American history. In contrast to other "red, white, and blue letter days," Labor Day was too "red" for business interests and occasionally the state; for those often marginalized or excluded from the labor movement, like African Americans and Latinos, Labor Day could be too white; and for working people themselves, who certainly sought to improve their wages and working conditions through public demonstrations but who also struggled for a shorter workday and workweek, Labor Day was sometimes best celebrated as a blue Monday, that is, less as a day of politics than as one of rest and leisure. Samuel Gompers, founder and longtime president of the American Federation of Labor, was largely correct when he declared, "Labor Day differs in every essential from the other holidays of the year in any country. . . . All other holidays are in a more or less degree connected with conflicts and battles of man's prowess over man, of strife and discord for greed and power, of glories achieved by one nation over another." Labor Day, on the other hand, "is devoted to no man, living or dead, to no sect, race, or nation."[41] In that distinctiveness resides both the power and the limitations of Labor Day as an American holiday.

If American Labor Day was invented on September 5, 1882, its origins are more remote and complex, extending even to the early American period, and intertwined with working-class efforts to assert a sense of their worth, to improve working conditions, and to win shorter workdays and workweeks. After the American Revolution, craftsmen in Boston, New York, Philadelphia, and other seaboard cities began to participate actively in political demonstrations and to celebrate their new republic, themselves, and their role as citizens. They did so in public demonstrations, in the streets and in cooperation with a range of other like-minded citizens, as in Philadelphia's Grand Federal Procession of July 4, 1788, which celebrated Pennsylvania's ratification of the United States Constitution. Of the five thousand marchers that day, many were working men, arrayed by trades and crafts, walking or riding on floats, carrying banners, displaying their tools, and exhibiting their crafts and products. In New York City too a Federal Procession mobilized some five thousand or six thousand craftsmen on July 23, 1788, in this case not only to celebrate the Constitution but to lobby New York state delegates to follow Pennsylvania in ratifying the new frame of national government. And on an annual basis, at potent political moments, such as the Fourth of July or (in New York City) on Evacuation Day (November 25), artisans and mechanics took to the streets to demonstrate pride in their work, their trade, their civic responsibilities, and their economic contributions as well as to promote their political and economic interests, although such promotion was always suitably clothed in the rhetoric of disinterestedness. Presenting themselves as consummate republicans, these workingmen stressed their independence, virtue, equality, citizenship, and commitment to community.[42]

Working people also began to challenge masters and owners of shops and factories; particularly as conditions of work and the organization of production changed, working people asserted interests that varied from those of their employers, with whom they had marched earlier in Federalist parades. As early as 1791, Philadelphia carpenters went on strike for a ten-hour day, hoping to cut their hours and work "from six to six!" (that is, from six o'clock in the morning until six in the evening, with two hours for lunch). These efforts—initially unsuccessful—continued into the nineteenth century, in Philadelphia and elsewhere, and culminated in notable labor successes in the 1830s. By then, a new consciousness of class had emerged among craft workers across trades, and artisans and laborers increasingly organized themselves into unions, articulated their mutual interests distinctive of their employers, fought for their common welfare, and expressed their own vision of American political economy. In spring 1834, workingmen came together in the General Trades' Union of the City and County of Philadelphia, which grew from seventeen affiliates and about two thousand members to an organization embracing some fifty unions and more than ten thousand wage earners. The following year, the General

Trades' Union staged a successful general strike for a ten-hour day. A key part of the strike proved to be spontaneous as well as orchestrated parades and rallies in Philadelphia's streets. These strike parades and other festive demonstrations, along with an established tradition of workers' public observation (even appropriation) of nationalist, patriotic occasions annually (like Independence Day) and more episodically (like Philadelphia's reception for the Marquis de Lafayette in 1824 or the George Washington Centennial Procession in 1832), established a traditional practice among workers in Philadelphia and elsewhere that proved critical to the advent of Labor Day.[43]

Trade unionists continued to invoke both the style and content of patriotic parades and fetes in their demonstrations for shorter hours and workweeks. The principles of the American Revolution stood behind claims to liberty and economic justice and helped to establish for working-class activists a right to strike. And in form, workers' protests associated themselves with both the militancy of the Revolution itself and the patriotic processions that later celebrated the new nation. As Susan G. Davis has noted, "the etymological connection between 'strike' and 'parade' is very close." To strike can mean "to set out on foot" or "to walk out," exactly what one does in a parade. To strike out on one's own is to assert independence and responsibility, exactly what working people hoped to do in antebellum America.[44]

By the late 1850s, labor leaders were able to amass huge numbers of demonstrators and mount spectacular events, sometimes ordered and respectable but sometimes more militant and less controlled. Increasingly, municipal authorities and propertied and business interests became concerned and sought new means of preserving order—particularly following the Great Strike of 1877—including the introduction of centralized city police forces and eventually the creation of militia units later transformed into the National Guard, as well as legislation more rigorously controlling public meetings and assembly.[45]

In the midst of an escalating battle between capital and labor in the last quarter of the nineteenth century, two organizations emerged to lead the labor movement, the Knights of Labor (founded 1869) and the Federation of Organized Trades and Labor Unions of the United States and Canada (later to become the American Federation of Labor). The Knights, with a membership of over 700,000 in the mid-1880s, organized both skilled and unskilled workers and embraced African Americans and women. Indeed their principles of inclusiveness extended membership even beyond wage earners to politicians and owners of small businesses. The Knights favored education and legislative activity over more direct action and avoided strikes at all costs. The first Labor Day in 1882 did not challenge the principles of the Knights' leadership; although the celebration represented virtually a one-day general strike, the

Knights had already arranged to be in New York for their annual meeting, and the day's broader message of worker solidarity unrelated to specific grievances spoke to the Knights' goals. But Terence V. Powderly, the Knights' grand master workman, proved reluctant to join with the Federation of Organized Trades and Labor Unions, or with more radical labor groups, in supporting a general strike campaign for an eight-hour day in 1885, which the trade unionists had proposed as the focus of a massive demonstration on May 1, 1886. Instead of such a demonstration—which in appearance resembled those designed for Labor Day but now yoked to a specific, concrete, militant message—Powderly favored an essay-writing effort to educate employers and the public, with the compositions to be published on Washington's Birthday. The Trades and Labor Unions proceeded with its plans, and in general, with the rapid decline of the Knights of Labor in the late 1880s, the new AFL became the chief promoter of Labor Day as an annual event. But May Day, as these 1886 plans suggest, appeared as a potential rival or alternative date for America's Labor Day—one that might challenge the moderate AFL's own hegemony among working-class activists.[46]

"Arouse, ye toilers of America!" a Federation of Organized Trades and Labor Unions circular entreated. "Lay down your tools on May 1, 1886, cease your labor, close the factories, mills and mines—for one day of the year. One day of revolt—not of rest!" In apparent distinction to the Labor Day holiday celebrated on the first Monday in September, which was beginning to achieve official recognition, this May Day demonstration was "a day not ordained by the bragging spokesmen of institutions holding the world of labor in bondage." Instead, it would be "a day on which labor makes its own laws and has the power to execute them! All without the consent or approval of those who oppress and rule." Organizers thus rebuffed not only capital and the state but the rival Knights of Labor as well and defined their event more militantly and purposefully as "a day of protest against oppression and tyranny . . . , a day on which to begin to enjoy 'eight hours for work, eight hours for rest, eight hours for what we will.' "[47]

The point of the Trade and Labor Unions' campaign was quite specific—to renew the fight for an eight-hour day—but as the immoderate rhetoric above suggests, the alliance sought to incorporate a wide range of labor groups, including those that would stage their own, more radical Labor Day events in Chicago in 1885. At its convention in 1884, the federation set May 1, 1886, for a general strike to culminate its efforts. It is not completely clear why they selected May Day (outside of New York City, the September Labor Day was not yet an obvious choice). But nearly twenty years earlier the Illinois legislature had passed an eight-hour law, which was set to take effect May 1, 1867, and to mark the occasion and encourage compliance among employers some forty-four Chicago unions had rallied and marched on the day. Employers found ways to evade the measure, which went largely unenforced, and the economic downturn of the 1870s further negated the efforts of workers to limit their workdays. But May Day 1867 may well have been remembered and employed to invoke the memory of a previous victory. Nearly all segments of the labor movement—even many Knights of Labor assemblies—embraced the campaign, and on May 1, 1886, some thirty to forty thousand workers struck in Chicago, with thousands parading through the streets with banners proclaiming their cause. In Chicago, the demonstrations were dominated by socialists and anarchists, although in other industrial cities trade unionists and Knights controlled the proceedings. Some workers won concessions, but the 1886 May Day strikes and their aftermath ended in tragedy and crisis, with the Haymarket Square incident in Chicago on May 4 and on May 5 the shooting of some nine strikers in Milwaukee. At Haymarket Square, while police were attempting to break up a rally protesting police repression of strikers at the McCormick reaper factory, a bomb exploded; a riot erupted, and police opened fire on the demonstrators. In the end, seven police officers and two protesters were killed, and some seventy people were injured. Inflamed, Chicago's civic and business elite acted to purge the city of labor radicalism.[48]

After the turmoil and repression associated with the Haymarket affair, the AFL, using May 1 as a day of national protest, returned to its campaign for the eight-hour day, which culminated in a mass strike on May 1, 1890. This May Day followed rallies strategically placed at key moments in the United States' commemorative and festive calendar: Washington's Birthday in 1889 and 1890, the Fourth of July in 1889, and Labor Day on September 2, 1889. Meanwhile in Europe, in July 1889, some four hundred delegates met at the Marxist International Socialist Congress in Paris and founded the Second International. A communiqué from AFL leader Samuel Gompers informed the meeting of the AFL's May Day plans; in solidarity and support for the eight-hour day, the Congress resolved to mark May 1, 1890, as an international labor day. As the date approached, the AFL abandoned the idea of a general strike and developed the alternate strategy of targeting particular unions to strike on labor's behalf (for 1890 it was the International Brotherhood of Carpenters and Joiners). The AFL, along with the Socialist Labor Party, sponsored rallies in many cities, including Chicago, where some thirty thousand working people, representing a hundred unions, turned out on May Day; in New York City, members of some seventy unions marched. An exaggerated headline in the New York *World* on May 2, 1890, proclaimed, "PARADE OF JUBILANT WORKINGMEN IN ALL THE TRADE CENTERS OF THE CIVILIZED WORLD. EVERYWHERE THE WORKMEN JOIN IN

DEMANDS FOR NORMAL DAY." Nonetheless, Labor's Emancipation Day was observed in numerous European cities—London, Paris, Madrid, Barcelona, Valencia, Seville, Lisbon, Copenhagen, Brussels, Budapest, Berlin, Prague, Turin, Geneva, Lugano, Warsaw, Vienna, Marseille, Reims, Amsterdam, Stockholm, Helsinki—as well as in Cuba, Peru, and Chile. In subsequent years, celebrations of labor continued internationally on May Day. Speaking in 1891, perhaps wishfully, at a time early in the process of the holiday's invention, Samuel Gompers said, "May 1st of each year is now looked upon by the organized wage-workers and the observing public as a sort of new Independence Day upon which they will every year strike a blow for emancipation and steadily weaken the shackles of wage slavery."[49]

Initially in the United States as elsewhere, May Day demonstrations grew larger and more enthusiastic. But the internationalization of the holiday, and its association with socialist and communist radicalism, rendered it suspect to many Americans. As the American Labor Day in September achieved a measure of popular legitimacy, its promoters increasingly sought to cleave more closely to acceptable symbolic forms of American nationalism and patriotism; wrapping the day in the American flag, leaders purged parades and rallies of red flags, foreign songs and slogans, and radical messages. May Day more baldly represented international class struggle, offering an alternative to the blander, more exclusively male and white, more nativist, but more American, Labor Day. At the founding convention of the radical International Workers of the World in 1905, the Wobblies resolved to adopt May Day—not the first Monday in September—as their Labor Day. Yet May Day was increasingly marginalized in the United States' public calendar as a day associated with the "European type," with "wild-eyed agitators," with "radicals, mostly socialists and anarchists," in contrast to Labor Day's "honest American workingmen," "sober, clean, quiet," "well-clothed and well-appearing men." The *New York Times*, in a typical description of May Day participants in 1901, observed, "Some few among the several thousand, unlike a meeting on Labor Day, seemed to be American-born, but accents and foreign mannerisms predominating." The *Ladies Garment Worker* commented in 1913, "From an International Holiday it has become quite a Jewish holiday, for with the exception of a few hundred stranded Italians, the gentiles in these demonstrations were conspicuous by their absence." After Labor Day's erection as a national holiday in 1894, May Day was increasingly construed as an un-American, class holiday, unlike the first Monday in September, which celebrated American labor and the nobility of work. By 1901, the AFL itself had abandoned May Day strikes and soon disowned the holiday altogether.[50]

Despite the events of the First World War and the Red Scare led by U.S. Attorney General A. Mitchell Palmer, and government repression of radical activity generally, celebrations of May Day continued in the United States. Organizers even attempted to redeem the day, presenting it as a festival "made in America"; a poem by Henry George Weiss, published in the *Daily Worker* in 1929, extolled:

> May Day!
> Labor's Day!
> Our day!
> Made in America!
> As American as the Fourth of July
> And the Declaration of Independence.
> Turned out of the crucible
> Of the suffering
> Of working men and women. . . .
> Bolshevik Russia didn't give May Day to the American working class,
> But the American working class gave May Day to the revolutionary
> workers of the world—
> Gave the world May Day.[51]

But it was an uphill battle to overcome the antagonism directed against May Day, which remained an occasion tainted red, and in the Cold War years better remembered (and disdained) for massive parades in Moscow's Red Square than for patriotic labor demonstrations in American city squares. Indeed, in 1947, membership in the New York United May Day Committee could subject one to loyalty investigations by the Justice Department. As early as the 1920s, conservatives attempted to counteract radical May Day observances by sponsoring patriotic days, an effort supported even by Samuel Gompers in 1923. In 1928, Congress resolved to create a Child Health Day for May 1. In endorsing the proposal, the AFL Executive Council commended its "worthy purpose" and observed, "May 1 will no longer be known as either strike day or Communist Day." In the 1930s, the Veterans of Foreign Wars similarly challenged the claims of leftists and radical labor activists to May Day and sought to counteract their messages by creating a new Loyalty Day. By 1949, forty-nine state and territorial governors had issued proclamations urging observance of Loyalty Day on May 1, and in 1955 President Dwight D. Eisenhower made Loyalty Day a national observance.[52]

If the radicalism of May Day frightened some Americans, the relative conservatism and self-conscious performances of loyalty of American Labor Day helped make the fete more acceptable to most Americans. Nonetheless, labor leaders continue to struggle with the dilemma that faced them from the start:

cultivating popular appeal came at the expense of more militant efforts to build solidarity and pursue the particular goals of improving wages, working conditions, and hours for working people. Moreover, if May Day proved much more suspect as an invented tradition—one supposedly originating among foreign radicals and imperiling American democracy—so did the less dangerous American Labor Day, which similarly lacked a sacred birth. Persistent efforts by labor activists to appropriate the Fourth of July—the most sacred of American holidays—suggest the continuing need to present labor's cause as consistent with America's founding principles and worthy of general support.

The AFL's Samuel Gompers and other labor leaders faced an additional problem: how to coax the rank and file to turn out for their Labor Day events. The advent of new leisure opportunities within the burgeoning mass culture of twentieth-century America offered alternatives to union parades and picnics. And as the day won popular recognition, athletic events, popular amusements, and excursions to parks, beaches, or other pleasure grounds enticed Americans generally, including working-class people, diverting them from organized labor observances. Gompers worried in 1914 that Labor Day would "lose its distinctive character and become a mere holiday for general meaningless purposes, and for the exploitation of private profit." His concerns were well-founded. Yet as historians Michael Kazin and Steven J. Ross have argued, who could blame workers? "Labor Day was not just an occasion to demonstrate their power; it was part of the larger struggle for a shorter workday and workweek." With the successes of organized labor—which included a considerable growth in union membership, increased wages from most union members, and a reduction in working hours—working people hoped to enjoy the fruits of their labors. Reluctance to march on Labor Day, when fishing, the barbeque, or shopping bargains beckoned, did not necessarily represent a diminished commitment to the labor movement; instead it suggested working people's success and confidence. Moreover, during times of crisis in the labor movement—as in the 1930s—and at moments of national emergency—as in the Second World War—Labor Day could be revived as an important political occasion for organized labor, an opportunity to define itself, to promote its interests, or to demonstrate its power and the magnitude of its contribution to American life. In less intense moments, organizers of union Labor Day programs sometimes attempted to compete directly for elusive participants and audiences by employing new forms of entertainment and spectacle themselves, but generally such efforts did little to educate the public, build working-class solidarity, or reverse the trend toward Labor Day as a generic, apolitical, leisure-filled three-day weekend, a last fling of summertime fun—St. Monday triumphant.[53]

NATIONAL HOLIDAYS. 61

hristmas as was made above in regard to Thanks-
iving, only in reversed order, since though Christ-
nas was prior to 1861 the greatest holiday in the
South, it was a very small one in the East and
Vest, and almost none at all in the New England
States. To-day, however, it everywhere prevails
n the Union, a fact borne witness to by the shopping done considerably ahead of time wherever
here is a shop with anything to sell. In the
South, as of yore, Christmas continues to flour-
sh, accompanied by free "eggnog," the dispens-
ng of gifts, the play of fireworks in towns and

Fig. 53. Labor Day parade (ca. 1887), from *Frank Leslie's Popular Monthly,* January 1892. Courtesy of Knight Library, University of Oregon.

In 1994, northeastern New Jersey celebrated the hundredth anniversary of Labor Day, with events, including a parade, centered on the American Labor Museum in Haledon. Here we see a patina of heritage covering the now traditional occasion, legitimating it as historical—that is, as a festival harkening back to olden times rather than one carrying a contemporary political message. The events mixed nostalgia with historical memory. In this New Jersey celebration, we can also observe the use of a national celebration to cultivate local pride, through recognition of the "founders" of Labor Day—Peter McGuire and Matthew Maguire—who were native sons, and in the selection of the parade's grand marshal—David Welsh, ninety-one, the son of a 1913 Paterson silk mill striker. In Haledon, Labor Day proved important in part simply because it was old but also because its antiquity helped to define the local community, both as Americans and as proud denizens of New Jersey. It is unlikely that the meaning Haledon found in Labor Day is transferable, even within northern or central New Jersey—the *New York Times*'s "New Jersey Guide" on the Saturday preceding Labor Day 1994, for example, noted that "The New Jersey State Sheepdog Trial" in Morris Township "is becoming a Labor Day weekend tradition." So much for historical tradition. Nonetheless, at least in one American community in the mid-1990s, Labor Day was more than a mere St. Monday. Its observance in Haledon suggests that Labor Day—its political power dormant—can at times function like other great American public holidays, connecting citizens to a collective past, allowing them to define themselves locally as Americans.

Americans know that summer officially begins on the weekend of the third Monday in May and ends on the first Monday in September. On Memorial Day, children anticipate their summer vacations and then, on Labor Day, bemoan their return to school, whereas parents make plans for summertime holidays and then, in September, celebrate the resumption of the school year. Although Memorial Day and Labor Day continue to hold real meaning on their own terms for some Americans, for most they define something else rather than call attention to themselves. These red-letter days are margins rather than centers of festive culture in the United States; they are bookends rather than books, embracing in fairly transparent fashion the tomes of summertime. We find it marginally reassuring that Memorial Day and Labor Day have some essential meanings (or at least we like to believe they do), which historians, journalists, and special constituencies announce and celebrate, often by decrying our lack of memory and appropriate commemorative reverence. But if meaning is made more popularly by the mass public—if holidays, like other cultural artifacts, mean what we take them to mean, not merely what their creators and promoters had in mind—then these two St. Mondays are (also) authentic celebrations of American abundance, material consumption, and leisure. Like all holy days, these too are not always honored devoutly: some Americans do not share in the country's wealth; some are unable to consume frivolously or even buy all that they need, let alone what they are supposed to want; and some have too little leisure, being forced to work on holidays, or too much, lacking jobs altogether. Nonetheless, Memorial Day and Labor Day stand as monuments to the success of the United States economy, and we treat these monuments as we treat most others—that is, we seldom pause to consider their prescribed meanings.[54] With a focus on relatively mindless, apolitical leisure, America's Labor Day is an appropriately ironic class holiday for America's supposedly classless society, and Memorial Day an appropriately ironic feast for a people not known for their historical consciousness or memory.

★ ★

CHAPTER 6

Martin Luther King Jr.'s Birthday

Inventing an American Tradition

King's image has often suffered a sad fate. His strengths have been needlessly exaggerated, his weaknesses wildly overplayed. King's true legacy has been lost to cultural amnesia. . . . The King we prefer [to remember] is easily absorbed into fast-food ads for his birthday celebration.

> Michael Eric Dyson, *I May Not Get There with You:*
> *The True Martin Luther King Jr.* (2000)

WHEN THE African American civil rights activist Muriel S. Snowden addressed a Martin Luther King Jr. Day audience at the Massachusetts Institute of Technology in January 1977, she revealed to them "a kind of bitter joke" she shared with her husband. In preparation for his march from Selma to Montgomery, Alabama, in 1965, the Rev. Martin Luther King Jr. had traveled north to Boston to raise money and support. Muriel Snowden and her husband, Otto, heard King speak, and Otto subsequently made the trip south to march with King across the bridge at Selma. But Snowden stayed home to participate in another march—the St. Patrick's Day parade in South Boston. What made this choice a joke, and why a bitter one? King's public career, particularly as he took his campaign for racial and economic justice north after his successes in the South, showed the depth and geographic range of racism and discrimination against African Americans and other people of color in the United States. Although a cradle of the American Revolution, in a state that had abolished slavery in the eighteenth century and that had been the hub of antebellum abolitionism, Boston itself in the 1960s was a place of de facto (rather than de jure, or legal) segregation and the locus of intense hostility and violence directed toward blacks. In 1965, the Massachusetts legislature passed a law that required districts to desegregate schools in which more than half of the students were black, yet eight years later some 85 percent of Boston's African American children attended schools with black majorities, often overwhelming ones. To combat this failure to desegregate, a federal judge in 1974 ordered that integration of Boston's schools be achieved through busing, the controversial tactic of using school buses to redistribute school children in a way that realized racially balanced school populations. Boston erupted in anger, protest, and violence. In heavily Irish American South Boston, a white boycott reduced first-day attendance rolls at a high school from an expected fifteen hundred to less than one hundred students, and enraged whites stoned the procession of yellow buses carrying young blacks to formerly all-white schools. In January 1977, Muriel Snowden's memories of these events were fresh. Her march in an earlier South Boston St. Patrick's Day parade had been no mere stroll in the park. Instead, it had been a challenge, a provocation even, performed in the interest of fighting racism and racial discrimination. Its potential for producing a violent reaction—despite her own commitment to nonviolence—was considerable, if not on a par with that seen in Selma. The joke was not only on the Snowdens but on America itself.[1]

St. Patrick's Day, of course, is more an ethnic and political holiday than a religious holy day in the United States. Like Columbus Day, which began as a celebration of Catholic Americans, including those ethnically Irish, and became an occasion that publicly recognized the legitimacy of Italian Americans and their double status in the United States, St. Patrick's Day allowed Irish Americans to celebrate themselves and their achievements as Americans, to cultivate ethnic pride and solidarity, and to command public respect. African Americans, unlike the Irish, Italians, or Norwegians (who trumped Columbus as "discoverer" of America with their own Leif Eriksson), had no broadly recognized patron saint of their own (Abraham Lincoln was the Great Emancipator, but he was not black) and no publicly sanctioned holiday. As we have seen, blacks—like other Americans—had advanced their claims on the Fourth of July and celebrated other particular African American holidays, such as Juneteenth and Emancipation Day, but they lacked a Columbus or St. Patrick's Day, occasions when they could perform their doubleness—as both African Americans and Americans—publicly, without contradiction, and when others, nonblacks, marched in African American parades. By the second half of the twentieth century, as numerous scholars have shown, the Irish had "become white"—that is, they had overcome earlier racist distinctions and discrimination, and achieved sufficient social and political power to become invisible within the white, American mainstream, except when they chose to call attention to their ethnicity. Ironically, then, Muriel Snowden was an interloper, not merely in a local, Irish American event but in an American institution.[2]

When Snowden addressed her audience in January 1977 at MIT in Cambridge, Massachusetts, less than a decade after King's assassination, the event she marked remained local and particular. Yet ironically, within less than another decade, King's birthday achieved the status of a national public holiday; indeed it became a St. Monday, a moveable feast culminating a three-day weekend observed in the middle of each January. Does such status confer on the day the legitimacy, the moral authority, and the popular appeal of such events as Presidents' Day, Memorial Day, or Labor Day? Keepers of King's memory fear such "success." Indeed, one might ask, does such federal holiday status, even as it institutionalizes the day, actually diminish it, orchestrating leisure and historical amnesia rather than memory, civic education, reverence, and social action?

A key to the power of special occasions such as Columbus Day or Labor Day is their dual function and legitimacy—as particular fetes for particular groups (defined ethnically, politically, or socially) and as general American festivals, appropriate for and commanding attention and respect among a majority of citizens. A monument to African American achievement and to the modern civil rights movement generally, one that celebrated a great *American* hero, emerged, then, in the creation of an annual national holiday honoring Martin Luther King Jr. on his natal day, beginning in 1986. But what is the meaning— and what will be the ultimate fate—of that new red-letter day? Although all traditions must originate in particular times and places, however obscure, as E. J. Hobsbawm has argued, traditions derive their legitimacy and sanctity in part from their apparent timelessness.[3] Yet Martin Luther King Jr.'s birthday, an invented tradition erected conspicuously so recently, in the penultimate decade of the twentieth century, lacks that patina of antiquity. The holiday's youth and historical transparency—in addition to its focus on the most troubling dilemma in United States history, the conflict between American ideals of equality and the endurance of discrimination and inequality, based particularly on race—thus make it a telling case study in our efforts to understand the creation of the American public calendar, the public negotiation of identity and historical memory in the United States, and the historical challenges of pluralism in America—especially strains between the particularism of diverse Americans and the claims of a more universal American nationalism.

Inventing Martin Luther King Jr. Day

Within four days of Martin Luther King Jr.'s assassination on April 4, 1968, outside the Lorraine Motel in Memphis, Tennessee, U.S. Representative John Conyers Jr. introduced legislation seeking to make King's birthday a federal holiday. The bill failed initially to garner the necessary support, but within fifteen years both houses of Congress endorsed the proposal, and a skeptical President Ronald Reagan signed it into law on November 3, 1983. Just over two years later, on the third Monday in January—January 20, 1986—the United

States celebrated the birthday of Martin Luther King Jr. for the first time as a national holiday. If promoters of the observance felt frustration over delays in achieving their objective, historians can only be struck by the velocity of this development.⁴ But then King's public career—lasting a mere thirteen years—was itself a whirlwind, as was its impact on American life. At the time of his death, King—only thirty-nine years old—was world famous, the recipient of the 1964 Nobel Prize for Peace. Yet he was nonetheless at the ebb of his popularity, as he moved from the "glory years" of the civil rights struggle in the South in the early 1960s to tackle the even more obstinate problems of racial and economic inequality in the North as well as the South and to become an outspoken critic of the United States' involvement in Vietnam. In 1967, King failed to

Fig. 54. Dr. Martin Luther King Jr. at a press conference at the Capitol, Washington, D.C., March 26, 1964. Photograph by Marion S. Trikosko. Library of Congress, Prints and Photographs Division, LC-U9–11696. Reproduced from the Collections of the Library of Congress.

make a Gallup poll list of the ten most popular Americans. Yet by 1986, as reflected in the *New York Time*'s January 15 editorial, King was conventionally placed in an American holy trinity with America's two loftiest heroes: "If George Washington symbolizes the creation of the Union and Abraham Lincoln its preservation, Martin Luther King symbolizes the continuing effort to confer its benefits on every citizen."⁵

Like King's life, his public holiday emerged amid controversy and continues to evolve in surprising and unpredictable ways. Conyers's bill encountered opposition, from Representative Larry P. McDonald of Georgia, for example, who declared that King was "not the caliber of person suitable to be made into a national hero." The arguments of McDonald and other detractors aside, the

Georgia congressman assumed too much in his suggestion that a national hero can be "made" by any legislative or executive action. In fact, heroes and holidays are not simply erected by government or business but are produced in untidy cooperation with a mass public, which influences officials and then revises their acts through the improvisations of life. The meaning of Martin Luther King Jr. Day, in other words, is not merely what its inventors prescribe but what the American public has and will make of it.

America's immediate reaction to King's assassination was despair, fear, anger, and violence. The militant leader of the Student Nonviolent Coordinating Committee, Stokely Carmichael, who had called for Black Power in a 1966 rally in Mississippi and had lost patience with King's more moderate, integrationist tactics, concluded, "When white America killed Dr. King, she declared war on us." Riots erupted in more than a hundred cities across the country. In Chicago, with some twenty blocks on the West Side in flames, Mayor Richard J. Daley ordered police officers to shoot to kill arsonists. In Washington, D.C., President Lyndon Baines Johnson proclaimed a day of national mourning, while U.S. Army troops set up to defend the Capitol and White House with machine guns. Some 24 people died in riots in the District of Columbia, with 46 deaths reported nationally; within a week, 27,000 people nationwide, mostly African Americans, had been arrested. These 1968 riots capped a series of urban insurrections that had begun in the summer of 1964, in Harlem, Rochester, New York, and Philadelphia, continuing in the August 1965 rebellion in the Watts section of Los Angeles (leaving some 34 dead and 900 injured), in the 1966 riots in San Francisco, Milwaukee, Chicago, Dayton, and Cleveland, and in the July 1967 uprisings in Newark (incurring some 25 African American deaths) and Detroit (costing 43 deaths, more than 1,000 wounded, and nearly 17,000 arrests).[6]

Such violence defied Martin Luther King's gospel of nonviolent social change. The shock and turmoil of King's terrible death, as well as the tumult of the 1968 national election and the unruly debates over the United States' involvement in the Vietnam War, were conflagrations that eventually burned themselves out. As they did so, Martin Luther King in death—as a symbol and inspiration—became part of a hoped-for solution, a means of restoring peace through justice and reform. As historian Harvard Sitkoff concluded, "the loss of Martin Luther King Jr. robbed the nation of its last best hope for fundamental change, without violence, without hatred." Yet some hoped the designation of a day to honor his memory, to remember his public life, and to promote his message would advance this goal by claiming a place in the calendar where Americans might suspend normal activities, reflect, and focus attention on America's continuing struggle to achieve equality. If no other living African

American leader could "keep hope alive, could galvanize the struggle, could inspire dreams," then perhaps a deceased King still could.[7]

Memorial events on January 15 emerged spontaneously and without official sanction, even as elected officials in Washington, D.C., and states throughout the country pushed for government recognition of King's birthday. In the immediate aftermath of King's assassination, some black employees unilaterally took the day off, and motorists drove with their headlights on as an act of remembrance. Black autoworkers in Detroit told Congressman Conyers, regarding January 15, that "[even] if it is not in the bargaining contract, one does not come to work anyway. It is a holiday already." As early as January 15, 1969, many schools with large black enrollments closed or stayed in session for only half the day; among schools that remained open, assemblies often honored King with special programs, speeches, and moments of silence. School absenteeism marked January 15 in the days before official recognition of the holiday; at Boys' High School in Brooklyn, New York, 80 percent of its twenty-six hundred students failed to appear on King's birthday in 1969. At Long Beach, New York, in the same year, students skipped school to attend a service at a youth center—only about seventy of the nearly three hundred participating had their parents' permission—and black students in Washington, D.C., boycotted schools that failed to close in honor of King. According to Cornelius Williams, student body president at Federal City College in the District of Columbia, "We have declared classes suspended today in honor of a great man. We have not waited for someone else to declare this a national holiday. We must establish our own heroes and holidays of our own."[8]

African Americans mobilized to do just that. In 1971, the Southern Christian Leadership Conference (SCLC)—the group Martin Luther King had helped found in 1957—delivered a petition to Congress containing three million signatures calling for a King holiday. While locally January 15 events continued to take place, ebbing and flowing according to the energies of Americans dispersed in various communities nationwide, several states sanctified the day, beginning with Illinois in 1973, Massachusetts and Connecticut in 1974, and New Jersey in 1975. Led by black members, labor unions—beginning with the American Federation of State, County and Municipal Employees (AFSCME)—recognized King's birthday and encouraged locals with some success to negotiate contracts designating the day as a paid holiday. At colleges and universities throughout the United States, teach-ins and other programs commemorated King's birthday, often becoming institutionalized in annual observances like those at the Massachusetts Institute of Technology, which began in 1975 and continue today. From 1978 to 1982, African Americans from across the country traveled to Washington to commemorate Martin Luther King's birthday, and in marches to the Lincoln Memorial and speeches delivered there they appealed for the creation of a national day of observance. In 1979, President Jimmy Carter lobbied Congress to pass a King holiday bill, but the legislation met defeat in the House later that year.[9]

Lobbying continued, led by the Martin Luther King Jr. Center for Nonviolent Social Change, founded in 1968 by King's widow Coretta Scott King to carry on her late husband's work. The pop-music artist Stevie Wonder supported these efforts with the release in 1980 of his song "Happy Birthday," dedicated to King's memory. That year, a King holiday bill failed to pass the U.S. House of Representatives by a mere five votes. In 1982, the King Center gathered more than six million signatures on a petition again calling for the creation of a federal holiday honoring Martin Luther King, and soon thereafter the House complied, voting overwhelming in favor of the legislation. A year later, in October, the Senate followed suit, and President Reagan signed the bill on November 3, 1983.[10]

With some notable exceptions, those states that had yet to create a day honoring King quickly followed the federal government's lead. By 1990, only Arizona, Montana, and New Hampshire had yet to mandate the holiday in some form; by 1995, in only the ninth year as an official national event, the holiday was observed at least in some fashion on the third Monday in January by all fifty states and four territories. Yet the rapid success of the new American holiday was neither easy nor complete. Reluctant states offered various explanations of their reticence to create a specific day recognizing Martin Luther King. These reservations fell into two rough categories: those concerning the holiday's economic impact and those assessing the relative worthiness of King the hero (both could work together as well). Although it simmered as subtext, the issue of race virtually never surfaced in the statements provided by King holiday antagonists as they justified their opposition. Proponents, on the other hand, frequently interpreted such opposition as racially motivated. The economic objection usually accepted, for the sake of argument, King's worthiness but countered that the economic impact of another paid holiday, for whatever noble purpose, was simply too costly to absorb. The objection to King as a worthy hero, in its most benign form, credited King for his contributions to the struggle for civil rights but suggested that he failed to merit his own official day relative to scores of other deserving champions not similarly honored. In more caustic critiques, King's contributions were obliterated by his alleged shortcomings—particularly the charges of plagiarism and philandering—which rendered him an inappropriate idol.

In some states (Kentucky and North Dakota, for example), King's birthday was recognized but not as a paid holiday. New Hampshire created a state Civil

Rights Day for the third Monday in January, self-consciously avoiding recognition of Martin Luther King Jr. A 1997 bill to add King's name to the annual event failed in the New Hampshire House of Representatives by a 177–178 margin, after it had passed the state senate. After the defeat, and a vote to prevent reconsideration until 1999, Representative Jane Kelley observed in disappointment, "New Hampshire will stand as a beacon light for bigotry." Utah similarly refused to recognize King by name, celebrating instead Human Rights Day beginning 1986, until Utah governor Mike Leavitt signed a bill in 2000 renaming the January holiday. By the century's end, South Carolina was the only state without an official celebration of Martin Luther King's birthday. The state permitted its employees the option of taking off either the day of the federal holiday or one of three Confederate holidays spread throughout the year. On Monday, January 17, 2000, South Carolina state offices remained open, and later that year legislation designed to create, explicitly, a Martin Luther King Day in South Carolina was amended in the House of Representatives to remove King's name and instead designate the occasion Civil Rights Day.[11]

Until the South Carolina controversy—enveloped in a battle to remove or defend the Confederate battle flag flying over the statehouse—the most conspicuous conflict over the King holiday occurred in Arizona. Attempts to erect a state Martin Luther King birthday commemoration began as early as 1972, but a Senate bill to sponsor such an event never emerged from committee. Efforts continued unsuccessfully, and in 1986 a House bill—which added a Martin Luther King holiday while combining the state observances of Washington's and Lincoln's Birthday into an Arizona Presidents' Day—failed by a single vote. Governor Bruce Babbitt then took matters into his own hands, issuing an executive order creating a paid holiday honoring King. But in 1987, Evan Mecham succeeded Babbitt as Arizona's governor, and he quickly rescinded the executive order, revoking the holiday. Instead, he offered the state a Civil Rights Day, which Arizonans would observe annually on a Sunday. Governor Mecham's actions ignited an uproar, both in Arizona and among supporters of the King holiday nationally. In 1990, Arizona citizens placed two initiatives on the ballot to restore Martin Luther King Day. But both met defeat—the more popular Proposition 302 attracting 49 percent of the vote—and Arizona remained polarized. Meanwhile, Arizona became the focus of intense scrutiny and economic pressure, as boycotts organized against its tourist attractions and convention facilities expressed national displeasure with the state's actions. Most devastating was the National Football League's disqualification of Phoenix as a site for the 1993 Super Bowl, denying the city an estimated $200 million in revenue. In the face of debilitating boycotts and uncomfortable with the reputation they had acquired during the controversy,

Arizona citizens easily passed Proposition 300 in November 1992, creating an Arizona Martin Luther King Day. Ironically, although among the last states to adopt the holiday, Arizona became the only one to do so through a popular referendum, one that ultimately expressed broad support for the commemoration across races and ethnicities (Arizona's population is only 3 percent African American).[12]

Widespread celebration of Martin Luther King Day by federal, state, and local governments today does not necessarily ensure either the permanence or importance of the holiday in American social and political life. Private employers—particularly those whose employees are not members of labor unions—have been much slower in recognizing the occasion. In 1994, only some 22 percent of businesses surveyed by the Bureau of National Affairs gave employees a paid holiday on King's birthday; a 1990 survey of Fortune 500 companies found that only 18 percent offered their employees the day off. Some criticized Hollywood in 1993 for failing to honor the day, despite its supposed liberalism and expressed concern for the plight of inner-city residents in the year following the riots that had rocked nearby South Central Los Angeles. At least three major film studios—Disney, Universal, and Fox—did not recognize King's birthday. According to a spokesman for MCA, Universal's parent company, "This corporation has made the decision that Martin Luther King Day is not a holiday." On the other hand, observance of King's birthday may be increasing in the private as well as the public sector. The Martin Luther King Jr. Federal Holiday Commission, established by Congress in 1984 to promote the commemoration, found that participation increased from 23 percent in 1991 to 31 percent in 1993, for example. If such figures lag well behind those for Christmas, New Year's, Thanksgiving, Independence Day, Memorial Day, and Labor Day—which are paid holidays for nearly all workers (that is, those employed by some 99 percent of American businesses)—they compare favorably with the figures for Presidents' Day (45 percent in 1985) and Veterans Day (20 percent). Nonetheless, the holiday remains a work in progress, and only time will tell if and how Martin Luther King Day will become woven into the fabric of American life in the twenty-first century.[13]

The Meaning of St. Martin's Day

Disagreement over the holiday's rightful name, its proper means of celebration, and even the legitimacy of its claim to a place in the United States' public calendar all reflect an ambiguity or indeterminacy in the commemoration's meaning, as various Americans contest or collaborate in the invention of Martin Luther King Jr. Day. Is the holiday a forum for the expression of black pride and an occasion to recognize specifically the historical contributions of African Americans to the nation, as suggested in Prof. Hubert E. Jones's remarks to an MIT audience in 1975?[14] Is it, on the other hand, a day for all Americans to embrace King as their hero, celebrate his accomplishments simply as an American, and follow his prescriptions for the nation? Is Martin Luther King Day a time for education, inspiration, and reflection; should King be remembered for his dreams? Or is the holiday a call to action, a time for deeds—political activism or community service—over words? Is King primarily a symbol of racial integration, nonviolent social change, the fight for economic equality, resistance to the economic and human cost of militarism; is King an emblem of moderation and reform, or of radicalism and revolution? Is he a convenient or unsettling hero? Does Martin Luther King Day—or April 4, the day of his assassination—commemorate more than a mere political figure or mortal champion; is it as much holy day as holiday, dedicated to "St. Martin"? Or should Americans see the occasion as an opportunity to embrace a fully human hero, a great man despite—or even because of—his flaws? Or, finally, is King's birthday an opportunity to dispute his worthiness, challenge his status as hero, or revise the historical meaning of his life and the struggle for equality and justice, which he helped to lead?

The short historical record dictates that we answer yes to all these questions. Although tethered to a particular historical figure whose real life history constrains the range of potential meanings that might be assigned to his work and legacy, Martin Luther King Day, like all American holidays, is nonetheless a protean public festival, particularly because the holiday is young and the issues it raises are old and ongoing—racism, inequality, poverty, violence. King's birthday, as a complex public event celebrated variably across the country, expresses contradictory messages; whereas some of these contradictions may be resolved over time, others no doubt will linger, both because people often do not think and act with perfect consistency and because Americans continue to disagree politically and express those differences in the arena provided by the public calendar, on Martin Luther King Day as on other holidays.

King's birthday is thus an official commemoration in which African Americans celebrate themselves, build solidarity, and steel themselves for continuing battles against discrimination. In this sense, it builds on earlier commemorative occasions adopted by blacks—such as emancipation days—and parallels some of the goals of another recently invented African American fete, Kwanzaa. Coming out of the same struggle for freedom, civil rights, distinctive identity, and self-worth in the 1960s, Kwanzaa was the creation of Dr. Maulana Ron Karenga in 1966—a spiritual but nondenominational, family-based festival for African American people celebrated from December 26 to January 1. Kwanzaa rejects commercialization, particularly "the cultural and economic exploitation perpetrated against us during the months of October, November, and December (the Christmas season)." According to the Kwanzaa Information Center's website, "Kwanzaa seeks to enforce a connectedness to African cultural identity, provide a focal point for the gathering of African peoples, and to reflect upon the Nguzo Saba, or seven principles, that have sustained Africans." Through elaborate rites staged over seven days, and then lived "as a way of life for Black Americans," Kwanzaa is designed to strengthen collective identity, honor a common past, and critically evaluate the present, committing celebrants "to a fuller, more productive future." Kwanzaa's African American nationalist objective is thus congruent with one of the King holiday's purposes—to cultivate black pride and solidarity—but its particular ethnic or racial constituency makes its task easier. Unlike Martin Luther King's birthday, Kwanzaa neither seeks nor requires official endorsement; it need not be all things to all people. Indeed, it continues to exist in part because the King holiday cannot be an exclusively African American fete. As the Kwanzaa Information Center observed in 2001, fifteen years after Martin Luther King's birthday had become a federal holiday, "African-Americans did not observe a holiday that was specific to our needs. A review of the major holidays celebrated in the United States would reveal that not one related specifically to the growth and development of African-Americans."[15]

Martin Luther King's birthday is an African American festival, one that does express something vital about the growth and development of black people in the United States, but it is also an ecumenical, multicultural holiday, one that uses the exemplary public life of King to teach larger truths about America to all Americans. Are these two purposes of the festival at odds with each other? In 1986, Charles Stoudamire, executive director of the Oregon Commission on Black Affairs, expressed concern that King's birthday celebrations focused primarily on the black community. "I think what this man stood for transcends any individual event or group of people—his teaching and philosophy applies to everybody," Stoudamire observed. "I'd like to see the way we celebrate the holiday reflect that." Such sentiments accorded with a chief goal of the King Federal Holiday Commission, according to Alan Minton, its chief of staff, "to make sure it's an American holiday, not just an African-American holiday." And organizers have often worried that audiences at King commemorative events lacked diversity. A review of MIT's January 15 programs in 1989 concluded, "Our . . . Memorials should both celebrate Martin Luther King and African Americanism while also engaging white Americans with subject matter of substance and impact. Our events of the past fifteen years have, in fact, accomplished the former, but by-and-large have not achieved the latter."[16]

In a sense, Martin Luther King Day embodies the dilemma and possibility outlined brilliantly by W. E. B. Du Bois in *The Souls of Black Folk* (1903), which spoke of the "double-consciousness" of African Americans: "One ever feels his two-ness,—an American, a Negro; two souls, two thoughts, two unreconciled strivings; two warring ideals in one dark body, whose dogged strength alone keeps if from being torn asunder." Writing in the gendered language of his day, Du Bois argued that black Americans have struggled to merge these selves in a way that preserves them both: "He would not Africanize America," nor would he "bleach his Negro soul in a flood of white Americanism. . . . He simply wishes to make it possible for a man to be both a Negro and an American, without being cursed and spit upon by his fellows, without having the doors of Opportunity closed roughly in his face." As "co-worker[s] in the kingdom of culture," African Americans husband their "best powers" and "latent genius," and they bear essential gifts for American civilization. Du Bois asked, "Would America have been America without her Negro people?" In this spirit, on King's birthday in 1975, Hubert E. Jones told his audience, "We must rise now to the level of conceiving the black interest as a universal interest. . . . Blackness means expanding and widening the circle, absorbing and integrating instead of being absorbed and integrated. . . . Blacks must establish moral and cultural authority over the whole." Lewis's solution to the apparent paradox of Martin Luther King Day as both a black holiday and an American holiday built on Du Bois's concept of two-ness: the fete might be both things simultaneously and without contradiction by expressing African American experience as American experience, with African American moral leadership—exemplified by Martin Luther King—redeeming the entire American nation.[17]

It is not surprising that participants at Martin Luther King Day programs are often disproportionately black, given the significance of King as the sole African American hero celebrated prominently and officially by the United States. In their 1998 study of the popular uses of history in American life, historians Roy Rosenzweig and David Thelen found, in addition, that African Americans generally possessed greater historical consciousness than did white Americans. The former more frequently identified with historical figures (not simply with those from the histories of their own family)—particularly with Martin Luther King Jr.—and had a stronger sense of a public, American past than did white Americans. Asked to name a person from the past who had affected them, white Americans more often cited a parent than all national historical figures combined, whereas black Americans surveyed more frequently chose Martin Luther King Jr. than any relative. Rosenzweig and Thelen concluded, "white Americans simply do not have a shared, revered public figure comparable to Martin Luther King, Jr."; indeed, no public figures were "powerful living presences" within the lives of most whites. Compared with blacks in the United States, white Americans seem more apt to take their heroes for granted and less likely perhaps to consider them in terms of race. Such tendencies—reflecting perhaps the privileges of whiteness, the luxury of racial unselfconsciousness—help account for the poorer relative attendance of whites at King commemorative ceremonies. Even a holiday as old as Independence Day—one unmarked by particular racial or ethnic implication—means less to white Americans, who care less about its historical significance than the excuse it provides for a family party, than Martin Luther King Day means to African Americans. If some white Americans eschew King festivities out of their own bigotry, most who fail to attend express political apathy, not antipathy. Such disinterest keeps white Americans away from similar public functions—Columbus Day parades, Labor Day marches, or Fourth of July speeches (although not fireworks)—as they choose self-indulgent leisure over historical and political engagement.[18]

The establishment of King as an American hero and the designation of the third Monday in January as a red-letter day were a cause for celebration among African Americans, but they also produced some consternation within the black community. Talmadge Anderson, editor of the *Western Journal of Black Studies,* saw the King holiday as a form of tokenism, "a minor concession by whites." "Blacks have been given one hero, Martin Luther King," he told the *New York Times* in a 1986 interview. "It is as if the rest of the civil rights leaders, the others who were more radical and may have done more to push the cause of civil rights, have been shut out." Anderson and others feared that remembering King might allow the public to forget other black heroes. Others became suspicious of the very acceptance of King that a federal holiday signified. For some in African American circles, mainstream endorsement almost by definition undermined King's status as a champion of black resistance. Were white motives pure? Was King—or rather, the particular King sanctified in public—too convenient a hero? And a small number of black critics echoed the old charge of Malcolm X (which he later reconsidered) that King was a "twentieth-century Uncle Tom," "the best weapon that the white man has."[19]

Yet if some African Americans remained skeptical, blacks generally expressed annoyance at those who publicly challenged King's status not merely as a black hero but as an American hero. And if King's individual star threatened to eclipse other, less famous black champions, the metamorphosis of Martin Luther King's birthday into a more generic Civil Rights Day, or into a broader and more diffuse celebration of civil rights figures of various races, outraged African Americans afraid that their sacred day might be diluted. In

Arizona in 1994, after Martin Luther King Day had been created by state referendum just two years earlier, the festival's popular, multicultural approach
troubled some black Arizonans, who preferred not to share the spotlight. One
community activist called Phoenix's efforts to honor the late Cesar Chavez,
founder of the United Farm Workers, along with King "stupid": it "shows no
respect to the black community." Such sentiments clumsily expressed the
challenge that Martin Luther King day faces as a festival establishing itself
both as an African American and as an American holiday. The event continues,
paradoxically, to cleave the country, in both senses of the word—to divide as
well as to bind Americans.[20]

Martin Luther King Day embodies a certain doubleness in other ways. Promoters and participants are sometimes at odds over its function as an occasion for inspiration or perspiration. Is Martin Luther King Day a time for education, reflection, perhaps revelation? Sounding an old theme in American
discourse, Muriel Snowden argued in her 1977 speech observing King's birthday at MIT that caretakers of King's dream must cultivate education as a
means of opportunity and equality. And she urged listeners to burnish their
collective historical memory. Ignorance about the civil rights struggles, particularly among young blacks, was "unforgivable," she said. "Some of us need to
seek out the facts of our past and our present, tell the story, pass it along, and
hopefully, add our own part to it." Snowden concluded with lines for an old
hymn: "Lord, God of Hosts, be with us yet—lest we forget, lest we forget." On
the first federal observance of King's birthday, the United States secretary of
education, William J. Bennett, visited a third grade class in Atlanta and called
Martin Luther King "one of the greatest teachers who ever lived." Having
asked the children how they planned to celebrate the day, Bennett seemed
most pleased by Ronnica James's answer: "I'm going to keep the dream alive
in my heart." President Ronald Reagan, who initially opposed the holiday, also
emphasized the inspirational side of King's legacy and linked himself to the
civil rights leader in remarks to the Council for a Black Economic Agenda in
1986: "Dr. King believed in the great promise of America and an America in
which all of us can progress as fast and as far as our ability, our vision and our
heart will take us. . . . That is the very promise that I came to Washington to
restore."[21]

But Reagan's words provoked skepticism among black leaders like M. Carl
Holman, president of the National Urban Coalition, who said, "Frankly, it's
easier for a lot of people to honor Martin when he's safely dead and deal with
him as though he were just a visionary, and not a practical and very pragmatic
protester against the status quo." Indeed, a number of African American leaders and their political allies have emphasized action over words on Martin

Luther King Day. The Rev. Jesse Jackson told a Washington, D.C., audience on January 15, 1986, "Dr. Martin Luther King Jr. was not assassinated for dreaming. He was assassinated for acting and challenging the Government. . . . We honor Dr. King most by action for justice. His birthday should be celebrated by action, not just by speeches and songs about action."[22]

If idle words were problematic, so was idleness itself on Martin Luther King Day, according to many holiday promoters. Anthony C. Campbell, senior minister at Eliot Congregational Church in Roxbury, Massachusetts, told his listeners at a King's birthday observance in 1980, "You all act like you are spectators, and I can't let you get away with thinking that this is a show and you are the audience. . . . You are on the stage of history, and God is the audience. I think you better do something, even if it is difficult." As an editorial in the Eugene, Oregon, *Register-Guard* on January 15, 1996, observed, "More than any other holiday on the American calendar, Martin Luther King Jr. Day lends itself poorly to being a day of rest or recreation." In this spirit, on August 23, 1994, President Bill Clinton signed the King Holiday and Service Act, which honored King by proclaiming his birthday holiday as a national day of service. "Nothing could be more appropriate," Clinton declared, "for it was Dr. King who said everyone can be great because everyone can serve." "The King holiday should be a day on, not a day off," urged the bill's chief sponsor, Senator Harris Wofford.[23]

For the Eugene *Register-Guard* editorial writer, dedicating the day to community service would help make the holiday more universal and "less a political football." But others such as Jesse Jackson, while supporting community service (as well as education), were troubled by efforts to depoliticize King: "We must resist this weak and anemic memory of a great man"—as a "nonthreatening 'dreamer' rather than as a 'drum major for justice.'" From this viewpoint, Martin Luther King Day is nothing if not political, a day to engage in public, social action, community service, and political activism. In 1994, New York governor Mario Cuomo made King's birthday a work day for the state assembly, calling on them to consider gun control measures; for Cuomo, no greater tribute could be paid to the memory of King. Elsewhere, particularly since 1994, Americans have used the occasion to organize gun buy-back programs, volunteer at food banks, refurbish schools, clean up trash and plant trees, and engage in other community activities with liberal political agendas. The Baptist minister and scholar Michael Eric Dyson has argued eloquently that Americans must resist whitewashing King or the history of the civil rights movement in the United States, making it seem that racial progress was natural, even unavoidable, and that full equality is an accomplished fact: "We must rebel against the varieties of amnesia that compete to reduce King to an icon for the status quo or a puppet of civil and social order." Dyson echoed Vincent Gordon Harding's characterization of King as "an inconvenient hero": "For those who seek a gentle, non-abrasive hero whose recorded speeches can be used as inspirational resources for rocking our memories to sleep, Martin Luther King Jr. is surely the wrong man."[24] King and his holiday thus function as patron and resource for those on the American political left, as a hero not merely to remember but whose activism should be imitated.

Appearing at a King birthday observance at the Harlem headquarters of the Rev. Al Sharpton on January 17, 2000, Hillary Rodham Clinton affirmed this notion, declaring, "The Bible says, 'Be ye doers of the word, not hearers only.' . . . We should ask all our leaders: 'Are you doers? Will you solve our problems?'" Democrat Rodham Clinton was in the midst of a campaign for the United States Senate; her probable Republican opponent in the race at the time was New York Mayor Rudolph Giuliani (who later withdrew), but Giuliani declined invitations to the larger commemorative events (where he had been booed in the past) attended by Rodham Clinton, concluding that they would be "politically charged." A Giuliani spokesman later commented, "Regrettably, Hillary Clinton did exactly what we expected her to do: politicize the Martin Luther King celebration." Of course, for politicians and activists able to link themselves to King, politicizing was the point.[25]

Yet those populating other parts of the political spectrum have also appropriated King as a useful icon, Mayor Giuliani's inability to do so notwithstanding. President Reagan, as we have seen, managed to link himself to King and his vision during a meeting with conservative black business leaders in 1986, even though he had opposed the Civil Rights Act of 1964, the culmination of King's campaign against segregation. The chairman of the group of black businessmen proclaimed, "We're in a post–civil rights period right now. This does not mean racial discrimination has disappeared. . . . But it's incorrect to apply civil rights to what otherwise are economic problems." The Reagan administration also invoked King's message of nonviolence not as a recommended strategy for civil disobedience during social protest (which it did not seek to encourage) but rather to preach against youth violence, particularly within urban black communities. Ironically—and disturbingly to King's living compatriots—conservatives even cited King's inspirational "I Have a Dream" oration, delivered at the Lincoln Memorial in 1963, to challenge affirmative action. William Bradford Reynolds, assistant attorney general for civil rights in the Justice Department during the Reagan administration, criticized affirmative action policies as violations of King's hope for a color-blind society. Reynolds claimed, "the initial affirmative action message of racial unification—so eloquently delivered by Dr. Martin Luther King, Jr., in his famous

'I Have a Dream' speech—was effectively drowned out by the all too persistent drumbeat of racial polarization that accompanied the affirmative action preferences of the 1970s into the 1980s." Attempting to make a similar point in lighthearted fashion, the political comic strip "Mallard Fillmore," appearing on Martin Luther King Day in 1998, had its duck muse before a caricature of King, "I wonder what would seem more weird to Doctor King . . . that 'affirmative action' ignores 'the content of our character' . . . or that his birthday is always on a Monday." Such selective citation of King's words, of course, obscures other of his statements about affirmative action, for example, his insistence that it "is impossible to create a formula for the future which does not take into account that our society has been doing something special *against* the Negro for hundreds of years." But such manipulation of heroes' words and memories is the stuff of politics and will no doubt continue, particularly as King becomes more firmly established in the American pantheon of heroes. In apparent affirmation of the adage "What's good for the goose is good for the gander," the black conservative and businessman Ward Connerly, who as a University of California regent led the successful effort to dismantle affirmative action in California, officially opened his National Campaign Against Affirmative Action on Martin Luther King Day in 1997.[26]

If politicians like Clinton and Connerly paid homage to different Kings, for some Americans, Martin Luther King Day—or April 4, the day of his assassination, his *dia natalis* (birth in heaven)—celebrates even more than a mere political figure; this holy day reverentially recalls "St. Martin Luther King." According to the Rev. Joseph Lowery, Southern Christian Leadership Conference president in 1988, "To be sure, I'm excited about the holiday, but without the holy day, the holiday could be out of harmony with the honoree." While King lived, followers often cast him as a prophet, as Moses, as an apostle, even as a Christ-like figure, and in his violent death he became a sainted martyr. If King himself assumed the persona of the Apostle Paul in his famous "Letter from the Birmingham Jail" in 1963, and the role of Moses in his final sermon, "I've Been to the Mountaintop" on April 3, 1968, more remarkable is the way disciples made these metaphors their own. As early as 1956, King had been called Alabama's Modern Moses, and crowds conflated him with Christ as well, as when he emerged from the Montgomery, Alabama, courthouse in March 1956 to shouts of "Behold the King!" After his conviction for conspiracy for his role in leading the bus boycott, one Baptist preacher hailed King, "He who was nailed to the cross for us this afternoon approaches." Even rivals resentful of King's acclaim nonetheless recognized this popular deification in their derisive references to King as "De Lawd."[27]

King's assassination on April 4, 1968, occurred just before Palm Sunday; its proximity to Easter, like Abraham Lincoln's assassination in 1865, encouraged some to call King's death a crucifixion and to associate the murdered King with Jesus Christ. At King's funeral, Dr. Benjamin Mays ended his eulogy by imagining words of Christ coming from King's mouth: "Let us pray, as Martin Luther [King] would pray if he could: 'Father forgive them, for they know not what they do.' If we do this, Martin Luther King, Jr. will have died a redemptive campaign for which all mankind will benefit." And such references continued, as when Harry Belafonte sang "Black Prince of Peace" on a television special program marking the first federal Martin Luther King holiday in 1986. More frequently, however, King was revered as martyr and saint, as someone who died for Christ, not as Christ himself. As early as June 23, 1968, the archbishop of New York Terrence Cooke celebrated a mass commemorating St. John the Baptist before thousands of Puerto Ricans, but dominating the altar was a photograph of Martin Luther King, to whom the mass was dedicated. In closing schools in Westchester school district in New York on January 15, 1969, officials declared that King had taken his "place among the martyrs." And in that year on the first anniversary of King's assassination, the Disciples of Christ—not known for its invocation of saints—set aside the day as one of "repentance, reconciliation and action on the urban crisis"; self-consciously, the denomination explained, "recognition of contemporary martyrs is not inconsistent with a meaningful observation of the crucifixion of Christ."[28]

Memorials to King the martyr soon followed, and various Christian denominations enshrined King in their calendars of saints, as in the 1978 *Lutheran Book of Worship*, which included a commemoration on January 15, classified King as a "renewer of society, martyr," and designated red—the traditional color for martyrs—as the liturgical color of the day. If Protestants stopped short of canonization, and if similar efforts by African American Catholics were precluded because King himself was not a member of their church, King nonetheless wears the halo of a saint for devotees. Nowhere has this become more concrete than in London at Westminster Abby, where in 1998 a new life-size statue of King was installed in a niche that had remained empty for five hundred years. One of ten new statues, the King monument, carved in French Richemont limestone, stands along a stone archway some twenty feet above viewers and honors King as a modern-day Christian martyr. Today, worshippers of King need not travel to London or visit United States churches that depict King in stained glass; they can practice their adoration by purchasing a Martin Luther King icon, painted by Robert Lenz and available from a Vermont mail order company. With prison bars as background and a booking number around his neck, a halo adorns King's head, while below a Greek inscription reads "Holy Martin"—St. Martin Luther King." Here King has become, literally, an icon.[29]

In contrast to those who have beatified King or transformed him into a mythic hero, others—Michael Eric Dyson most eloquently—argue that King should be remembered and honored as a fully human, flawed champion: "King was undeniably a great American hero, but he did not become great by denying his mortality. . . . We do not have to make him a saint to appreciate his greatness. Neither should we deny his imperfections as we struggle to remember and reactivate his legacy." According to Dyson, "King's career, with all its flaws and failures, is simply the most faithful measure of American identity and national citizenship as we are likely to witness." Indeed, Dyson argues for a critical analysis of King, warts and all, not only in the interest of historical truth but to make King a more human, embraceable hero for Americans who, like King, themselves embody frailties and face obstacles in their real world.[30]

Martin Luther King's image "has suffered a sad fate," writes Dyson. "His strengths have been needlessly exaggerated, his weaknesses wildly overplayed." Those weaknesses—imagined and alleged as well as real—received considerable attention during King's lifetime, most notably through the efforts of J. Edgar Hoover and the Federal Bureau of Investigation, which kept King under surveillance and conducted a campaign to destroy his reputation. In the years after King's assassination, reassessments of the historical record have documented acts of plagiarism and philandering committed by King. His critics have seized on these transgressions and made numerous other, often wild allegations intended to undermine his heroic status. If King is a saint to some, then to others he is nothing but a sinner, a villain, perhaps the devil himself, and such detractors have used the occasion of Martin Luther King Day to besmirch King's reputation, belittle his legacy, and challenge the policies and programs of his followers.[31]

Opponents of the legislation to make King's birthday a national holiday gave vent to harsh criticism of King and his proposed day in Congress. The Liberty Lobby characterized King as "a man who deliberately brought violence to American streets, a subversive who was called 'the most notorious liar in America' by J. Edgar Hoover." The legislation itself, the lobby's legislative aid E. Stanley Rittenhouse said, was "very one-sided" and "racist." Congressman Larry P. McDonald, another conservative critic, claimed King taught "contempt for the law," and it was therefore "most unsuitable for his anniversary to be made a national holiday." Rittenhouse even charged that King was a communist or communist sympathizer: "The fact is he aided the Communist cause; he abetted it constantly, continuously. Since when does a Nation honor a man who honored its enemy?" A former Communist Party member, Julia Brown, declared before the congressional subcommittee, "If this measure is passed honoring Martin Luther King, we may as well take down the Stars and Stripes that fly over this building and replace it with a Red flag." King supporters successfully refuted each of these charges and managed as well to address the additional criticisms of the holiday proposal as too costly, which opponents raised continually, sometimes sincerely, sometimes as a cover for their lack of sympathy or their disdain for King and the causes he championed. During congressional hearings, Senator Birch Bayh of Indiana asked, "The cost? What are the costs of a national holiday? Perhaps more rightly, what are the costs of not having a holiday? What are the costs of second-class citizenship? What are the costs of a little black boy or a little black girl . . . not having the opportunity to share in a national holiday of some great leader that happens to look like them, to come from the same heritage that they came from?" And Coretta Scott King's response reminded legislators of the long-term economic exploitation of African Americans. Although she did not call for reparations—"No amount of money can compensate for the brutal injustice of slavery in the United States," she said—she inquired, "given the hundreds of years of economic sacrifice and involuntary servitude of American blacks, is it too much to ask that one paid holiday per year be set aside to honor the contributions of a black man who gave his life in an historic struggle for social decency?"[32]

Even after the successful erection of a federal King holiday, opponents continued to contest the day. Nowhere was this more vivid than in Memphis, Tennessee, on Saturday, January 17, 1998, when some fifty members of an Indiana branch of the Ku Klux Klan held a rally at the county courthouse to dispute the legitimacy of Martin Luther King Day. The Klan protest in turn attracted a crowd of at least twelve thousand black and white counterdemonstrators, while Klan speakers mocked King's "I Have a Dream" speech, demanded a return to racial segregation, and demeaned blacks, Jews, Asians, foreigners, and homosexuals. The confrontation eventually erupted in violence, after some fifteen to twenty young African American men, identified by police as gang members, attempted to break through police barricades. Later storefront windows were broken in the melee, including those of black businesses. Tony DeBerry's family's restaurant—Pearl Lee's, named after DeBerry's mother, a civil rights advocate who had marched with King in March 1968, just before his death—lost its front windows. DeBerry told a *New York Times* reporter, "King spoke of nonviolence and blacks uplifting each other. He died for us. In 1968, we didn't have the kind of rights and freedoms to have black-owned businesses in downtown Memphis. . . . The glass can be replaced. But those broken windows are a symbol of a misdirected, angry younger generation. Not only Memphis, but America, is going through a healing process, and I hope this is a wake-up call that we still have a lot of work to do." Another black man in the crowd observed, "A lot of older people . . . were just shaking their heads and saying, 'What a shame.' . . . The Klan accomplished just what they wanted. It is a sad day." In other parts of the city, meanwhile, more peaceful ceremonies took place as part of a series of events called "Memphis Remembers Martin," commemorating the thirtieth anniversary year of King's assassination. If these activities helped compensate for the violence of the Saturday riot, cultivating tolerance and healing in Memphis, the Ku Klux Klan rally nonetheless illustrated the political opportunities created by Martin Luther King Day, ironically and disturbingly, even for hate groups.[33]

More recently, and more peacefully, the King holiday served as a political battleground, a forum to restage symbolically the civil rights struggles of the 1960s, if not the Civil War of the 1860s. Beginning in January 2000, the NAACP imposed a tourism boycott on South Carolina to protest the state's display of the Confederate battle flag from its capitol dome in Columbia. Not only did the NAACP see the flag as an emblem of slavery and thus an affront to African Americans, but its display dated only to 1962—not to the Civil War itself—when it was hoisted as an expression of defiance to the civil rights movement. On January 8, 2000, a week after the NAACP boycott began, and as Martin Luther King's Birthday approached, defenders of the battle flag staged a rally at the statehouse, which attracted some six thousand people. Under hundreds of red Confederate battle flags, marchers paraded six blocks from a cemetery containing Confederate dead along Main Street to the statehouse. The group included troops of Confederate re-enactors outfitted with muskets and bayonets, and some three dozen women clad in Civil War–era costumes and widow's black. Incongruously, among those assembled was a ninety-three-year-old white woman, Alberta Martin, billed as a Confederate widow. If Mrs. Martin's birth some forty-two years after Appomattox (apparently followed by marriage at a young age to an elderly Civil War veteran) suggests to us a rather tenuous connection to a distant, nineteenth-century past, these demonstrators asserted a direct link to that bygone era and a commitment to protect their "southern heritage." In the coded language of popular politics in the South, "heritage" suggested much more than simply dashing gray uniforms and respect for elders. And a banner carried by a group of ministers reading "No King but Jesus" promoted not only dedication to an exclusive Christianity but derogation of Martin Luther King.[34]

South Carolina, as we have seen above, recognizes King's birthday in ambiguous fashion, allowing state employees the choice of taking the day off or of opting instead for one of three other Confederate holidays. Even for those South Carolinians who decide to take the third Monday in January off, they may do so not to honor King but to celebrate the birthday of Robert E. Lee, whose January 19 birthday is officially recognized by South Carolina as well as by other southern states. Opponents of the Confederate battle flag's place on the South Carolina statehouse countered its supporters' January 8 rally with one of their own on January 17, 2000, Martin Luther King Day. Some forty-six thousand people advanced down Washington and Main Streets to the capitol, in the largest march in the city's history, carrying signs that read "Your Heritage is My Slavery," and arguing, in the words of the Rev. John Hurst Adams, "The Civil War's been over a long time." Although flag supporters had derided the NAACP as "outsiders and agitators" (ironically, the Confederate widow herself hailed from Elba, Alabama), among the antiflag demonstrators were a number of white elected officials, business leaders, and clergy members. Addressing the crowd on the statehouse steps, the white mayor of Charleston, Joe Riley, declared, "The vast majority of South Carolina says it's time to bring down the flag now. . . . We cannot ignore that the Confederate battle flag was taken by hate groups. It was taken by the Klan. It became a banner of the segregation-forever movement, and we cannot be insensitive in South Carolina to the feelings of our African American brothers and sisters when they see that flag." Such rallies, representing contrasting positions along the American political spectrum, suggest the potential of Martin Luther King Day as a forum for political activity as well as the unfinished and still controversial nature of the American holiday.[35]

If the day can be employed to make trouble or make political hay, to promote community, tolerance, nonviolence, and equality, it can also function—sometimes to the distress of King Day supporters—as an occasion to promote consumption and indulge leisure. The Rev. Elliott Cuff of Mount Ararat Missionary Baptist Church in Ocean Hill–Brownsville, New York, speculating about the long-term prospects of the holiday, worried, "King's birthday, as we move into the next millennium, will probably go the way of the rest of the holidays, a day to rest and shop. That's unfortunate. I think it is vitally important because these are marks in the sand for what made America what it is today." Ironically, it is often controversy and political contention on public holidays—even challenges to their validity as days of official commemoration—that give these occasions vitality. As they become less contentious, less "political," holidays may become more entrenched and universal but also blander, less meaningful, more often moments of forgetting. Although it is impossible for historians to predict the future (the past is hard enough), it may be that some of the aspects of the recent observances of Martin Luther King Day that promoters find most troubling in fact signal the successful arrival of the holiday as an American tradition.[36]

In 1989, on the eve of King's birthday, residents of Memphis, Tennessee, were shocked by the local distribution of a whimsical promotional calendar by McDonald's restaurants. Through an embarrassing oversight, an advertising agency employee labeled the entry for January 16 (the Monday officially designated to honor King that year) as National Nothing Day. McDonald's quickly recalled the offensive calendars, but the African American community expressed outrage, calling the gaffe an "inexcusable thing." "It's an insult and an effort to degrade what is important to us," a Memphis NAACP official charged. McDonald's spokespersons, on the other hand, maintained that it was simply "a terrible, terrible oversight, . . . an innocent mistake." National Nothing Day was intended, according to the advertising agency, to mock all other holidays, to call attention to the clutter of the calendar, inundated with numerous silly occasions, like national pickle day. Three years later, a joke book-of-days published in 1992 and prominently featured by the national bookstore chain Walden Books more consciously ridiculed King on his birthday, offering the mildly offensive riddle, "What do you call a civil rights leader from another planet? Martian Luther King." The McDonald's Martin Luther King Day debacle in Memphis certainly reflected the youth of the holiday and its ongoing fight for full recognition. But, ironically, it may also presage the future fate of the day—as just another space on the calendar, ignored by most Americans or trivialized with tasteless humor—even as it achieved official status in the United States.[37]

For the first time in honor of King, Wall Street closed down on Monday, January 20, 1998. If stores continue to stay open on the holiday, they more often call attention to the special nature of the day, if less to salute King than to sell him. Increasingly, Martin Luther King figures in sales promotions in mid-January, and shoppers take advantage of the three-day weekend. A newspaper in Eugene, Oregon, carried an advertisement in a January 17, 2000, edition, for example, which featured a large picture of King and the words, "Help us celebrate Martin Luther King Jr. Day!" over a three-dollar-off coupon for any purchase more than ten dollars. In more sophisticated fashion, a computer company—Apple—has featured King (as well as Einstein and Gandhi) in its advertisements, under the banner "Think Different," exploiting King's image as an innovator without much concern that King's career predated the information revolution or that he might have been more critical than supportive of the corporate giant. A young man working in New York on King's birthday in 1998 reflected on the shoppers around him: "They think it's a day for recreation, part of a three-day weekend. . . . It surprises me. After everybody fought for it, there's a day of observance and nobody observes it."[38]

In fact, Americans observe it widely, both with reverence and nonchalance, as a serious political occasion and, unselfconsciously, as just another celebration of American capitalism, which has been successful enough to underwrite days of rest and commercial consumption for some—though clearly not all—its citizens. It is a further irony, perhaps, that if commercialization threatens to trivialize the King holiday, the power of commerce—or, rather, the threat to commerce through economic boycotts—proved crucial in its establishment.

The ambiguous Martin Luther King Day—as a federal holiday—is a sign of the times. As historians such as Michael Kammen and John Bodnar have argued, until late in the nineteenth century, government in the United States had proved hesitant to sanctify its heroes, only reluctantly authorizing funds for statues and monuments or creating public holidays. But since then, the state, as it grew in power, acted more frequently to endorse and underwrite the construction of public memory through memorials and red-letter days, culminating perhaps during the presidency of Franklin Delano Roosevelt, who sought to unify and regulate the national calendar in unprecedented fashion, declaring which days should be sacred, which should be available for shopping, and which should "live in infamy." John Bodnar draws a distinction between "official" and "vernacular" culture—the former represents elite leadership (professional and educational, not simply governmental) and its commitment to clear, ideal, nationalistic statements in commemoration, whereas the latter "represents an array of specialized interests that are grounded in parts of the whole." Vernacular culture is diverse,

Fig. 55. Poster listing Martin Luther King Day events at the University of Oregon, January 1996. Collection of the author.

changing, and divisive. In Bodnar's subtle analysis, the two cultures work together in complicated ways to fashion public memory.[39]

Yet the King holiday seems not to fit his formulation easily. Certainly Martin Luther King Day is both official and vernacular: official because it has been sanctioned by federal, state, and local governments, and vernacular because it emerged in the popular recognition of a martyr and hero—one who had often been at odds with official culture—and is celebrated regularly in private or nongovernmental exercises. In Arizona's 1992 referendum, the official and the vernacular merged as ordinary Arizonans approved the holiday overwhelmingly, yet throughout the United States, official endorsement did not necessarily translate into a paid holiday for many citizens because employers proved reluctant to cooperate. Nonetheless, even in such situations, some find ways to craft vernacular celebrations, whereas others manage to avoid official and vernacular fetes alike. Ironically, endorsement by the state of Martin Luther King Day—which made the vernacular official—carried liabilities or signaled the limitations of newly won African American status and power. On the one hand, some black critics feared co-optation, because they were unable to imagine that the King so harassed and abused by officials could be embraced by them without fundamental alteration of his memory. On the other hand, some may have wondered, how meaningful was federal endorsement in the 1980s, at a moment in American history when Americans were particularly wary of the national state, when leaders in the executive branch sought to dissolve agencies and promote a devolution of authority? And while the law decreed equality, and the executive branch seemed to support it, inequality and discrimination persisted. Perhaps it was less an irony than it had originally appeared, then, that Ronald Reagan—who as a presidential candidate promised to "get government off people's backs" and who cultivated unprecedented suspiciousness of Washington—had signed the new holiday into law.

If today St. Martin's day has become another St. Monday for some, the history of King's life and his official stature in America's pantheon of heroes remain as a resource for those who promote his legacy or who seek his posthumous support in shaping responses to present or future dilemmas, particularly those that concern the enduring problems of discrimination, inequality, limited opportunity, and poverty in the United States. Martin Luther King Day, its stakes clearer and higher than those of older national holidays, is a work in progress, still being shaped, still being contested, still in the process of becoming "traditional."

Epilogue

The Future of the Past

ENDING ON a less than final note—acknowledging that Martin Luther King Jr.'s Birthday, like the rest of the United States public calendar, remains a work in progress—seems to preclude a standard, definitive conclusion. Yet this may be the place to assess how and why and to what extent the established public holidays in this country's yearly cycle have achieved their success and to speculate about the future of American red-letter days. Each of the fetes examined in these pages emerged to perform critical cultural and political work for Americans and the United States—to explain, celebrate, and even to cultivate the national birth of the country; to nurture or repair a sense of national union; to assuage grief and explain loss; to revise Americans' definition of their society and polity, acknowledging and accepting its ethnic and racial diversity; and similarly to express appreciation of the American working class, while paradoxically imagining the United States as a classless, or middle-class, society. If these holidays were officially recognized or even officially erected, they emerged and remain vernacular as well—the product and property of diverse Americans. Of course, not all citizens or residents possessed the power to influence particular holidays equally, just as some were more able than others to fashion new, more favorable identities as Americans. Still, each holiday provided a potential temporal arena within the public sphere in which to challenge the definition of America and of first-class citizenship, or in which to question the achievement of American promise. On all of these festivals, Americans practiced politics, sometimes without any particular consciousness of doing so, and through both consensual rites and noisy confrontations they shaped the contours of American nationalism.

The weight and density of these commemorative political occasions have shifted over time. That absence makes the heart grow fonder has not necessarily proved true with American holidays, as their origins grow more distant. Washington and Lincoln are recognized and respected still, but these heroes no longer move Americans as they once did. The Fourth of July remains a celebration of the United States' nativity but has become as much a festival of summer as one of sacred political origins. And Memorial Day and Labor Day—although they can still stir some Americans to express their grief and patriotism, their sense of worth and solidarity—are merely for many the spring and autumn bookends of summer. Wars and similar crises turn Americans' attention to their political feasts and encourage some to reexamine what their nation stands for, but the memory of each successive American war and the contemplation of its human and material costs seem to obscure memories of earlier conflicts and sacrifices. With the increasing accumulation of red-letter days in the American calendar, individual holidays sometimes compete for citizens' affections; indeed, to a certain extent, individuals and communities specialize through a sort of division of labor in the production of American public festivals. And in a world of greater complexity, in which Americans embody multiple interests and identities, they have much to distract them, including new forms of commercialized entertainment and media.

The national holidays that have succeeded have been those that have proved to be politically amphibious. They express universal American themes (Independence and national birth, liberty, democracy, opportunity), while they simultaneously (and without apparent contradiction) express the particular hopes and dreams of Americans both individually and within groups that are defined ethnically, religiously, racially, regionally, or by class or gender. Such fetes are national and localized, often realized as national through local—even partisan—political practice. For each national holiday that has become ensconced in the United States calendar, numerous others have remained provincial or have faded away altogether. Patriots' Day in Massachusetts, for example, celebrates the "shot heard 'round the world" at Lexington on April 19, 1775—a plausible birth date for the American republic—but it never became a national festival (except perhaps to American running enthusiasts who eagerly watch the Boston Marathon, staged annually on the third Monday in April) because it was defined as too sectional. Evacuation Day was a still more proximate and circumscribed holiday, celebrating the withdrawal of British troops from New York City in 1783 and celebrated there but nowhere else on November 25. Pioneer Days, in Utah, Idaho, and other western states, commemorate localized American origin myths, but, although participants often conflate their experience with the Pilgrims' landing at Plymouth Rock, these festivals seem to lack larger national significance. Cinco de Mayo—commemorating a short-lived Mexican military victory over French invaders at the Battle of Puebla in 1862—has recently moved onto the American festive calendar as an occasion similar to St. Patrick's Day, although in this case the holiday is celebrating Mexican American ethnicity; given its referent event, however, it seems unlikely the holiday will ever become another Columbus Day. As one disgruntled man asked in a letter to the editor of an Oregon newspaper following May 5, 1997, "why is it [Cinco de Mayo] being celebrated in the United States, when even more important battles fought by us go unmarked and forgotten?" "If we're to have holidays, official or unofficial, let us mark U.S. historical dates, not foreign ones, and keep alive our own heritage."[1] Few today celebrate Arbor Day or Bird Day on April 22 or May 4, Flag Day on June 14, American Indian Day on the fourth Friday in September, or a number of other holidays that once showed promise as potential American fetes.[2] These occasions lacked wide popular support as well as a committed group of patrons who might have promoted them to a wider public audience. Ironically, letters like the one above rejecting Cinco de Mayo by calling it foreign and alien to "our own heritage" are more likely to inspire an assertive defense and elevation of the holiday rather than persuade Americans to ignore it. For a public holiday, the next best thing to a strong constituency is a set of vocal critics.

What might the twenty-first century bring to the United States' public calendar? With President George W. Bush's ascension to the presidency, might the chief executive follow his initiative as Texas governor and declare June 10 as Jesus Day? Such a move would bring the nation full circle, conflating the political and religious calendar in a manner reminiscent of the colonial period, before the U.S. Constitution with its First Amendment prohibition against the establishment of religion. Governor Bush's proclamation claimed, surprisingly, that "Throughout the world, people of all religions recognize Jesus Christ as an example of love, compassion, sacrifice and service. Reaching out to the poor, the suffering and the marginalized, he provided moral leadership that continues to inspire countless men, women and children today." Universalizing Christ as an American hero, Governor Bush then enshrined him and "faith-based" social and political activism in the state calendar: "Jesus Day challenges people to follow Christ's example by performing good works in their communities and neighborhoods." Jesus Day makes clear—as does Martin Luther King Day—that despite secular trends, the United States remains a religiously charged political world. The evangelical Christian fete certainly has zealous supporters as well as adamant critics, but it is likely to fail both judicial and popular scrutiny in a country committed to religious freedom and the separation of church and state. New England Puritans would have seen Jesus Day as blasphemous and redundant; for them, Christ should rule over all 365 days, and the designation of one particular day would make devotion inappropriately formulaic. Today most Christians seem satisfied with what they have: a sacred, if unofficial, place in the weekly public calendar—the Sabbath.[3]

Jesus, then, already has his day, but who or what might win a future spot in the United States' yearly cycle of political festivals? If American history has seen a steadily widening claim to membership in the political nation, then we might expect newer, historically marginalized parties to forward their interests, assert their rights, and celebrate themselves into first-class citizenship through a new American public holiday. Women remain unrepresented in the American calendar (Mother's Day remembers women as mothers, not as citizens). International Women's Day and women's history month are celebrated enthusiastically by some but do not attract wide attention as American festivals. Perhaps in the future American women will find their own Washington, Lincoln, Columbus, or King. If in Arizona some celebrate Cesar Chavez along with King on the third Monday in January, could the Mexican American leader, or some other Latino champion, get his or her own day as the ethnic composition of the United States continues to change? Might Asian Americans make a similar case? Or would the American public perceive such initiatives—even when cast in universal terms—as too particularistic and fragmenting?

Will new wars or unprecedented economic crises produce new American heroes, or has the heroic age waned? No public holiday marks the United States' victory in the Second World War or any of its leaders. Might a new fete commemorate or cultivate the American environmental movement or one of its idols? Earth Day—first celebrated on April 22, 1970 (on the day Nebraska marked Arbor Day)—remains an episodic festival, but one with the potential to garner wider, official endorsement. American holidays have frequently been born of crisis. Independence Day and Washington's Birthday grew out of the travail of revolution, Lincoln's Birthday and Memorial Day followed the Civil War, and Martin Luther King Day emerged from the civil rights struggle and King's martyrdom. Given the dire consequences of pollution, species extinctions, exhaustion of nonrenewable resources, and the impact of global warming, the challenge of environmental problems looms large nationally and internationally. Might an environmental champion or martyr merit a red-letter day, or might a renewed Earth Day become a more prominent and regular feature of the United States political calendar?

If "the past is a foreign country," what does that make the future? A New World? In that new world, Americans will continue to observe festive moments in the public sphere, although in changing venues and media, and in the process they will act politically, celebrating themselves into the future.

NOTES

Introduction. Identity, History, and the American Calendar

1. Among the most important recent works in American history are Susan G. Davis, *Parades and Power: Street Theater in Nineteenth-Century Philadelphia* (Philadelphia, 1986); Paul A. Gilje, *The Road to Mobocracy: Popular Disorder in New York City, 1763–1834* (Chapel Hill, N.C., 1987); Peter Shaw, *American Patriots and the Rituals of Revolution* (Cambridge, Mass., 1981); Mary P. Ryan, *Women in Public: Between Banners and Ballots, 1825–1880* (Baltimore, Md., 1990); David Waldstreicher, *In the Midst of Perpetual Fetes: The Making of American Nationalism, 1776–1820* (Chapel Hill, N.C., 1997); Simon P. Newman, *Parades and the Politics of the Street: Festive Culture in the Early American Republic* (Philadelphia, 1997).

2. Barry Bearak, "Kashmir Endures Its Holiday of Contradictions," *New York Times*, Aug. 16, 2000.

3. T. G. Fraser, ed., *The Irish Parading Tradition: Following the Drum* (London, 2000); "Protestant Protests in Ulster Begin Peacefully but Turn Violent," *New York Times*, July 10, 2000; Conor Cruise O'Brien, "Blocking the Road and Paying the Price," *New York Times*, July 16, 1998, op-ed page.

4. Among the most significant recent works, see Maurice Halbwachs, *The Collective Memory*, trans. F. J. Ditter (New York, 1980); Eric Hobsbawm and Terence Ranger, eds., *The Invention of Tradition* (Cambridge, U.K., 1983); Natalie Zemon Davis and Randoph Starn, eds., special issue, "Memory and Counter-Memory," *Representations* 26 (spring 1989), esp. Pierre Nora, "Between Memory and History: *Les Lieux de Mémoire*," 7–25; and Nora, *Realms of Memory: The Construction of the French Past*, 3 vols., ed. Lawrence D. Kritzman, trans. Arthur Goldhammer (New York, 1996–98); Yael Zerubavel, *Recovered Roots: Collective Memory and the Making of Israeli National Tradition* (Chicago, 1995); John R. Gillis, ed., *Commemorations: The Politics of National Identity* (Princeton, N.J., 1994); Michael Kammen, numerous pathbreaking works but esp. *Mystic Chords of Memory: The Transformation of Tradition in American Culture* (New York, 1991); John Bodnar, *Remaking America: Public Memory, Commemoration, and Patriotism in the Twentieth Century* (Princeton, N.J., 1992); David Glassberg, *American Historical Pageantry: The Uses of Tradition in the Early Twentieth Century* (Chapel Hill, N.C., 1990); Roy Rosenzweig and David Thelen, *The Presence of the Past: Popular Uses of History in American Life* (New York, 1998); Karal Ann Marling, *George Washington Slept Here: Colonial Revivals and American Culture, 1876–1986* (Cambridge, Mass., 1988); Leigh Eric Schmidt, *Consumer Rites: The Buying and Selling of American Holidays* (Princeton, N.J., 1995); Stephen Nissenbaum, *The Battle for Christmas: A Cultural History of America's Most Cherished Holiday* (New York, 1996); Ellen M. Litwicki, *America's Public Holidays, 1865–1920* (Washington, D.C., 2000).

5. Pierre Nora, "General Introduction: Between Memory and History," in *Realms of Memory* 1:1, 3.

6. Ibid., 12.

7. The philosopher George Santayana (1863–1952) most famously said, "Those who cannot remember the past are condemned to repeat it." He also cynically observed, "History is a pack of lies about events that never happened told by people who weren't there."

8. W. E. B. Du Bois, *The Souls of Black Folk* (1903), in *Writings*, ed. Nathan Huggins (New York, 1986), 364–65.

Chapter 1. Political Fireworks

1. Quoted in Charles Warren, "Fourth of July Myths," *William and Mary Quarterly*, 3d ser., 2 (July 1945): 242.

2. David Waldstreicher, *In the Midst of Perpetual Fetes: The Making of American Nationalism, 1776–1820* (Chapel Hill, N.C., 1997), 30–35; Jay Fliegelman, *Declaring Independence: Jefferson, Natural Language, and the Culture of Performance* (Stanford, Calif., 1993), 5–26; Simon P. Newman, *Parades and the Politics of the Street: Festive Culture in the Early American Republic* (Philadelphia, 1997), 33–34. See also Pauline Maier, *American Scripture: Making the Declaration of Independence* (New York, 1997), 155–60; Len Travers, *Celebrating the Fourth: Independence Day and the Rites of Nationalism in the Early Republic* (Amherst, Mass., 1997).

3. John Adams to Abigail Adams, July 3, 1776, in *The Adams Family Correspondence*, 6 vols., ed. L. H. Butterfield, Wendell D. Gararet, and Marjorie E. Sprague (Cambridge, Mass., 1963–73), 2:30. See also Adams to Samuel Chase, July 9, 1776, in *Letters of the Delegates to Congress, 1774–1789*, 4 vols., ed. Paul H. Smith (Washington, D.C., 1976–79), 4:414.

4. Adams to Chase, July 9, 1776, in *Letters of the Delegates*, 4:414.

5. Maier, *American Scripture*, 159; Warren, "Fourth of July Myths," 242n. 8. North Carolina received news of the Declaration on July 22; see Fletcher M. Green, "Listen to the Eagle Scream," *North Carolina Historical Review* 31, 3–4 (1954): 295–320, 529–49, esp. 297.

6. Jürgen Habermas, *The Structural Transformation of the Public Sphere: An Inquiry into a Category of Bourgeois Society*, trans. Thomas Burger (Cambridge, Mass., 1989); Craig Calhoun, ed., *Habermas and the Public Sphere* (Cambridge, Mass., 1992); Michael Warner, *The Letters of the Republic: Publication and the Public Sphere in Eighteenth-Century America* (Cambridge, Mass., 1990), quotation at xiii; Mary P. Ryan, *Women in Public: Between Banners and Ballots, 1825–1880* (Baltimore, 1990), esp. 10–13; Benedict Anderson, *Imagined Communities: Reflections on the Origins and Spread of Nationalism*, rev. ed. (London, 1991).

7. Williams quoted in Warren, "Fourth of July Myths," 255; continental officer quoted in Travers, *Celebrating the Fourth*, 24.

8. See Henrietta C. Ellery, ed., "Diary of the Hon. William Ellery, of Rhode Island, June 28–July 23, 1778," *Pennsylvania Magazine of History and Biography* 11 (1887): 477–78.

9. Saul Cornell, "Aristocracy Assailed: The Ideology of Backcountry Anti-Federalism," *Journal of American History* 76, 4 (March 1990): 1150–56; Waldstreicher, *In the Midst of Perpetual Fetes*, 93–96; events can be followed in the *Carlisle Gazette*, Jan. 2, 9, 16, 23, 1788, and in accounts reprinted in Merrill Jensen, John P. Kaminski, and Gaspare J. Saladino, eds., *The Documentary History of the Ratification of the Constitution*, 16 vols. (Madison, Wisc., 1976–), 2:670–708.

10. *Account of the Grand Federal Procession, Philadelphia, July 4, 1788. To which are added, Mr. Wilson's Oration, and a letter on the Subject of the Procession* (Philadelphia, 1788). For insightful readings of the Philadelphia and similar processions, see esp. Waldstreicher, *In the Midst of Perpetual Fetes*, 1–2, 90–107; Susan G. Davis, *Parades and Power: Street Theatre in Nineteenth-Century Philadelphia* (Philadelphia, 1986), 117–25; Whitfield J. Bell Jr., "The Federal Processions of 1788," *New-York Historical Society Quarterly* 46 (January 1962): 5–39.

11. *Account of the Grand Federal Procession, Philadelphia*, 17.

12. Waldstreicher, *In the Midst of Perpetual Fetes*, 91, 93, 103–4; New York's procession is detailed in Kenneth Silverman, *A Cultural History of the American Revolution* (New York, 1976), 585.

13. Silverman, *Cultural History of the American Revolution*, 585–87.

14. John Wilkes, as quoted in Maier, *American Scripture*, 162.

15. Ibid., 190–91.

16. Richard D. Brown, ed., *Major Problems in the Era of the American Revolution, 1760–1791* (Lexington, Mass., 1992), 310.

17. Maier, *American Scripture*, 192–93, 197, quotation at 192.

18. Ibid., 198; Leonard Sweet, "The Fourth of July and Black Americans in the Nineteenth Century: Northern Leadership Opinion with the Context of the Black Experience," *Journal of Negro History* 61 (July 1976): 258. Nat Turner's rebellion had been planned to erupt on July 4, 1831; Denmark Vesey's uprising had been scheduled for July 14, 1822, some have argued, after blacks suffered mistreatment while attending a white Independence Day celebration.

19. Sweet, "Fourth of July and Black Americans," 260, 261. For a ringing indictment of colonizers by a prominent African American leader, see the Rev. Peter Williams Jr.'s July 4, 1830, address to his congregation at St. Philip's Protestant Episcopal Church in New York, in *Lift Every Voice: African American Oratory, 1787–1900*, ed. Philip S. Foner and Robert James Branham (Tuscaloosa, Ala., 1998), 114–21. Quotation from *The American Anti-Slavery Almanac, for 1843*, comp. L. M. Child (New York, [1842]), n.p. Margaret Fuller, "Fourth of July," *New-York Daily Tribune*, July 4, 1845, 2, in *Margaret Fuller: Essays on American Life and Letters*, ed. Joel Myerson (Schenectady, N.Y., 1978), 297–300.

20. Sweet, "Fourth of July and Black Americans," 262–63.

21. Graham Russell Hodges, *Root and Branch: African Americans in New York and East Jersey, 1613–1863* (Chapel Hill, N.C., 1999), 222–23.

22. William B. Gravely, "The Dialect of Double-Consciousness in Black American Freedom Celebrations, 1808–1863," *Journal of Negro History* 67 (winter 1982): 303–4; Shane White, "'It Was a Proud Day': African Americans, Festivals, and Parades in the North, 1741–1834," *Journal of American History* 81 (June 1994): 13–50; Austin Steward, "Termination of Slavery," in Foner and Branham, *Lift Every Voice*, 104–9, quotation at 107.

23. Frederick Douglass, "What, to the Slave, Is the Fourth of July?" in Foner and Branham, *Lift Every Voice*, 246–68, quotations at 255–56.

24. Ibid., 258.

25. Boycotts rely on conspicuousness—ceremonies on July 5 thus explicitly marked and called attention to blacks' absence from the Fourth of July, while allowing African Americans to celebrate their own version of Independence Day. Note, however, that Douglass's famous 1852 oration was delivered on July 5, not to boycott the Fourth but because Independence Day celebrations were traditionally moved to July 5 when the Fourth fell on a Sunday, as it did in 1852.

26. Gravely, "Black American Freedom Celebrations," 303–4; Sweet, "Fourth of July and Black Americans," 269, 271; Waldstreicher, *In the Midst of Perpetual Fetes*, 328–29. See also Geneviève Fabre, "African-American Commemorative Celebrations in the Nineteenth Century," in *History and Memory in African-American Culture*, ed. Geneviève Fabre and Robert O'Meally (New York, 1994), 77–80.

27. Gravely, "Black American Freedom Celebrations," 304, 311 (Banneker Committee quotation); Fabre, "African-American Commemorative Celebrations," 82–86; Sweet, "Fourth of July and Black Americans," 270–71.

28. Gravely, "Black American Freedom Celebrations," 304–5, 319n. 19; first Douglass quotation at 305. Douglass's 1857 West Indian Emancipation Day speech is in Foner and Branham, *Lift Every Voice*, 308–12, quotations at 311 and 309–10.

29. Quoted in Gravely, "Black American Freedom Celebrations," 311–12.

30. Samuel L. Horst, ed., *The Fire of Liberty in Their Hearts: The Diary of Jacob E. Yoder of the Freedmen's Bureau School, Lynchburg, Virginia, 1866–1870* (Richmond, Va., 1996), 55; National Lincoln Monument Association, *Celebration by the Colored People's Educational Monument Association in Memory of Abraham Lincoln, on Fourth of July, 1865, in the Presidential Grounds, Washington, D.C.* (Washington, D.C., 1865), Douglass quotation at 5. On the continuing celebration of Emancipation Day,

see Randal C. Archibold, "Celebrating a New Year, and a Milestone for Freedom. Black Americans Commemorate Anniversary of Lincoln's Historic Proclamation to End Slavery," *New York Times*, Jan. 1, 2000, A27.

31. For an evocative sketch of Juneteenth in the twentieth century, see Ralph Ellison's novel *Juneteenth*, ed. John F. Callahan (New York, 1999), esp. chap. 7, 116–40.

32. William H. Wiggins Jr., *O Freedom! Afro-American Emancipation Celebrations* (Knoxville, Tenn., 1987), Mrs. Bass quotation at 18; William H. Wiggins Jr. and Douglas DeNatale, eds., *Jubilation: African American Celebrations in the Southeast* (Columbia, S.C., 1993), esp. 17–21 and 61–67, quotation at 21.

33. Wiggins and DeNatale, *Jubilation*. On Juneteenth in Eugene, Oregon, see Paul Neville, "Black Coalition Plans Expansion of 'Juneteenth,'" *Register-Guard* (Eugene, Ore.), June 14, 1994, 3B; "Juneteenth Picnic Commemorates Freedom," *Register-Guard*, June 12, 1997, B1, 3, which comments on the holiday's revival in the past decade. William Raspberry, "America's Black Island Faces Depopulation, Not Integration," nationally syndicated column, *Register-Guard*, July 4, 1997.

34. Henry D. Thoreau, *Walden* (1854), in *Walden and Resistance to Civil Government*, 2d ed., ed. William Rossi (New York, 1992), 57.

35. Henry David Thoreau, "Slavery in Massachusetts," an address delivered at Framingham Grove, July 4, 1854, reproduced in various published and unpublished versions in Henry A. Hawken, *Trumpets of Glory: Fourth of July Orations, 1786–1861* (Granby, Conn., 1976), 207–22.

36. Wendell Phillips, "Oration Delivered at Framingham Grove," July 4, 1854, in Hawken, *Trumpets of Glory*, 224. The address was printed in the *Liberator*, July 14, 1854.

37. *Almanac of the American Temperance Union, for the year of our Lord 1845* (New York, [1844]), 26, 33. Temperance reform is well summarized in Ronald G. Walters, *American Reformers, 1815–1860* (New York, 1978), 123–43.

38. *Almanac of the American Temperance Union, 1845*, 33.

39. Clementina Smith, as quoted in Anthony F. C. Wallace, *Rockdale: The Growth of an American Village in the Early Industrial Revolution* (New York, 1978), 297–98, quotation at 312.

40. Thomas Starr King, "Fourth of July Address, San Francisco, July 4, 1860," published with variant texts in Hawken, *Trumpets of Glory*, 252–59, quotations at 252, 258.

41. See, for example, Dr. Ezra Stiles Ely's Fourth of July sermon, July 4, 1827, *The Duty of Christian Freemen to Elect Christian Rulers* (Philadelphia, 1828).

42. "Declaration of Sentiments and Resolutions, by the Woman's Rights Convention [Seneca Falls, New York], July [19], 1848," in *We, the Other People: Alternative Declarations of Independence by Labor Groups, Farmers, Women's Rights Advocates, Socialists, and Blacks, 1829–1975*, ed. Philip S. Foner (Urbana, Ill., 1976), 77–83.

43. Rosemarie Zagarri, "The Rights of Man and Woman in Post-Revolutionary America," *William and Mary Quarterly*, 3d ser., 55, 2 (April 1998): 203–30; Nancy Isenberg, *Sex and Citizenship in Antebellum America* (Chapel Hill, N.C., 1998), esp. 1–13, 15–16. And see Lydia Maria Child, "Home and Politics," *Union Magazine*, August 1848, 63–68.

44. On women's roles in Independence Day celebrations, and politics more generally, see Waldstreicher, *In the Midst of Perpetual Fetes*, 82–84, 157, 166–70, 234–41, quotation at 239; Newman, *Parade and Politics of the Street*, 87, 95, 101–2; Ryan, *Women in Public*, esp. 24–37; Isenberg, *Sex and Citizenship*.

45. See Foner, *We, the Other People*, 105–14, quotations at 105, 106. The woman's declaration in 1876 was a more liberal paraphrase of the Declaration of Independence than was the 1848 Seneca Falls declaration. Less confined by the original script and format, it offered a detailed bill of impeachment after its prologue. In addition to demanding the vote, it advocated women's service on juries, deletion of the word "male" in state constitutions and judicial codes (which prohibited women from holding offices, for example), and more equitable rules of divorce.

46. Davis, *Parades and Power*, esp. 23–48. Although sympathetic to working people, Davis analyzes them in all their complexity, showing for example how such raucous celebrations could at times become virulently racist and violent. By the 1820s, middle-class people who chose not to confront the working class and their festivities on the Fourth simply left town for country celebrations. See also Bruce Laurie, *Working People of Philadelphia, 1800–1850* (Philadelphia, 1980). Roy Rosenzweig, *Eight Hours for What You Will: Workers and Leisure in an Industrial City, 1870–1920* (Cambridge, U.K., 1983), esp. 65–90, insightfully examines the working-class Fourth of July in Worcester, Massachusetts, later in the century.

47. Foner, *We, the Other People*, 47–50 (Working Man's Declaration), 51–55 (Declaration of Rights of the Trades' Union of Boston), 6–9 (*Mechanics' Free Press* quotation at 6–7).

48. See ibid. for these and other re-declarations of independence. See also Herbert Gutman, *Work, Culture and Society in Industrializing America* (New York, 1977), 51. The Fourth of July became the site of later labor conflicts as well. See Paul Krause, "Rethinking the Homestead Lockout on the Fourth of July," *Pittsburgh History* 45, 2 (1992): 53–55.

49. Foner, *We, the Other People*, 26–28.

50. Quoted in Gutman, *Work, Culture, and Society*, 30.

51. Davis, *Parades and Power*, 150–51; Edwin G. Burrows and Mike Wallace, *Gotham: A History of New York City to 1898* (New York, 1999), 828.

52. Rosenzweig, *Eight Hours for What You Will*, 77–90.

53. Edward L. Ayers, Patricia Nelson Limrick, Stephen Nissenbaum, and Peter S. Onuf, *All over the Map: Rethinking American Regions* (Baltimore, 1996); see especially Peter S. Onuf's essay, "Federalism, Republicanism, and the Origins of American Sectionalism," 11–37. And see David Waldsteicher's brilliant chapter, "Regionalism, Nationalism, and the Geopolitics of Celebration," in *In the Midst of Perpetual Fetes*, 246–93.

54. John M. Murrin, "A Roof without Walls: The Dilemma of American National Identity," in *Beyond Confederation: Origins of the Constitution and American National Identity*, ed. Richard Beeman, Stephpen Botein, and Edward C. Carter II (Chapel Hill, 1987), 333–48, quotation at 347.

55. Ayers et al., *All over the Map*, esp. 8–9.

56. Onuf, "Federalism, Republicanism, and the Origins of Sectionalism," 17, 31; Waldstreicher, *In the Midst of Perpetual Fetes*, 250.

57. Quoted from the Washington *National Intelligencer*, July 15, 1854, in Green, "Listen to the Eagle Scream," 314.

58. *The Writings and Speeches of Daniel Webster*, 18 vols. (Boston, 1903), 4:297; quoted in Green, "Listen to the Eagle Scream," 315–16; Waldsteicher, *In the Midst of Perpetual Fetes*, 274.

59. John Bakeless, ed., *The Journals of Lewis and Clark: A New Selection* (New York, 1964), 30. See also Stephen E. Ambrose, *Undaunted Courage: Meriwether Lewis, Thomas Jefferson, and the Opening of the American West* (New York, 1996), 149.

60. Other Fourth of July celebrations among the Corps of Discovery are described in Ambrose, *Undaunted Courage*, 247, 380.

61. Argonauts on the Oregon Trail generally needed to reach Independence Rock by the Fourth of July in order to reach the Oregon Country successfully.

62. Drew R. McCoy, "James Madison and Visions of American Nationality in the Confederation Period: A Regional Perspective," in Beeman, Botein, and Carter, *Beyond Confederation*, 226–58; Madison quoted at 227, 248.

63. See ibid.; and see generally Drew R. McCoy, *The Elusive Republic: Political Economy in Jeffersonian America* (Chapel Hill, N.C., 1980). The toasts are quoted in Waldstreicher, *In the Midst of Perpetual Fetes*, 291; Green, "Listen to the Eagle Scream," 547. If an American Empire of Liberty was designed to avoid the creation of a colonial system in the West that would have replicated the British system Americans had rebelled against, it was successful only for white citizens of the repub-

lic. For Native people in the lands being claimed and settled, of course, this was colonialism pure and simple.

64. Green, "Listen to the Eagle Scream," 534–36. See also Cynthia A. Kierner, "Genteel Balls and Republican Parades: Gender and Early Southern Civic Rituals, 1677–1826," *Virginia Magazine of History and Biography* 104, 2 (spring 1996): 196–204.

65. On southern nationalism, see Drew Gilpin Faust, *The Creation of Confederate Nationalism: Ideology and Identity in the Civil War South* (Baton Rouge, La., 1988).

66. Green, "Listen to the Eagle Scream," 538–40, 295; Mamie Garvin Fields with Karen Fields, *Lemon Swamp and Other Places: A Carolina Memoir* (New York, 1983).

67. Lyn Spillman, *Nation and Commemoration: Creating National Identities in the United States and Australia* (Cambridge, U.K., 1997), 37–49, 70–73; Philip S. Foner, "Black Participation in the Centennial of 1876," *Negro History Bulletin* 39 (February 1976): 532–38. By contrast, the fiftieth anniversary of Independence was a simpler, less conflicted event; see Andrew Burstein, *America's Jubilee: How in 1826 a Generation Remembered Fifty Years of Independence* (New York, 2001).

68. G. Kurt Piehler, *Remembering War the American Way* (Washington, D.C., 1995), 61, 76, argues that southerners again embraced the Fourth of July after the end of Reconstruction and especially with the rise of a new patriotism (and patriotic organizations such as the Sons of the American Revolution and the Daughters of the American Revolution) in the 1890s, which emphasized a common Revolutionary heritage. See especially Nina Silber, *The Romance of Reunion: Northerners and the South, 1865–1900* (Chapel Hill, 1993); and Kirk Savage, "The Politics of Memory: Black Emancipation and the Civil War Monument," in *Commemorations: The Politics of National Identity*, ed. John R. Gillis (Princeton, N.J., 1994), 127–49, on the elision of African Americans in the commemoration of the Civil War.

69. See, for example, L. Bradford Prince, "Holiday Ceremonies in New Mexico," *Independent* 53 (Sept. 19, 1901): 2225.

70. Ken Verdoia and Richard Firmage, *Utah: The Struggle for Statehood* (Salt Lake City, 1996); Gustive O. Larson, *The "Americanization" of Utah for Statehood* (San Marino, Calif., 1971); Orson F. Whitney, *History of Utah . . . in Four Volumes* (Salt Lake City, 1892).

71. Verdoia and Firmage, *Utah*, 21–22, 59–70; Special Order No. 2, Adjutant-General's Office, G.S.L. City, July 1, 1859, reprinted in Whitney, *History of Utah*, 1:718–19.

72. See Verdoia and Firmage, *Utah*, 79, 82, 115–17, 124–25, 127, 136–37, 140–42. The Morrill Act is better know for its land grant program designed to create a national system of agricultural colleges.

73. *Salt Lake Tribune*, July 4 and 5, 1885, and *Deseret News*, July 6 and 7, both quoted in Larson, *"Americanization" of Utah*, 139–42. See also Verdoia and Fermage, *Utah*, 136.

74. Larson, *"Americanization" of Utah*, 195–96; on the "Pen" community generally, see 183–206. See also Verdoia and Firmage, *Utah*, 129–32.

75. On Mormon holiday celebration, particularly Independence Day, see also Bruce L. Campbell and Eugene E. Campbell, "Early Cultural and Intellectual Developments," in *Utah's History*, ed. Richard D. Poll (Provo, Utah, 1978), 311. On celebration following statehood, see Verdoia and Firmage, *Utah*, 176–82, 196–97.

76. The answer to this question, of course, is complex and variable, as it is when posed for African Americans. The great diversity among North America's Native peoples contributes to this complexity and forces any serious student of Native American experience to conclude that there is no such single entity as *the* American Indian. On the peculiar relationship of white Americans to Indians, see esp. Philip J. Deloria, *Playing Indian* (New Haven, 1998). See also Emily Greenwald's unpublished paper "'Hurrah! 4th of July!': The Ironies of Independence Day on the Reservations."

77. Colin G. Caloway, *The American Revolution in Indian Country: Crisis and Diversity in Native American Communities* (Cambridge, U.K., 1995), is the standard treatment of the subject. Clark de-

clared that "to excel them [Indians] in barbarity was and is the only way to make war upon the Indians" (quoted at 48).

78. William Apess, *On Our Own Ground: The Complete Writings of William Apess, a Pequot*, ed. Barry O'Connell (Amherst, Mass., 1992). All Apess quotations are taken from O'Connell's definitive edition.

79. Ibid., 276.

80. Ibid., 286. Apess's efforts to contest the notion that Indians had vanished in the eastern part of the United States, or that their disappearance was inevitable, paralleled those of African Americans in New England who struggled against their invisible status and erasure from the region's history; see esp. Joanne Pope Melish, *Disowning Slavery: Gradual Emancipation and "Race" in New England, 1780–1860* (Ithaca, N.Y., 1998).

81. Quoted in Apess, *On Our Own Ground*, 192.

82. Ibid., 195.

83. See Barry O'Connell's introduction to Apess, *On Our Own Ground*, esp. xviii–xxii, lxxiv.

84. John Wannuaucon Quinney, "Fourth of July Oration" (1854), in *The Heath Anthology of American Literature*, 2d ed., 2 vols., ed. Paul Lauter (Lexington, Mass., 1994), 1:1789–92, quotation at 1789. See also Wolfgang Hochbruck, "'I Ask for Justice': Native American Fourth of July Orations," in *The Fourth of July: Political Oratory and Literary Relations, 1776–1876*, ed. Paul Goetsch and Gerd Hurm (Tübingen, Germany, 1992), 155–65.

85. Quinney, "Fourth of July Oration." Quinney not only critiqued this nationalist white history but challenged more generally the supposed superiority of written over oral history, which remained a common obligation and endured through repeated recitation (see ibid., 1:1790, 1791).

86. Ibid., 1:1792. Quinney contested the exclusive identification of whites as pioneers, because his narrative traced Mahican migrations—pioneering—over a period of two hundred years.

87. Quoted in Hochbruck, "Native American Fourth of July Orations," 163.

88. "A Mission to the Menominee: Alfred Cope's Green Bay Diary," part 3, *Wisconsin Magazine of History* 50 (winter 1967): 135–38.

89. "Vinita, C.[herokee] N.[ation], July 4th, 1881," *Cherokee Advocate*, July 20, 1881, quoted in Hochbruck, "Native American Fourth of July Orations," 163–64.

90. T. J. Morgan, Commissioner of Indian Affairs, "Instructions to Indian Agents in Regard to Inculcation of Patriotism in Indian Schools," Dec. 10, 1889, in *The Fifty-Ninth Annual Report of the Commissioner of Indian Affairs to the Secretary of the Interior* (Washington, D.C., 1890), 167, see also 18–19. The national holidays enumerated included Washington's Birthday, Decoration Day, Fourth of July, Thanksgiving, and Christmas, as well as the anniversary of passage of the Dawes Act (1887)—Franchise Day—designed to allot Indian land in severalty, on February 8. On Pratt, and on educational means toward assimilationist ends more generally, see David Wallace Adams, *Education for Extinction: American Indians and the Boarding School Experience, 1875–1928* (Lawrence, Kans., 1995), esp. 51–55.

91. Alice Fletcher to the Commissioner of Indian Affairs, in *Fifty-Ninth Annual Report*, 19.

92. Henry Lyman, "Speech of Henry Lyman: Our Fourth of July," *Southern Workman*, Aug. 16, 1887, 89, quoted in Hochbruck, "Native American Fourth of July Orations," 165.

93. Quoted in Hochbruck, "Native American Fourth of July Orations," 164.

94. On the Crows, see Frederick E. Hoxie, *Parading through History: The Making of the Crow Nation in America, 1805–1935* (Cambridge, U.K., 1995), 209–10, 213–15, 363–65.

95. Carolyn Gilman and Mary Jane Schneider, *The Way to Independence: Memories of a Hidatsa Indian Family, 1840–1920* (St. Paul, Minn., 1987), 182. The place-name Independence could take on crueler ironies, of course, as it may have at Camp Independence, established July 4, 1862, to quell "disturbances" among the Native Americans in the Owens Valley in California. Here white independence, not Native autonomy and self-determination, was the objective. By 1915, Native people

had been gathered at Fort Independence Reservation. See Sven Liljeblad and Catherine S. Fowler, "Owens Valley Paiutes," in *Handbook of North American Indians: Great Basin*, ed. Warren L. D'Azevedo (Washington, D.C., 1986), 11:430.

96. Superintendent Ernest Jermark, circular to Indians of Fort Berthold Reservation, Jan. 30, 1922, reproduced in Gilman and Schneider, *Way to Independence*, 224.

97. Gilbert L. Wilson, Diary, vol. 4, Wilson Papers, Minnesota Historical Society, quoted ibid., 303.

98. *The Seventieth Annual Report of the Commissioner of Indian Affairs to the Secretary of the Interior* (Washington, D.C., 1901), 342–43, as quoted in Adams, *Education for Extinction*, 205–6; Hochbruck, "Native American Fourth of July Orations," 164. The anthropologist Gilbert L. Wilson observed Mandan and Hidatsa men at a Fourth of July celebration in 1907 in symbolic enactments of warfare during an evening dance; see Gilman and Schneider, *Way to Independence*, 303. Hoxie, *Parading through History*, 209, 209n. 32, 325, describes similar demonstrations by Crows early in the 1890s, as well as in the 1930s. These sorts of sham battles had become standard in Buffalo Bill's Wild West and were performed throughout the United States by Indian actors. On Wild West shows, see L. G. Moses, *Wild West Shows and the Images of American Indians, 1883–1933* (Albuquerque, N.M., 1996); and Don Russell, *The Wild West: A History of the Wild West Shows* (Fort Worth, Tex., 1970).

99. On the origins of Buffalo Bill's Wild West, see Russell, *Wild West*, esp. 1–30; Moses, *Wild West Shows*, esp. 21–41; Richard White, "Frederick Jackson Turner and Buffalo Bill," in *The Frontier in American Culture: An Exhibition at the Newberry Library, August 26, 1994–January 7, 1995, with Essays by Richard White and Patricia Limerick*, ed. James R. Grossman (Berkeley, 1994). See Carolyn T. Foreman, *Indians Abroad, 1493–1938* (Norman, Okla., 1943), on the larger history of Indians on display in Europe.

100. White, "Frederick Jackson Turner and Buffalo Bill," 35. Amos Bad Heart Bull, *A Pictographic History of the Oglala Sioux*, with drawings by Amos Bad Heart Bull, text by Helen H. Blish, and introduction by Mari Sandoz (Lincoln, Neb., 1967), esp. 42–43, 79; see plates 326–54 and 373–411, pp. 423–46, 464–97; some color plates appear between pp. 10 and 11. The evocative photographs of John A. Anderson at Rosebud, especially those taken between 1895 and 1915, similarly show Lakotas celebrating the Fourth of July through pageantry influenced by the Show Indian experience. See Don Doll and Jim Alinder, eds., *Crying for a Vision: A Rosebud Sioux Trilogy, 1886–1976* (Dobbs Ferry, N.Y., 1976), unpaginated.

101. Bad Heart Bull, *Pictographic History*, 42–43.

102. Ibid., 424 (quotation). Elements of the Smoothing-the-Place Dance are depicted in plates 376–89, 406–7 (pp. 467–80, 492–93). Warrior charges are shown in plates 391–405 (pp. 482–91). Plate 408 shows the commemoration of He Dog (pp. 494–95).

103. Gilman and Schneider, *Way to Independence*, 159–63, 223, 310. Hoxie, *Parading through History*, 363–65. See also the Grass Dance performances depicted in Bad Heart Bull, *Pictographic History*, plates 409–11 (pp. 495–97); a color plate showing the Oglala Grass Dance on July 4, 1903, faces p. 11.

104. On the powwow, see George P. Horse Capture, *Powwow* (Cody, Wyo., 1989); "Powwows of Interest" are listed at 57. See *Handbook of North American Indians: Great Basin*, 11:276, for a James Sherman photograph of a footrace that was part of the 1906 Fourth of July celebration at Duck Valley Reservation. On other reservations, Indian rodeos fulfill some of the same purposes. The Navajo Nation schedules its rodeo annually on the Fourth of July, for example. In 1995, their Fourth of July celebration ran from June 30 to July 4 at Window Rock.

105. Horse Capture, *Powwow*, 34. See also Gilman and Schneider, *Way to Independence*, 303–5, on appreciation of veterans and reverence for the United States flag among Hidatsas especially during the period of World War I. See also the essay by Howard Bad Hand (Brulé-Lakota from the Rosebud Reservation), "The Flag in American Indian Art," *Cross Paths* (publication of the Ma-

shantucket Pequot Museum and Research Center) 2, 3 (fall–winter 1999): 1, 7; and Toby Herbst and Joel Kopp, *The Flag in American Indian Art* (Cooperstown, N.Y., 1993).

106. See esp. Thomas A. Britten, *American Indians in World War I: At Home and at War* (Albuquerque, N.M., 1997), esp. 51–71; Parker quoted at 64. See also Russel L. Barsh, "American Indians in the Great War," *Ethnohistory* 38 (summer 1991): 276–303. Parker's distinguished relative Ely S. Parker had served as a general under Ulysses S. Grant in the Civil War.

107. Quoted in Herman J. Viola, *After Columbus: The Smithsonian Chronicle of the North American Indians* (Washington, D.C., 1990), 21. On the Vietnam era, see Tom Holm, *Strong Hearts, Wounded Souls: Native American Veterans of the Vietnam War* (Austin, Tex., 1996). While instilling a particular patriotism, military service, especially experience in battle, could on the other hand (or in addition) be profoundly unsettling for Native men and women. My analysis is not meant to challenge this point. See, for example, N. Scott Momaday's powerful novel *House Made of Dawn* (New York, 1968), or Leslie Marmon Silko, *Ceremony* (New York, 1977), both of which explore this theme.

108. Indian patriotism and nationalism are surely gendered, as emphasis on warrior traditions suggests. Nonetheless, women as well as men supported American war efforts in both twentieth-century world wars, and women demonstrated their own patriotism in other ways, as for example through participation in the Daughters of the American Revolution (founded in 1890). According to Holm, *Strong Hearts, Wounded Souls*, 23–25, Indian men fought in Vietnam (even though often against the war themselves) for a complex set of reasons: to fight for their Native country; to understand combat; to honor their families; and to maintain their own notion of peoplehood. Albert Smith as quoted in Bruce Watson, "*Jaysho, moasi, dibeh, ayeshi, hasclshnih, beshlo, shus, gini,*" *Smithsonian* 25, 5 (August 1993): 34–43; quotation at 36. This article discusses the famed Navajo code-talkers, whose Native language communication in the Pacific theater proved indecipherable by the Japanese.

109. "Monument for Warriors Challenges Stonemasons," Associated Press story, *Register-Guard* (Eugene, Ore.), June 24, 1996; obituary of Leon Shenandoah, by David Stout, *New York Times*, July 1996, B7.

110. Andy Newman, "Buffeted by Sea and by Fame, Dreaming of Home in Ukraine," *New York Times*, July 6, 2000, B7; Michael Kimmelman, "Why Settle for the Real Fireworks?" *New York Times*, July 4, 2000, E1. For Independence Day 2000, in fact, I witnessed two fireworks displays—the one in New York City as well as one sponsored by Branford, Connecticut, held over a week before the Fourth, indeed occurring even before the month of July, on Saturday, June 25.

111. Suzanne Boorsch, *Fireworks! Four Centuries of Pyrotechnics in Prints and Drawings* (New York, 2000).

112. Dirk Johnson, "Amid Flags and Fireworks, New Meanings of Patriotism," *New York Times*, July 4, 1996, A1, A7.

113. William H. Cohn, "A National Celebration: The Fourth of July in American History," *Cultures* 3, 1 (1976): 150–51. See David Glassberg, *American Historical Pageantry: The Uses of Tradition in the Early Twentieth Century* (Chapel Hill, N.C., 1990), 52ff., on the playground movement, including its nationwide "Safe and Sane July Fourth" campaign; Rosenzweig, *Eight Hours for What You Will*, 153–68. And see Raymond W. Smilor, "Creating a National Festival: The Campaign for a Safe and Sane Fourth, 1903–16," *Journal of American Culture* 2 (1979): 611–22.

114. Glassberg, *American Historical Pageantry*, esp. 24–35, 52–60, 93–107.

115. Don DeLillo, *White Noise* (New York, 1985), 218–19.

116. Pierre Berton, *Niagara: A History of the Falls* (New York, 1998); Alfred Runte, *National Parks: The American Experience* (Lincoln, Neb., 1979), 163–65.

117. Runte, *National Parks*, 163–65. Finally, in 1968, the National Park Service abolished the fire-fall, but Yosemite Valley remained a crowded place, filled with less-than-natural wonders during the Fourth of July; indeed, it was the scene of a riot during the Fourth weekend of 1970 (176).

118. "The Fourth. Grand Patriotic Demonstration in This City Yesterday. Mount Hood Illuminated," *Oregonian* (Portland, Ore.), July 5, 1887, from the scrapbooks of the Mazamas, a Pacific Northwest mountaineering club. Thanks to Erik Weiselberg for sharing this material with me; see also Weiselberg, "The Ascendancy of the Mazamas: Environment, Identity, and Mountain Climbing in Oregon, 1854–1930," Ph.D. dissertation, Department of History, University of Oregon, 1999.

119. *Indianapolis News* story, reprinted in the *Portland News*, July 18, 1887; "Mount Hood Illumination," *New Northwest*, July 7, 1887; J. M. Baltimore, "Illumination of Mount Hood," *Frank Leslie's Illustrated Newspaper*, July 30, 1887. These and other clippings are collected in the Mazama scrapbook.

120. "Watch Out for the Rockets' Red Glare," *New York Times*, July 2, 2000.

121. Shana Cohn, "Add Caution to July 4th Celebration, Experts Urge," *Register-Guard*, June 28, 1996, 1C, 2C; "8 Die as Blaze Erupts at Fireworks Store," *New York Times*, July 4, 1996, A7; Appelbaum, *Glorious Fourth*, 156–58; "CPSC Holds Fireworks Safety Press Conference on Mall in Washington," June 28, 2000; also see the CPSC website at http://www.cpsc.gov/prerel/prhtm100/00130.html.

122. "Aryan Nations Plan Another Idaho Parade," *Register-Guard*, Oct. 2, 1998; John Higham, *Strangers in the Land: Patterns of American Nativism, 1860–1925*, rev. ed. (New York, 1977 [1955]), 194–222, quotation at 195.

123. John Bodnar, *Remaking America: Public Memory, Commemoration, and Patriotism in the Twentieth Century* (Princeton, N.J., 1992), 83–84, 95–96. The Ku Klux Klan—at the height of its power in the 1920s—infamously marched on Independence Day, massively in Indianapolis and prominently in other cities outside the South. Yet in these cities the Klan was actively condemned by the press and clergy and as early as 1921 in Cleveland suppressed by city government (see 84–85, 96).

124. "Holiday Marked with Bells, Oaths," *Register-Guard*, July 5, 1997; Celia W. Dugger, "In Historic Surge to be Americans, 5,000 Take Oath," *New York Times*, July 5, 1997, A1, A27; "A Pledge of New Allegiance," *New York Times* photo, July 5, 2000, A15; Appelbaum, *Glorious Fourth*, 159.

125. Ben Ratliff, "Struttin' with a Big Band (but Hold Satchmo's Growl)," *New York Times*, July 6, 2000, E1, E3; Ralph Blumenthal, "Digging Deeply at Satchmo's Early Roots," *New York Times*, Aug. 15, 2000, B1, B2.

126. Patricia Leigh Brown, "Higher and Drier, Illinois Town Is Reborn," *New York Times*, May 6, 1996, A1, A10.

127. Lyn Spillman, "The Question of a Common Culture and the American Revolution Bicentennial Celebration," paper, Department of Sociology, University of California, Berkeley; Spillman, *Nation and Commemoration*, 94–135, examines the Bicentennial in comparison with Australia's 1988 bicentenary of European settlement. The official assessment was quoted in *Bicentennial Times*, a newsletter of the American Revolution Bicentennial Authority, Dec. 3, 1976, 1.

128. Ron Kovic, *Born on the Fourth of July* (New York, 1976), [xi], 46. "Collective effervescence" is Lyn Spillman's term (*Nation and Commemoration*, 130).

Chapter 2. Haven in a Heartless Calendar

1. [Finley Peter Dunne], "Thanksgiving," in *Mr. Dooley's Opinions* (New York, 1901), 125.

2. Presidential Thanksgiving Day Proclamation, Oct. 19, 1984, printed in the *Register-Guard* (Eugene, Ore.), Oct. 20, 1984. In 1988, however, in a decidedly anti-multicultural and self-parodying fashion, President Reagan mused, in response to university students in Moscow, who questioned him about the dismal living conditions of American Indians in the United States, "We have provided millions of acres of land for what are called preservations—or the reservations, I should say. [The Indians], from the beginning, announced that they wanted to maintain their way of life, as they had always lived there in the desert and the plains and so forth. But maybe we made a mistake. Maybe we should not have humored them in that, wanting to stay in that kind of prim-

itive lifestyle. Maybe we should have said, 'No, come join us. Be citizens along with the rest of us'"; quoted in Michael Dorris, "Mr. Reagan and the Indians," *Los Angeles Times*, June 12, 1988, reprinted in Dorris, *Paper Trails: Essays* (New York, 1994), 255.

3. See William T. Davis, *Plymouth Memories of an Octogenarian* (Plymouth, Mass., 1906), 28–29.

4. See esp. Ann Uhry Abrams, *The Pilgrims and Pocahontas: Rival Myths of American Origin* (Boulder, Colo., 1999); "What's Happening in . . . El Paso," *USA Today*, Apr. 12, 1996, 8D. On similar claims to the first Thanksgiving by Texas, Florida, Maine, and Virginia, see Diana Karter Appelbaum, *Thanksgiving: An American Holiday, an American Tradition* (New York, 1984), 14–17. In 1998, New Mexico and Texas celebrated the four hundredth anniversary of Oñate's *entrada*—establishing the first European settlement in North America and predating the 1607 settlement at Jamestown, Virginia—but not without its own controversy; see James Brooke, "An Anniversary Brings Pride and Resentment," *New York Times*, May 3, 1998, A19.

5. See chapter 3 in this volume as well as Matthew Dennis, "America Discovers Columbus: Centenary Celebrations of the Columbian Voyage of 'Discovery,' 1792–1992," paper delivered at Yale University, Oct. 23, 1992, and the American Historical Association annual meeting, December 1992. Burnishing their historical reputation, historian Evarts Boutell Greene made a representative case for the Pilgrims as America's forefathers in his keynote address at the Pilgrim Tercentenary Celebration's Convocation at the University of Illinois, Dec. 21, 1920; see Greene, *The Place of the Pilgrim in American History* ([Champaign, Ill.], 1921), esp. 15–22, 37, 41–42. On the "snide business of 'firstness,'" see Michael Kammen, *Mystic Chords of Memory: The Transformation of Tradition in American Culture* (New York, 1991), 384–92. See also Appelbaum, *Thanksgiving*, esp. 126–27, an excellent general guide to Thanksgiving's history.

6. Davis, *Plymouth Memories*, 28–29. And see John Seelye, *Memory's Nation: The Place of Plymouth Rock* (Chapel Hill, N.C., 1998), a mammoth cultural history that analyzes Plymouth Rock as a political symbol over the centuries.

7. Davis, *Plymouth Memories*, 264; Pilgrim celebrations of the Old Colony Club, the town, the Pilgrim Society, the first and third parishes, the Robinson Society, and the Fire Department of Plymouth, 1770–1895, are listed (356–57). Note that none was observed in 1821 or 1871.

8. These dates represent an adjustment from the Julian to the Gregorian calendar, inaugurated in 1582 but adopted in Great Britain and its colonies only in 1752. Ten days were added to dates occurring before 1700, with eleven days added to those after 1700. Plymouth's Old Colony Club, however, incorrectly added eleven days to the date of the December 11 landing, erroneously setting December 22 as Forefathers' Day. The error became a matter of debate, sometimes acrimonious, beginning in 1832. Although mathematics was not on their side, some traditionalists who resisted further adjustment declared, "We much prefer established error to novel truth." Although the date of the commemoration shifted back and forth between December 22 and 21 in the nineteenth century, the Pilgrim Society eventually determined that December 22 (the traditional if wrongly adjusted day) was preferable. See George F. Willison, *Saints and Strangers: Being the Lives of the Pilgrim Fathers and Their Families, with Their Friends and Foes; and an Account of Their Posthumous Wanderings in Limbo, Their Final Resurrection and Rise to Glory, and the Strange Pilgrimages of Plymouth Rock* (New York, 1945), 425–26.

9. James Baker, "Haunted by the Pilgrims," in *The Art and Mystery of Historical Archaeology: Essays in Honor of James Deetz*, ed. Anne Elizabeth Yentsch and Mary C. Beaudry (Boca Raton, Fl., 1992), 346–48. Davis, *Plymouth Memories*, provides personal recollections of numerous celebrations; see, for example, 361; 375–84 describes the 1870 commemoration; Daniel Webster, *A Discourse Delivered at Plymouth, December 22, 1820 in Commemoration of the First Settlement of New England* (Boston, 1821); *An Account of the Pilgrim Celebration at Plymouth, August 1, 1853* (Boston, 1853); *The Proceedings at the Celebration by the Pilgrim Society at Plymouth, December 21, 1870, of the Two Hundred and Fiftieth Anniversary of the Landing of the Pilgrims* (Cambridge, Mass., 1871). New England

Societies by 1870 had spread to Cincinnati, New York, Chicago, Montreal, New Orleans, St. Louis, San Francisco, and Aurora, Nevada. On the spread of Thanksgiving—rather than Forefathers' Day—beyond New England to the South and West, see Appelbaum, *Thanksgiving,* 89–127.

10. Davis, *Plymouth Memories,* 357–60, quotations from 359 and 127; Webster, *Discourse Delivered at Plymouth.*

11. Davis, *Plymouth Memories,* 365–70, 372–75; Baker, "Haunted by Pilgrims," 348. The eighty-one-foot granite monument to the Pilgrims was completed in 1889. That Plymouth Rock had become a national talisman was clear by the 1830s, when Alexis de Tocqueville found local people and tourists treating fragments as sacred relics (347).

12. See Appelbaum, *Thanksgiving,* 129–34. The antislavery message conveyed in New England sermons can be seen, for example, during the year of the Missouri Compromise and Plymouth's bicentenary, in Joseph Dana, *A Sermon, Delivered at Ipswich [Mass.] on the Day of the Annual Thanksgiving, November 23, 1820* (Newburyport, Mass., 1820), 15; and David Elliott, *The Causes of Our Fear, and the Grounds of our Encouragement. A Sermon, Preached August 31st, 1820. Being a Day of Humiliation, Thanksgiving and Prayer* (Chambersburg, Pa., 1820), esp. 7–8. Edward Payson, *God's Praises Sung; His Works Forgotten. A Sermon, Preached on the Public Thanksgiving, November 30, 1820* (Portland, Me., 1820), celebrates New England's forefathers generically and Maine's admission into the union specifically as a result of the Missouri Compromise, while not mentioning the slavery question.

13. See *Proceedings at the Celebration by the Pilgrim Society;* Davis, *Plymouth Memories,* 375–80.

14. Abraham Lincoln, "By the President of the United States of America. A Proclamation," in *Speeches and Writings, 1859–1865,* ed. Don E. Fehrenbacher (New York, 1989), 520–21.

15. On the 1921 commemoration, see Frederick W. Bittinger, *The Story of the Pilgrim Tercentenary Celebration* (Plymouth, Mass., 1923). See also Kammen, *Mystic Chords of Memory,* 384–85. To multiply the ironies, William T. Davis's *Plymouth Memories,* published only fifteen years earlier, did not even include an index item for "Thanksgiving." In contrast to the 1920 tercentenary, the 1820 bicentenary and the 1870 susquecentenary celebrated 1620 rather than 1621 (there were no Landing Day festivities recorded for 1821 or 1871). Forefathers' Day would be resurrected in the 1880s and 1890s, during an unprecedented surge of patriotism, religious nationalism, and filio-piety, by cultural elites who founded numerous new lineage-based patriotic societies, including the Society of Mayflower Descendants.

16. Jacob Abbott, as quoted in Jane C. Nylander, *Our Own Snug Fireside: Images of the New England Home, 1760–1860* (New York, 1994), 281 (my emphasis).

17. John Marsh, "A Sermon," dated pamphlets, American Antiquarian Society, 14 (my emphasis); here Marsh quotes scripture—Numbers 11:12, a passage in which Moses complains about his role as a "nursing father" required to carry the "suckling child," that is, the people Israel. Marsh thus suggests that, like the feminized Moses, the feminized Pilgrim Fathers—at least retroactively—accept their role as the leaders of a Chosen People who settled a Promised Land. For other biblical allusions to nursing fathers, see Isaiah 60:16 and Esther 2:7. Lydia Maria Child, "Thanksgiving-Day," manuscript of *A New Flower for Children* (New York, 1856), letter file, Beinecke Rare Book and Manuscript Library, Yale University, New Haven, Conn. The historical literature on the shifting place of women in late-eighteenth-century and nineteenth-century New England and the United States generally is extensive, but see esp. Elaine Forman Crane, *Ebb Tide in New England: Women, Seaports, and Social Change, 1630–1800* (Boston, 1998), esp. 63–64, 86; and Nancy F. Cott, *The Bonds of Womanhood: "Women's Sphere" in New England, 1780–1835* (New Haven, Conn., 1977). On the "feminization" of American Protestantism, see Richard D. Shiels, "The Feminization of American Congregationalism: 1730–1835," *American Quarterly* 33 (1981): 46–62; Ann Douglas, *The Feminization of American Culture* (New York, 1977).

18. Sarah Josepha Hale's story has been told in various places. See, for example, Appelbaum, *Thanksgiving;* and, of course, see Hale's own writings as editor of *Godey's Lady Book;* Hale, *North-*

wood: A Tale of New England (Boston, 1827); Hale, *Traits of American Life* (Philadelphia, 1835). Hale's biographers include Patricia Okker, *Our Sister Editors: Sarah J. Hale and the Tradition of Nineteenth-Century American Women Editors* (Athens, Ga., 1995); Ruth E. Finley, *The Lady of Godey's: Sarah Josepha Hale* (Philadelphia, 1931); and Sherbrooke Rogers, *Sarah Josepha Hale: A New England Pioneer, 1788–1879* (Grantham, N.H., 1985). See also Harriet Beecher Stowe's chapter, "How We Kept Thanksgiving at Oldtown," in her historical novel *Oldtown Folks* (Boston, 1868), in Stowe, *Three Novels*, ed. Kathryn Kish Sklar (New York, 1982), 1207–23, which offers a classic, nostalgic, and prescriptive account of the New England Thanksgiving. On Mother's Day and the feminization of the calendar that accompanied American commercialization, see Leigh Eric Schmidt, "The Commercialization of the Calendar: American Holidays and the Culture of Consumption, 1870–1930," *Journal of American History* 78 (December 1991): 887–916; and Schmidt, *Consumer Rites: The Buying and Selling of American Holidays* (Princeton, N.J., 1995), esp. 244–92.

19. The Salem *Observer*, quoted in the *Columbian Centinel*, Nov. 23, 1825, as quoted in Nylander, *Our Own Snug Fireside*, 261.

20. See Mary P. Ryan, *Women in Public: Between Banners and Ballots, 1825–1880* (Baltimore, Md., 1990), esp. 19–57; Schmidt, *Consumer Rites*. And see Stephen Nissenbaum's captivating *The Battle for Christmas: A Cultural History of America's Most Cherished Holiday* (New York, 1996), which builds on the work of Susan G. Davis, "'Making Night Hideous': Christmas Revelry and Public Order in Nineteenth-Century Philadelphia," *American Quarterly* 34, 2 (summer 1982): 185–99.

21. Sarah Josepha Hale, *Northwood: A Tale of New England* (Boston, 1827); Hale to President Abraham Lincoln, Sept. 28, 1863, with an enclosed, annotated editorial from *Godey's Lady's Book*, July 1859, 81, one of many written by Hale advocating a national Thanksgiving; Manuscripts Division, Library of Congress, Washington, D.C. See also Appelbaum, *Thanksgiving*, 153; and see Hale's 1860 editorial, "Editor's Table," *Godey's Lady's Book*, November 1860, 271.

22. Mrs. Sarah Josepha Hale, *Northwood; or, Life North and South: Showing the True Character of Both* (New York, 1852). Lincoln, "A Proclamation," 520–21. On the reconciliation of North and South after the Civil War, with particular attention to gender, see Nina Silber, "Intemperate Men, Spiteful Women, and Jefferson Davis," in *Divided Houses: Gender and the Civil War*, ed. Catherine Clinton and Nina Silber (New York, 1992), 283–305; and Silber, *The Romance of Reunion: Northerners and the South, 1865–1900* (Chapel Hill, N.C., 1993).

23. William DeLoss Love, *The Fast and Thanksgiving Days of New England* (Boston, 1895); David Cressy, *Bonfires and Bells: National Memory and the Protestant Calendar in Elizabethan and Stuart England* (London, 1989), esp. 190–206, on the English calendar in colonial America; see also Richard P. Gildrie, "The Ceremonial Puritan: Days of Humiliation and Thanksgiving," *New England Historical and Genealogical Register* 136 (January 1982): 3–16; David D. Hall, *Worlds of Wonder, Days of Judgment: Popular Religious Belief in Early New England* (New York, 1989), 166–212; Nissenbaum, *Battle for Christmas*, esp. 3–48.

24. Sabbatarianism marks the Sabbath—observed sometimes on Saturday and sometimes on Sunday, the latter day among American Protestants and Catholics—as a day of rest and worship. English and Low Country Puritans remodeled their liturgical calendars in the sixteenth and seventeenth centuries to pivot weekly around the Sabbath, which became a significant holy day as numerous saints' feasts were purged from the calendar. In colonial America, the Sunday Sabbath established itself, and blue laws—named supposedly for the color of the paper on which they were printed in Connecticut—enforced strict Sunday observance by banning work and mandating business closures. See Alexis McCrossen, *Holy Day, Holiday: The American Sunday* (Ithaca, N.Y., 2000), esp. 9–12.

25. Love, *Fast and Thanksgiving Days*, 41–42. The Belgic Confession (1561) and Second Helvetic Confession (1566) quoted at 41–42.

26. Gildrie, "Ceremonial Puritan," 3–4 (quotation); Hall, *Worlds of Wonder*, 169–72.

27. Love, *Fast and Thanksgiving Days*, 156.

28. Ibid., 159–61.

29. Hall, *Worlds of Wonder*, 171–72; Love, *Fast and Thanksgiving Days*, 122–28, 199–200.

30. Love, *Fast and Thanksgiving Days*, 221–27, quotations on 227.

31. Ibid., 230–36, quotations 230, 232; see also Gildrie, "Ceremonial Puritan," 11–13.

32. Appelbaum, *Thanksgiving*, 62–64.

33. Margaret Fuller, "Thanksgiving," *New-York Daily Tribune*, Dec. 12, 1844, 2, in *Margaret Fuller: Essays on American Life and Letters*, ed. Joel Myerson (Schenectady, N.Y., 1978), 248–53.

34. Governor P. Hansborough Bell, as quoted in Appelbaum, *Thanksgiving*, 131. Antislavery ministers built on a Thanksgiving tradition established earlier in the century by black as well as white preachers. See esp. Absalom Jones, "A Thanksgiving Sermon, Preached January 1, 1808 . . . on Account of the Abolition of the African Slave Trade, on That Day, by the Congress of the United States," in *American Sermons: The Pilgrims to Martin Luther King Jr.*, ed. Michael Warner (New York, 1999), 538–45.

35. Governor John Geary, as quoted in Appelbaum, *Thanksgiving*, 135.

36. Ibid., 142–45, 164.

37. See esp. Silber, *Romance of Reunion*.

38. George S. May, "The Thanksgiving Day Race of 1895," *Chicago History* 11, 3 (1982): 175–83; "Turkey Race," *Times-Picayune*, Nov. 20, 1994, 2D1; James R. Kuykendall and Elizabeth S. Howard, "Turkey Trot Days at Oliver Hall's Store," *Alabama Review* 38, 2 (1985): 105–18. Variations of the turkey trot remain popular today among American runners; the November 2000 issue of *Runner's World* contained some ninety Thanksgiving or turkey-trot road races throughout the country in its Race Calendar section (95–107).

39. Richard C. Crepeau, "Sport and Society Broadcast for Friday, Nov. 29, 1996," WUCF-FM 89.9, Orlando, Fla.; Elliott J. Gorn and Warren Goldstein, *A Brief History of American Sports* (New York, 1993), 131, 154. See also Appelbaum, *Thanksgiving*, 198–205.

40. See James Deetz and Jay Anderson, "The Ethnogastronomy of Thanksgiving," *Saturday Review of Science*, Nov. 25, 1972, 29–38; Deetz, *In Small Things Forgotten* (Garden City, N.Y., 1977); and see James Deetz and Patricia Scott Deetz, *The Light Here Kindled: Life, Love and Death at Plymouth Colony* (New York, 2000). Deetz quotation from Stanley Hock, "Thanksgiving: The Shocking Truth," *Express* (San Francisco Bay area), Nov. 21, 1986, 6.

41. "Why Turkey on Holidays? Marketing, of Course," Associated Press story, *Register-Guard*, Nov. 24, 1988, B1; "Our Thanksgiving Bird," *Harper's Weekly*, Dec. 2, 1871, 1132; Mark Fritz, "Are Growers Breeding Disaster?" *Register-Guard*, Nov. 19, 1995, 1A, 4A; Margaret Visser, "One Strange Bird," *New York Times*, Nov. 26, 1992, op-ed page; Suzanne Hamlin, "Sleepy? Maybe It's the Turkey," *New York Times*, Nov. 23, 1994, C1, C5.

42. Franklin Benjamin Hough, *Proclamations for Thanksgiving, Issued by the Continental Congress, President Washington, by the National and State Governments on the Peace of 1815, and by the Governors of New York since the Introduction of the Custom; with Those of the Governors of the Several States in 1858. With an Historical Introduction and Notes* (Albany, N.Y., 1858). Greeley's poem is quoted in Appelbaum, *Thanksgiving*, 119. On the New York Thanksgiving exodus to New England, see "The Thanksgiving Dinner. Annual Exodus of New Englanders Who Want to Eat It at Home," *New York Times*, Nov. 29, 1888.

43. Rev. R. F. Putnam, as quoted in Appelbaum, *Thanksgiving*, 118. E. A. Pearson, a young woman of Boston, wrote mournfully to her brother, the Rev. Ephraim Abbot, on November 24, 1811, lamenting that "this season found us all *scattered*." She nonetheless observed, "yet there is a center, where, (however separated) the pious souls often meet—there we had reason to join in extolling the unreasoned goodness of Heaven—how much mercy have we received the year's past!" Ephraim Abbot letters, manuscript collections, American Antiquarian Society, Worcester, Mass.

(I am grateful to Jonathan Sassi for bringing these letters to my attention); Edwin McDowell, "Many Turn Holiday into Mini-Vacation," *New York Times*, Nov. 24, 1994, B24.

44. See, for example, the FTD Florist advertisement in the national Sunday newspaper supplement, *Parade*, Nov. 20, 1994, 12: "Beauty and the Feast: This Thanksgiving let your professional FTD florist create a gift that's a match for the holiday feast." Mobil Corporation offered "A Note of Thanks" on the op-ed page of the *New York Times*, Nov. 24, 1994, A33, for "what's *right* with us and our world." Included, among many other gifts, were the democratic system, humor, volunteers, tolerance, and the wonders of nature; no mention was made of gasoline consumption to facilitate holiday travel.

45. Ronette King, "The Holiday Stretch; Retailers Are Vying Valiantly to Get Pockets Jingling, Registers Ringing," *Times-Picayune*, Nov. 20, 1994, F1, F3; Carl Bybee, "Northwest Prime for New Holiday: Buy Nothing Day," *Register-Guard*, Nov. 24, 1999, op-ed page.

46. Yuri Rasovsky, "Reioyce Together: An Aural Historie . . . [of Thanksgiving]," a proposal for a radio documentary program on the history of Thanksgiving, xiii–xvi.

47. Ibid. See also Appelbaum, *Thanksgiving*, esp. 233–44.

48. Schmidt, "Commercialization of the Calendar," 890.

49. Quoted in Appelbaum, *Thanksgiving*, 239.

50. See Schmidt, "Commercialization of the Calendar," 915.

51. See, for example, Appelbaum, *Thanksgiving*, 222–24. For more recent examples of Americanization associated with Thanksgiving, and the creativity demonstrated by immigrants in forging an American identity that conserves their particular heritages, see Sara Rimer, "For Immigrants, English Helps Them Feel at Home," *New York Times*, Nov. 28, 1991, A1, A5; and Elsa Brenner, "West Indians in Pursuit of the American Dream," *New York Times*, Nov. 28, 1993, Westchester County sec., 13.

52. Eve Bunting, *How Many Days to America? A Thanksgiving Story*, illus. by Beth Peck (New York, 1988), n.p.

53. Mike Clary, "Saving Grace Comes to Child Adrift at Sea; Rescue: on Thanksgiving Morning," *Los Angeles Times*, Nov. 26, 1999, A1; Clary, "Two Nations Tug at 5-Year-Old Survivor," ibid., Nov. 30, 1999, A1; Traci Watson, "Cubans Drown Trying to Reach USA," *USA Today*, Nov. 26, 1999, 3A; Sue Anne Pressly, "Young Refugee at Center of International Dispute; Rather, Cuba Wants Return of Boy Rescued at Sea," *Washington Post*, Nov. 30, 1999, A03. Clary reported that according to a hospital spokesperson, Elian had a Thanksgiving plate, including turkey and mashed potatoes, but in nonconformity with tradition, "he didn't like the stuffing—he spit it out."

54. See, for example, Paul Rudnick, "Sailing through a Skyful of Thanksgiving Reveries; Goyim and Indians," *New York Times*, Nov. 28, 1991, C6; James Bennet, "Pilgrims' Progress: In Bronx, Plucky Settlers Give Thanks," ibid., Nov. 27, 1992, A1. On the perceived appropriateness of Thanksgiving for Jews, see, for example, Don Plonsky, "Three Rabbis Say Thanksgiving Is a Holiday for Jews Too," *Northern California Jewish Bulletin*, Nov. 21, 1986, 1.

55. Anzia Yezierska, "America and I," in *The Open Cage: An Anzia Yezierska Collection*, ed. Alice Kessler-Harris (New York, 1979), 20–33, quotation at 32–33.

56. Pearl Kazin's story is reproduced in the Jewish Reconstructionist prayer book *Kol Haneshamah: Shabbat Vehagim* (Wyncote, Pa., 1994), 825–26; the Jewish Reconstructionist movement has also distributed a pamphlet to its members, *Tefilah for Thanksgiving in Two Civilizations* (Wyncote, Pa., 1998), which sanctions American Thanksgiving and infuses it with religious meaning for Jews, while emphasizing the holiday's multiculturalism.

57. Andrew R. Heinz, *Adapting to America: Jewish Immigrants, Mass Consumption, and the Search for American Identity* (New York, 1990).

58. Rudnick, "Sailing through a Skyful of Thanksgiving Reveries," C6; Jenna Weissman Joselit, *The Wonders of America: Reinventing Jewish Culture, 1880–1950* (New York, 1994), 5.

59. Joan Nathan, *Jewish Cooking in America* (New York, 1998), 210.

60. Plonsky, "Thanksgiving Is a Holiday for Jews Too"; Joe Sexton, "Three Thanksgivings in Brooklyn Help Survivors Defy Stings of Disaster," *New York Times*, Nov. 24, 1995, A17.

61. "Indian March Marks Bittersweet Holiday," *New York Times*, Nov. 28, 1991, B9.

62. "Indian Protest Turns Violent in Plymouth," Associated Press story, *Register-Guard*, Nov. 28, 1997.

63. See, for example, "Indian March Marks Bittersweet Holiday," *New York Times*, Nov. 28, 1991, B9 (quotation); Diane Ketcham, "Long Island Journal: A Gathering of Tribes," *New York Times*, Nov. 28, 1993, Long Island sec., 3; Kathleen Teltsch, "Chronicle," *New York Times*, Aug. 26, 1992, B6, which describes the fifth annual A Giving of Thanks. The late Modoc-Irish anthropologist and writer Michael Dorris has criticized Thanksgiving, at least in its mythologized version, in "For Indians, No Thanksgiving," *New York Times*, Nov. 24, 1988, op-ed page, reprinted in Dorris, *Paper Trails*, 228–31. Nonetheless, he celebrated the redeemable holiday himself, as becomes clear in his essay "Thankfulness," reprinted from *Parents*, October 1992, at 74–76.

64. William Apess, *Eulogy on King Philip, as Pronounced at the Odeon, in Federal Street, Boston* (1836), in *On Our Own Ground: The Complete Writings of William Apess, a Pequot*, ed. Barry O'Connell (Amherst, Mass., 1992), 286.

65. "Indian Protest Turns Violent," Associated Press, Nov. 28, 1997; Jill Lepore, "Revenge of the Wampanoags," *New York Times*, Nov. 25, 1998, op-ed page; Eliza Wells Smith, "Op-Art" feature, *New York Times*, Nov. 27, 1997, A23. For other examples of Native celebration, see the *Yakima Nation Review*, Nov. 19, 1993, notice of a Thanksgiving mini-powwow at the Toppenish, Washington, longhouse; or see "UAA Sponsors Thanksgiving Celebration," *Tundra Times*, Nov. 17, 1993: "Give thanks by joining the Native American Thanksgiving celebration hosted by the University of Alaska Anchorage (UAA) Native Student Club." For evidence that Thanksgiving is being transformed increasingly into a multicultural holiday that appreciates the history of Native Americans, see Pam Belluck, "Pilgrims Wear Different Hats in Recast Thanksgiving Tales," *New York Times*, Nov. 23, 1995, A1, A20.

66. Quoted in Love, *Fast and Thanksgiving Days*, 88.

67. Jennifer Lenhart, "Feast Helps Take the Chill out of the Air," *Houston Chronicle*, Nov. 26, 1993, A37; Marty Graham, "Food Plentiful, So Are Volunteers at Holiday Superfeast for Hungry," *Houston Post*, Nov. 26, 1993, A44. See also David Lundy, "Hosea Delivers Dinner Again," *Atlanta Journal Constitution*, Nov. 26, 1993, D2; Sarah Taladay, "Gifts of Food Answer Prayers of the Homeless," *Chicago Tribune*, Nov. 26, 1993, 2C3. Note also that Thanksgiving is the occasion when the American Indian Relief Council launches its Operation Turkey Dinner, which calls attention to the nearly four-hundred-year history of Indian-white relations, beginning with the Pilgrims and Wampanoags, and supplies turkey dinners to more than ten thousand Native people; fund-raising letter, Brian J. Brown to members, 1995. On nineteenth-century charity and benevolence associated with Thanksgiving, see Nylander, *Our Own Snug Fireside*, 277–78.

68. I am grateful to Margaret McBride for bringing this word, *radiidin*, and these works to my attention. Melanie Wallendorf and Eric J. Arnould, "'We Gather Together': Consumption Rituals of Thanksgiving Day," *Journal of Consumer Research* 18, 1 (June 1991): 13–31, esp. 16, 25–26; on the responsibilities similarly placed on women to nurture families—and arrange reunions and feasts like Thanksgiving—see Micaela DiLeonardo, "The Female World of Cards and Holidays: Women, Families, and the Work of Kinship," *Signs: Journal of Women in Culture and Society* 12, 3 (spring 1987): 440–53.

69. John Bebow, "Santa Has New Helpers: Mail Carriers," *Detroit News and Free Press*, Nov. 19, 1993, B1; see also the story detailing the parade, ibid., Nov. 26, 1993, A8. The story of St. Louis's Thanksgiving Day Parade was described under the headline "Christmas in St. Louis," *St. Louis Post-Dispatch*, Nov. 26, 1993, B1. See also Holly Morris, "It Gets Me in the Spirit," *Atlanta Journal*

Constitution, Nov. 26, 1993, D1. Notwithstanding Detroit's parade, Tony Snow, "A Nation Blessed with Spirit," *Detroit News and Free Press*, Nov. 25, 1993, E3, marvels that the holiday has not been "messed up" by advertisers, arguing that it has remained mercifully personal, private, and informal.

70. Note that retail establishments that do not sponsor parades often advertise themselves by calling attention to the fact that they are closed on Thanksgiving, in keeping with the spirit of the day. For example, in the *New York Times* (Nov. 28, 1996, A6), next to an ad for Macy's—reading "Happy Thanksgiving (Did we mention we're having a Parade today!)"—Bloomingdale's proclaimed in its own ad, "Happy Thanksgiving. Bloomingdale's is closed today. We're enjoying the holiday with family and friends, and we hope you are too. Look for our 8-page insert in today's paper, then shop early tomorrow during our big Thanksgiving Sale."

71. By "postmodern" I mean to emphasize the inclusiveness and heterogeneity of the occasion, with its multiple, conflicting, sometimes contesting meanings, what the Russian cultural theorist Mikhail Bakhtin termed "heteroglossia." The holiday is produced popularly through plural forms and genres, mixed in unpredictable combinations.

Chapter 3. Reinventing America

1. Quoted in J. H. Elliott, *The Old World and the New, 1492–1650* (Cambridge, U.K., 1970), 10.

2. A number of recent works have reexamined Columbus the man as well as the myth. Among the most significant are the following: Felipe Fernandez-Armesto, *Columbus* (Oxford, U.K., 1991); William D. Phillips Jr. and Carla Rahn Phillips, *The Worlds of Christopher Columbus* (Cambridge, U.K., 1992); Kirkpatrick Sale, *The Conquest of Paradise: Christopher Columbus and the Columbian Legacy* (New York, 1990), the exemplary anti-Columbus history; John Noble Wilford, *The Mysterious History of Columbus: An Exploration of the Man, the Myth, the Legacy* (New York, 1991); Claudia L. Bushman, *America Discovers Columbus: How an Italian Explorer Became an American Hero* (Hanover, N.H., 1992).

3. David Beers Quinn, *England and the Discovery of America, 1481–1620* (New York, 1974). In one of the most dramatic recent challenges, Yale University Press, on Columbus Day 1965, published a volume about the Vinland Map, purported to be a genuine pre-Columbian European map of the New World lands discovered by Leif Eriksson in the eleventh century; see R. A. Skelton, Thomas E. Marston, and George D. Painter, *The Vinland Map and Tartar Relation*, with a foreword by Alexander O. Vietor (New Haven, Conn., 1965).

4. Alfred W. Crosby Jr., *The Columbian Exchange: Biological and Cultural Consequences of 1492* (Westport, Conn., 1972), 44–45.

5. Christopher Columbus, *The Four Voyages of Christopher Columbus: Being His Own Log-book, Letter, and Dispatches*, ed. and trans. J. M. Cohen (London, 1969), 59.

6. Quoted in Fernandez-Armesto, *Columbus*, 138; on the number of casualties resulting from Columbus's pacification campaign, see 112–13.

7. Thus priority asserted for Leif Eriksson constitutes, for Italian American boosters, a slap in the face. Those counterclaims by Norse immigrants and their descendants function essentially like those of Catholic hyphenated Americans: to establish their legitimate claim to American citizenship, bypassing the seventeenth- and eighteenth-century Anglo-American past and linking themselves instead to the "first American," that is, an eleventh-century discoverer. Norwegian identity and its representation through connections to ancient Norse discovery are discussed perceptively in April R. Schultz, *Ethnicity on Parade: Inventing the Norwegian American through Celebration* (Amherst, Mass., 1994), esp. 74–78.

8. Quoted in Bushman, *America Discovers Columbus*, 107. Washington Irving's biography, *The Life and Voyages of Christopher Columbus*, first appeared in English and American editions in 1828, and it was reprinted repeatedly thereafter. Its influence on Americans' understanding of Colum-

bus is unmatched by any other writing on the Admiral. For good assessments of the work and its impact, see Bushman, *America Discovers Columbus*, 107–26, and Sale, *Conquest of Paradise*, 342–45.

9. Samuel Sewall, *Phaenomena quaedam Apocalyptica Ad Aspectum* NOVI ORBIS *configurata. Or some few lines toward a description of the New* HEAVEN, *As It makes to those who stand upon the* NEW EARTH (Boston, 1697), 47; see also 49. And see *The Diary of Samuel Sewall, 1674–1729, newly edited from the manuscript at the Massachusetts Historical Society*, ed. M. Halsey Thomas, 2 vols. (New York, 1973), 2:630, 960, 1039.

10. *Diary of Samuel Sewall*, 2:960; on October 11, 1720, Sewall wrote, rather awkwardly and obscurely, to the widow he was courting, "I thank you for your Unmerited Favours of yesterday; and hope to have the Happiness of Waiting on you tomorrow before Eight a-clock after Noon. I pray GOD to keep you, and give you a joyfull entrance upon the Two Hundred and twenty ninth year of Christopher Columbus his Discovery."

11. Jonathan Edwards, "Thoughts on the Revivals in 1740," in *The Works of President Edwards, in Ten Volumes* (New York: S. Converse, 1829–30), 4:129. See also Delno C. West and August Kling, "Columbus and Columbia: A Brief Survey of the Early Creation of the Columbus Symbol in American History," *Studies in Popular Culture* 12, 2 (1989): 48.

12. Michael Warner, *The Letters of the Republic: Publication and the Public Sphere in Eighteenth-Century America* (Cambridge, Mass., 1990), quotation at xiii. On the original concept of the public sphere, perceptively applied and reworked by Warner and others, see Jürgen Habermas, *The Structural Transformation of the Public Sphere: An Inquiry into a Category of Bourgeois Society*, trans. Thomas Burger (1962; reprint, Cambridge, Mass., 1989). On the idea of nationalism, see Benedict Anderson, *Imagined Communities: Reflection on the Origins and Spread of Nationalism*, rev. ed. (London, 1991); and see David Waldstreicher, *In the Midst of Perpetual Fetes: The Making of American Nationalism, 1775–1820* (Chapel Hill, 1997). Jay Fliegelman, *Declaring Independence: Jefferson, Natural Language, and the Culture of Performance* (Stanford, Calif., 1993), esp. 25–26, emphasizes the performative aspect of publishing in revolutionary America. Thus, not only did texts recapitulate events not witnessed by readers, but some, like the Declaration of Independence, could produce events.

13. Philip Freneau [and Hugh Henry Brackenridge], *A Poem, on the Rising Glory of America (1772)*, in *Poems Written between the Years 1768 and 1794*, a facsimile edition (Delmar, N.Y., 1976), 36–46. See also Kenneth Silverman, *A Cultural History of the American Revolution: Painting, Music, Literature, and the Theatre in the Colonies and the United States . . . , 1763–1789* (New York, 1976), 232–34. The community, or nation, that these poets and others typically imagined before 1775 was Great Britain.

14. Joel Barlow, *Columbiad* (Philadelphia, 1807), bk. 1, ll. 176–84. The complete poem, in facsimile reproduction of the enlarged and revised 1825 edition, is in *The Works of Joel Barlow*, 2 vols. (1825; reprint, Gainesville, Fla., 1970), 2:371–866.

15. David S. Shields, *Oracles of Empire: Poetry, Politics, and Commerce in British America, 1690–1750* (Chicago, 1990), 26–32.

16. Sylvanus Americus [Samuel Nevill], "The History of the Northern Continent of *America*," serialized in *The New American Magazine* (Woodbridge, N.J., 1758). On Nevill's history and loyalist verses, see Bushman, *America Discovers Columbus*, 28–30, 42–43.

17. Silverman, *Cultural History of the American Revolution*, 116–17.

18. Bushman, *America Discovers Columbus*, 41. See also Philip J. Deloria's *Playing Indian* (New Haven, Conn., 1998), 36, 51–54; see also John Higham, "Indian Princess and Roman Goddess: The First Female Symbols of America," *Proceedings of the American Antiquarian Society* 100 (1990): 45–79.

19. Mercy Otis Warren, "A Political Reverie," first published in the *Boston Gazette*, and subsequently in *Poems, Dramatic and Miscellaneous by Mrs. M. Warren* (Boston, 1790), reproduced in facsimile in *The Plays and Poems of Mercy Otis Warren*, comp. Benjamin Franklin V (Delmar, N.Y.,

1980), 188–97. Phillis Wheatley, "His Excellency, Gen. Washington," written at Providence, R.I., October 26, 1775, and later published in the *Pennsylvania Magazine*; also see *The Poems of Phillis Wheatley*, ed. Julian D. Mason Jr. (Chapel Hill, N.C., 1966), 87–90. On these poets, see Bushman, *America Discovers Columbus*, 41–42, 46, 48–50, 62–75; see also Silverman, *Cultural History of the Revolution*, 227, 284–85, 320. The Yale poets Timothy Dwight and Joel Barlow, also described in this volume (402–3), and in Bushman, *American Discovers Columbus* (50–53, 75–80), similarly deployed the idea of Columbia in their popular, nationalist works.

20. David C. Humphrey, *From King's College to Columbia, 1746–1800* (New York, 1976), 270–72.

21. See Sale, *Conquest of Paradise*, 338–39; West and Kling, *Columbus and Columbia*, 52–54; Bushman, *America Discovers Columbus*, 54–55. On the goddess Columbia, see Deloria, *Playing Indian*, 51–53; Higham, "Indian Princess and Roman Goddess"; and see E. McClung Fleming, "The American Image as Indian Princess, 1765–1783," *Winterthur Portfolio* 2 (1965): 65–81; and Fleming, "From Indian Princess to Greek Goddess: The American Image, 1783–1815," ibid., 3 (1967): 37–66.

22. See Edwin Patrick Kilroe, *Saint Tammany and the Origin of the Society of Tammany or Columbian Order in the City of New York* (New York, 1913); and see Deloria, *Playing Indian*, 38–70. Edward G. Porter discusses "The Ship Columbia and the Discovery of Oregon," *New England Magazine* (June 1892): 370–71.

23. See Higham, "Indian Princess and Roman Goddess," 45–79, esp. 56–58; Deloria, *Playing Indian*, 53; Fleming, "American Image as Indian Princess," 66. The dual-gendered Columbia (feminine)/Columbus (masculine) became a multivocal symbol, expressing almost simultaneously stability and passivity, on the one hand, and dynamism and expansion on the other.

24. On the Northwest Ordinance, see Peter S. Onuf, *Statehood and Union: A History of the Northwest Ordinance* (Bloomington, Ind., 1987). Of course, the denial that expansion of white Americans into the American interior was colonial required a willful disregard of Native peoples and their occupation of these lands. The myth of the Vanishing Indian in the old Northwest became a self-fulfilling prophecy, the realization of which came only at great trouble, expense, and loss of life. It is also clear that this common reading of the West as destiny was, in fact, exclusive, leaving out, for example, African Americans, most of whom remained slaves. For a provocative analysis of the potent intersection of nationalism and regionalism, esp. western regionalism, see Waldstreicher, *In the Midst of Perpetual Fetes*, 246–93. And see Edward L. Ayers, Patricia Nelson Limerick, Stephen Nissenbaum, and Peter S. Onuf, *All over the Map: Rethinking American Regions* (Baltimore, 1996).

25. Silverman, *Cultural History of the American Revolution*, 576, 579, 585.

26. *Account of the Grand Federal Procession, Philadelphia, July 4, 1788. To which are added, Mr. Wilson's Oration, and a letter on the Subject of the Procession* (Philadelphia, 1788), 17.

27. Silverman, *Cultural History of the American Revolution*, 580. If such an event as the Grand Procession can be read as a text, the reverse seems also true: the published account read by nonparticipants, in a sense, might produce an event, an experience of nationalism for its readers. Susan G. Davis, *Parades and Power: Street Theatre in Nineteenth-Century Philadelphia* (Philadelphia, 1986), perceptively examines this and similar events in early national Philadelphia.

28. Edward F. De Lancey, "Columbian Celebration of 1792: The First in the United States," *Magazine of American History* 29, 1 (January 1893): 12; Charles T. Thompson, "Columbus Day One Hundred Years Ago," *Chautauquan: A Monthly Magazine*, n.s., 16, 7 (November 1892): 192–93. Philadelphia's commemoration may have been celebrated publicly only in print, with the publication of a "Columbia edition" of Dunlap's *Daily American Advertiser*. In nearby Princeton, Philadelphia patriot Joseph Reed delivered a celebratory oration on Columbus, which was reproduced in Dunlap's paper. Near Baltimore, on his private estate, Charles Francis Adrian le Paulmier, Chevalier d'Anmour, French consul and American patriot, dedicated an obelisk some twenty-eight-feet tall to the sacred memory of Columbus. See William Eleroy Curtis, "The Columbus Monuments," *Chautauquan: A Monthly Magazine*, n.s., 16, 7 (November 1892): 138–39; J. M. Dickey, comp., *Chris-*

topher Columbus and His Monument Columbia (Chicago, 1892), 73–78. See also Bushman, *America Discovers Columbus,* 92–94, on the Baltimore monument.

29. *The Independent Chronicle, and the Universal Advertiser* (Boston), Oct. 25, 1792. See Massachusetts Historical Society, *Proceedings,* vol. 1 [1791–1835] (Boston, 1879), 28–29, 31, 44–46; Louis Leonard Tucker, *Clio's Consort: Jeremy Belknap and the Founding of the Massachusetts Historical Society* (Boston, 1990), 134–35. And see "The Last Columbian Century Anniversary," *Harper's Weekly,* Aug. 17, 1889, 655; De Lancey, "Columbian Celebration of 1792," 2–5; Thompson, "Columbus Day One Hundred Years Ago," 190–91. See also Bushman, *America Discovers Columbus,* 81–97, esp. 88–91.

30. Tucker, *Clio's Consort,* 134–35.

31. *Journal and Patriotic Register* (New York), Oct. 17, 1792.

32. Ibid.

33. On the Tammany monument to Columbus, see ibid.; Kilroe, *Saint Tammany,* 184–86 and 173–77. And see De Lancey, "Columbian Celebration of 1792," 6–11; Thompson, "Columbus Day One Hundred Years Ago," 189–90. Other more permanent Columbian monuments were described in Curtis, "Columbus Monuments."

34. See Kilroe, *Saint Tammany,* 84–87. Appendices (209ff.) list the various Tammany Societies in the colonies and United States, their celebrations, and their orations, dating from 1771. See also Deloria, *Playing Indian,* esp. 38–70. Deloria carefully distinguishes the New York from the Philadelphia Tammany Society, the latter conceived in the very different terms required by postrevolution America (47–50). On the rituals of the New York Tammany Society, see also Alfred F. Young, *The Democratic Republicans of New York: The Origins, 1763–1797* (Chapel Hill, N.C., 1967), 398–99.

35. Ironically, pledges to inclusiveness notwithstanding, the New York Tammany Society exhibited a strong anti-Catholic, anti-Irish sentiment in its early years and worked to keep "foreigners" out. Needless to say, women and blacks—free or otherwise—were similarly excluded. The Irish came to dominate the Tammany Society in Pennsylvania; the collision between these immigrants and older members, filled with ethnic, nativist prejudices, caused the fragmentation and demise of most older Tammany Societies. Later, the New York society too would be dominated by Irish immigrants and their descendants; see Kilroe, *Saint Tammany,* 142–46; Deloria, *Playing Indian,* 45–47.

36. *Journal and Patriotic Register* (New York), Oct. 17, 1792.

37. See, for example, Belknap's *Discourse,* as well as his treatment of Columbus in his *American Biography, or An Historical Account of Those Persons Who Have Been Distinguished in America* (Boston, 1794–98), 123–28. Blacks in the urban North suffered continued exclusion, even with abolition and the enlargement of the public sphere. See esp. Shane White, " 'It Was a Proud Day': African Americans, Festivals, and Parades in the North, 1741–1834," *Journal of American History* 81 (June 1994): 13–50.

38. On the impact of the French Revolution in the United States, see Simon P. Newman, *Parades and the Politics of the Street: Festive Culture in the Early American Republic* (Philadelphia, 1997), esp. 120–51.

39. On *Tammany, or the Indian Chief,* see George O. Seilhamer, *History of the American Theatre: New Foundations* (Philadelphia, 1891), 85–86, quotation at 86. On Morton's play *Columbus, or the World Discovered,* see ibid., 366; George C. D. Odell, *Annals of the New York Stage* [to 1798] (New York, 1927), 1:463–64; *Diary of William Dunlap (1766–1839), Collections of the New York Historical Society for the Year 1929,* 3 vols., ed. Dorothy C. Barck (New York, 1930), 1:146–47. On William Dunlap's play *Andre/The Glory of Columbia,* see Jared Brown, *The Theatre in America during the Revolution* (Cambridge, U.K., 1995), 169.

40. Poem quoted in Francis Von A. Cabeen, "The Society of the Sons of St. Tammany of Philadelphia," *Pennsylvania Magazine of History and Biography* 27, 1 (1903): 36. Because Irish Americans would later adopt Columbus as their Catholic patron, this early-nineteenth-century opposition

between Columbus and St. Patrick, and the derogation of the latter as an ethnic hero, is ironic. On the later relationship between these two figures in ethnic, festive culture, see Timothy J. Meagher, "'Why Should We Care for a Little Trouble or a Walk through the Mud': St. Patrick's and Columbus Day Parades in Worcester, Massachusetts, 1845–1915," *New England Quarterly* 58 (1985): 5–26.

41. Higham, "Indian Princess and Roman Goddess," 57, 63. And see Deloria, *Playing Indian*, 38–70. The Indian problems of the 1790s, and their resolution through successful conquest and peace (and expansion) "with honor," can be surveyed concisely in John K. Mahon, "Indian–United States Military Situation, 1775–1848," in *Handbook of North American Indians: Indian–White Relations*, ed. Wilcomb Washburn (Washington, D.C., 1988), 4:149–52; "Columbian Tragedy," illustrated in Washburn, *Handbook of North American Indians*, 151; see also Reginald Horsman, "United States Indian Policies, 1776–1815," ibid., esp. 32–35.

42. See Paul Semonin, "'Nature's Nation': Natural History as Nationalism in the New Republic," *Northwest Review* 30, 2 (1992): 6–41; Deloria, *Playing Indian*, 44–45, 50, 58; Higham, "Indian Princess and Roman Goddess," 66; Belknap, *American Biography*, 128.

43. Reported in the *Journal and Patriotic Register* (New York), Aug. 10, 1790; see Deloria, *Playing Indian*, 54–55.

44. Philip Freneau, "The Indian Burying Ground" (1787). The 1812 anti-British cartoon (drawn probably by William Muldaux and possibly published in a Pennsylvania newspaper) is illustrated in Horsman, "United States Indian Policies," 38.

45. John W. Reps, *The Making of Urban America: A History of City Planning in the United States* (Princeton, N.J., 1965), 225, 227; see 229, fig. 135, for the plan of Columbus, Ohio. Generally, on Columbianization of the landscape, see George R. Stewart, *Names on the Land: A Historical Account of Place-Naming in the United States* (New York, 1945). See Anne E. Bentley, "The Columbia-Washington Medal," *Proceedings of the Massachusetts Historical Society* 101 (1990): 120–27.

46. Kilroe, *Saint Tammany*, 145–46, quotation at 186.

47. The counterclaims of Scandinavian immigrants—that it was actually Leif Eriksson who first discovered and settled America—functioned essentially in the same way as did Irish Catholic or Italian claims for Columbus as the discoverer and their patron. Scandinavian Americans first began to argue their case in the 1870s, nearly contemporaneous with the Italians; see, for example, Rasmus Bjorn Andersen, *America Not Discovered by Columbus: A Historical Sketch of the Discovery of America by the Norsemen* (Chicago, 1874). In each case, ethnic Americans—that is, those from a non-Anglo tradition—established their legitimate claim to American citizenship.

48. Chauncey Depew, as quoted in R. Reid Badger, *The Great American Fair: The World's Columbian Exposition and American Culture* (Chicago, 1979), 85.

49. See *Harvard Encyclopedia of American Ethnic Groups*, ed. Stephan Thernstrom (Cambridge, Mass., 1980), esp. 490–95 on immigrant restriction legislation.

50. See Christopher J. Kauffman, *Faith and Fraternalism: The History of the Knights of Columbus, 1882–1982* (New York, 1982), for the standard historical account of the organization.

51. *New York Times*, July 28, 1879, from Knights of Columbus Archives, New Haven, Conn.

52. Matthew C. O'Connor, "Early History of the Knights of Columbus," handwritten manuscript, undated (SC-7-1-2), Knights of Columbus Archive, New Haven, Conn.

53. See Edwin G. Burrows and Mike Wallace, *Gotham: A History of New York City to 1898* (New York, 1999), 159, 193; Carl Solana Weeks, *Savannah in the Times of Peter Tondee: The Road to Revolution in Colonial Georgia* (Columbia, S.C., 1997), 115–16, 166.

54. See Burrows and Wallace, *Gotham*, 248, 513, 543, which traces the rise of the Irish in New York City and their use of St. Patrick's Day as an ethnic celebration, in the rich context of the city's larger history.

55. Ibid., 828; Meagher, "Why Should We Care for a Little Trouble or a Walk through the Mud," 6–7.

56. Meagher, "Why Should We Care for a Little Trouble or a Walk through the Mud," quotations at 18.

57. Ibid., esp. 20–24.

58. For an example of the continuing use of Columbus by Catholics to identify themselves with the American mainstream, see Supreme Knight Virgil C. Dechant's message in "Christopher Columbus: His Achievements, Times, and Faith," a quincentenary pamphlet issued by the Knights of Columbus in 1992.

59. "The Influence of Italians of Boston," *Boston Sunday Globe*, Oct. 2, 1910, Columbus Day file (KC-1-3-49), Knights of Columbus Archive, New Haven, Conn.; David Glassberg, *American Historical Pageantry: The Uses of Tradition in the Early Twentieth Century* (Chapel Hill, N.C., 1990), 22–23. On Columbus Day, see Jane M. Hatch, ed. and comp., *The American Book of Days*, 3d ed. (New York, 1978), 918–21; Hennig Cohen and Tristram Potter Coffin, eds., *The Folklore of American Holidays* (Detroit, 1987), 301–2. Columbus Day has also been a Hispanic-American celebration, but the Spanish-speaking peoples of the United States have been more divided in their assessment of the Discoverer than have the Italians.

60. On events in New York, see Bushman, *America Discovers Columbus*, 165–68, 173–74, 179–83. See also *The Unveiling of the Columbus Statue, New York, May 1894* (New York, ca. 1894), commemorating the Columbus statue sculpted by Jeronimo Sunol, commissioned by New York's elite, which competed (tardily) with the one raised at Columbus Circle by the Italian American community. Some of Boston's 1892 pageantry is described in *A Memorial to Christopher Columbus from the City of Boston in Honor of His Discovery of America* (Boston, 1893). New Haven's great parade of some six thousand marchers, featuring the Knights of Columbus prominently, is described in the *New Haven Union*, Oct. 11, 1892 (KC-1-1-53), Knights of Columbus Archive, New Haven, Conn. The Chicago World's Columbian Exposition of 1893 is analyzed by Robert Rydell, *All the World's a Fair: Visions of Empire at American International Expositions, 1876–1916* (Chicago, 1984), 38–71; Alan Trachtenberg, *The Incorporation of America: Culture and Society in the Gilded Age* (New York, 1982), esp. 208–34; Badger, *Great American Fair*.

61. *Official Souvenir Programme, New York Columbian Celebration, October 8th to 15th, 1892* (New York, 1892). A wealth of material—newspaper clippings, programs, mementoes, and other ephemera—regarding the four hundredth anniversary celebrations of Columbus's voyage are contained in the several scrapbooks in the Bowen Family Papers, American Antiquarian Society, Worcester, Mass.; see esp. octavo vols. 9 and 13. Clarence W. Bowen, the collector of this material, was a member of New York's elite, grandson of Lewis Tappan and son of Henry C. Bowen, who published the New York *Independent*. The younger Bowen, a historian and founder of the American Historical Association, was intimately involved in the festivities in both Chicago and New York. See also Bushman, *America Discovers Columbus*, 165–68.

62. See Rydell, *All the World's a Fair*, 46; Bushman, *America Discovers Columbus*, 170–75. Note, however, that Bellamy, a socialist as well as a Baptist minister, originally drafted an expansive and inclusive pledge, more democratic and more disposed toward women's rights, than the one that was widely promulgated. Bellamy's lines "I pledge allegiance to my flag and the Republic for which it stands" made less a fetish out of the flag, while his inclusion of "equality"—"one Nation indivisible with Liberty, Equality, and Justice for all"—was not only more democratic but implicitly recognized the struggles of women and African Americans for equal rights. Later additions and emendations included the specification that "the United States of America" was the particular republic to which allegiance was being pledged, and the inclusion of the words "Under God," which were added in 1954.

63. These themes are developed in Rydell, *All the World's a Fair*, 38–71. See also Trachtenberg, *Incorporation of America*, 11–17, 208–34.

64. Among the photographs in Badger, *Great American Fair*, are those showing both Dahomey

"cannibals" and Sioux people, among other exotic peoples on display. Indians had become a fixture in late-nineteenth-century anniversary parades, like the United States Centennial Parade of
1876 and the grand procession marking the centennial of the Constitution in 1887.

65. See Rydell, *All the World's a Fair*, esp. 52–59; David Ewing Duncan, "The Object at Hand: A
Baby Rattle Invokes the Frenzy of Adulation That Once Made Columbus an American Hero for All
Seasons," *Smithsonian*, October 1993, 26.

66. Justin Winsor, *Christopher Columbus, and How He Received and Imparted the Spirit of Discovery*,
5th ed. rev. (Boston, 1892), 500, 512.

67. Quoted in Rydell, *All the World's a Fair*, 43.

68. Hatch, *American Book of Days*, 920; *Columbiad* (June 1910), *Boston Globe*, Oct. 2, 1910 (contained in "Columbus Day, 1910" file, KC-1-3-49, Knights of Columbus Archives, New Haven,
Conn.). See also Bushman, *America Discovers Columbus*, 179. On Utah's Columbus Day, beginning
as a state holiday in 1919, see Philip F. Notarianni, "Italians in Utah," in *Utah History Encyclopedia*,
ed. Allan Kent Powell (Salt Lake City, 1994), 280. Italians in the state appropriated ceremonial
space on Utah's Pioneer Day (July 24) to celebrate Columbus as the "First Pioneer of America."

69. See, for example, Spyros Cateras, *Christopher Columbus Was a Greek and His Real Name Was
Nikolaos Ypshilantis* (Manchester, N.H., 1937); Brother Nectario Maria, *Juan Colón . . . Was a Spanish Jew* (New York, 1971); Manuel Luciano de Silva, *Columbus Was 100% Portuguese* (Providence,
R.I., 1988). See also Andersen, *America Not Discovered by Columbus*; a *New York Times* advertisement
for Bergen Line and Scandinavian Airlines (Sept. 26, 1991, A7) asked, beneath a picture of three Viking ships (due to visit the South Street Seaport in New York), "Which country discovered America when the rest of Europe firmly believed the world was flat? That's right. That's Norway." And
see Newton Frohlich, "Was the Discoverer of America Jewish?" *Moment*, December 1991, 35–43
(Frohlich seems to answer yes to this question, but he also asks in a sidebar, "Do We Really Want
to Claim Columbus?"); "Did Chinese Discover America before Columbus?" Associated Press
story, *Register-Guard* (Eugene, Ore.), May 7, 1993, 16A. Finally, see Mirta Ojito, "On Columbus Day,
2 Rival Groups Vie for Ownership of a Man and His Feat," *New York Times*, Oct. 14, 1996, B12,
which details the continuing appeal of Columbus to both Hispanic and Italian Americans, as well
as the rivalry between these groups in New York, who often attempt to claim him exclusively.

70. Letter to the editor, *New York Times*, Nov. 4, 1989; Jose Gonzalez, letter to the editor, *New
York Times*, Sept. 1, 1990.

71. Quoted in "Columbus Commission on the Rocks," *huracan* (summer 1991), a publication of
the Alliance for Cultural Democracy.

72. "Phyllis Diller as Green Zombie Gill-Woman," "Datebook," *San Francisco Chronicle and Ex-
aminer*, June 2, 1991, 27.

73. On the Vinland Map controversy, see the *New York Times*, Oct. 12, 1965, and subsequent is-
sues during the next week. Skelton, Marston, and Painter, *Vinland Map*; Helen Wallis et al. trace
"The Strange Case of the Vinland Map," *Geographical Journal* 40 (1974): 183–214. See also Wilcomb
Washburn, ed., *The Vinland Map Conference* (Chicago, 1971). The matter of the Vinland Map's au-
thenticity remains unsettled, although more scholars now see it as a fake than as genuine; see John
Noble Wilford, "Disputed Medieval Map Held Genuine after All," *New York Times*, Feb. 13, 1996,
B7, 12; John Noble Wilford, "Study Casts Disputed Map as False Link to Vikings," *New York Times*,
Feb. 26, 2000, A8. On the other hand, a clear consensus does exist among scholars accepting as
fact the eleventh-century exploration and settlement at L'Anse aux Meadows in Newfoundland
by Norse people.

74. It is striking that the recent indictments of Columbus rest on virtually no new information
but instead on a rereading of the documentary record in terms of current interests and concerns.
Until the early 1990s, for example, historians and others made little of the sexual assaults that accompanied the discovery and conquest, although the evidence of such conduct is clear in the ex-

plorers' and colonists' own writings. See, for example, Stephanie Wood, "Rape as a Tool of Conquest in Early Latin America," *CSWS Review* (Center for the Study of Women in Society, University of Oregon) (1992): 18–20.

75. The strange history of the Columbus Quincentenary Jubilee Commission is described in "Columbus Commission on the Rocks." See also Rick DelVecchio, "A Cloud on Columbus Celebration Plans," *San Francisco Chronicle*, May 6, 1991. By December 1990, the commission's first chair, John Goudie, had resigned, after the commission fell well short of its private fund-raising goals, sinking it some $700,000 in debt, and after it had lost most of its corporate sponsors following financial irregularities. Even when not officially licensed by the commission, services and products were eagerly promoted through (often strained) references to Columbus and the Discovery. See, for example, the special quincentenary issue of *Newsweek* (fall / winter 1991), in which Embassy Suites promoted its hotels with the cat cartoon character Garfield dressed up like Columbus, and with the slogan, "Garfield's American Adventure: Twice the Adventure, Twice the Hotel." A Ford Motor Company advertisement for its Explorer vehicle invited readers to become latter-day Columbuses: "You want to go where no one has gone before. This weekend. Your Explorer is ready."

76. Rayna Green, interview with Gabrielle Tayac (Apr. 6, 1989), *Northeast Indian Quarterly* 7, 3 (fall 1990): 12–13. See also Kyle Kajihiro, "Columbus Revisited: Uncovering the History of His Commemoration, Discovering a People's History," *Portland Alliance*, for similar thoughts about the unique "teaching moment" offered by the quincentenary and the possibilities for political mobilization. And see Meredith Sommers, "A Teachable Moment," *Radical Historians Newsletter*, no. 67 (November 1992): 3, 16.

77. Jimmie Durham, *Columbus Day: Poems, Drawings and Stories about American Indian Life and Death in the Nineteen-Seventies* (Minneapolis, 1983), 10, 11.

78. Jose Barreiro, "View from the Shore: Toward an Indian Voice in 1992," *Northeast Indian Quarterly* 7, 3 (fall 1990): 14; Dirk Johnson, "As Discoverer Is Hailed, the Discovered Protest," *New York Times*, Oct. 14, 1991. See also Suzan Shown Harjo, "My Turn: I Won't Be Celebrating Columbus Day," special quincentenary issue, *Newsweek* (fall / winter 1991): 32.

79. See esp. James Riding In, "The Politics of the Columbus Celebration: A Perspective of Myth and Reality in United States Society," *American Indian Culture and Research Journal* 17, 3 (1993): 1–9; the entire issue of the journal is devoted to this subject.

80. Kajihiro, "Columbus Revisited." African Americans, on the other hand, played a limited role in anti-Columbus dissent. Some, like June Jordan, urged African Americans to ignore the hoopla: "Christopher Columbus is a dead man. And anybody who gives that guy more than a minute of attention of any kind is either brain-dead or seriously misled at the least" ("Let the Dead Bury Their Dead," *Essence*, October 1992, 158). Cf. Marable Manning, "1492: A Personal Perspective," *The Witness*, January 1992.

81. One of the reasons for the disintegration of the official celebration was that given the unanticipated controversy and the surprising dominance of these new voices in quincentenary planning, federal funding largely dried up; see "Columbus Commission on the Rocks."

82. See, for example, the environmentalist critique of Columbus and the ecological heritage he carried with him in Sale, *Conquest of Paradise*, 74–91.

83. For another example of the collision of academic and popular history—another battle in the culture wars of the 1990s—that confronted a more proximate, controversial episode, see Edward T. Linenthal and Tom Engelhardt, eds., *History Wars: The Enola Gay and Other Battles for the American Past* (New York, 1996); and see Mike Wallace, *Mickey Mouse History and Other Essays on American Memory* (Philadelphia, 1996).

84. Johnson, "As Discoverer Is Hailed, the Discovered Protest."

85. Ari L. Goldman, "Religious Notes," *New York Times*, Sept. 7, 1991.

86. Michael Janofsky, "Voyage down Fifth Avenue Is Full of Political Maneuvers," *New York Times*, Oct. 13, 1992; David Gonzalez, "A Poet Finds a New Muse in Columbus," *New York Times*, Oct. 11, 1997, B1; Viscusi articulated his position in an epic poem, "An Oration upon the Most Recent Death of Christopher Columbus," which he recited on Columbus Day 1997 at the Columbus Expo in New York.

87. John Lombardo, "Italian *and* Native Americans Forge Historic Link," *Fra Noi*, September 1991, 1, 34. I am indebted to Susan Pezzino for bringing this Italian–Native American rapprochement to my attention and for providing me with photocopies of various issues of *Fra Noi*. Thanks as well to Marie Gallo for searching the newspaper's archives.

88. Judith Cortese Fosco, "An Historic Journey: Native Americans to Visit Sicily," *Fra Noi*, March 1992, 1, 32; Tom Laue, "A Hero's Welcome: Italy Embraces Native Americans," *Fra Noi*, May 1992, 1, 28.

89. Judith Cortese Fosco, "Sun Shines on Parade: 500th a Celebration of Diversity," *Fra Noi*, November 1992, 1, 28; Sam Dillon, "Schools Growing Harsher in Scrutiny of Columbus," *New York Times*, Oct. 12, 1992, A1, B5.

90. Flemington Furs advertisement, "Queen Isabella Sale," *New York Times*, Oct. 9, 1994, New Jersey sec., 9; Todd S. Purdum, "Emphasizing the Environment, Clinton Signs Water Measure," *New York Times*, Oct. 13, 1996, A16; Don Terry, "Columbus Divides Ohio's Capital City," *New York Times*, Dec. 26, 1993.

91. Mercedes-Benz advertisement, *Register-Guard*, Nov. 3, 1998, 5A.

Chapter 4. Washington, Lincoln, and the Unheroic Presidents' Day

1. The Monday Holiday Act of 1968, passed by the 90th Cong., 2d sess., was signed by President Johnson on June 28, 1968; *Public Papers of the President of the United States* (Washington, D.C., 1970), Lyndon B. Johnson, 1968, 342.

2. Among the answers to this question is that James A. Garfield—also a Civil War general and United States president—seems to be missing. Note that Garfield was shot by an assassin in July 1881 and died that September, the year Field completed this portrait. Is the artist thus offering a comment on Garfield's tragic demise after only four months in office by leaving him out of the painting?

3. See Barry Schwartz, *George Washington: The Making of an American Symbol* (New York, 1987), esp. 17–20 on the early emergence of Washington as national hero. On Lincoln, see Merrill D. Peterson, *Lincoln in American Memory* (New York, 1994); and Barry Schwartz, *Lincoln and the Forge of National Memory* (Chicago, 2000).

4. Certainly this generalization is more accurate for Washington than for Lincoln, who remained a controversial figure in the South, even if spokesmen for the New South such as Henry Grady, late in the nineteenth century, embraced Lincoln as a symbol of mercy and reconciliation; Michael Davis, *The Image of Lincoln in the South* (Knoxville, Tenn., 1971).

5. Note, for example, that in New Orleans in 1997, Washington's name was removed from an elementary school, after passage of a law forbidding the naming of public places for slaveholders. See Kevin Sack, "Blacks Strip Slaveholders' Names Off Schools," *New York Times*, Nov. 12, 1997, A1, A21; Sack, "Today's Battles Topple Yesterday's Heroes," ibid., Nov. 16, 1997, sec. 4, 5; see also *Time Magazine*, Nov. 24, 1997, 4. For a positive assessment of Washington's struggle with slavery, in time for his birthday, see Robert F. Dalzell Jr., "George Washington, Slaveholder," *New York Times*, Feb. 20, 1999, A27.

6. Ironically although appropriately, the ambiguity of the holiday is such that we lack consensus on how to spell it. Sometimes it appears as Presidents Day, sometimes in the plural possessive as Presidents' Day (although it is not always clear how many presidents are so honored—two or forty-one?), and sometimes in the singular possessive, President's Day. Samuel Adams and John

Adams are quoted in Rush, *The Autobiography of Benjamin Rush*, ed. George W. Corner (Princeton, N.J., 1948), 139, 141.

7. Washington, his cult, and its meaning in American history have been illuminated by the impressive work of a number of scholars beginning in the mid-1970s. See especially Lawrence J. Friedman, *Inventors of the Promised Land* (New York, 1975), 44–78; Catherine L. Albanese, *Sons of the Fathers: The Civil Religion of the American Revolution* (Philadelphia, 1976), 143–81; Michael Kammen, *A Season of Youth: The American Revolution and the Historical Imagination* (New York, 1978); George B. Forgie, *Patricide in the House Divided* (New York, 1979); Margaret Brown Klapthor and Howard Alexander Morrison, *G. Washington: A Figure upon the Stage* (Washington, D.C., 1982); Garry Wills, *Cincinnatus: George Washington and the Enlightenment* (New York, 1984); Schwartz, *George Washington*; Paul K. Longmore, *The Invention of George Washington* (Berkeley, Calif., 1988), quotation at 204–5; Karal Ann Marling, *George Washington Slept Here: Colonial Revivals and American Culture, 1876–1986* (Cambridge, Mass., 1988); Simon P. Newman, "Principles or Men? George Washington and the Political Culture of National Leadership, 1776–1801," *Journal of the Early Republic* 12 (1992): 477–507; Newman, *Parades and the Politics of the Street: Festive Culture in the Early American Republic* (Philadelphia, 1997); David Waldstreicher, *In the Midst of Perpetual Fetes: The Making of American Nationalism, 1776–1820* (Chapel Hill, N.C., 1997); Fritz Hirschfeld, *George Washington and Slavery: A Documentary Portrayal* (Columbia, Mo., 1997).

8. Schwartz, *George Washington*, 7–28.

9. Adams to Benjamin Rush, Mar. 19, 1812, in *Spur of Fame: Dialogues of John Adams and Benjamin Rush, 1805–1813*, ed. John A. Schutz and Douglass Adair (1966; reprint, San Marino, Calif., 1980), 211–12 (italics in original).

10. Adams recalled the thirdhand insult in a letter to Rush, Jan. 8, 1812, ibid., 206; Rush's prospective response and evaluation of Washington's military accomplishments was written in his letter to Adams, Feb. 12, 1812, ibid., 210–11, 209. Adams lampooned the adoration of Divus Washington in his letter to Rush, Feb. 25, 1808, ibid., 104.

11. Quoted in Schwartz, *George Washington*, 23.

12. The destruction of the statue of George III is treated in chapter 1 of this volume. See also Klapthor and Morrison, *G. Washington: Figure upon the Stage*, 18–21, for illustrations. John Trumbull's painting *Washington and the Departure of the British Garrison from New York City* (1790) shows Washington standing beside his horse with the empty pedestal in the background. On George Washington's succession to the "throne" previously occupied by George III, see esp. Schwartz, *George Washington*, 31–38; Newman, *Parades and Politics*, esp. 33–38, 46–73. Washington Irving, "Rip Van Winkle: A Posthumous Writing of Diedrich Knickerbocker," from Irving's *The Sketch Book of Geoffrey Crayon, Gent.* (originally published serially, 1819–20), in *History, Tales and Sketches*, ed. James W. Tuttleton (New York, 1983), 769–85, incident is at 779.

13. Quoted in Schwartz, *George Washington*, 32. On Washington's aversion to monarchy and Jefferson's firm belief about American commitment to republicanism, see Thomas Jefferson, "The Anas—Selections," Feb. 4, 1818, in *Writings*, ed. Merrill D. Peterson (New York, 1984), 664; see also Jefferson to John Melish, Jan. 13, 1813: "General Washington did not harbor one principle of federalism. He was neither an Agloman, a monarchist, nor a separatist. He sincerely wished the people to have as much self-government as they were competent to exercise themselves" (1270).

14. Waldstreicher, *In the Midst of Perpetual Fetes*, 118–24, quotation at 118.

15. Andrew Burstein, *Sentimental Democracy: The Evolution of America's Romantic Self-Image* (New York, 1999), esp. 3–21, quotation at 3.

16. Waldstreicher, *In the Midst of Perpetual Fetes*, 118–23.

17. See Newman, *Parades and Politics*, 58–68. See also Schwartz, *George Washington*, 77–79, 82–84. In 1792, for example, both the old City Dancing Assembly and the new City Dancing Assembly gave similar, elegant balls in honor of Washington's birthday, on February 21 and 22. The

former group represented "aristocratic members of families of wealth and position," whereas the latter were "active tradesmen" unable to gain admission to the old Assembly. President Washington diplomatically attended both; see Thomas Wescott, *A History of Philadelphia from the Time of the First Settlement on the Delaware to the Consolidation of the City and District in 1854,* 5 vols. (Philadelphia, 1886), 3:603–5. On celebrations of Washington's birthday during his lifetime, see David M. Matteson, *George Washington Every Day: A Calendar of Events and Principles of His Entire Lifetime* ([Washington, D.C., 1932?]), 352–53, a volume published by the United States George Washington Bicentennial Commission.

18. *Gazette of the United States* (Philadelphia) 9, 1078 (Feb. 22, 1796).

19. Ricketts advertisement, ibid., 9, 1079 (Feb. 23, 1796); "Extract of a letter from a gentleman in Philadelphia, to his friend in Charleston," ibid., 9, 1085 (Mar. 1, 1796).

20. Ibid., nos. 1085–96, quotation in no. 1096. On the geographical range of Washington's birthday celebrations throughout the United States in the 1790s, from Maine to Georgia, and west to Kentucky, see Newman, *Parades and Politics,* 59–60.

21. James Miltimore, *A Discourse Delivered in Newmarket, at the Particular Request of a Respectable Musical Choir, to a Numerous Assembly, convened for celebrating the Birth-Day of the Illustrious Washington . . . Published by desire of the hearers* (Exeter, N.H., 1794).

22. See Newman, *Parades and Politics;* Waldstreicher, *In the Midst of Perpetual Fetes.*

23. See "THE PRESIDENT'S BIRTHDAY," *Independent Chronicle* (Boston), Feb. 18, 1790; Mirabeau [pseudonym], "Forerunners of Monarchy and Aristocracy in the United States," *Aurora* (Philadelphia), Dec. 7, 1792; A DEMOCRAT, "For the GENERAL ADVERTISER," ibid., Feb. 18, 1793; *Massachusetts Mercury* (Boston), Feb. 23, 1796. Quoted in Newman, *Parades and Politics,* 62–63.

24. *Gazette of the United States,* Feb. 29, 1796; ibid., Mar. 7, 1797.

25. The Lay Preacher of Pennsylvania, "OBSERVATIONS on the death of Washington," *Independent Gazette* (Worcester, Mass.), Jan. 7, 1800.

26. *Independent Gazette* (Worcester, Mass.), Jan. 14, 28, and Feb. 25, 1800. Hundreds of eulogies were published in the United States and conformed generally to common conventions (although the fact of a formula does not necessarily imply they were less than genuine and heartfelt in their sentiments). For an exemplary eulogy, see Enos Hitchcock, *A Discourse on the Dignity and Excellence of the Human Character; Illustrated in the Life of General George Washington, . . . in Commemoration of the Afflictive Event of his Death. Delivered February 22, 1800, in the Benevolent Congregational Church in Providence* (Providence, R.I., 1800), quotation at 13; or see Charles Humphrey Atherton, *EULOGY on GEN. GEORGE WASHINGTON, late president of the United States, who died December 14, 1799; Delivered at Amherst, N.H. before the inhabitants of the town of Amherst, the inhabitants of the town of Milford, and the Benevolent Lodge, on the 22d day of February, 1800, at the request of the committee of the selectmen and other respectable citizens* (Amherst, N.H., 1800).

27. Adams to Rush, June 21, 1811, in Schutz and Adair, *Spur of Fame,* 181–82. Waldstreicher, *In the Midst of Perpetual Fetes,* 212–14.

28. James Morton Smith, *Freedom's Fetters: The Alien and Sedition Laws and American Civil Liberties* (Ithaca, N.Y., 1956), 270–74. The city of Quincy, Massachusetts, nonetheless has made the best of the creation of Presidents' Day by organizing a Presidents' Day Winter Festival—fulfilling John Adams's dreams some two hundred years later—featuring its two favorite-son presidents, John Adams and John Quincy Adams.

29. Jefferson to Dr. Walter Jones, Jan. 2, 1814, in *Writings,* 1320.

30. The legend and facts of Jefferson's inauguration are briefly analyzed in Joseph J. Ellis, *American Sphinx: The Character of Thomas Jefferson* (New York, 1997), 200–202. Jefferson as quoted in Waldstreicher, *In the Midst of Perpetual Fetes,* 190–91.

31. English practices are well analyzed by David Cressy, *Bonfires and Bells: National Memory and the Protestant Calendar in Elizabethan and Stuart England* (Berkeley, Calif., 1990).

32. The celebration of the March 4 is analyzed in Waldstreicher, *In the Midst of Perpetual Fetes*, 190–94. Bascom's diary is quoted at 194.

33. Benedict Anderson, *Imagined Communities: Reflections on the Origins and Spread of Nationalism*, rev. ed. (London, 1991), convincingly analyzes the rise of modern nationalism in terms of development of a national imagination, cultivated especially through print culture. Anderson's focus on the importance of these imaginative acts should not lead students to conclude that such nation building was merely imaginative, nor should it necessarily imply that political participation within the public sphere, even in such festive events, which have often been treated as ephemeral and unimportant, was necessarily qualitatively inferior to other forms of political activity. They were different and transitional, and if these fetes could sometimes contain dissent, they also facilitated its expression. See Jürgen Habermas, *The Structural Transformation of the Public Sphere: An Inquiry into a Category of Bourgeois Society*, trans. Thomas Burger (Cambridge, Mass., 1989), which suggests such decline in the quality of politics as participation broadens; and see his revised views in "Further Reflections on the Public Sphere," in *Habermas and the Public Sphere*, ed. Craig Calhoun (Cambridge, Mass., 1992).

34. Waldstreicher, *In the Midst of Perpetual Fetes*, 214–15; Conrad Edick Wright, *The Transformation of Charity in Postrevolutionary New England* (Boston, 1992), 74–75, 162–68, quotations at 162, 163; according to Wright, some 150 Washington Benevolent Societies were formed in New England between 1811 and 1815. The Washington Benevolent Society in Ohio, founded in 1813, is treated in Donald J. Ratcliffe, *Party Spirit in a Frontier Republic: Democratic Politics in Ohio, 1793–1821* (Columbus, Ohio, 1998), 187–89, 204–5. For just one example of a Washington Benevolent Society constitution, see *The Constitution of the Washington Benevolent Society of the Town of Charlton, in the County of Saratoga. To which is added, the Farewell Address of George Washington, and the Constitutions of the United States and the State of New-York* (Albany, N.Y., 1811). On the Washingtonians, see also David Hackett Fischer, *The Revolution of American Conservatism: The Federalist Party in the Era of Jeffersonian Democracy* (New York, 1965), 110–28; and Howard B. Rock, *Artisans of the New Republic: The Tradesmen of New York City in the Age of Jefferson* (New York, 1979), 84–89.

35. *An Historical View of the Public Celebrations of the Washington Society, and those of the Young Republicans, from 1805, to 1822, compiled by order of the Washington Society, for the use of the Members* (Boston, 1823), quotations at 13, 33, 67, 93.

36. Thomas A. Budd, Esq., *An Oration before the Washington Benevolent Society of Pennsylvania. Delivered in the Olympic Theatre, on the 22nd of February, 1828* (Philadelphia, 1828), 20–23; Herbert G. Gutman, *Work, Culture and Society in Industrializing America: Essays in American Working-Class and Social History* (New York, 1976), 51.

37. *The Foundation, Progress and Principles of the Washington Temperance Society of Baltimore, and the influence it has had on the Temperance Movement in the United States. By a member of the Society* (Baltimore, 1842). By the time of publication, the Washington Temperance Society claimed vigorous, flourishing societies in Maryland, New England, and the midwestern, southern, and western states. The society seemed to target adult men—gentlemen—unlike other temperance organizations, which sought particularly to reform youth. According to its manifesto, however, some societies were composed entirely of females or youth (21). On Martha Washingtonian Societies, composed of working-class women and pursuing reform on their behalf, see Ruth M. Alexander, "'We Are Engaged as a Band of Sisters': Class and Domesticity in the Washingtonian Temperance Movement, 1840–1850," *Journal of American History* 75 (1988–89): 763–85.

38. Abraham Lincoln, "Address to the Washington Temperance Society of Springfield, Illinois," Feb. 22, 1842, in Lincoln, *Speeches and Writings, 1832–1858*, ed. Don E. Fehrenbacher (New York, 1989), 81–90.

39. Hirschfeld, *Washington and Slavery*; John Rhodehamel, *The Great Experiment: George Washington and the American Republic* (New Haven, Conn., 1998), 95; Ira Berlin, *Many Thousands Gone:*

The First Two Centuries of Slavery in North America (Cambridge, Mass., 1998), 259, 232–33, 268–69; David Brion Davis, *The Problem of Slavery in the Age of Revolution, 1770–1823* (Ithaca, N.Y., 1975), 170–71; Graham Russell Hodges, *Root and Branch: African Americans in New York and East Jersey, 1613–1863* (Chapel Hill, N.C., 1999), 155–58.

40. Hodges, *Root and Branch,* 211–12; Hirschfeld, *Washington and Slavery,* 71. When Washington retired to Mount Vernon for the last time in 1797, his cook Hercules, in contrast to Mary Simpson Washington, remained behind in Philadelphia as a free man not because voluntarily manumitted by Washington but because he ran away.

41. Richard Allen, "Eulogy for Washington," Dec. 29, 1799, reprinted from the *Philadelphia Gazette,* Dec. 31, 1799, in *Lift Every Voice: African American Oratory, 1787–1900,* ed. Philip S. Foner and Robert James Branham (Tuscaloosa, Ala., 1998), 56–58.

42. Lemuel Haynes [pastor of the church in West Rutland], *Dissimulation Illustrated. A Sermon delivered at Brandon, Vermont, February 22, 1813, before the Washington Benevolent Society; it being the Anniversary of Gen. Washington's Birth-Day, published at the request of the society* (Rutland, Vt., 1814). On Haynes, see esp. John D. Saillant, "Lemuel Haynes and the Revolutionary Origins of Black Theology, 1776–1801," *Religion and American Culture* 2 (winter 1993): 79–102.

43. W[illiam]. D[exter]. Wilson, *A Discourse on Slavery: Delivered before the Anti-Slavery Society in Littleton, N.H., February 22, 1839, being the Anniversary of the Birth of Washington* (Concord, N.H., 1839), quotations at 3, 4, 33

44. Frederick Douglass, "What, to the Slave, Is the Fourth of July?" in Foner and Branham, *Lift Every Voice,* 254–55.

45. Harriet Beecher Stowe, *Uncle Tom's Cabin; or, Life among the Lowly* (1853), in *Three Novels,* ed. Kathryn Kish Sklar (New York, 1982), 1–519, quotation at 33. The novel first appeared in installments in the *National Era* during 1851.

46. "Extract from Mr. Cram's Journal," *Massachusetts Missionary Magazine* 3, 10 (March 1806): 389–90.

47. Thomas S. Abler and Elisabeth Tooker, "Seneca," in *Handbook of North American Indians: Northeast,* ed. Bruce G. Trigger (Washington, D.C., 1978), 15:507–8; Barbara Graymont, *The Iroquois in the American Revolution* (Syracuse, N.Y., 1972), 213; Anthony F. C. Wallace, *The Death and Rebirth of the Seneca* (New York, 1970), 141–48.

48. "Washington to the Chiefs of the Seneca Nation," Dec. 29, 1790, in George Washington, *Writings,* ed. John Rhodehamel (New York, 1997), 772–73. Although Washington speaks of brotherhood here, he speaks elsewhere of a fatherly relationship to the Indians—"the fatherly care the United States intend to take of the Indians" (774). If Iroquois people would continue to insist on a brotherly relationship, for most Native people the president became the Great Father. The implications (even limitations) of father status, particularly among matrilineal Indian societies, were not always clear to U.S. diplomats asserting patriarchal authority.

49. Lewis H. Morgan, *League of the HO-DÉ-NO–SAU-NEE, Iroquois,* ed. William N. Fenton (1851; new edition, Secaucus, N.J., 1962), 256–57. Morgan's account is based on a translation of his informant, the Seneca Ely S. Parker, who recorded it from a discourse by the Seneca religious leader Sose-há-wä on October 4–6, 1848, at Tonawanda. Morgan discusses Seneca reverence for Washington at 178–79; he concludes, "Surely the piety and the gratitude of the Iroquois have, jointly, reared a monument to Washington above the skies, which is more expressive in its praise, than the proudest recitals on the obelisk, and more imperishable in its duration, than the syenite which holds up the record to the gaze of centuries" (179).

50. Named by his parents simply Washington Grayson in 1843, he added the George when he left home to attend a white school, at about age sixteen. It's likely that the addition of George to Grayson's name was a gesture of acculturation as well as an attempt to appropriate a measure of the distinction residing in the name of the white hero Washington. See *A Creek Warrior for the Con-*

federacy: The Autobiography of Chief G. W. Grayson, ed. W. David Baird (Norman, Okla., 1988); Mary Jane Warde, *George Washington Grayson and the Creek Nation, 1843–1920* (Norman, Okla., 1999).

51. On the Washington Monument, see Frank Freidel, *George Washington: Man and Monument*, 3d ed. (Washington, D.C., 1988), 42. On Apess, see *On Our Own Ground: The Complete Writings of William Apess, a Pequot*, ed. Barry O'Connell (Amherst, Mass., 1992), 277 (quotation), 305–6. See Frederick E. Hoxie, *Parading through History: The Making of the Crow Nation in America, 1805–1935* (Cambridge, U.K., 1995), 210. On Native American military service—and their particular sort of patriotism—see Tom Holm, *Strong Hearts, Wounded Souls: Native American Veterans of the Vietnam War* (Austin, Tex., 1996); in addition to joining numerous Indian veterans' groups, Native American veterans have joined other national veterans' groups, including the Order of the Purple Heart (181–82). Although the Purple Heart originated in the Revolutionary War, it was not awarded subsequently until revived and issued as a new medal on the bicentennial of Washington's birth in 1932, with the War Department announcing the award on February 22.

52. See David Wallace Adams, *Education for Extinction: American Indians and the Boarding School Experience, 1875–1928* (Lawrence, Kans., 1995), 191–206, esp. 201–2, quotations at 201, 202.

53. The anonymous Oglala man is quoted in Roy Rosenzweig and David Thelen, *The Presence of the Past: Popular Uses of History in American Life* (New York, 1998), 168. Given the disastrously high unemployment at Pine Ridge—among the highest in the United States—the Monday holiday to commemorate Presidents' Day would have been cruelly ironic for many Sioux residents.

54. On Washington as an American place-name, see George R. Stewart, *Names on the Land* (Boston, 1967), 164, 168, 189, 192, 198, 235–36, 286–88, 318, 358, 382–83.

55. Charles Caldwell, *A Discourse on the First Centennial Celebration of the Birth-Day of Washington, delivered by request* (Lexington, Ky., 1832), containing also "An Ode composed for the first Centennial Celebration of the Birth-day of WASHINGTON," by Josiah Dunham. Daniel Webster's remarks are printed in *Speeches and Other Proceedings at the Public Dinner in Honor of the Centennial Anniversary of Washington* (city of Washington, 1832).

56. Henry Adams, *The Education of Henry Adams* (completed and privately circulated 1907; first published 1918), in *Novels, Mont Saint Michel, The Education*, ed. Ernest Samuels and Jayne N. Samuels (New York, 1983), 762–63.

57. See Gary Wills, *Lincoln at Gettysburg: The Words That Remade America* (New York, 1992), esp. 213–47. Everett wrote to Lincoln the next day, "I should be glad, if I could flatter myself that I came as near to the central idea of the occasion, in two hours, as you did in two minutes"; Peterson, *Lincoln in American Memory*, 115.

58. Forgie, *Patricide in the House Divided*, 168–72, quotation at 171; Marling, *George Washington Slept Here*, 78–79.

59. [Henry T. Tuckerman], "Holidays," *North American Review* 84 (1857): 363.

60. Douglass, "What, to the Slave, Is the Fourth of July?"; Drew Gilpin Faust, *The Creation of Confederate Nationalism: Ideology and Identity in the Civil War South* (Baton Rouge, La., 1988), 14, 24, image of seal shown at 25. See also Marling, *Washington Slept Here*, 103–4.

61. *New York Times*, Feb. 23, 1865, quoted in Schwartz, *George Washington*, 195–96.

62. *Memorial Exercises on the Occasion of the Semi-Centennial Anniversary of the Assassination of Abraham Lincoln* (Springfield, Ill., 1915), 35–36; Marcus Cunliffe, *The Doubled Image of Lincoln and Washington*, 26th Annual Robert Fortenbaugh Memorial Lecture, Gettysburg College (Gettysburg, Pa., 1988), 12, 7.

63. This phrase is Peterson's, in *Lincoln in American Memory*, 17. Peterson nicely narrates and analyzes the assassination and public reaction, 3–35.

64. Ibid., 8, 27–28; one poet wrote, "His [Lincoln's] blood is freedom's eucharist" (8); Cunliffe, *Doubled Image*, 22–23; according to Cunliffe, Lincoln's assassination "solemnized and almost sanctified him" (22).

65. *Addresses delivered at the Lincoln Dinners of the Republican Club of the City of New York, in response to the toast Abraham Lincoln, 1887–1909* (New York, 1909); Peterson, *Lincoln in American Memory*, 142–43, 157–58, 182–85; Michael Kammen, *Mystic Chords of Memory: The Transformation of Tradition in American Culture* (New York, 1991), 109.

66. Quoted in Peterson, *Lincoln in American Memory*, 263.

67. Ibid., 362–63; Kammen, *Mystic Chords of Memory*, 589–90; Stewart, *Names on the Land*, 299, 311, 318–21, 330, 358 (at various times, the name of Lincoln was proposed for the new states that ultimately entered the union as Wyoming, South and North Dakota, and New Mexico). According to a *Rand McNally Road Atlas* published in the early 1980s, most states, including Alabama, Arkansas, Georgia, Kentucky, Mississippi, Missouri, Oklahoma, Tennessee, West Virginia, and Virginia (Lincolnia Heights, near Washington, D.C.), were listed as having a town or city named Lincoln. Roosevelt is quoted in Cunliffe, *Doubled Image*, 7.

68. George Washington, "Farewell Address," Sept. 19, 1796, in *Writings*, 966–67.

69. Abraham Lincoln, "Second Inaugural Address," Mar. 4, 1865, in *Speeches and Writings, 1859–1865*, ed. Don E. Fehrenbacher (New York, 1989), 686–87; Lincoln to Greeley, Aug. 22, 1862, ibid., 357–58.

70. Abraham Lincoln, Speech at New Haven, Connecticut, Mar. 6, 1860, ibid., 147; Lincoln, "Second Inaugural Address," 687.

71. James Russell Lowell, "Ode Recited at the Harvard Commemoration, July 21, 1865," in *The American Tradition in Literature*, ed. Sculley Bradley, Richmond Croom Beatty, and E. Hudson Long, 3d ed. (New York, 1967), 1673–75.

72. Stewart, *Names on the Land*, 299, 318; by the end of the nineteenth century, twenty-three counties had taken the name Lincoln, mostly in the West.

73. Archbishop Glennon of St. Louis, in a 1915 tribute to Lincoln in Springfield, Illinois, on Lincoln's birthday, naturalized Lincoln as a "gnarled . . . oak tree of the forest" but also feminized him: "Abraham Lincoln was a man with a heart as tender as a woman's"; see *Addresses Delivered at the Celebration of the One Hundred and Sixth Anniversary of the Birth of Abraham Lincoln, under the Auspices of the Lincoln Centennial Association* (Springfield, Ill., 1915), quotation at 19.

74. Davis, *Image of Lincoln in the South*, esp. 166–70.

75. Quoted in Peterson, *Lincoln in American Memory*, 191–92.

76. Ibid., 48–49; Nina Silber, *The Romance of Reunion: Northerners and the South, 1865–1900* (Chapel Hill, N.C., 1993), 164–65; Kammen, *Mystic Chords of Memory*, 109. On the origins of Decoration Day, see Silber, *Romance of Reunion*, 58–61; Gaines Foster, *Ghosts of the Confederacy: Defeat, the Lost Cause, and the Emergence of the New South, 1865–1913* (New York, 1987), 42–45; Charles Reagan Wilson, *Baptized in Blood: The Religion of the Lost Cause, 1865–1920* (Athens, Ga., 1980); G. Kurt Piehler, *Remembering War the American Way* (Washington, D.C., 1995), 48–49, 58–62.

77. *New York Tribune*, Dec. 23, 1886; Grady's remarks were often quoted and reprinted, as in Daniel Hall's eulogy from 1887, published in *Addresses Commemorative of Abraham Lincoln and John P. Hale, delivered by Daniel Hall of Dover, N.H., with a biography and other speeches and writings of the orator* (Concord, N.H., 1892), 23. Robinson's speech is published in *Addresses Delivered at the Celebration of the One Hundred and Fifth Anniversary of the Birth of Abraham Lincoln* (Springfield, Ill., c. 1914), 10, 11.

78. *Addresses Delivered at the Celebration of the One Hundred and Fifth Anniversary of the Birth of Abraham Lincoln*, 25–26, 30–31, 33. Some celebrants made much of Lincoln as a native son of the South, on the basis of his birth in Kentucky, and the log cabin in which he was allegedly born, in Hodgenville, Kentucky, became a national shrine.

79. See Peterson, *Lincoln in American Memory*, 156–60, 316–17, 372; Vanderberg quoted at 316. And see, among numerous examples of Lincoln's appropriation, Lincoln depicted as an anti-imperialist in Col. H. O. S. Heistand, *Abraham Lincoln, being an address delivered before the Men's League*

of the Broadway Tabernacle, February 13, 1908 (New York, 1909), 36. Heistand advocated, "before acting on great public questions, ask ourselves 'What would Lincoln do?'" Or, for example, see the address by John Grier Hibben, president of Princeton University, in which he invokes Lincoln on his birthday in 1917 as an advocate of wartime unity and Americanization, in *Addresses Delivered at the Celebration of the One Hundred and Eighth Anniversary of the Birth of Abraham Lincoln* (Springfield, Ill., c. 1917), 27–28.

80. Wills, *Lincoln at Gettysburg*, esp. 84–87; Pauline Maier, *American Scripture: Making the Declaration of Independence* (New York, 1997), 201–8. Lincoln, Speech on the Dred Scott decision at Springfield, Ill., June 26, 1857, in *Speeches and Writings, 1832–1858*, 390–403, quotation at 398–99; Lincoln to Henry L. Pierce and Others, Apr. 6, 1859, in *Speeches and Writings, 1859–1865*, 19; Speech at Chicago, Illinois, July 10, 1858, in *Speeches and Writings, 1832–1858*, 439–58, quotation at 456.

81. Stewart, *Names on the Land*, 330; *Oration by Frederick Douglass, Delivered on the Occasion of the Unveiling of the Freedmen's Monument, in Memory of Abraham Lincoln, in Lincoln Park, Washington, D.C., April 14, 1876*, in Frederick Douglass, *Autobiographies*, ed. Henry Louis Gates (New York, 1994), 915–25; W. E. B. Du Bois, "Abraham Lincoln" (first published in *Crisis*, May 1922), in Du Bois, *Writings*, ed. Nathan Huggins (New York, 1986), 1196; Du Bois, "Again, Lincoln" (first published in *Crisis*, September 1922), in *Writings*, 1197–99.

82. Peterson, *Lincoln in American Memory*, 372, 355–58, quotation at 357. Kirk Savage, "The Politics of Memory: Black Emancipation and the Civil War Monument," in *Commemorations: The Politics of National Identity*, ed. John R. Gillis (Princeton, N.J., 1994), 127–49.

83. Dr. Stephen S. Wise, "Lincoln: Man and American," in *Addresses Delivered at the Celebration of the One Hundred and Fifth Anniversary of the Birth of Abraham Lincoln*, 37, 66.

84. Cunliffe, *Doubled Image*, 8, 21, 24. An ode eulogizing Washington is recycled for Lincoln in Dr. William Jayne, *Abraham Lincoln: Personal Reminiscences of the Martyred President, by his neighbor and intimate friend Dr. William Jayne* (Chicago, 1908), 58. See *Memorial Exercises on the Occasion of the Semi-Centennial Anniversary of the Assassination of Abraham Lincoln*, 35, on both Washington and Lincoln as the First American.

85. Marling, *Washington Slept Here*, 44–51, 105–14; Kammen, *Mystic Chords of Memory*, 215–21.

86. Marling, *Washington Slept Here*, 105–38, esp. 107–8, 117.

87. Ellen M. Litwicki, *America's Public Holidays, 1865–1920* (Washington, D.C., 2000), 153–64, quotations at 157.

88. Ibid., 76, 91–92; Marling, *Washington Slept Here*, 132–38, esp. 134–35. See also Clarence Winthrop Bowen, ed., *The History of the Centennial Celebration of the Inauguration of George Washington as First President of the United States* (New York, 1892). Clarence W. Bowen was a member of the executive committee of the Centennial Celebration. The Bowen Family Papers, including numerous scrapbooks, at the American Antiquarian Society, Worcester, Mass., contain an astonishing wealth of clippings and memorabilia related to this and other festive events, including the family's legendary Fourth of July celebrations; see esp. scrapbook octavo vols. 9 and 31. The Centennial was not uncontested; see "Women Protest. Alleged Injustices to the Sex by the Centennial Committee," *New York World*, Apr. 26, 1889. Women delegates complained of the exclusion of their sex, except as passive admirers. They declared, "The century which closes next week, to be celebrated with such pomp and show by men, has been for women a century of injustice."

89. Lincoln as quoted in Kammen, *Mystic Chords of Memory*, 221. Newspaper clipping, scrapbook vol. 9, Bowen Papers, American Antiquarian Society. February 22 oratory would continue to sound such notes, as in former senator Albert Beveridge's 1921 speech to the New York Sons of the Revolution, which recruited Washington to the fight against the "insidious wiles" of foreign radicals in America's cities (see Marling, *Washington Slept Here*, 191).

90. See Dion Dennis, "Washington's Birthday on the Texas Border," at http://www.ctheory. com/e36.html, examined Mar. 12, 2000. See also Elliott Young, "Red Men, Princess Pocahontas,

and George Washington: Harmonizing Race Relations in Laredo at the Turn of the Century," *Western Historical Quarterly* 29 (spring 1998): 48–85.

91. The German-American Bund rally, with its appropriation of Washington, is depicted in Klapthor and Morrison, *G. Washington: Figure upon the Stage*, 86, fig. 45. Washington to the Hebrew Congregation in Newport, Rhode Island, Aug. 18, 1790, in *Writings*, 766–67.

92. Arthur H. Landis, *The Abraham Lincoln Brigade* (New York, 1967); Edwin Rolfe, *The Lincoln Battalion* (New York, 1974); Robert Rosenstone, *Crusade of the Left: The Lincoln Battalion in the Spanish Civil War* (New York, 1969).

93. Du Bois, "Again, Lincoln," 1198; Peterson, *Lincoln in American Memory*, 379.

94. Earl Browder, *Lincoln and Communism* (New York, 1936); Harvey Ginsberg, "Everyone Owned a Lincoln," *New York Times*, Feb. 20, 1995, op-ed page; Peterson, *Lincoln in American Memory*, 379; Marling, *Washington Slept Here*, 374–76, quotation at 376; William E. Woodward, *George Washington: The Image and the Man* (New York, 1926); and see Marling's critique of Woodward, in *Washington Slept Here*, 250–54. George Babbitt, of course, was the "hero" of the 1922 novel by Sinclair Lewis, *Babbitt*. Woodward, author of the novel *Bunk* (1923), coined the term "debunk," which entered common usage as a synonym for slanders against George Washington (see Marling, *Washington Slept Here*, 354).

95. Klapthor and Morrison, *G. Washington: Figure upon the Stage*, 70–87; Marling, *Washington Slept Here*, 121 (quotation). And see, for example, ad campaigns employing Washington irreverently, such as those by Pioneer Electronics in 1986, Anheuser-Busch in 1989, and Pietro's Pizza in February 1992. An ad for Century Furniture in *Smithsonian*, September 1990, inside cover, explained "How George Washington dealt with China. He tabled it. On an exquisite Chippendale-style mahogany china table." Maurer quoted in Marling, *Washington Slept Here*, 368; see fig. 12.4 for Maurer portrait (369).

96. Leigh Eric Schmidt, *Consumer Rites: The Buying and Selling of American Holidays* (Princeton, N.J., 1995), 297, 301–2, with the *American Florist* quoted at 301.

97. Peterson, *Lincoln in American Memory*, 197. See "Washington Week in Review" advertisement in the *New Yorker*, Mar. 18, 1996, 62. Actually, by the year 2000, Martin Luther King Jr. birthday sales had begun to appear, a tasteless exploitation of the martyred hero that perhaps signals the full incorporation of the holiday into the United States public calendar.

98. See, for example, George Lipsitz, *Time Passages: Collective Memory and American Popular Culture* (Minneapolis, Minn., 1990). On the commercialization of American holidays generally, see Schmidt, *Consumer Rites*; Rosenzweig and Thelen, *Presence of the Past*, esp. 153, 168. On the other hand, African Americans still celebrate Lincoln at Emancipation Day (or Jubilee Day) celebrations (January 1); see, for example, Randall C. Archibold, "Celebrating a New Year, and a Milestone of Freedom," *New York Times*, Jan. 1, 2000, A27. On Negro History Week and Black History Month, see Kammen, *Mystic Chords of Memory*, 441, 630. An Oglala Sioux woman from the Pine Ridge reservation in South Dakota interviewed for Rosenzweig and Thelen's study expressed disappointment that Lincoln was, in her view, just like other presidents in their disregard for Native rights and welfare. Particularly offensive was his role as commander in chief during the suppression of the Great Sioux Uprising in Minnesota, which resulted in the hanging of some thirty-eight Santee Sioux in December 1863. In fact, local and military figures sought to execute a greater number, some 303 Indians (*Presence of the Past*, 275n. 22); Lincoln was a detached chief executive with regard to Indian affairs, acting humanely when encountering Indians and their problems personally but proving an indifferent advocate for Native people when politically preoccupied; see esp. David A. Nichols, *Lincoln and the Indians: Civil War Policy and Politics* (Columbia, Mo., 1978).

99. Peterson, *Lincoln in American Memory*, 380; Michael Kernan, "Renovating Washington's Monument, Designer-Style," *Smithsonian*, June 1999, 30–32; "Mount Vernon to Mourn Washington Again," *New York Times*, Nov. 28, 1999, Travel sec., 3; Schwartz, *George Washington*, 199.

100. Bruce Handy, "*Ich Bin ein* Magazine Editor," *Time*, Sept. 18, 1995, 127; *George*, October 1995. In the United States Mint's 1999 advertising campaign to promote its new series of state quarters, it employed the muppet Kermit the Frog posing as George Washington crossing the Delaware: "Kermit the Frog here, as George Washington, bringing you the biggest thing to happen to our country since Betsy Ross learned how to sew." On the cover of a recent edition of *Kids Discover* magazine 10, 8 (2000), devoted to George Washington, Washington is reduced to introducing himself in a cartoon dialogue bubble with the words, "I'm the one-dollar man."

101. James Bennet, "Exultant Buchanan Pushes Economic Insecurity Theme," *New York Times*, Feb. 22, 1996, A1, A16.

102. Bill Bryson, *I'm a Stranger Here Myself: Notes on Returning to America after Twenty Years Away* (New York, 1999), 163. In February 1999, a puzzled five-year-old speculated about the meaning of Presidents' Day: "that's the day celebrating Clinton's impeachment?"

Chapter 5. St. Monday

1. Edmund S. Morgan, *The Puritan Family: Religion and Domestic Relations in Seventeenth-Century New England*, rev. ed. (1944; reprint, New York, 1966), 69–71. Daniel T. Rodgers, *The Work Ethic in Industrial America, 1850–1920* (Chicago, 1978), traces the later history of the work ethic.

2. Benjamin Franklin, *Autobiography, Poor Richard, and Later Writings*, ed. J. A. Leo Lemay (New York, 1987), 463, 556, 644–45.

3. Leigh Eric Schmidt, *Consumer Rites: The Buying and Selling of American Holidays* (Princeton, N.J., 1995), 24–25; Stephen Nissenbaum, *The Battle for Christmas: A Cultural History of America's Most Cherished Holiday* (New York, 1996). On the English religious and political calendar and its revision, see David Cressy, *Bonfires and Bells: National Memory and the Protestant Calendar in Elizabethan and Stuart England* (Berkeley, Calif., 1990). William Bradford, *Of Plymouth Plantation: The Pilgrims in America*, ed. Harvey Wish (New York, 1962), 82–83. Dickinson to Mabel Loomis Todd, Dec. 24, 1883, in *Austin and Mabel: The Amherst Affair and Love Letters of Austin Dickinson and Mabel Loomis Todd*, ed. Polly Longsworth (New York, 1984), 174–75.

4. Rodgers, *Work Ethic*, is an indispensable guide in tracing these transformations. See esp. 7–17, 27–29. See also David M. Potter, *People of Plenty: Economic Abundance and the American Character* (Chicago, 1954), esp. 166–88. And see George Lipsitz, *Time Passages: Collective Memory and American Popular Culture* (Minneapolis, Minn., 1990), on mass consumption, leisure, and popular culture in the second half of the twentieth century.

5. Diana B. Henriques, "New Take on Perpetual Calendar," *New York Times*, Aug. 24, 1999, C1, C2.

6. For the perspective of a scholar of American religion on the decline of Memorial Day, see Catherine Albanese, "Requiem for Memorial Day: Dissent in the Redeemer Nation," *American Quarterly* 26 (October 1974), 386–98. See also William Lloyd Warner, *The Living and the Dead* (New Haven, Conn., 1959), on Memorial Day; and see generally Gary Laderman, *The Sacred Remains: American Attitudes toward Death, 1799–1883* (New Haven, Conn., 1996).

7. Paul H. Buck, *The Road to Reunion, 1865–1900* (Boston, 1937), 116–21; James M. McPherson, "When Memorial Day Was No Picnic," *New York Times*, May 26, 1996, op-ed page, 11; C. F. Horner, *The Life of James Redpath* (New York, 1926), 111–19. And see especially Ellen M. Litwicki, *America's Public Holidays, 1865–1920* (Washington, D.C., 2000), which devotes its first chapter to Memorial Days, 9–49; and Cecilia Elizabeth O'Leary, *To Die For: The Paradox of American Patriotism* (Princeton, N.J., 1999), 52–87, 91–97, 100–109, 145–46. *A History of the Origins of Memorial Day as Adopted by the Ladies' Memorial Association of Columbus, Georgia* (Columbus, Ga., 1898) recites the southern mythic origin tale.

8. Buck, *Road to Reunion*, 117; G. Kurt Piehler, *Remembering War the American Way* (Washington, D.C., 1995), 57–59, 61–62; Litwicki, *America's Public Holidays*, 12–14. See generally the Grand Army

of the Republic, *National Memorial Day*, 2 vols. (Washington, D.C., 1868, 1869). And see Nina Silber, *The Romance of Reunion: Northerners and the South, 1865–1900* (Chapel Hill, N.C., 1993), 58–61.

9. On Memorial Day in the South, see especially Charles Reagan Wilson, *Baptized in Blood: The Religion of the Lost Cause, 1865–1920* (Athens, Ga., 1980), 28; Gaines Foster, *Ghosts of the Confederacy: Defeat, the Lost Cause, and the Emergence of the New South, 1865–1913* (New York, 1987), 42–45; Drew Gilpin Faust, "Altars of Sacrifice: Confederate Women and the Narratives of War," in *Divided Houses: Gender and the Civil War*, ed. Catherine Clinton and Nina Silber (New York, 1992), 171–99, esp. 184, 196; Piehler, *Remembering War*, 61–62, 64–65.

10. Piehler, *Remembering* War, 19, 49–52; Frank Moore, *Memorial Ceremonies at the Grave of Our Soldiers: Saturday, May 30, 1868* (Washington, D.C., 1869).

11. "Memorial Days Past," the reminiscences of the late Charles V. Stanton, longtime editor of the Roseburg, Oregon, *News-Review*, in *Register-Guard* (Eugene, Ore.), May 29, 2000, 10A.

12. Silber, *Romance of Reunion*, 59; Buck, *Road to Reunion*, 118; McPherson, "Memorial Day."

13. Buck, *Road to Reunion*, 119–20. On Civil War monuments, see Kirk Savage, "The Politics of Memory: Black Emancipation and the Civil War Monument," in *Commemorations: The Politics of National Identity*, ed. John R. Gillis (Princeton, N.J., 1994), 129–31; and see Piehler, *Remembering War*, 64–75.

14. Silber, *Romance of Reunion*, 61–62; McPherson, "Memorial Day"; Buck, *Road to Reunion*, 121. And see David W. Blight, *Race and Reunion: The Civil War in American Memory* (Cambridge, Mass., 2001); Litwicki, *America's Public Holidays*, 44–49.

15. Savage, "Politics of Memory," 131–32; Kansas *Star Ledger* as quoted in Silber, *Romance of Reunion*, 157. See also Piehler, *Remembering War*, 68–69; William H. Wiggins Jr., *O Freedom! Afro-American Emancipation Celebrations* (Knoxville, Tenn., 1987); Frederick Douglass's Decoration Day Address at Arlington, 1871, inserted by Douglass in his *Life and Times of Frederick Douglass Written by Himself* (first pub. 1881; rev. ed. 1893), in Douglass, *Autobiographies*, ed. Henry Louis Gates Jr. (New York, 1994), 850–51.

16. Frederick Douglass, "There Was a Right Side in the Late War: An Address Delivered in New York, New York, on 30 May 1878," in *The Frederick Douglass Papers, Ser. 1: Speeches, Debates, and Interviews*, ed. John W. Blassingame and John R. McKivigan (New Haven, Conn., 1991), 4:480–92.

17. Alessandra Lorini, *Rituals of Race: American Public Culture and the Search for Racial Democracy* (Charlottesville, N.C., 1999), 28–31; Douglass, *Life and Times*, 884–86; Douglass, "There Was a Right Side in the Late War," 4:480–92; Piehler, *Remembering War*, 65–66. Litwicki, *America's Public Holidays*, 36–42.

18. William H. Wiggins Jr. and Douglas DeNatale, eds., *Jubilation! African American Celebrations in the Southeast* (Columbia, S.C., 1993), 18, 28–29, 77.

19. Carolyn Gilman and Mary Jane Schneider, *The Way to Independence: Memories of a Hidatsa Indian Family, 1840–1920* (St. Paul, Minn., 1987), 277; *Fifty-Ninth Annual Report of the Commissioner of Indian Affairs to the Secretary of the Interior, 1890* (Washington, D.C., 1890), 18–19.

20. David Wallace Adams, *Education for Extinction: American Indians and the Boarding School Experience, 1875–1928* (Lawrence, Kan., 1995), 204–5.

21. Tom Holm, *Strong Hearts, Wounded Souls: Native American Veterans of the Vietnam War* (Austin, Tex., 1996), 101–2; on honoring and reintegration ceremonies, see 185–97. See the following photographs reproduced in Don Doll and Jim Alinder, eds., *Crying for a Vision: A Rosebud Sioux Trilogy, 1886–1976* (Dobbs Ferry, N.Y., 1976). On Indian patriotism, see also Herman J. Viola, *After Columbus: The Smithsonian Chronicle of the North American Indians* (Washington, D.C., 1990), 18–24, 220–25.

22. Litwicki, *America's Public Holidays*, 33–34.

23. Silber, *Romance of Reunion*, 58–60.

24. Wilson, *Baptized in Blood*, 28; Foster, *Ghosts of the Confederacy*, 29, 31, 38–46; Faust, "Altars of Sacrifice," esp. 184, 196; Litwicki, *America's Public Holidays*, 14–21.

25. Oliver Wendell Holmes, as quoted in Silber, *Romance of Reunion*, 161; Michael Kammen, *Mystic Chords of Memory: The Transformation of Tradition in American Culture* (New York, 1991), 103; see Jack Santino, *All around the Year: Holidays and Celebrations in American Life* (Urbana, Ill., 1994), 119–20, on Memorial Day as a general American Day of the Dead; John Bodnar, *Remaking America: Public Memory, Commemoration, and Patriotism in the Twentieth Century* (Princeton, N.J., 1992), 79–85, 90–92 (on Indianapolis), 95–107, esp. 96 (on Cleveland).

26. Piehler, *Remembering War*, 111–14; Woodrow Wilson, "An Armistice Day Statement," in *The Papers of Woodrow Wilson*, ed. Arthur S. Link (Princeton, N.J., 1991), 64:7; Making Armistice Day a Legal Holiday, U.S. 76th Cong., 3d sess., H. Report 2156 (1938).

27. Richard E. Oberdorfer, "'Practical Patriotism': Armistice Day and the Suppression of American Radicalism," seminar paper, University of Oregon, 1996; "Radical Lynched by Centralia Mob," *Morning Oregonian* (Portland, Ore.), Nov. 12, 1919, 1–2; and see Tom Copeland, *The Centralia Tragedy of 1919: Elmer Smith and the Wobblies* (Seattle, Wash., 1993). Armistice Day 1919 was also the occasion of the U.S. House of Representatives' refusal to seat the prominent socialist Victor L. Berger, elected from Milwaukee, Wisconsin, but still facing charges stemming from the Espionage Act. The American Legion, meeting on Armistice Day in Minneapolis, called for the cancellation of Berger's citizenship.

28. Bodnar, *Remaking America*, 85–85, 88–89.

29. Piehler, *Remembering War*, 117–18; dedication day events, 118–20. Note the participation in this ceremony of the Crow Indian leader Plenty Coup, who, despite instructions to remain silent, spoke (in Crow): "I am glad to represent all the Indians of the United States in placing on the grave of this noble warrior this coup stick and war bonnet, every eagle feather of which represents a deed of valor by my race"; see Frederick E. Hoxie, *Parading through History: The Making of the Crow Nation in America, 1805–1935* (Cambridge, U.K., 1995), 345.

30. Piehler, *Remembering War*, 141; Robert J. Myers, *Celebrations: The Complete Book of American Holidays* (Garden City, N.Y., 1972), 265–70.

31. *New York Times*, Oct. 29, 1974, A29; ibid., Oct. 28, 1975. On the shift in the date of Veterans Day observances, see Piehler, *Remembering War*, 171.

32. I witnessed the dedication events personally, during a research trip to Washington, D.C., in 1982. Much has been written on these events and the Vietnam Veterans Memorial, but see esp. Piehler, *Remembering War*, 171–78; Bodnar, *Remaking America*, 2–9.

33. See Michael Kazin and Steven J. Ross, "America's Labor Day: The Dilemma of a Workers' Celebration," *Journal of American History* 78, 4 (March 1992): 1294–1323; Litwicki, *America's Public Holidays*, 70–112.

34. Kazin and Ross, "America's Labor Day," 1299–1302; Jonathan Grossman, "Who Is the Father of Labor Day?" *Labor History* 14, 4 (fall 1973): 612–23; Richard P. Hunt, "The First Labor Day," *American Heritage* 33, 5 (August–September 1982), 109–12. Estimates range from the New York *Sun*'s number of 12,500 to the *Irish World*'s 15,000 to 20,000. See also Estelle M. Stewart, "Origins and Significance of Labor Day," *Monthly Labor Review* 43, 2 (August 1936): 279–84; Philip S. Foner, *May Day: A Short History of the International Workers' Holiday* (New York, 1986), esp. 3–4.

35. *Herald*, as quoted in Kazin and Ross, "America's Labor Day," 1302; McCabe, as quoted in Hunt, "First Labor Day," 112.

36. Grossman, "Father of Labor Day," 621; Kazin and Ross, "America's Labor Day," 1302.

37. Kazin and Ross, "America's Labor Day," 1302–3; Grossman, "Father of Labor Day," 622.

38. Kazin and Ross, "America's Labor Day," 1296.

39. Ibid., 1315–18; Foner, *May Day*, esp. 75–77. On the first Labor Day in Chicago, see Litwicki, *America's Public Holidays*, 83–87.

40. U.S. Department of Labor, "History of Labor Day," website at http://www.dol.gov; Myers, *Celebrations*, 210.

41. Gompers, as quoted in "History of Labor Day," U.S. Department of Labor website.

42. *Account of the Grand Federal Procession, Philadelphia, July 4, 1788. To which is added, Mr. Wilson's Oration, and a letter on the Subject of the Procession* (Philadelphia, 1788); Whitfield J. Bell Jr., "The Federal Processions of 1788," *New-York Historical Society Quarterly* 46 (January 1962): 5–39; Sean Wilentz, *Chants Democratic: New York City and the Rise of the American Working Class, 1788–1850* (New York, 1984), 87–97.

43. Wilentz, *Chants Democratic*, esp. 219–54; Bruce Lurie, *Working People of Philadelphia, 1800–1850* (Philadelphia, 1980), 85–104 (the economic crisis of the Panic of 1837 reversed the gains of labor in the general strike of 1835); Susan G. Davis, *Parades and Power: Street Theatre in Nineteenth-Century Philadelphia* (Philadelphia, 1986), 113–53.

44. Davis, *Parades and Power*, 133.

45. Ibid., 166–68.

46. Foner, *May Day*, 14–19; Melvyn Dubofsky, *Industrialism and the American Worker, 1865–1920* (Arlington Heights, Ill., 1975), 54–61, briefly summarizes the rise and fall of the Knights of Labor.

47. Quoted in Foner, *May Day*, 19.

48. Litwicki, *America's Public Holidays*, 75, 87–91.

49. On the impact of Haymarket on Labor Day, see Paul Avrich, *The Haymarket Tragedy* (Princeton, N.J., 1984), 93–94; Foner, *May Day*, 40–46, 56.

50. Foner, *May Day*, 75–77; *New York Times*, May 2, 1901; *Ladies Garment Worker*, June 4, 1913, 26, quoted in Kazin and Ross, "America's Labor Day," 1305n. 25; see ibid., 1304–5. In selecting May Day over Labor Day, the IWW complained about the latter holiday, "Labor Day has completely lost its class character. The very fact that 'Labor Day' was legally, formally and officially established by the capitalist class itself, through its organized government, took the 'starch' out of it." May Day, however, "was not disgraced, contaminated and blasphemed by capital's official sanction and approval, as has Labor Day" (quoted in Foner, *May Day*, 77).

51. Quoted in Foner, *May Day*, 103–4.

52. Ibid., 132–33. On Loyalty Day, see ibid., 134–36; Myers, *Celebrations*, 141–42.

53. See Kazin and Ross, "America's Labor Day," esp. 1307–8, quotation at 1307. On the use of popular entertainment in Labor Day events, see esp. 1313–15.

54. Bob Herbert, "Working Harder, Longer," *New York Times*, Sept. 4, 2000, op-ed page, noted that "There's a lot of good news to report this Labor Day," including low unemployment and rising wages. But, he noted, citing a report, *The State of Working America, 2000/2001* (Ithaca, N.Y., 2000), families "are more indebted, working more and more hours, and the stock market boom has largely passed them by." The poor have not disappeared, with a national poverty rate of 12.7 percent, just one-tenth of a percentage point less than in 1989 and one full percentage point higher than in 1979. A 2001 report issued by the International Labor Organization found that Americans worked more hours annually per person—some 1,979 hours per year—than did residents of any other industrialized country; Steven Greenhouse, "Report Shows Americans Have More 'Labor Days,'" *New York Times*, Sept. 1, 2001, A6.

Chapter 6. Martin Luther King Jr.'s Birthday

1. Muriel S. Snowden, "The Dream: Education Is Freedom," in *Reflections of the Dream, 1975–1994: Twenty Years of Celebrating the Life of Dr. Martin Luther King Jr. at the Massachusetts Institute of Technology*, ed. Clarence G. Williams (Cambridge, Mass., 1996), 56.

2. See Noel Ignatiev, *How the Irish Became White* (New York, 1995); David Roediger, *Wages of Whiteness: Race and the Making of the American Working Class* (London, 1991); and Roediger, *Toward the Abolition of Whiteness: Essays on Race, Politics, and Working Class History* (London, 1994).

3. See E. J. Hobsbawm, introduction to *The Invention of Tradition*, ed. Eric Hobsbawm and Terrence Ranger (Cambridge, U.K., 1983), 1–14.

4. Michael Eric Dyson, *I May Not Get There with You: The True Martin Luther King, Jr.* (New York, 2000)—the best treatment of King's reputation and representation in American life—briefly traces the events leading to the creation of King's birthday as a national holiday (see esp. 286–90). And see "Looking Back at a Man Ahead of His Time. A Conversation: Andrew Young on Rev. Martin Luther King, Jr.," *New York Times*, Jan. 12, 1986, E5.

5. Dyson, *I May Not Get There with You*, 303; "How to Honor Dr. King—and When," *New York Times*, Jan. 15, 1986, A22.

6. Harvard Sitkoff, *The Struggle for Black Equality, 1954–1992*, rev. ed. (New York, 1993), 185–89, 208–9.

7. Ibid., 209. Invocation of King as a guiding spirit continues into the present, as in then Vice President Al Gore's comments from the pulpit of the Ebenezer Baptist Church in Atlanta on King's birthday in 2000; see "Nation Celebrates Holiday Honoring Martin Luther King, Jr.," *Jet* 97, 9 (Feb. 7, 2000): 5.

8. William H. Wiggins, *O Freedom! African-American Emancipation Celebrations* (Knoxville, Tenn., 1987), 137; *New York Times*, Jan. 16, 1969, A30; *Washington Post*, Jan. 16, 1969, A2. On the origins of the holiday, see U.S. Congress, House, Subcommittee on Census and Population of the Committee on Post Office and Civil Service, *Designate the Birthday of Martin Luther King, Jr., as a Legal Public Holiday*, 94th Cong., 1st sess., H.R. 1810 (Washington, D.C., 1975); U.S. Congress, House, Subcommittee on Census and Statistics of the Committee on Post Office and Civil Service, *Martin Luther King, Jr., Holiday Bill*, 98th Cong., 1st sess., H.R. 800 (Washington, D.C., 1983); and see esp. Wiggins, *O Freedom!* 134–51.

9. Wiggins, *O Freedom!* 134, 137–38; Dyson, *I May Not Get There with You*, 286–88. On the establishment of Martin Luther King Day in Oregon (the legislation was first introduced in 1969 but not signed into law until 1985), see Paul Neville, "Honoring a Legacy for Us All," *Register-Guard* (Eugene, Ore.), Jan. 15, 1996, A1, A6.

10. Dyson, *I May Not Get There with You*, 287–88.

11. Richard M. Merelman, *Representing Black Culture: Racial Conflict and Cultural Politics in the United States* (New York, 1995), 79–80; Peter Applebome, "King Holiday Seeks Wider Acceptance in U.S.," *New York Times*, Jan. 16, 1994, A1, A10; Nicholas O. Alozie, "Political Tolerance Hypotheses and White Opposition to a Martin Luther King Holiday in Arizona," *Social Science Journal* 32, 1 (January 1995): 1–16; "New Hampshire Denies King Holiday Again," *Jet* 91, 20 (Apr. 7, 1997): 16; "Utah Designates Dr. King's Birthday a Holiday; Last State to Adopt the Day," *Jet* 97, 20 (Apr. 24, 2000): 4; David Firestone, "46,000 March on South Carolina Capitol to Bring Down Confederate Flag," *New York Times*, Jan. 18, 2000, A12; "S.C. Strips King's Name from Holiday," Associated Press story, *Daily Emerald* (University of Oregon, Eugene, Ore.), Mar. 2, 2000, 1.

12. Alozie, "Martin Luther King Holiday in Arizona"; see also Leah Landrum, "The Martin Luther King Jr. Holiday in Arizona: When Politics Becomes Theater," master's thesis, Arizona State University, 1991.

13. Applebome, "King Holiday Seeks Wider Acceptance in U.S.," A1, A10; Janice Castro, "Thanks for the Memories: Walt Disney Studios, Universal Studios and Twentieth-Century Fox Film Corp. Do Not Honor Martin Luther King Day," *Time*, Jan. 25, 1993, 15.

14. Hubert E. Jones, "Martin Luther King, Jr., What Does He Mean to Me?" in *Reflections of the Dream*, 37.

15. Melanet's Kwanzaa Information Center, at http://www.melanet.com/kwanzaa, accessed Mar. 18, 2001; Leigh Eric Schmidt, *Consumer Rites: The Buying and Selling of American Holidays* (Princeton, N.J., 1995), 300–301.

16. Clarence G. Williams, "Introduction," in *Reflections of the Dream*, 26–27; Neville, "Honoring a Legacy for Us All," 6A; Applebome, "King Holiday Seeks Wider Acceptance in U.S.," A1.

17. W. E. B. Du Bois, *The Souls of Black Folk* (1903), in *Writings*, ed. Nathan Huggins (New York, 1986), 364–65, 371, 545; Jones, "What Does He Mean to Me?" 39.

18. Roy Rosenzweig and David Thelen, *The Presence of the Past: Popular Uses of History in American Life* (New York, 1998), 151–62, esp. 153–54.

19. Susan F. Rasky, "Black History Struggles to Keep Up with the Demand," *New York Times*, Jan. 12, 1986, E28; Dyson, *I May Not Get There with You*, 284–85, 104.

20. Applebome, "King Holiday Seeks Wider Acceptance in U.S.," A10.

21. Snowden, "The Dream," 56, 60; William E. Schmidt, "Top U.S. Educator Calls Dr. King a Fine Teacher," *New York Times*, Jan. 15, 1986, A8; Bernard Weinraub, "Reagan Opens Observances Leading to Dr. King's Birthday," *New York Times*, Jan. 14, 1986, A16.

22. Weinraub, "Reagan Opens Observances," A16; Jesse Jackson, "Required Reading. On Dr. King's Birthday," an excerpt from a speech by Jackson, delivered Jan. 12, 1986, *New York Times*, Jan. 15, 1986, B10.

23. Anthony C. Campbell, "Do You Remember?" in *Reflections of the Dream*, 81; "Give King Day Meaning," *Register-Guard*, Jan. 15, 1996, 10A; President Bill Clinton, "Remarks on Signing the King Holiday and Service Act of 1994," *Weekly Compilation of Presidential Documents* 30, 34 (Aug. 29, 1994): 1701–3.

24. "Give King Day Meaning," 10A; Jackson, "Required Reading. On Dr. King's Birthday," B1; Applebome, "King Holiday Seeks Wider Acceptance in U.S.," A10; Neville, "Honoring a Legacy for Us All," 6A; "Nation Celebrates Holiday Honoring Martin Luther King, Jr.," 5; Dyson, *I May Not Get There with You*, 3, 305; Vincent Gordon Harding, "Beyond Amnesia: Martin Luther King, Jr. and the Future of America," *Journal of American History* 74, 2 (September 1987): 468–76, quotation at 476.

25. Adam Nagourney, "On King Day, Crash Course for First Lady," *New York Times*, Jan. 18, 2000, A20.

26. Dyson, *I May Not Get There with You*, 22–25, Reynolds quoted at 22; "Mallard Fillmore," *Register-Guard*, Jan. 19, 1998; Edward W. Lempinen, "Connerly Widens Anti-Affirmative Action Campaign; He Announces New Effort on King Birthday," *San Francisco Chronicle*, Jan. 16, 1997, A17. The most offensive appropriation of King's famous "I Have a Dream" speech may be that of John Callahan, the syndicated cartoonist of "Callahan," who in April 1995—in the anniversary month of King's assassination—drew a comic that showed a frowning woman standing in the doorway of her son's bedroom, while her son stood over his bed, with a puddle in the middle. At the top, a caption read, "Martin Luther King, age 13," while near the boy it read, "I had a dream." See Ann Oldenburg, "A Cartoonist on the Offensive," *USA Today*, Nov. 14, 1995, 8D. Callahan has also published the cartoon in his *Freaks of Nature* (New York, 1995).

27. Ronald Smothers, "Bigotry's Persistence," *New York Times*, Jan. 19, 1988, B3; Scott W. Hoffman, "Holy Martin: The Overlooked Canonization of Dr. Martin Luther King, Jr.," *Religion and American Culture: A Journal of Interpretation* 10, 2 (summer 2000): 123–48, esp. 126–31; Dyson, *I May Not Get There with You*, 302–3.

28. Hoffman, "Holy Martin," 132–38; see also Rev. Anthony Campbell's 1980 King Day remarks, when he told his audience that God "finds one person. When the world was flooded with wickedness, Noah was found. When a new religion was called forth . . . He found Abraham. People were struggling, and He found Moses. He bypassed generations of slavery and found Martin Luther King, Jr." (Campbell, "Do You Remember?" 82).

29. Ibid., 123, 138–41; Jenny E. Heller, "Westminster Abbey Elevates 10 Foreigners," *New York Times*, Sept. 22, 1998, D4; "Rights Activist among Martyrs Honored in Stone," Associated Press story, *Register-Guard*, July 10, 1998, 16A.

30. Dyson, *I May Not Get There with You*, 5, 8, 301, see also 103.

31. Ibid.; David J. Garrow, *The FBI and Martin Luther King, Jr.: From "Solo" to Memphis* (New York, 1981).

32. Coretta Scott King as quoted in Wiggins, *O Freedom!* 141–47. The objection to a King holiday on economic grounds—as too costly to states, counties, or municipalities—continues to be raised, as in Wallingford, Connecticut's recent, unsuccessful bid to substitute King Day for Lincoln's Birthday rather than accept the former as an additional paid holiday. See Ann DeMatteo, "Wallingford Loses Ruling on MLK Day," *New Haven Register*, Aug. 26, 2000, A1, A6; and see note in "Metro Briefing: Hartford, Connecticut: Dispute over King Holiday," *New York Times*, July 27, 2000, B7.

33. Emily Yellin, "A City Strives to Balance Its Role in King Legacy," *New York Times*, Jan. 19, 1998, A10.

34. Jim Davenport, "S. Carolinians Rally 'round the Rebel Flag," Associated Press story, *Register-Guard*, Jan. 9, 2000, 5A.

35. Ibid.; Firestone, "46,000 March on South Carolina Capitol to Bring Down Confederate Flag," A12; David Firestone, "Unfurling a Battle Cry and Its Last Harrah," *New York Times*, Jan. 23, 2000, sec. 4, 5. In 1996, South Carolina's governor, David Beasley, along with two former governors and two congressmen, including Senator Strom Thurmond (all Republicans), called for removal of the flag to another site on the state capitol grounds. According to former governor Carroll A. Campbell Jr., "The flag is being used now to sow hate. . . . This [moving the flag], in my opinion, will end the controversy and bring people closer" (Rick Bragg, "Political Heavyweights Back Governor on Confederate Flag," *New York Times*, Nov. 28, 1996, A13). See also Paul Greenberg, "Dual Lee, King Holiday Would Weave All Americans Together," syndicated column that first appeared in 1986, reprinted in *Register-Guard*, Jan. 19, 1998, which suggests, problematically and unrealistically, the merger of the two holidays in the interest of multiculturalism. For another example of the political use of King's birthday, see Alexander Reid, "Town Targets Ugly Image: Braintree Sees King as Key," *Boston Globe*, Dec. 6, 1992, South Weekly, 1; for Braintree—a town becoming more racially diverse—a King Day festival became a means of cultivating racial and ethnic harmony, atoning for previous insensitivity, and (officials hoped) restoring substantial state funding eliminated by the Massachusetts Commission Against Discrimination for earlier transgressions.

36. Randal C. Archibold, "Celebrating a New Year, and a Milestone for Freedom," *New York Times*, Jan. 1, 2000, A27.

37. Isabel Wilkerson, "Memphis Blacks Charge Calendar Slurs Dr. King," *New York Times*, Jan. 15, 1989, sec. 1, pt. 1, 16; Alex Chadwick, "Waldenbooks Fires Three over Nasty Calendar," National Public Radio, *Weekend Edition*, Sept. 5, 1992.

38. Barry Bearak, "On Day to Honor Dr. King, Some Pause as Others Shop," *New York Times*, Jan. 20, 1998, A1, A12; advertisement for Value Village, in *Register-Guard*, Jan. 12, 2000, 3A. This ad generated at least one objecting letter, which urged readers not to commercialize King: "How demeaning and degrading to honor his contribution and achievements by shopping," wrote Marybeth M. Nessler, letter to the editor, *Register-Guard*, Jan. 19, 2000, 10A. A criticism by the Turning Point Project of the use to which King's words and image have been put appeared in the *New York Times*, July 10, 2000, A13. See also Dyson, *I May Not Get There with You*, 6.

39. Michael Kammen, *Mystic Chords of Memory: The Transformation of Tradition in American Culture* (New York, 1991); John Bodnar, *Remaking America: Public Memory, Commemoration, and Patriotism in the Twentieth Century* (Princeton, N.J., 1992), 13–14.

Epilogue. The Future of the Past

1. John A. Hutchinson to the editor, *Register-Guard* (Eugene, Ore.), May 8, 1997, 12A.

2. American Indian Day has been celebrated on various days, sometimes in September, some-

times in February—tied to passage of the Dawes Act (1887), which allotted Indian reservations in severalty and expropriated "extra" land, resulting in the loss of millions of acres—and sometimes in May. Generally, the holiday has not been popular among Native Americans. See Nicolas G. Rosenthal, "Building a Better Indian: The Promotion and Commemoration of American Indian Day in the Early Twentieth Century," unpublished paper.

3. Laurie Goodstein, "Bush's Jesus Day Is Called Insensitive and a Violation of the First Amendment," *New York Times*, Aug. 6, 2000, A16.

Stern, Elizabeth, 111
Steward, Austin, 25
Steward, Ira, 37
Stoner, Winifred Sackville, Jr., 154
Stoudamire, Charles, 266
Stowe, Harriet Beecher, 115, 184
St. Patrick's Day, 3–4, 142–44, 256–57
Student Nonviolent Coordinating Committee, 260
Stuyvesant, Peter, 83
Suffrage movement, 34–35
Sullivan, James, 132
Sullivan, John, 185
Sunday school movement, 31–32

Taft, William Howard, 230
Tallmadge, Frederick S., 207–8
Tammany, or the Indian Chief (Hatton), 135
Tammany Society, 143, 304 nn. 34, 35
    and Columbus Day, 129, 133–34, 140
    and Independence Day, 35
Taylor, Hamilton, 50
Taylor, Zachary, 48, 69–70
Temperance movement, 30–31, 36, 179–80, 312 n. 37
Terry, Clark, 78
Thacher, James, 85
Thanksgiving, 10
    alternate claims, 83–85, 295 n. 4
    and American Revolution, 94–95
    antebellum era, 86–87, 95–96, 295 n. 8, 298 n. 34
    and antislavery movement, 86, 87, 96, 296 n. 12, 298 n. 34
    and charity, 82, 91, 112, 114, 300 n. 67
    and Christmas, 116–17
    and Civil War, 96–98
    and colonial era, 83, 85–86, 91–94, 112, 295 n. 5, 297 n. 24
    and consumerism, 104–5, 106–7, 114–15, 117, 299 n. 44, 301 nn. 69, 70
    early republic, 85–86, 95
    and immigrants, 107–11, 299 n. 53
    and Jews, 109–12, 299 n. 56
    late nineteenth century, 98–104, 296 n. 15
    and Native Americans, 4, 82, 112–14, 300 nn. 63, 65, 67
    official establishment of, 87–88, 90–91, 96
    and Pilgrim images, 85–86, 91–92, 108, 110, 295 n. 5
    and postmodernity, 118, 301 n. 71
    and reconciliation, 87, 90–91, 98
    Roosevelt's date change, 105–6

sports events, 99–100
    travel, 101, 103–4, 298 n. 43, 299 n. 44
    turkey consumption, 100–101, 102
    women's roles, 88–91, 115–16, 296 n. 17
Thatcher, Moses R., 49
Thelen, David, 214, 267–68
Thompson, Maurice, 197–98
Thoreau, Henry David, 30
Tomb of the Unknown Soldier, 236, 237, 320 n. 29
Travel, 101, 103–4, 298 n. 43, 299 n. 44
Treaty of Canandaigua (1794), 185
Tsereteli, Zurab K., 160–61
Tuckerman, Henry T., 190
Turkey trots, 99
Turner, Frederick Jackson, 46, 148
Turner, Nat, 287 n. 18
Tyler, Lyon G., 198

Uncle Tom's Cabin (Stowe), 184
Union League Club, 206
United Daughters of the Confederacy, 224, 230

Valentine's Day, 162
Vandenberg, Arthur, 200
Vaynshteyn, Zhana, 112
Vesey, Denmark, 287 n. 18
Veterans Day, 236–37, 238. *See also* Armistice Day
Veterans of Foreign Wars, 237, 251
Vietnam Veterans Memorial, 237
Vietnam War
    and Independence Day, 79–80
    Native American military service, 66–67, 231–32, 238, 293 n. 108
    and Veterans Day, 237
Viscusi, Robert, 158

Waldstreicher, David, 21, 42, 169, 170, 176
Wallendorf, Melanie, 115
Warner, Michael, 18, 125
War of 1812, 44
Warren, Mercy Otis, 128
Wasden, Bill, 112
Washington, George
    and Declaration of Independence, 17
    and Evacuation Day, 207–8
    and national identity, 164, 184, 189, 195–96
    and patriotic rhetoric, 52
    and slavery, 181–82, 309 n. 5, 313 n. 40
    See also Presidents' Day; Washington's Birthday
Washington, Mary Simpson, 182